WOMEN AND GENDER IN JEWISH PHILOSOPHY

Jewish Literature and Culture
Series Editor, Alvin H. Rosenfeld

WOMEN
AND
GENDER
IN JEWISH
PHILOSOPHY

Edited by Hava Tirosh-Samuelson

INDIANA UNIVERSITY PRESS
Bloomington and Indianapolis

This book is a publication of

Indiana University Press
601 North Morton Street
Bloomington, IN 47404-3797 USA

http://iupress.indiana.edu

Telephone orders 800-842-6796
Fax orders 812-855-7931
Orders by e-mail iuporder@indiana.edu

The paper used in this publication meets the minimum requirements of American National Standard for Information Sciences—Permanence of Paper for Printed Library Materials, ANSI Z39.48-1984.

Manufactured in the United States of America

Library of Congress Cataloging-in-Publication Data

Women and gender in Jewish philosophy / edited by Hava Tirosh-Samuelson.
p. cm. — (Jewish literature and culture)
Proceedings of a conference held Feb. 25–26, 2001 at Arizona State University.
Includes index.
ISBN 0-253-34396-8 (cloth) — ISBN 0-253-21673-7 (paper)
1. Philosophy, Jewish—Congresses. 2. Feminist theory—Israel—Congresses.
3. Sex role—Philosophy—Congresses.
4. Sex role—Israel—Congresses. I. Tirosh-Samuelson, Hava, date II. Series.
B5800.W66 2004
181'.06'082—dc22
2003021946

1 2 3 4 5 09 08 07 06 05 04

To my twin sister, Dr. Ada Schein,
a dedicated scholar and a close friend.

CONTENTS

Acknowledgments

The essays in this volume were either presented in or solicited for a conference held at Arizona State University on February 25–26, 2001. The funding for the conference came from the generous support of the Harold and Jean Grossman Chair of Jewish Studies at Arizona State University. I wish to thank Norbert M. Samuelson, Professor of Religious Studies and the holder of the Grossman Chair, for making this support possible and for providing advice about the running of the conference. Other units at ASU contributed to the conference: the Department of History, the Department of Philosophy, the Department of Religious Studies, the Lincoln Center for Applied Ethics, and the Women's Studies Program. To the chairs of these units thanks is hereby given. The essay by Suzanne Last Stone appeared first in *Cardozo Studies in Law and Literature* 8 (1996). I thank the editors of the journal for allowing me to bring this essay, in a revised form, to the readers of the volume. I could not have accomplished the work on the manuscript without the help of my research assistant, Mary Egel. Her meticulous copyediting made it possible for me to bring the volume to press sooner rather than later. Finally, my gratitude is conveyed to my editor at Indiana University Press, Janet Rabinowitch, who enthusiastically supported this project and made the volume as good as it could possibly be.

The project was funded by a grant from the Academy of Jewish Philosophy.

WOMEN AND GENDER IN JEWISH PHILOSOPHY

HAVA TIROSH-SAMUELSON

Editor's Introduction: Jewish Philosophy in Conversation with Feminism

Toward a Conversation

Feminism has thoroughly transformed contemporary Judaism. After centuries of being excluded, Jewish women have finally become active interpreters of their own tradition as rabbis, teachers, academic scholars, and communal leaders. Feminism has also transformed the academic discipline of Jewish studies. The flourishing of the field of Jewish studies in North America in the 1970s coincided with and was influenced by the emergence of women's studies and black studies. The discipline of Jewish studies was transformed in response to a simple question—what about women? In the attempt to answer this question, all aspects of Jewish Studies—Bible, rabbinics, history, Hebrew literature, political science, sociology, ethnography, and other sub-fields such as Holocaust studies, Israel studies, and film studies—have been profoundly changed.[1]

Of all the disciplines within Jewish studies, Jewish philosophy has been least affected by feminism. Although several women, including Colette Sirat, Sarah Heller-Willensky, Sara Klein-Braslavy, and Rivkah Horwitz, are well-known historians of Jewish philosophy, their scholarship has not been informed by feminism in general or by feminist philosophy in particular. They have instead been influenced by the standards and conventions of the academic study of Judaism. Aware of this situation, in 1986 Heidi Ravven published an essay titled "Creating a Jewish Feminist Philosophy."[2] She challenged Jewish women philosophers "to contribute to the philosophic definition and analysis of the central beliefs and praxis of women,"[3] and argued that "women's ethical, social, erotic, and spiritual expressions ought to influence the choice of a philosophic approach to integrate them into Jewish philosophy."[4] Ravven proposed the Hegelian notion of "concrete universality" as an overarching principle within which feminists could find "a systematic way of integrating their experiences and formations of Judaism into Jewish philosophy." In the late 1980s and 1990s, a few (male) scholars of Jewish philosophy did take note of feminism and acknowledged its potential influence on the field, but even these sympathetic voices have had but a limited familiarity with feminist philosophic literature.[5] Their less sympathetic colleagues have simply ignored feminist philosophy, presumably because they regard it as irrelevant or philosophically inconsequential.[6]

In 1994, I (then writing under the surname "Tirosh-Rothschild") attempted to account for this state of affairs in an essay titled "'Dare to Know': Feminism and the Discipline of Jewish Philosophy."[7] To introduce the reader to the discipline of feminist philosophy, this essay summarized the main strands of feminist philosophy and attempted to explain why the field has failed to make an impact on Jewish philosophy. I argued that the failure reflects a debate about the meaning of philosophy. Practitioners of Jewish philosophy have not taken either feminist philosophy or Jewish feminism seriously because they have not regarded it as philosophy proper. Rather, feminism has been viewed as a political ideology or a social theory that is either irrelevant to Jewish philosophy or that does not have philosophical merit. Furthermore, my essay noted that the indifference to feminist philosophy arises from the fact that Jewish philosophy is committed to the very modernist assumption about knowledge, the so-called Enlightenment Project, which feminist philosophy has challenged. Conversely, feminist philosophers were paying no attention to Jewish philosophy, reflecting the marginal status of Jewish philosophy among practitioners in the academy. The essay went on to show that Jewish philosophy and feminist philosophy have much in common: both believe that philosophy must take into consideration the identity of the knower; both philosophize on the basis of concrete, space-time bound experiences; and both critique the totalizing, presumably universalistic claims of Western philosophy. Given the shared ground, the essay called on Jewish philosophers, Jewish feminists, and feminist philosophers to enter a conversation that could transform all three discourses. Such conversation could potentially correct some of the excesses in feminist philosophy, broaden the scope of Jewish philosophy, and deepen the vision of Jewish feminism.

To date, however, the discourse of Jewish feminism has been theological and hermeneutical rather than philosophical.[8] Feminist Jewish theologians such as Judith Plaskow and Ellen Umansky exposed the gender biases of traditional Judaism and gave rise to a distinctive feminist spirituality and midrash.[9] While Jewish feminism brought creative innovations to Jewish religious life in North America, the Jewish feminist academic discourse continues to lack philosophical rigor, in part because its framers were trained in religious studies rather than in departments of philosophy. One exception to this generalization is Susan E. Shapiro. In an essay on Moses Maimonides,[10] she focuses on the gendered language of Maimonides's metaphysics that equates form with male and matter with female.[11] Shapiro argues that although Maimonides's genderized language reflects the actual, uneven power relations between men and women, his own use of rhetoric in the teaching of philosophy might instruct contemporary Jewish philosophers to rethink the relationship between philosophy and rhetoric along lines similar to the feminist critique of the Western masculine conception of reason. Although Shapiro's attempt to include rhetoric in philosophy is problematic, her essay marked an important contribution to the emerging conversation between Jewish philosophy and feminism. Yet Shapiro did not address the challenge I posed in "'Dare to Know.'"

This volume is an attempt to bring about a new conversation between feminism and Jewish philosophy. The volume originated in a conference that took place at Arizona State University[12] and includes essays that were either delivered in or solicited for the conference. While feminism informs the conversation of the volume, *the volume does not constitute a feminist Jewish philosophy.* Rather, this is a collection of essays by Jewish women philosophers who think about Jewish philosophy and within the Jewish philosophical tradition in light of feminist philosophy.

The volume reaches no consensus about the merits of feminism and feminist philosophy. Several contributors either critique or express deep ambivalence and discomfort about feminist philosophy. A few contributors, who see themselves first and foremost as philosophers, find the feminist critique of the ideal of rationality quite disturbing, since it frustrates the very commitment to truth that is the hallmark of philosophy. And still others treat feminist philosophy with respect, but regard their primary identification to be with Judaism and Jewish philosophy rather than with feminism or feminist philosophy. While maintaining that Jewish philosophy can be enriched through the conversation with feminist philosophy, these contributors also believe that Jewish philosophy can correct and challenge some aspects of feminist philosophy. Finally, there are those who endorse the feminist claim that gender is a useful category in philosophical analysis and proceed to show the centrality of concepts such as *mother*, or *the feminine* in the works of (male) Jewish philosophers.

The lack of consensus about feminism is paralleled by a lack of consensus about the meaning of Jewish philosophy. For some, Jewish philosophy is the pursuit of abstract, universal truths regardless of any particularistic considerations such as sex or class, even though the discipline is limited to Jewish topics. For others, Jewish philosophy is an analytic inquiry into the assumptions, beliefs, and practices of Judaism.[13] This inquiry can be undertaken for the sake of understanding the Jewish past, in which case Jewish philosophy is akin to the history of ideas or intellectual history; or it can be carried as a constructive, hermeneutical endeavor, in which case Jewish philosophy is inseparable from Jewish theology. Several participants, however, denied the validity of this distinction and claimed that the very act of retelling the history of Jewish philosophy is to engage in constructive philosophical activity. And for still others, Jewish philosophy is primarily an exegetical endeavor whose goal is to fathom the meaning of the divinely revealed tradition that must be true, since God is truth.

The diversity of viewpoints reflects each contributor's location in the spectrum of modern Judaism, her philosophical training, her views on modernism and postmodernism, the extent of her familiarity with feminist philosophy, her biological age, and her academic career. But beyond all these factors, I believe that the lack of consensus among the contributors illustrates the liberating power of philosophy. When women exercise their innate ability to think and dare to know about their selves, the world, and truth, they challenge all forms of dogmatic thinking, get rid of clichés and unreasoned opinions, and expose untruths. Regardless of how the commitment to truth is expressed, it is evident that the very pursuit enables women to actualize their full human potential in ways that were traditionally closed to all women, including Jewish women.

Reflections on the meaning of being human frame the volume and give it coherence. That theme is engaged historically, analytically, methodologically, and constructively. Arranged chronologically, Part One includes essays that examine individual Jewish philosophers or a particular philosophical school. These essays bring to light the use of gender categories by Jewish philosophers, the potential relevance that Jewish philosophy bears to feminist philosophy, and critical reflections about feminist philosophy from the perspective of Jewish philosophy. Part Two includes essays that discuss the various sub-fields of Jewish philosophy—metaphysics, philosophy of mind, ethics, political philosophy, philosophy of law, and theology. These essays wrestle with the theoretical challenges that feminist philosophy poses to Jewish philosophy and, conversely, propose potential contributions of Jewish philosophy to feminist thought. Out of this discussion emerge three main themes: the problem of knowledge and human embodiment, the relationship between the self and the other, and the problem of power.

🌸 *The Main Themes*

HUMAN EMBODIMENT AND KNOWLEDGE

The human body, especially the body of women, has stood at the center of the feminist agenda, both politically and philosophically.[14] Feminism began as a political revolution by focusing on the body of the female as a vehicle of liberation from male oppression. In the 1960s and 1970s, women demanded greater control over their bodies and the freedom to choose what is appropriate for their bodies. The locus of the debate was the right of women to abortion, which gave rise to feminist philosophical reflections on all areas in which the female body itself is involved, be they abortion, rape, women's labor, and any practice that limits the freedom of the female to control her body or to express herself through the body. The *material* body of the female was the locus of self-assertion and philosophical reflection.

In the 1980s and 1990s, feminist philosophy shifted the interest from the material body to *representation* of the female body in Western culture.[15] The argument was that the very association of women with body in Western culture has been oppressive to women, because the body was that which the male philosopher had to transcend in order to be fully human.[16] Much of feminist philosophy has focused on the pervasiveness of the mind–body dichotomy in Western philosophy, medicine, law, literature, and the arts, documenting the resulting negative perceptions of women. The feminist focus on the *represented body* went hand in hand with the claim that "body" is not a natural entity, but a social construct imposed on women by the dominant male-made culture.[17] Generally speaking, feminists who followed Derrida have treated the female body as a text with multiple meanings, many of them subversive to the dominant culture. And feminists who adopted the analysis of Foucault treated the female human body as itself a politically inscribed entity, its physiology and morphology shaped by the histories and practices of containment and control.

Feminist reflections on human embodiment and its relationship to knowledge went deeper when feminists focused on the connection between the female body and the way women think and express themselves. Several postmodern French feminists, including Hélène Cixous, Julia Kristeva, and Luce Irigaray, have recommended "embodied thinking." Crossing the boundaries between philosophy, literary theory, and psychoanalysis, they have criticized not only the dominant order (in particular its patriarchal aspect) and valorized the feminine, but they went even further, striving to dissolve any form of binary thinking, any *ism*, including feminism. Feminine sexuality itself should provide the model for a non-binary thinking since it is, as Irigaray has put it, "not one" but multiple and plural. By thinking from the female body, feminists expose the phallocentric nature of traditional philosophy, with its false dichotomies and hierarchic strategies liberating women from oppressive patterns of thought.[18]

Several essays in this volume consider the problem of human embodiment and knowledge: How did Jewish philosophers understand human embodiment? Did Jewish philosophers equate embodiment with "the feminine?" Did they regard anatomical differences between men and women to be relevant to thinking? How do passions, emotions, and the imagination shape human cognition according to Jewish philosophers? Are humans able to transcend their embodiment by virtue of philosophy? And what are the political implications of the conceptualization of human embodiment in Jewish philosophy?

The volume commences with an essay by Sarah Pessin, a scholar of medieval Jewish philosophy, who specializes in its Neoplatonic strand. She goes to the core of the problem that Western philosophy (including Jewish philosophy) poses to women—the association of the feminine with evil and valuation of the feminine as loss. From its beginning in the fifth century B.C.E., Greek philosophy thought about *good* and *bad* in gender categories, associating the former with *male* and the latter with *female*. The gender inflection of Western philosophy is evident in two examples: in the way Plato construed the myth of creation and in Aristotle's metaphysics and biology. For Plato, while the female functions as Creator and Sustainer, she is still subordinated to the masculine principle of Reason, the *true* Creator and Sustainer in the *Timaeus*. For Aristotle, form is active, male, and good, whereas matter is passive, female, and evil. By the same token, the male of the human species defines the standard of humanity, whereas the human female is viewed as an "incomplete male." In Greek philosophy, then, the feminine is construed both as *negation of goodness* and as *the locus of loss*.

Pessin traces the impact of Greek philosophy on Jewish philosophy by looking at Philo, Maimonides, and Kabbalah. For all three, the feminine is identified with "privation, deprivation and depravity" and identified with the chaotic, the weak, and the passive. But Pessin's concern is not limited to exposing the negative perception of the feminine in medieval Jewish philosophy. In the eleventh-century philosopher-poet Solomon ibn Gabirol, she finds a different conception of matter and of passivity, one that departs from the dominant theme of feminine-as-loss. Gabirol's works enables Pessin to "ground a feminist voice" within Jewish philosophy. This is not to say that Gabirol was a feminist, but that in Gabirol's philosophy one can find a positive valuation of matter and passivity and a different understanding of desire. Instead of defining the masculine as the locus of power and hence regarding the feminine as representing the desire to become masculine, Gabirol's discourse on matter understands it as a "receptive longing for completion." In identifying the most sublime grade of matter with the feminine, and positing matter as ontologically superior to form, Gabirol offers a different view of humanity, one based on love and on erotic receptivity. While Pessin shows how Gabirol's teachings were indebted to an obscure textual tradition in Islamic philosophy wrongly attributed to Empedocles, she also insightfully hints that Gabirol's metaphysics anticipates Levinas's teachings on relationality and the feminist "ethics of care." Both of these themes will be explored at length in this volume.

Like Pessin, Idit Dobbs-Weinstein specializes in medieval Jewish philosophy, but if Pessin discovers feminist possibilities in the Neoplatonic teachings of Gabirol, Dobbs-Weinstein focuses on the Aristotelian tradition and finds in it the inspiration for a feminist stance within Jewish philosophy. Like other feminist critics of the Western philosophical canon, Dobbs-Weinstein reminds us that the act of philosophizing and the telling of the history of philosophy are always political acts. Most sensitive to patterns of oppression, suppression, or exclusion, Dobbs-Weinstein shows that they are present not only in the way Western philosophy has constructed its own history but also in the way that feminists have critiqued the Western canon. Indeed, she argues that Western philosophy is rooted in a fusion of Platonism and Christianity and that traces of it are manifested also in the feminist critique of Western philosophy. As a historian of philosophy Dobbs-Weinstein seeks to set the record straight by focusing on the Aristotelian strand, especially as understood by medieval Jewish and Muslim philosophers. This literature, Dobbs-Weinstein holds, "can provide an invaluable resource to the feminist critique of the philosophical canon."

Dobbs-Weinstein turns to Levi ben Gershom, known as Gersonides (1288–1344), and to Spinoza (1632–1675) as two examples of marginalization and exclusion in Jewish philosophy and in Western philosophy. Gersonides's *Wars of the Lord* was placed under a ban and his technical philosophical discourses on human knowledge were never published. Spinoza was excommunicated by the Jewish community of Amsterdam. In Gersonides and Spinoza, Dobbs-Weinstein finds "concrete examples for a critique of the modern universal (male) subject, whose disembodied knowledge implicitly underlies all modern ethics and political philosophy." She wishes to recover a materialist theory of knowledge that could serve as an antidote to the dualistic tendencies of Western (Christian) philosophy. Gersonides provides such a theory when he claims that all acts of knowledge are embedded: there is no knowledge without sensation. Continuing this line of thinking, Dobbs-Weinstein argues, Spinoza goes further when he exposes the political consequences of all philosophical activity. In agreement with contemporary feminists, Spinoza teaches that it is absurd to base "politics on an abstract ideal of the human being, as an escape from nature that neither has not nor could exist." In the anti-utopian, anti-totalitarian, and democratic vision of Spinoza, Dobbs-Weinstein finds meaningful vision for women and Jews in the post-Holocaust age.

Spinoza's philosophy is also the point of departure for Heidi Ravven's vision for women and Jews in contemporary, democratic societies. Ravven, too, rejects a distinction between the history of Jewish philosophy and constructive Jewish philosophy, because for her telling the story of the past necessarily involves the teller in interpretation; all historians of Jewish philosophy are necessarily commentators. She considers the act of commenting to be a Jewish activity *par excellence* and rejects a narrow understanding of Jewish philosophy as an endeavor just for Jews, about Jews, and by Jews. The value of Jewish philosophy lies in its universal truths about the human condition, including truths about women. Ravven finds Spinoza most relevant to women and to Jews because he "envisioned the philosophic life, which was also the consummate ethical life, as aiming at the liberation from all forms of oppression, and particularly, internalized oppression." Spinoza was neither a proto-feminist nor an anti-feminist, but he was concerned with "the plight of the powerless and proposed a remedy for the internal emotional and cognitive effects of such powerlessness." In Spinoza, then, feminists and Jews could find a way to think about human embodiment that denies Descartes's mind/body dualism.[19] Taking Spinoza as her model for the liberation from oppression, Ravven agrees with the feminist maxim that "the personal is political," but she also takes feminist "ethics of care" to task.[20] Not only are feminist philosophers insufficiently aware of their own continued commitments to Cartesian and Kantian models, but they also fall short of Spinoza's ideal of intellectual love and of his ethical project of full liberation and freedom. Through analysis of Spinoza's understanding of the human Self, and especially his concept of "passivity," Ravven presents a view of philosophy that could be meaningful to women and Jews.

The main example of materialist philosophy, of course, is Karl Marx. Marx's place in the history of Jewish philosophy is even more problematic than Spinoza's. If Spinoza was informed about his Jewish philosophical predecessors and refused to convert to Christianity after his excommunication, Marx was baptized as a young child and wrote one of the most virulent anti-Semitic attacks on Jews and Judaism as part of his scathing critique of religion. Historically speaking, however, no account of modern Jewish history and Jewish intellectual life is complete without consideration of Marxist thought, because Jews flocked in great numbers to Socialist and Communist movements and became leading theoreticians. Similarly, no account of modern philosophy can ignore the fact that leading Marxist philosophers, for example, followers of the Frankfurt School, were Jews. Furthermore, a Marxist-based analysis of history and of the human condition was at the foundation of Labor Zionism that shaped Israeli culture before and after the establishment of the State of Israel. With the notable exception of Steven Schwarzschild, Jewish philosophy rarely refers to Marxism, because most Jewish philosophers hold the very religious beliefs that Marx so vehemently critiqued.

Unlike Jewish philosophy, feminist thought is deeply indebted to Marxism.[21] Marxist theories of human nature, society, economics, politics, and the family have inspired a rich body of feminist literature as well as fierce debates among feminists. Philosophically, the most significant impact of Marxism on feminism was the development of "feminist standpoint theory" on the basis of Marxist epistemology.[22] Diemut Bubeck summarizes it as such:

> Two premises generate the idea of different standpoints. First different material conditions, especially different kinds of work and work relations, generate not only different experiences but also different conceptualizations and perspectives, and thus ultimately different theories about the world. Secondly there are systematic divisions between different groups in society with respect to material conditions of their lives. Given these groups' different material locations, stand point theorists conclude that their experience of the world is characteristically different, and therefore their beliefs and theories are also different: they have different standpoints.[23]

On this basis, feminists have articulated a "feminist standpoint epistemology" as a major challenge to the conventions of philosophy that claim to know what is universally true regardless of the identity of the knower.[24]

Trained in Marxist philosophy, Jean Axelrad Cahan reflects on Jewish philosophy and on Jewish feminism from that perspective. In agreement with Jürgen Habermas, who denounced the French critique of rationality and modernity,[25] Cahan commends the Marxist "mode of critique of history and politics . . . its retention of universal concepts and capacity for abstraction . . . its analyses of commodification and of daily life; and its overall critical and oppositional stance toward dominant forces and powers of a given epoch." Cahan criticizes feminists for "so heavily emphasizing the bodily dimensions of existence," at the expense of "the possibilities of abstraction" that men and women share. For Cahan, rational thinking is the foundation of equality between men and women. Cahan accuses contemporary Jewish feminism of "philosophical myopia" and she presents classical Marxist theory as a way to recover the very philosophical thinking that feminists find oppressive to women. Furthermore, Cahan claims that the feminist preoccupation with sex difference has obscured the economic origins of many forms of oppression of women, especially in late capitalism. Many of the problems that women face, including their problematic status in traditional Jewish societies, Cahan argues, are not due to philosophy but to social and economic factors. As a philosopher, however, Cahan rejects the Marxist claim that universal ideas are but social constructs. Deeply committed to the Enlightenment Project, Cahan proceeds to engage three contemporary Jewish feminists—Miriam Peskowitz, Daniel Boyarin, and Susan Shapiro—from a Marxist perspective. Cahan argues that they uncritically employ Marxist categories, on the one hand, and that they fail to engage the task posed by Marxist philosophy, on the other hand.

A different engagement of the "feminist standpoint epistemology" is offered by T. M. Rudavsky, a historian of medieval Jewish philosophy who is also conversant with Anglo-American analytic philosophy. Rudavsky's essay "analyzes the implications of feminist critiques of metaphysics and epistemology with respect to the development and self-perception of Jewish philosophy." In line with my "'Dare to Know,'" Rudavsky summarizes the main claims of feminist philosophy and notes the overlap between them and Jewish philosophy. However, she rejects the radical feminist critique of allegedly "masculinist" philosophy, because it fails to abide by the criteria of rationality that guide the philosophical pursuit of truth.[26] Furthermore, the feminist critique does not do justice to the complexity of the Western philosophical tradition. In the case of medieval Jewish philosophy, for example, a close examination indicates its ambivalence with regard to the primacy of reason, the espousal of objectivity, and the postulation of metaphysical essentialism. As for perception of women, medieval Jewish philosophy had a mixed record, including negative perceptions as well as egalitarian possibilities. Thus, exoterically Maimonides's *Guide of the Perplexed* associated the female with negative characteristics, thereby contributing to the exclusion of women from philosophy or their social marginalization. But esoterically, Maimonides presented the prophetess Miriam to have "penetrated the mysterious that is defended by negative predicates." Maimonides then posited a "philosophical spirituality" that is, in principle, accessible to women. The upshot of Rudavsky's analysis is that when a Jewish philosopher engages the philosophic past openly and critically, the study exposes harmful negative perceptions of women while offering women the spiritual benefits of philosophical activity.

THE SELF AND THE OTHER: HUMAN RELATIONALITY

If pre-modern Jewish thinkers looked at rationality as the mark of humanity, Jewish existentialist (male) philosophers regarded relationality as the core of being human. A second cluster of reflections about being human surrounds the relationship between the self and the other. Does Jewish philosophy view the self as an autonomous entity that strives toward self-realization or rather as a subjectivity that responds to the presence of the other? If for some Jewish philosophers being human means possessing a capacity to respond to the presence of the other, what do they share with feminist philosophers and where do they differ?

Feminist reflections on the human self emerge as a critique of Kant, who linked moral agency to the autonomy of reason and to the ideal of impartial normativity. Feminists have charged that Kant "neglects matters of care and close personal relationship"[27] and insisted that "moral reasoning is grounded in social life" and that emotions are a legitimate ingredient of moral understanding. Emotional sensitivity to the feelings and attitudes of others emerges through interpersonal relations among individuals who communicate with each other within social communities.[28] Moreover, several feminist philosophers have argued, this type of moral reasoning is exercised especially by women who find themselves in the position of caregivers and nurturers, as mothers, wives, and daughters. Feminist philosophy of care has thus been promoted as a major alternative to Kantian moral philosophy and its more recent formulation by John Rawls.

Leora Batnitzky, who specializes in modern Continental philosophy, shows that the feminist critique of Kantian ethics has much in common with the views of Franz Rosenzweig (1896–1929), Martin Buber (1878–1965), and Emmanuel Levinas (1906–1992), albeit with important differences. Batnitzky analyzes the use of the category of "the feminine" in their works and explores their claim that ethics and responsibility emerge from human dependence and vulnerability. She shows that "Jewish existentialist thinkers have a greater affinity with contemporary 'women-centered' feminist philosophies and with feminist philosophies of care . . . than they do with either Sartre or de Beauvoir's existentialism." Like the feminist ethics of care, Jewish existentialist philosophers hold that caring is the response to human vulnerability. However, Batnitzky also maintains that Jewish philosophy can call into question the post-liberal rhetoric that permeates feminist philosophy (often unconsciously) and she is critical of the notion of "the feminine." Looking closely at Levinas's construal of "the feminine," Batnitzky argues that "Levinas's use of 'the feminine' is a de-theologized and de-politicized version of Rosenzweig's arguments about the relation between Judaism and Christianity." Since she finds the equation of Judaism and "the feminine" and of women and "the feminine" to be historically and philosophically problematic, she concludes that "Jewish philosophy and feminist philosophy will do better without the use of 'the feminine.'" Through conversation with feminist philosophers of care, Batnitzky proceeds to correct the problems in Jewish existentialist philosophy and in feminist philosophy by turning to the Neo-Kantian virtue ethics of Hermann Cohen (1842–1918) to reconfigure the relationship between autonomy, freedom, and equality.

If vulnerability and dependence capture the core of being human, it is not surprising that Emmanuel Levinas viewed the relationship between mother and child as the paradigm of the ethical. Claire E. Katz, who writes on French philosophy and on philosophy of education, analyzes the role that the figure of "the feminine" plays in his philosophy. Like Batnitzky, Katz presents the philosophy of Levinas as a Jewish critique of Western, masculine philosophy and of its notion that philosophy is a preparation for one's own death. Shifting the focus of philosophy from ontology to ethics, Levinas "replaces the concern for my own death with the concern for the other's death." In doing so, Levinas signals that "subjectivity is always already inter-subjective." While this point is in accord with the tenor of feminist ethics, Levinas has been criticized by feminists, especially by Luce Irigaray, for being a sexist, for privileging heterosexual marriage, and for marginalizing women. Engaging several feminist readers of Levinas, Katz refutes their misreadings by situating Levinas's phenomenology in its proper Jewish matrix, especially noting his indebtedness to Rosenzweig, and by looking closely at his reading of biblical narratives.

Most instructively, Katz reminds us that for Levinas, in contrast to Sartre and Simone de Beauvoir, the other is *not* that which threatens the self, seeking to control, manipulate, and even annihilate the self. Rather, the other is "the one to whom I am most responsible." To be a human is to stand in an ethical relationship with the other who places obligations on the self that are neither cognitive nor chosen. "The feminine" is the central trope of Levinas's philosophy because it captures the irreducible alterity of the other. For this reason, Jacques Derrida criticized Levinas on the grounds that he is limited to one sex, and that he privileges the male over the female. Contrary to Derrida, Katz presents Levinas as a thinker who understands the human as a sexed being from the very moment of creation. However, the distinction between male and female in created humans is not meant to teach us about equity between the sexes. The other, signified by "the feminine," can never be equal to the self, because the other always places obligations on the self to which the self responds without choice or cognition. Because of the inequality between self and other in the ethical relationship, maternity plays such a major role in Levinas's philosophy. Katz analyzes this trope and presents Levinas's ethics as a Jewish critique to the Christian understanding of charitable love (*agapē*).

The centrality of maternity for feminist and Jewish existentialist philosophers is challenged by a startling fact: mothers sometimes do kill their children. How can feminists account for this evil act? Laurie Zoloth, a scholar of social ethics and bioethics, who is informed by and sympathetic to postmodernist philosophy and Jewish postmodernism, takes up the issue in the context of her wrestling with the problem of evil. Zoloth charges that feminist theory suffers from a "terrible lacuna" because it does not address the problem of evil adequately.[29] In their determination to expose patterns of suppression and victimization, feminists have ignored the fact that women do perpetrate abominable crimes, including killing their own children. Rejecting rule ethics, Zoloth closely examines some of the most notorious cases of mothers who have killed, and critiques the attempts of feminists to excuse these cases by appealing to insanity or oppression. Calling on feminists to face the problem of evil more honestly and deeply, Zoloth engages the reflections on evil by John Kekes, Alain Badiou, and Hannah Arendt in order to glean from them useful ways of thinking about evil. Most instructively, Zoloth suggests that the rabbinic conception of the Evil Inclination (*yetzer hara*) can be useful to feminist social ethics because it acknowledges the human proclivity to do evil while placing moral boundaries and demanding that humans exercise choice and responsibility.

POWER, LAW, AND JUSTICE

Reflections on the problem of evil are necessarily linked to reflections about power (both human and divine) and about justice. Since Judaism posits the existence of a just God whose will is revealed in the Law—the Torah—it is understandable that the third cluster of issues in the volume concerns the problem of power and its relationship to law. These essays are written in an attempt to think through how feminist political theory, jurisprudence, and theology could enrich Jewish philosophy and, conversely, how the Jewish philosophical tradition could respond to some of the claims of feminist philosophy.

The uses and abuses of power have been a major concern for Jews and for women. In their long history, Jews have experienced short periods of political power alternating with the long durations of Jewish political powerlessness and social marginalization. Sensitivity to the needs of the oppressed and the powerless has been at the center of the prophetic teaching, calling Israel to speak truth to abusive human powers and seek justice. The revealed Torah itself defines the boundaries of justice and prescribes specific acts to curb the abuses of power and to address the needs of the powerless in Israelite society. The attention to the suffering of the powerless in Judaism was so prevalent that the rabbis depicted God as a caring, suffering God who shares in the pain of the People of Israel.

The implications of this portrayal for the conversation between Jewish philosophy and feminist legal theory are discussed by Suzanne Last Stone, a scholar of American constitutional law and of Jewish law. Stone analyzes the gender inflection of the central divine attributes—mercy and judgment—in order to illustrate how "feminist jurisprudence would benefit from a less polemical, more nuanced confrontation with the rabbinic legal tradition," and conversely, how "Jewish legal studies would be enriched by incorporating feminist methodologies that take gender categories seriously in understanding law and that focus on the emotional and socio-sexual aspects of law." Treating midrash as "philosophical expression" of general legal principles, Stone looks carefully at a midrash from Lamentations Rabbah and shows that its gender categories are very fluid. Divine justice itself does not conform to the "masculine" stereotype and God is depicted as Israel's wife, acting out of mercy and through attention to emotional considerations. The complex use of gender categories problematizes the feminist claim that a monotheistic conception of a masculine God lies at the root of the modernist notion of law as impartial, objective, and rational. Yet Stone is not ready to conclude that Jewish law is "written in a feminist voice." Instead, she argues that in rabbinic literature, "the masculine, like the feminine, is constantly redefined" because the male rabbis delineated their identity not just in reference to women but also in reference to non-Jews. Thus the trait of mercy was ascribed to Israel (to both men and women) but the "aggressive masculine characteristics such as vengeance and violence, were attributed to non-Jews." The complex depiction of God leads, in turn, to a complex legal theory, one that addresses many of the concerns of feminist legal theory.

Whereas feminist legal theorists in the 1990s criticized the modernist theories of judging as masculine and feminist philosophers charged that the adversarial method of analytic philosophy is itself masculine,[30] feminist political theorists exposed male domination in all social structures. When the "second wave" of feminism emerged in the late 1960s it was an angry rebellion against all forms of male domination and male oppression of women. Feminist political activism thus intended to bring an end to patterns of exclusion, domination, and exploitation and, at the same time, to empower women to take their rightful place in the public sphere. Concomitantly, feminist theorists highlighted the limits of liberal democracy and its inadequate dealing with the power imbalance between men and women in the public and private spheres.[31] While feminist activism led to the transformation of politics, economics, law, education, and culture, the very access of power itself accentuated the problem of responsibility noted by Zoloth. Do women wield power differently than men? Do women use power more justly and responsibly? Can the victims of the past avoid becoming victimizers once they have access to power? Only time will provide the answers to these questions. At present, feminist theoretical discourse does not address these questions because it is still committed to expositing the subtle ways in which women, more than most oppressed groups, have suffered and are suffering the covert and overt faces of power. The determination to liberate themselves from the abuses of power has led feminists to embrace the democratic principle, to be deeply committed to consensus building and decision through persuasion, and to insist on sharing institutional power. Indeed, feminists have argued that the political realm itself could and should be transformed, if it is modeled after relations formed in the private, domestic, and particular realm, for example, in mothering.[32] This was one reason for the feminist denunciation of the dichotomy between private and public and their utopian vision of politics without power.

In Judaism, any analysis of the uses and abuses of power must be undertaken within the parameters of halakhah. Yet, it was Jewish law itself that caused the unjust exclusion of Jewish women from the public sphere and their negative portrayal in traditional Judaism, according to Jewish feminists.[33] For contemporary Jewish religious women who accept the authority of the Jewish legal tradition, the rabbinic sources had to be examined anew and reinterpreted. Thus Judith Hauptman, a Talmud scholar, analyzed rabbinic texts and came to the conclusion that its (male) framers were open to the concerns and needs of women and the rabbis actually overcame some of the problems left open by the Torah.[34] Rachel Adler, among the founders of Jewish feminism, articulated a hermeneutics of rabbinic texts that allows for rethinking of their views of women and the relations between the sexes.[35] While Adler, whose views are discussed in this volume by Randi Rashkover, pioneered a new way of thinking of power relations in Judaism, much more theoretical work is necessary before a Jewish feminist political theory can be articulated. Nancy Levene's essay addresses this task.

Levene correctly notes that within Jewish philosophy "political philosophy is one of the most promising areas for feminist research," and that "Jewish political thought is potentially very fertile ground on which to nourish feminist philosophical insights." Yet such engagement should not be limited to merely noting the "affinities [that] exist between the subjects of feminist philosophy and Jewish political philosophy. Rather, a feminist Jewish political philosophy should raise the most penetrating questions about personhood, political agency, equality and freedom within Judaism." Such engagement is admittedly difficult given the religious nature of Jewish sources and the political history of the Jews in the diaspora and in the State of Israel, but it is necessary if a Jewish political feminist philosophy is to emerge.

Levene begins to address the task by arguing that Jewish law itself is much more amenable to the concerns of women and feminists than is commonly understood. Building on the work of the biblical scholar Bernard M. Levinson, Levene presents a reading of the biblical covenant that "brings into existence the radical and utopian argument that the existence of the nation is conditional upon the people's assent and ongoing commitment to the covenant." This understanding of the covenant is not only inclusive of women, but it is also the basis of a communitarian reinterpretation of the covenant. For Levene, then, "there are no Jewish political questions that are not also feminist questions." With this in mind, Levene then turns to examine Spinoza's understanding of the relationship between religion and politics and shows how his analysis of the ancient Hebrew past could help contemporary Jews to challenge the privatization of religion in modern nation-state, and "to preserve Jewish law (the 'thickness' of the tradition) by reconceiving its connection to political life and [by] highlight[ing] its fluidity, egalitarianism, and openness." Seeking to repoliticize our understanding of religion, Levene suggests that Jewish communal life in the premodern period is another fruitful source for democratic proclivities within traditional Judaism. Since Jewish legal sources recognized key democratic concepts such as consent and majority rule, it is not true that Judaism and democracy are necessarily mutually exclusive. Articulating the theoretical questions that Jewish feminist philosophy should wrestle with, Levene poses a covenantal, democratic, communitarian and egalitarian vision of Judaism.

The problem of power is theological no less than it is political or legal and the problem has become exceedingly acute after the Holocaust. Sandra B. Lubarsky engages post-Holocaust Jewish theologians—Martin Buber, Eliezer Berkowitz, and Irving (Yitz) Greenberg—who sought to understand "how power could have become so deeply perverted." Although these Jewish theologians spoke about "divine hiddenness" or absence of God, and limited the power of God, their understanding of power remains a traditional one: power's primary form is coercive.[36] Feminist philosophers, by contrast, not only critiqued dominating power, but also showed that the notion of divine hiddenness is problematic as a theological strategy. Seeking to formulate "multiple forms of alternative power," feminists proposed a relational form of power, "the quiet, gentle power of sympathy, patience, care and support." The feminist critique of dominating or coercive power (i.e., of power-over) is in accord with the analysis of power by process philosophers, such as Alfred North Whitehead and Charles Hartshorne, and their main Jewish follower, Hans Jonas. They do not confine power to the Godhead and they speak about God's power as the power of persuasion. Lubarsky considers process philosophy to be the most appropriate response to the problem of evil and to the challenges that women and Jews face today. She invites Jewish theologians to reject the notion of omnipotence and to think about persuasion as power, but a power that is "exercised in response to the integrity of other beings." With a new understanding of power based on process philosophy, it is possible to reconceptualize the covenant between Israel and God as a covenant of love, "love that encourages both self-determination and the continuity of all beings."

The historical, methodological, and constructive perspectives of the volume are woven together in the final essay by Randi Rashkover. Against the exegetical grain of postmodern Jewish philosophy, Rashkover speaks for a Jewish philosophy that is systematic, rigorous, and critical, on the one hand, and religiously committed and informed, on the other hand. For Rashkover, the midrashic orientation of postmodern Jewish philosophy is problematic because it is not sufficiently systematic, even as it takes for granted the authority of Jewish religious texts and their surplus of meaning. For this reason, she, contrary to Cahan, looks favorably at the rabbinic critique by Jewish feminists such as Miriam Peskowitz and Rachel Adler.

According to Rashkover, their engagement with rabbinic sources should be recognized as philosophical; and she defines philosophy as "conscious reflections upon the drama of human inter-subjective engagement." This definition of philosophy is indebted to the Neo-Hegelian philosophy of the British Jewish philosopher, Gillian Rose.[37]

Rashkover finds Rose most inspiring because of her attempt "to resuscitate philosophy against . . . the postmodern 'renunciation of reason.'" Yet Rose was also very aware that knowledge is a product of inter-subjective relations. Rose differs from other postmodern writers in her Neo-Hegelian claim that the form of inter-subjective relations is law. Through law, one learns "that life is a perpetual process of desire, risk, engagement and investment with others." Rashkover finds this insight instructive for the rethinking of Jewish philosophy for the twenty-first century. Rose also provides Rashkover with a model of dealing with the problem of power and the realization that law is necessary as a limit on power. Rose's own analysis of rabbinic texts enables Rashkover to approach them as "expressions of law and the politics of power," while defining the task of philosophy as "[taking] note of law and the endless repetition of its perpetual cycle from desire to loss, to reflection, back to desire." To be human, according to Rashkover, means to experience the anxiety of the law, an anxiety that can be overcome only through the life of faith. While Rashkover endorses the works of Peskowitz and Adler, because she reads them through the lens of Rose's philosophy, Rashkover also believes that they do not accomplish the task of Jewish philosophy. Peskowitz's work is blatantly secular, and Adler is not sufficiently open about her own theological commitments. If Jewish feminism is going to produce philosophical theology that can overcome the problems of the exegetical modality, then a new model is necessary. Rashkover finds the paradigm in the philosophical theological of David Novak.

Endorsing Novak's critique of Cohen, Buber, and Levinas, Rashkover explores his notion of natural law in light of Rose's philosophy, whose main concept is "theological desire." Theological desire means the existential yearning for a God who creates the world as a home for us and who establishes a relationship with us through which we feel secure. Through theological desire, Rashkover explains, we become persons of faith. Can there be room for rationality in this model of faith? Rashkover answers in the affirmative, calling on feminists to appreciate the religious significance of a philosophically rigorous feminist hermeneutics. Philosophical analysis, Rashkover maintains in contrast to Ravven, Cahan, and Rudavsky, cannot remain devoid of theology.

Jewish Philosophy in Conversation with Feminism

🌀 Implications

As rich and suggestive as these essays are, the conversation between feminist philosophy and Jewish philosophy has just begun. Further analysis and creative thinking are yet to be undertaken before feminist Jewish philosophy can fully address the challenge Heidi Ravven posed in 1986. Nonetheless, on the basis of this volume we can look ahead and spell out the messages of its contributors to Jewish philosophy, feminist philosophy, and Jewish feminism.

To practitioners of Jewish philosophy, the volume makes clear that there are Jewish women who teach, study, and do Jewish philosophy. The question, Are there women Jewish philosophers? should now be put to rest. Women practitioners of Jewish philosophy should not only be included in all professional activities, but their views, claims, and arguments should also be debated, critiqued, and challenged. No interpretation of Jewish philosophy offered herein is above dispute and no reading is necessarily true. As the contributors to this volume invite scholars of Jewish philosophy to engage them, they also call on Jewish philosophers (both men and women) to become familiar with the rich feminist philosophic literature cited in the essays, and to address its philosophical significance. Such familiarity could lead to a more accurate and rich understanding of feminist thought and can stimulate the avoidance of global and superficial generalizations about "feminism." For Jewish philosophers to continue to dismiss feminist philosophy on the grounds that it is philosophically derivative or shallow is but a convenient way to perpetuate either ignorance or laziness. The volume also makes it clear that no analysis of Jewish philosophy (historical and constructive) can be complete without attention to gender categories. *By including women in Jewish philosophy, this volume also ensures that gender is included in the purview of Jewish philosophy.*

Concomitantly, the volume invites feminist philosophers both to become familiar with Jewish philosophy and to recognize what the two discourses have in common. Encountering Jewish philosophy might lead feminist philosophers to become conscious of their own "blind spots" and their own continued loyalty to some of the unspoken assumptions of the Western philosophical tradition. Since Jewish philosophy itself developed as a critique of Western philosophy, some of the limitations of philosophy criticized by feminists are not applicable to Jewish philosophy. Feminist philosophers will do well to engage with another way of conceptualizing difference, and thereby to recognize that for feminism to be truly emancipatory it must not only endorse a plurality of voices, but must make room for religious self-understanding.

Lastly, this volume calls on Jewish men, women, and especially on Jewish feminists to become philosophically informed. The cultivation of philosophy is good for Jews because the critical thinking involved in the pursuit of truth enables Jews to discard all forms of conscious and unconscious self-deception, to challenge harmful uses of ideology, indoctrination, and dogmatism, and to become more honest and subtle in the practice of Judaism.[38] Jewish feminism has succeeded in transforming the practices of Jewish public life. Yet if Jewish feminism is to continue to grow, it must include philosophical awareness and must continue to examine itself in light of what we know to be true about being human. The analysis of the human condition itself should be undertaken in light of what we know in evolutionary psychology, genetics, and the cognitive sciences. And when such examinations are undertaken, we may find that gender identity and preferences are not just a matter of social construction; they have also much to do with the nature of human beings. Biology may play a larger role in shaping humans than feminists have been willing to admit.[39] With this volume, we have come closer to formulating a feminist Jewish philosophy, but the task is not yet complete.

NOTES

1. For an overview of the impact of feminism on Jewish studies, see Lynn Davidman and Shelly Tenenbaum, eds., *Feminist Perspectives on Jewish Studies* (New Haven, Conn.: Yale University Press, 1994); Renee Levine Melammed, ed., *"Lift Up Your Voice": Women's Voices and Feminist Interpretation in Jewish Studies* (Hebrew) (Tel Aviv: Yediot Aharonot and Sifrei Hemed, 2001).

2. Heidi Ravven, "Creating a Jewish Feminist Philosophy," *Anima* 12, no. 2 (1986): 99–112.

3. Ibid., 100.

4. Ibid., 101.

5. See Kenneth Seeskin, "Jewish Philosophy in the 1980s," *Modern Judaism* 11 (1991): 160; Steven Katz, "Jewish Philosophy in the 1980s: A Diagnosis and Prescription," in *Studies in Jewish Philosophy*, ed. Norbert M. Samuelson (Lanham, Md.: University Press of America), 61–100; Eugene B. Borowitz, *Renewing the Covenant: A Theology of the Post-Modern Jew* (Philadelphia: Jewish Publication Society, 1991). For the most sustained engagement of a male Jewish philosopher with feminist philosophy and with Jewish feminism, consult Michael Oppenheim, "To Notice the Color of Her Eyes: Facing the Feminist Jewish Critique," in his *Speaking/Writing of God: Jewish Philosophical Reflections on the Life with Others* (Albany: State University of New York Press), 53–82.

6. A notable exception is Elliot R. Wolfson, who has absorbed the feminist critique of Luce Irigaray in his analysis of gender imagery in Kabbalah. Among Wolfson's numerous writing on gender we may note *Circle in the Square: Studies in the Use of Gender in Kab-*

balistic Symbolism (Albany: State University of New York Press, 1995); idem, "Occultation of the Feminine and the Body of Secrecy in Medieval Kabbalah," in *Rending the Veil: Concealment and Secrecy in the History of Religion,* ed. Elliot R. Wolfson (New York and London: Seven Bridges Press, 1999), 113–54; idem, "Woman—The Feminine as Other in Theosophic Kabbalah: Some Philosophical Observations on the Divine Androgyne," in *The Other in Jewish Thought and History: Construction of Jewish Culture and Identity* (New York: New York University Press, 1994), 166–204. While Wolfson's studies have been hotly debated by scholars of Kabbalah, they have not attracted criticism from scholars of Jewish philosophy, even though some could agree with Wolfson's contention that Kabbalah is an integral part of Jewish philosophy. See Elliot R. Wolfson, "Jewish Mysticism: A Philosophical Overview," in *History of Jewish Philosophy,* ed. Daniel H. Frank and Oliver Leaman (New York and London: Routledge, 1997), 450–98.

7. The essay was published in *Feminist Perspectives on Jewish Studies,* 85–119. The essay elicited several responses: see Heidi M. Ravven, "Observations on Jewish Philosophy and Feminist Thought," *Judaism* 46 (1997): 422–38; Michael Oppenheim, "Feminism, Jewish Philosophy and Religious Pluralism," *Modern Judaism* 16, no. 2 (1996): 147–60.

8. See Judith Plaskow, "Jewish Feminist Thought," in *History of Jewish Philosophy,* 885–94.

9. See Judith Plaskow, *Standing Again at Sinai* (San Francisco: Harper and Row, 1990); Ellen Umansky, "Creating a Jewish Feminist Theology," in *Weaving the Visions: New Patterns in Feminist Spirituality,* ed. Judith Plaskow and Carole P. Christ (San Francisco: Harper and Row, 1989); Ellen Umansky and Diane Ashton, eds., *Four Centuries of Jewish Women's Spirituality: A Sourcebook* (Boston: Beacon, 1992); Elyse Goldstein, *ReVisions: Seeing Torah Through a Feminist Lens* (Woodstock, Vt.: Jewish Lights Publications, 1998); Rachel Adler, *Engendering Judaism: An Inclusive Theology and Ethics* (Boston: Beacon, 1998).

10. Susan E. Shapiro, "A Matter of Discipline: Reading for Gender in Jewish Philosophy," in *Judaism since Gender,* ed. Miriam Peskowitz and Laura Levitt (New York: Routledge, 1997), 158–73.

11. It is instructive to compare Shapiro's feminist analysis of Maimonides's use of gender category with the non-feminist, detailed analysis of the same terms and the same passages by Sara Klein-Braslavy, *Maimonides' Interpretation of the Adam Stories in Genesis: A Study in Maimonides' Anthropology* (in Hebrew) (Jerusalem: Reuben Mass, 1986). To wit, mere attention to gender category does not necessarily manifest feminist sensibilities or commitments.

12. The conference was held at Arizona State University on February 25–26, 2001 with the support of the Harold and Jean Grossman Chair in Jewish Studies and the departments of History, Philosophy, Religious Studies, and Women Studies. The conference included (male) Jewish philosophers as respondents to the papers. Their responses are not included herein because one of the goals of this volume is to feature Jewish women who study, teach, and do Jewish philosophy.

13. For theoretical analyses of the various approaches to Jewish philosophy, see the essays in Norbert M. Samuelson, ed., *Studies in Jewish Philosophy: Collected Essays of the Academy of Jewish Philosophy 1980–1985* (Lanham, Md.: University Press of America, 1987).

14. For a philosophical analysis of the feminist discourse on embodiment see Elizabeth Grosz, "Bodies and Knowledges: Feminism and the Crisis of Reason," in *Feminist Epistemologies,* ed. Linda Alcoff and Elizabeth Potter (New York and London: Routledge, 1993), 187–215, esp. 194–210.

15. For example see Susan Rubin Suleiman, ed., *The Female Body in Western Culture: Contemporary Perspectives* (Cambridge, Mass.: Harvard University Press, 1985); Susan

Bordo, *Unbearable Weight: Feminism, Eastern Culture and the Body* (Berkeley: University of California Press, 1993).

16. This claim was first formulated by Jenevieve Lloyd, *The Man of Reason: "Male" and "Female" in Western Philosophy* (Minneapolis: University of Minnesota Press, 1984). The masculinity of Western philosophy is now taken for granted by many feminist philosophers, although some women philosophers have also challenged it. See note 26 below.

17. For an overview of the philosophical implications of this argument, see Sally Haslangar, "Feminism in Metaphysics: Negotiating the Natural," in *The Cambridge Companion to Feminism in Philosophy,* ed. Miranda Fricker and Jennifer Hornsby (Cambridge: Cambridge University Press, 2000), 107–26, esp. 117–19.

18. An illuminating but critical analysis of Irigaray and Kristeva is offered by Allison Weir, *Sacrificial Logics: Feminist Theory and the Critique of Identity* (New York and London: Routledge, 1996), 90–111 and 145–83.

19. Such re-evaluation of Spinoza has already been called for by some feminist philosophers. See Moira Gatens, "Toward a Feminist Philosophy of the Body," in *Crossing Boundaries: Feminisms and the Critique of Knowledge,* ed. Barbara Caine, Elizabeth Grosz, and Marie de Lepervanche (Sydney; Boston: Allen and Unwin, 1988); Genevieve Lloyd, *Part of Nature: Self-Knowledge in Spinoza's Nature* (Ithaca, N.Y.: Cornell University Press, 1994).

20. For an overview of feminist philosophy of care, see Marilyn Friedman, "Feminism in Ethics: Conceptions of Autonomy," in *Feminism in Philosophy,* 205–24; Joan C. Tronto, *Moral Boundaries: A Political Argument for an Ethics of Care* (New York and London: Routledge, 1993).

21. An excellent overview is provided by Rosemarie Putnam Tong, *Feminist Thought: A More Comprehensive Introduction,* 2nd ed. (Boulder: Westview Press, 1998), 94–129.

22. See Nancy C. M. Hartsock, "The Feminist Standpoint: Developing the Ground for a Specifically Feminist Historical Materialism," in *Feminism and Philosophy: Essential Readings in Theory, Reinterpretation and Application,* ed. Nancy Tuana and Rosemarie Tong (Boulder: Westview Press, 1995), 69–90.

23. Diemut Bubeck, "Feminism in Political Philosophy: Women's Difference," in *Feminism in Philosophy,* 187.

24. The "feminist standpoint epistemology" results necessarily in a pluralistic notion of knowledge and in attention to the social nature of all knowledge claims. In other words, instead of epistemology, there are only epistemological communities. A good example of this line of thought is found in *Feminist Epistemologies,* ed. Linda Alcoff and Elizabeth Potter, cited above.

25. It is instructive to compare Cahan's engagement with Habermas with Nancy Frazer's. The difference indicates both the limited impact of Critical Theory on Jewish philosophy, on the one hand, and the reticence of Jewish female philosophers to accept feminist claims, on the other hand. See Nancy Fraser, "What's Critical about Critical Theory? The Case of Habermas and Gender," in *Feminism and Philosophy: Essential Readings in Theory, Representation, and Application,* ed. Nancy Tuana and Rosemarie Tong (Boulder: Westview Press, 1995), 272–98.

26. Rudavsky's critique of feminist philosophy is similar to that of Janet Radcliff Richards, *The Skeptical Feminist* (New York: Routledge & Kegan Paul, 1980). In the summary of Andrea Nye, "Richards ridiculed feminists' suggestions that logic is male, that superior reasoning power as defined in philosophy should not be respected and that there should be no privilege attached to what is 'well argued and consistent.'" Nye, *Philosophy and Feminism: At the Border* (New York: Twayne Publishers, 1995), 28. Richards's critique

of feminism as antirational has been well received by the philosophical establishment in the United States.

27. Marilyn Friedman, "Feminism in Ethics: Conceptions of Autonomy," in *Feminism in Philosophy,* 212.

28. For an excellent examination of the role of emotion's philosophical activity, see Alison M. Jaggar, "Love and Knowledge: Emotion in Feminist Epistemology," in *Women and Reason,* ed. Elizabeth D. Harvey and Kathleen Okruhlik (Ann Arbor: University of Michigan Press, 1992), 115–42, and the bibliography cited therein.

29. Feminist philosophers, we must note, did pay attention to the problem of evil, but they did so in the context of reflecting about evil done to women rather than about the capacity of women to cause evil. For an overview of the feminist discourse on the problem of evil, see Andrea Nye, *Philosophy and Feminism,* 154–59.

30. See, for example, Janice Moulton, "A Paradigm of Philosophy: The Adversary Method," in *Discovering Reality,* ed. Sandra Harding and Merrill Hintikka (Dordrecht: D. Reidel, 1983), 149–64.

31. For an overview of feminist critique of liberal democracy, see Anne Philips, *Democracy and Difference* (University Park: Pennsylvania State University Press, 1993).

32. See Anne Philips, *Feminism and Politics* (Oxford and New York: Oxford University Press, 1998), 149–50.

33. The most celebrated example of feminist critique of Jewish law is Rachel Biale, *Women in Jewish Law: An Exploration of Women's Issues in Halakhic Sources* (New York: Schocken Books, 1984). See also Judith Romney Wegner, *Chattel or Person? The Status of Women in the Mishnah* (New York: Oxford University Press, 1988).

34. Judith Hauptman, *Rereading the Rabbis: A Woman's Voice* (Boulder: Westview Press, 1998).

35. Rachel Adler, *Engendering Judaism: An Inclusive Theology and Ethics* (Boston: Beacon Press, 1998).

36. For a recent philosophical and theological analysis of the problem of divine hiddenness, consult Daniel Howard-Snyder and Paul K. Moser (eds.), *Divine Hiddenness: New Essays* (Cambridge, England: Cambridge University Press, 2002).

37. The fact that Gillian Rose converted to Christianity on her deathbed may make Jewish philosophers uncomfortable with Rashkover's treatment of Rose as an inspiration for rethinking Jewish philosophy.

38. The role of philosophy and critical thinking in the struggle against self-deception is analyzed with great clarity by Roderick R. Hindery, *Indoctrination and Self Deception or Free and Critical Thought* (Lewiston, N.Y.: Edwin Mellen Press, 2001).

39. On the challenge to feminist theory from cognitive psychology and evolutionary biology, see Steven Pinker, *How the Mind Works* (New York and London: W. W. Norton, 1997), passim.

RE-READING JEWISH PHILOSOPHERS

Part One

ONE

❦

SARAH PESSIN

Loss, Presence, and Gabirol's Desire: Medieval Jewish Philosophy and the Possibility of a Feminist Ground

> *dew drops ambiguously*
> *withering saplings adrift*
> *opening mouths asunder*
> *(reception in revelation {receive / reveal})*
> *(conception in concealment {conceive / conceal})*
> *outpouring and indwelling*
> *the pooling tears of eros*[1]

❦ *Introduction*

As placeholder for the secondary, the subordinate, and the recalcitrant, the *feminine* survives ancient and medieval philosophy, Jewish medieval philosophy notwithstanding, under a suppressive stronghold. Despite Dillon's optimistic conclusion that *"Chercher la femme* can be a rewarding activity for the Platonic philosopher,"[2] even the most well-intentioned glance at the Greek roots of medieval Jewish philosophy seems to suggest otherwise.

Subjugating the feminine principle to the masculine from its very beginnings, and plotting a conceptual space in which the history of philosophy grows, there stands the well-known Pythagorean "Table of Opposites" in which the pair "male and female" is structurally correlated with the pair "good and bad." As recounted by Aristotle at the very start of his *Metaphysics,* [the Pythagoreans] say there are ten principles, which they arrange in two columns of cognates—limit (*péras*) and unlimited (*ápeiron*), odd (*perritón*) and even (*ártion*), one (*hen*) and plurality (*pleithos*), right (*deksión*) and left (*aristerón*), male (*árren*) and female (*theilu*), resting (*eimeroun*) and moving (*kinoumenon*), straight (*euthú*) and curved (*kampúlon*), light (*phōs*) and darkness (*skótos*), good (*agathón*) and bad (*kakón*), square (*tetrágōnon*) and oblong (*heterómeikes*).[3]

Translated also as "good and evil," this *agathón/kakón* coupling sets a stage upon which the feminine signals the negation of goodness. Standing in her opposition to the *árren,* the masculine Strongman (*árren* from *érrōmai,* "to put forth strength"), the feminine *theilu* is the Nurturer (*theilu* from *thaō,* "to suckle"). And yet, despite the positive connotations of nurturing, she is made to become the locus of loss. Here, *theilu* emerges under her definition as "soft," "yielding," and "*weak.*" And so, the feminine lives on as correlate of evil on the Pythagorean table of opposites, as impotent mother and erratic nurse in Plato's *Timaeus,* as obedient helper (and mother of recalcitrant temptation) in Philo, and as the imaginationary whore-of-matter in Maimonides. We have entered upon the "feminine-as-loss" dynamic.

The main question of our study is whether the feminine can in any way be redeemed through an engagement with such texts. I suggest that in the philosophy of Solomon ibn Gabirol, especially his discourse on matter, we may uncover the possibility of a feminist ground. I will show how there emerges in Gabirol, rather unexpectedly, (a) a championing of materiality, (b) a conceptual coupling of material passivity with divine essentiality, and as such, (c) a positive valuation of passivity. In this way, while he himself does not draw out implications for the feminine, the very pages of Gabirol's metaphysics can be shown to invite a reversal of the feminine-as-loss thematic. From marker of loss, the feminine as passive can be revaluated now as the locus of presence—as that which is most sacred, as the very mark of the Divine Essence itself. This reversal of passivity from loss to presence will be further linked to what I will argue is an existential stance of erotic receptivity in Gabirol's philosophy, a stance in which the expectant potency of *eros* (signaled, I will suggest, by the feminine) replaces the active potency of power (or, the masculine stance) in the estimation of the highest existential possibility of human being. Through an engagement with the metaphysics of Gabirol in which we encounter a positive valuation of the material as the receptive mark of *eros* itself, I find the grounds for redeeming the feminine passive—from loss to presence.

A brief word about my methodology and goals is in order. Except for a comment on Aristotle's biological theory, this paper does not discuss actual remarks about women, nor does it impute misogynist assumptions—or conversely, feminist intents—to the authors in question. In finding a feminist ground in Gabirol's metaphysics, I am not suggesting that Gabirol was himself a feminist. Rather, I uncover a feminist ground by allowing the textual constructions—including the valuation of the feminine therein—to speak for themselves. Gabirol's text is thus seen to signal a moment of rupture within the medieval Jewish philosophical (as well as kabbalistic) corpus, offering an internal critique of the feminine-as-loss motif in medieval Jewish thought.

🌐 Feminine-as-Loss: The Rupture of the Feminine

In the feminine-as-loss symbolic order, there emerges a triple rupture: the feminine is correlated with evil, Womb-Creation emerges as a devalued False-Creation, and maternal/material creative sustenance is completely subordinated to paternal/seminal universalizing form and function. In addition to the correspondence of the feminine (*theilu*) with evil (*kakón*), we also find the devaluation of maternality/materiality. In depictions of maternal lifegiving itself, feminine vitality is suppressed. Despite her portrayal as both the nurturing suckler, as well as the birth-giving womb—the very source of life itself—the feminine is still devalued and robbed of all her life-giving energy. In Plato's *Timaeus,* she is *both* the suckling wet nurse (*tithēnē*)[4] *and* the lifegiving mother.[5] And yet, it is precisely in this dual role as Creator (mother) and Sustainer (wet nurse) that she is subordinated to the masculine principle of Reason—that which, in the context of the *Timaeus,* is made to emerge as the *true* Creator and Sustainer. Whereas the feminine role of mother (and not simply wet nurse) invokes, to be sure, the conceptual space of vitality and creation, the philosophical imagination, in its insistence on subordinating the feminine, construes the maternal creation as a "mere creation"—an organic Womb-Creation (which we might call "Internal Creation") to be subordinated to the Demiurgic paradigm of contra-natural, rule-imposing ordering (which we might call "External Creation"). Ironically, it is the female character Diotima who, in Plato's *Symposium,* emerges as the champion of this "external creation" over the maternal business of "internal creation." It is Diotima, after all,[6] who puts forth the value of philosophy as a kind of spiritually procreative act, as the "soul's conception of wisdom and virtue" over and above the maternal, internal creation, viz. being "pregnant in the body only" (here, interestingly, described by Diotima as a characteristic not of women per se, but of men whose powers of reasoning are weak).[7]

Aristotle's developmental biology further illustrates this feminine-as-loss theme in Greek philosophy. For Aristotle, the formal principle, which is associated with reason, is given to the developing fetus by the father's sperm, whereas the mother provides only the material element to the future human.[8] She at once serves as the material receptacle for the child during its gestation, as she additionally gives to the child the "material stuff" of its bodily constitution; the father's sperm, on the contrary, is the forming principle that makes this "lump of blood and tissue" into a human being with the capacity for rational thought. In the making of a new life, the father is the true generator of that life; the mother, on the contrary, can be said only to be "that in which" the new life is generated:

> For there must needs be that which generates and that from which it generates; even if these be one, still they must be distinct in form and their essence must be different; and in those animals that have these powers separate in two sexes the body and nature of the active and the passive sex must also differ. If, then, the male stands for the effective and active, and the female, considered as female, for the passive, it follows that what the female would contribute to the semen of the male would not be semen but material for the semen to work upon.[9]

In describing semen's communicating to the embryo its power to move and grow (into a human being), Aristotle adds:

> the female, as female, is passive, and the male, as male, is active, and the principle of the movement comes from him. Therefore, if we take the highest genera under which they each fall, the one being active and motive and the other passive and moved, that one thing which is produced comes from them only in the sense in which a bed comes into being from the carpenter and the wood.[10]

While, to be sure, both the maternal and paternal elements (the material and formal causes) are necessary (as is seen more broadly in the Aristotelian hylomorphic metaphysics in the joint presence of a formal and a material element in any substance), it is clear that the maternal plays not only the passive and receptive, but as such, the *subordinate* role in the formula. She provides raw material; he provides functional coherence. She is the wood; he is the carpenter. Hers is the realm of reason-deprived materiality; his is the realm of rational ordering.[11] In the registers of Creation, it is the male Demiurgic father who, in his external role as inseminator of order (or tamer of chaos), has title to True Creator. Once again, as above, the organic Internal Creation of the womb is erased; no principle of creation per se, the mother is merely *site of* creation; she is simply the *condition for* the True Creation of a human in the unfolding of the male seminal principle of human Form in the developing embryo.[12]

Even though form and matter both emerge as necessary elements within Aristotle's thought—both in his biological theory and in his metaphysics more broadly—it becomes clear that form trumps matter, and that matter corresponds to the female.[13] Contributing to a devaluation of the feminine, this opposition between matter and form[14] parallels oppositions between disorder (or chaos) and reason, as well as between potency and act. Flourishing in the Neoplatonic tradition, we find this dynamic in Plotinus's own focus on materiality-as-source-of-evil (itself related to a discourse of matter as privation). In Plato's work, while absent a "form-over-matter" discourse per se, a similar dynamic surfaces. Returning again to the *Timaeus,* we find the masculine reasoning principle of order claiming victory over the feminine principle of chaos and/or disorder. The order—or Reason[ing]— principle of the cosmos (itself aligned with the masculine Demiurge, or Craftsman) is described in contrast to the Nurse of Becoming—the Receptacle principle, itself sometimes described as chaotic[15] and at other times described as purely inactive.[16] While itself not necessarily best equated with matter,[17] the receptacle mother—as passive inactivity and/or chaos—is here clearly devalued—devalued, moreover, qua emasculated other—to the take-charge Demiurge.[18] What's more, the negative depiction of the feminine passivity comes in stages. As inactivity, the feminine takes on a relationally negative valence (as compared to the activity of the masculine principle), and as chaos, the feminine takes on an essential—and not merely relational—negative valence all her own. Linked with the feminine, passivity as privation of activity is a negative and subordinate state: it is at best a *deprived* state (of inactivity, in relational contrast to the Craftsman's [demi]urging), and it is at worst a *depraved* state (of chaotic, essential disorder). Here, privation, deprivation, and depravity all go hand in hand.[19] The victory here, as in the Pythagorean table of opposites above, clearly goes to the masculine, and to the victor go the spoils: Reason, Stability, Truth, and Being belong to the Demiurge, and the mother-of-all may enjoy only anticipatory glances at the weak reflections of his riches as their shadowy reflections cast themselves upon her lap.

This construal of the feminine as the ground between deprivation and depravity resonates with the dual-edged devaluation of the feminine described by Luce Irigaray:

> [T]he articulation of the reality of my sex is impossible in discourse, and for a structural, eidetic reason. My sex is removed, as least as the property of a subject, from the predicative mechanism that assures discursive coherence.

> I can thus speak intelligently as sexualized male . . . or as asexualized. Otherwise, I shall succumb to the illogicality that is proverbially attributed to women. All the statements I make are thus either borrowed from a model that leaves my sex aside— . . . signifying . . . that . . . I must be quite inferior to someone who has ideas or models on his own account—or else my utterances are unintelligible according to the code in force. In that case they are likely to be labeled abnormal, even pathological.[20]

Enabling the virile acts of Demiurgic creation by receiving his order[ing]s within herself, the Receptacle is "quite inferior to someone who has ideas or models on his own account." Relationally, she is deprived—precisely inferior, moreover, to the one whom Timaeus describes as having the Model, as having the Paradigm, as having the Platonic Ideas before him. But yet, in the description of her which leaves out the relational fact of her receptivity (her waiting-to-be-filled by the Demiurge), the Receptacle, in being identified as sheer chaos, is, we might say, "labeled abnormal, even pathological"; she is identified in this way with the sheer disordered hysteria of Irigaray's feminine other.

This feminine-as-loss thematic in encounter with Irigaray's feminine other poignantly emerges from Maimonides's own metaphorical depiction of matter as the "married harlot" of Proverbs 6:26.[21] While the whore image in one sense does not implicate the feminine as such (after all, the married harlot is contrasted with another feminine image, viz. the woman of valor of Proverbs 31:10), there is yet another sense in which the married harlot image speaks quite directly to what is a conception of the feminine essence in general: viz. she is (a) in need of being ruled, but also (and this really isolates her inferiority), she is (b) recalcitrant to that rule. The notion of feminine otherness is complete. She must be subordinated, and the proof of that is that she does not easily submit to subordination. Quite a bind, and conceptually airtight: if she is submissive, that shows that her nature must be submissive; if she is not submissive, that shows that her nature must be recalcitrant (again, with the assumption still in place, and unshakeable, that she is supposed to submit). And so, even the positive valuation of the material in the feminine image of the woman of valor continues along within these parameters, only here, she is praised for finally embracing and living up to her submissive nature; here, she is praised for finally allowing herself to be dominated by the masculine-centric Forms/Reason. matter is negatively valenced when seen in her recalcitrance as the unstable, fickle taker-on of many different forms; in this regard, she is the faithless married harlot who takes on many different partners, and, as such, the destructive Siren who lures men to their undoing:

All man's acts of disobedience and sins are consequent upon his matter.[22]

And further,

> Whenever the impulses of matter impel such an individual toward the dirt and the generally admitted shame inherent in matter, he feels pain because of his entanglement, is ashamed and abashed because of what he has gone through, and desires to diminish this shame with all his power and to be preserved from it in every way.[23]

Matter is, on the other hand, positively valenced when seen in her eventual submission to the powers of Reason; in this regard, she is the woman of valor who quietly submits to her master's rule:

> For if it so happens that the matter of a man is excellent, and suitable, neither dominating him nor corrupting his constitution, that matter is a divine gift.[24]

Here, then, it is ultimately a phallocentric foundation that grounds even the most positive feminine image of the Maimonidean woman of valor, in that, ultimately, the very identity of the feminine is defined in relation (in fact, in *subordination*) to the masculine. The feminine thus emerges as the masculine's other—in fact, as the masculine's subordinated other—with the masculine emerging as the primary and central source of identity and value.[25]

This motif is radicalized in medieval Kabbalah. Far from breaking away from the feminine-as-loss dynamic, even the *Zohar*'s own elaboration of a divine femininity actively devalues the feminine. As Elliot Wolfson has clearly shown, the feminine aspect of God in the *Zohar* is ultimately fulfilled through a conversion:

> Erotic yearning for the feminine is indicative of the beginning of the redemptive process, which overcomes duality and division, but the consummation is marked by the restoration of the feminine to the masculine, which entails the transformation of the *Shekhinah* from feminine other to the sign of the covenant or the corona of the phallus.[26]

Here, the full completion of the feminine emerges as a self-eradication, clearing the way for a new locus of masculinity. Wolfson speaks of a "crossing of gender identities"[27] in which the feminine *Shekhinah* aspect of the Godhead transforms from "impoverished feminine"[28] into the "enriched feminine" precisely in metamorphosizing into a male. Stressing the implications of this, Wolfson adds that these feminine images "must be seen as part of an androcentric, indeed phallocentric, perspective whereby the female is part of the masculine."[29] Despite initial appearances to the contrary, the kabbalistic text does not break through the feminine-as-loss dynamic. Indeed, Kabbalah actively contributes to the feminine-as-loss dynamic precisely in its giving voice to its vision of the divine within phallocentric parameters in which "the female is part of the masculine."

In his forthcoming *Language, Eros, Being: Kabbalistic Hermeneutics and Poetic Imagination,*[30] Wolfson further examines kabbalistic images of divine femininity, cautioning us to remember that "even these images must be understood as expressive of a prevailing phallocentric worldview." Wolfson cites Elizabeth Grosz's own insightful formulation of the problem:

> Phallocentrism is explicitly *not* the refusal of an identity for women (on the contrary, there seems to be a proliferation of identities—wife, mother, nun, secretary, etc.), but rather, the containment of that identity by other definitions and identities.[31]

While Jewish medieval philosophy does not rehearse the kabbalistic idea of the feminine's complete eradicating absorption into the masculine, the phallocentrism of its feminine-as-loss dynamic is itself, as we have seen, quite strong. A case in point, Maimonides's "matter-as-woman-of-valor" discourse not only privileges the masculine, but phallocentrically defines the feminine in relation to him. The feminine is not only that in need of being broken by the masculine, but is herself essentially a kind of broken-masculine.

Maimonides is not the first Jewish philosopher to engage the feminine-as-loss dynamic. We find in Jewish philosophy as early as Philo an employment of the feminine image to demarcate that aspect of soul which is, although necessary, itself subordinated to the truly ideal soul-state, viz. Reason—itself symbolized through the male figure of Adam:

> First [God] made mind, the man, for mind is most venerable in a human being, then bodily sense (*aisthēsis,* or perception), the woman.[32]

In his allegorical interpretation of Genesis 2:18–3:1, Philo explicates scriptural Adam as the rational part of soul. By contrast, Eve emerges as the symbolic placeholder for the Senses (sense perception), as well as the symbolic mother of the Passions (the main passion, pleasure, itself symbolized by the Serpent). Both Sense and Passions are treated as aspects of soul that are subordinate to the reasoning aspect of soul, and, furthermore, as irrational:

[T]he princely (*hēgemonikón,* lit. "ruling") part of the soul is older than [in the sense of ontologically prior to] the soul as a whole, and the irrational portion younger [in the sense of ontologically posterior]. . . . The irrational portion is sense and the passions which are the offspring of sense.[33]

Reason, symbolized by Adam, is, then, also described through further images as the "princely," literally, the "*hēgemonikón,*" or, the one who leads and/or commands,[34] as well as soul's "starting principle," or "ruling part" (*árchon*).[35] In Philo's account, these concepts become inextricably linked to Adamic masculinity, and hence the very notions of *starting, leading,* and *ruling* become undisputedly engendered as masculine (and, desirable) traits. The Adamic ruler, himself symbolizing the Reasoning part of soul, emerges as authoritarian and controlling, the husband and father who, as lord of the household, must keep the wife and children in line.

In its relation to the mother (Sense) and the offspring (Passions), the symbolic Adam/male takes on the role of both husband and father. Interestingly, Philo also labels God himself as *Father.*[36] This clearly illustrates a most positive valuation of the masculine, including a particular championing of fatherhood (itself an act of External Creation, as above). As maker and keeper of souls, God is the Father of each individual soul; as orderer of the individual soul, Reason—as the vestige of Divine Logos—is described as soul's father as well.

Returning to the idea that the masculine lord's virtue lies in keeping the wife and children in line, of Sense, we are told:

[F]or none of the things which perception experiences [as impressions] are submitted to without the mind, for it is a fountain-head (*pēgē*) to it and a foundation (*themélios*) upon which it leans (*epereidetai*).[37]

Philo further says:

[W]hen bodily sense (*aisthēsis,* or perception) is in command, the mind is in a state of slavery heeding none of its proper objects; but when the mind is in the ascendant, the bodily sense (*aisthēsis,* or perception) is seen to have nothing to do and to be powerless to lay hold of any objects of sense perception (*aisthēsis*).[38]

Eve-as-Sense stands in reverse correlation to Adamic Reason's ascendancy; his strength entails her powerlessness; in his mastery, her enslavement is complete. And, in similar manner, Adamic Reason must sublimate the Passions, those Eve-begotten offspring. In a brilliant moment of exegetical artistry, Philo joins the Genesis 3:1 Serpent to the later Mosaic "serpent of brass," expositing the first as pleasure and the second as self-mastery, pleasure's cure:

> The man [i.e., reasoning soul] whose eyes are open determines to run away from this serpent [viz. pleasure], and he fashions another, the principle of self-mastery (*sōphrosúnē*), that serpent of brass, in order that the man who has been bitten by pleasure may, on seeing self-mastery, live the real life (*ton alēthē bíon*).[39]

Phallocentrically identified, the wife and daughter (Sense and Passions)[40] share no power with masculine Reason. The irrational mother–daughter coupling of Sense and Passions is only brought into the conceptual fold to the extent that they serve as "helpers" towards Reason's proper function.

> [I]t was requisite (*édei*) that the creation[41] of mind (*nous*) should be followed immediately by that of sense perception (*aisthēsis*), to be a helper (*boēthós*) and ally (*súmmaxos*) to it.[42]

To be true to themselves, the mother–daughter pair of Sense and Passions must be "helpers," an identification that is itself only possible if they become "the ruled" (*to archómenon*).[43] Revealingly, Philo exposits this notion of *to archómenon* with the further term *to laôdes*—the masses (from *laô*, to look or to behold, together with the term *eidos*, or "that which is seen").[44] In effect, the populace are "the ones who see that which is seen." In a Platonic–Philonic context, this takes on a decidedly negative connotation, conjuring up the contrast between the ones who have opinions (*doxa*) only as opposed to the ones who know what is true. In this context, "the ones who see what is seen" takes on the sense of "those who don't know." They are the "vulgar masses." And in our current context, it is Sense and Passions, the mother and her offspring, who are, as those ruled and in need of being ruled, the vulgar masses. Their functional success is, in this sense, relational and subordinating: to be what they are designed (by God) to be is for them to submit willingly to (masculine) Reason and, in so doing, to help Reason be all that it can be.

In the very claim that Eve/Sense is a helper designed to be part and parcel of the properly functioning Adam/Reason, we have a phallocentric construction of the feminine in terms of the masculine (a dynamic appropriately mirroring the very Genesis account of Eve's own creation from Adam's side). Additionally subordinating the feminine, and here similar to Maimonides's own sense of the harlotry of matter, Philo stresses how Eve/Sense in fact stands opposed to Reason's function. While, to be sure, Eve/Sense provides

Adam/Reason with important information about the outside world, it would appear, nonetheless, that her very existence represents a threat of sorts to Reason: her very activity signals the inactivity—we might say, the death—of Reason:

> As a matter of fact it is when the mind has gone to sleep that perception begins, for conversely, when the mind wakes up perception is quenched (*sbénnutai*). A proof of this is afforded by the fact that whenever we wish to get an accurate understanding of a subject (*hótan ti boulōmetha akribōs noē-sai*)[45] we hurry off to a lonely spot; we close our eyes; we stop our ears; we say "good-bye"[46] to our perceptive faculties (*apotattómetha tais aisthēsesin*). So then, we see that, when the mind is astir and awake, the power of perception is suppressed (*phtheiretai aisthēsis*).[47]

Here we have the hint that the feminine, in her proper role, must ultimately not only submit, but be eradicated. Translated above as "is suppressed," the actual Greek "*ptheiretai*" may simply be translated as "is destroyed."[48] And so, the terms of Adamic Reason's ascendancy are themselves predicated upon the destruction, the death, of Eve-as-Sense. In similar fashion, reconsider the claim that, "[a]s a matter of fact it is when the mind has gone to sleep that perception begins, for conversely, when the mind wakes up perception is quenched (*sbénnutai*)." More than a mere "quenching," we might note that when used of persons, the verb "*sbénnutai*" can metaphorically mean "to die." Again, it is not merely subordination or suppression, but the demise of the feminine other that marks the Adamic vitality.

In light of such harsh reverse correlations between the very life of the one and the very death of the other, might we not add the converse sentiment? Might we not at least be led to wonder whether the moment of her ascendancy marks for him a moment of death? Taken in this further converse sense, Eve emerges as the locus of Adam's death: in her very birth from the life of Adam, it would appear that Eve has signaled his death. This stark theme might be found in Maimonides's matter-as-married-harlot discourse as well, in his reminder that

> every living being dies and becomes ill solely because of its matter.[49]

Where matter is seen as the faithless feminine harlot, we here too find the dramatic suggestion that the feminine marks the spot of man's death. To the notion, then, that the death of femininity marks the birth of the masculine (a dynamic at play most dramatically in the Kabbalah's suggestion that the feminine become the masculine, but also in Philo's own suggestion of Eve-as-Sense's death and destruction in the face of Adamic Reason), we have found a complementary phallocentric trope: from the conceptual possibility of Eve as vital, life-affirming mother-to-all, the philosophical imagination has instead come to find in the feminine the roots of man's demise.

On the Possibility of a Feminist Ground: Solomon Ibn Gabirol and the Transfiguration of Erotic Longing

The Neoplatonic writings of Solomon ibn Gabirol (d. 1056) reveal a blend of philosophical and mystical Jewish and Islamic influences, featuring many standard Platonic and Neoplatonic themes. In many respects, Gabirol's works can be seen to engage the feminine-as-loss dynamic just as robustly as the authors we have already considered. And yet, amongst those standard tropes (including ideas of matter as disordered and privative), he additionally develops a very unique doctrine of matter that offers a philosophical departure from the standard Pythagorean, Platonic, Aristotelian, and Neoplatonic discussions. Developing an idea of various grades of matter (along with various grades of form), Gabirol's discourse couples the standard negative estimations of regular (corporeal) materiality with a decidedly positive evaluation of a higher, sublime grade of materiality. More exalted than either terrestrial or celestial materiality, Gabirol's highest conception of matter offers us an unexpected space for turning the standard table of oppositions on its head, for privileging the passivity of the material, and in this way, we will argue, the passivity of the feminine.

PRIVILEGING MATTER

Gabirol's systematization of matter is complex and manifold, and many of the negative associations of materiality can still be found in his arrangement. Nonetheless, there does emerge an important sense in which, within Gabirol's discourse, materiality—divorced from and prior to any form—is sublime. In fact, in its pre-form state, matter emerges as more sublime than form within Gabirol's analysis. An extended analysis of this theme goes beyond the scope of this paper, but the sublimity of matter over form can begin to be seen in the following claim in Gabirol's *magnum opus,* the *Fons Vitae (Fountain of Life,* or *Meqōr Hayyīm):*[50]

> *materia est creata ab essentia, et forma est a prorprietate essentiae, id est sapientia et unitate. . . .*[51]
>
> . . . Matter is created from Essence, and form is from the property of Essence, that is to say, from Wisdom and unity.

"Essence" here refers to the Divine Essence, as Gabirol (following on Muta-zilite as well as Sufi leads)[52] describes God as *al-Dhāt al-'ūlā* (the First Essence). Here, then, Gabirol's account is clear: where God Himself is construed in terms of two "moments"—an essential moment, and an active one—then, it is to the more essential moment of divine reality that we must connect materiality, with form being related, rather, to God's second—or active—moment.

In a move that turns the treatment of matter in the bulk of Platonic, Aristotelian, and Neoplatonic traditions on its head,[53] Gabirol thus creates a conceptual space in which matter trumps form. Given the usual correlation within these traditions of matter and the feminine (as we have already seen), Gabirol's move provides an unexpected space: from a correlation of matter/ feminine at best with what is secondary in reality and at worst with the very origin of evil itself, we find here instead her identification as the very outgrowth of Divine Essence. As outgrowth of God's own most essential nature, the material here emerges under the positive valence as the hidden reality in which the moment of divine truth is most fully encountered— encountered, that is, in the shadow of unknowing. It is in the darkness of the "nothing" of matter that God most fully is revealed—revealed, that is, through matter's own nature as "the concealed." As Elliot Wolfson has taught us in the context of kabbalistic sources, we must understand God's own hidden nature as concealed in being revealed, and revealed through concealment.[54] Reflecting this idea, Gabirol links the material to the divine through what we may call a "discourse of hiddenness" in which both matter[55] and God are the *occulta*—the hidden aspects of reality, with form (and actuality) instead taking second place as the manifest aspect of encountered reality. And so, regarding the hiddenness of matter, we learn that

> the more remote [something] is from the senses, the more similar it is to matter, and as such it is more hidden according to the hiddenness of matter.[56]

Linking the material to the divine through a continuation of this "discourse of hiddenness," we may turn to the pages of Gabirol's *Keter Malkhūt*[57] poem to be reminded of the link between the divine and the hidden:

> *Keter Malkhūt* §24: Who can understand the *hidden* secrets (*sōdōt*) of your creation . . . the *concealed* (*ḥevyōn*) lies therein.

> *Keter Malkhūt* §26: Who can approach your dwelling place (*tekhūnatekha*), in your having raised the Throne of Glory (*Kissē ha-Kavōd*) above the sphere of Intellect. There lie the fields of *concealment* (*ha-ḥevyōn*) and the *hidden* secret (*sōd*).

Clearly, in its link to the divine both through a "discourse of hiddenness," but also more overtly in the claim that matter is derived from God's own essence, Gabirol has privileged the material. And so, in the most immediate sense, given the ancient and medieval association of the feminine with matter, Gabirol's discourse of matter can be seen as providing a space for the feminine voice. However, let us take this a step further.

EROTIC TRANSFIGURATION

In coming to appreciate the fuller implications of Gabirol's privileging of the material, we arrive at the moment of erotic transfiguration, an even deeper feminist ground. In the erotic transfiguration, we go from an active (masculine) desire-for-power to a passive, feminine desire-to-become, a longing for receptivity and presence. Here, a feminist voice emerges not by denying the coupling of passivity and the feminine, but by redeeming the passive stance[58] as an essentially erotic desire-to-be-completed. Unlike the masculine desire-for-power, here the erotic stance is one of receptivity—*a receptive willingness to engage the self through an engagement with the other.*[59]

The contours of this sort of receptive stance within Neoplatonism can already be seen in Pierre Hadot's own description of Plotinus's existential comportment (and the difference that may hence be discerned between Platonic and Plotinian desire). While, in the case of Plotinus, this receptive stance is not engaged through a discourse on matter (as we argue is the case for Gabirol), it might help to hear Hadot's own reflections on the Plotinian desire-to-be-filled. In his careful treatments of Plotinus,[60] Hadot describes Plotinus's own philosophical endeavor in terms of an erotic receptivity to divine presence. Hadot explains the core of Plotinian metaphysics as an erotic or receptive—in the sense of "desiring-to-be-filled"—comportment to the world; it is, in Hadot's language, an "intuition of the mystery of Life."[61] This erotic ground is itself a state of receptivity, of openness—something that Hadot describes as a "complete passivity" and readiness to "receive the divine invasion."[62] This erotic composure is what, for Plotinus, gives the human being its essential starting and end point.[63]

In my own reading of Gabirol's discourse on matter, it is precisely this receptive desire-to-be-filled—as a most genuine description of the self in its highest, most sublime essence—that emerges as key. In Gabirol's description of the sublime nature of passive materiality as the hidden site of divinity, we have opened a space for privileging the passive as the receptive stance of openness-in-the-face-of-the-other. Existentially speaking, this receptive comportment is an erotic stance, a starting place in the world in which we ask to be filled, in which we ask to become—because acknowledging the necessity of becoming—created by the other. This erotic longing is no longer a (masculine) desire for (masculine) power, but a desire for being desired—a presence open to receive the presence of the other. An existential receptivity, this presence and openness to receive presence is a desire to be loved.

A careful investigation of Gabirol's text—and in particular, its philosophical underpinnings—allows us to explicitly uncover not only a positive valuation of materiality/passivity, but also this fuller notion of material-as-erotic-presence. For, struck by Gabirol's notion of a first, purest occurrence of matter derived directly from the Divine Essence, Shem Tov ibn Falaquera (Gabirol's thirteenth-century Hebrew translator and editor), is led to remark that Gabirol is following in the tradition of the Empedoclean *Book of Five Substances*. Referred to in contemporary scholarship as "Pseudo Empedoclean" for its false attribution to the Greek philosopher Empedocles, the precise nature of this textual tradition, and its doctrine of a First Matter between God and the existent universe, remains something of a mystery. Yet traces of such a tradition surface in a number of Islamic and some Jewish mystical sources, such as the writings of ibn Masarra (tenth century), al-Sijistānī (d. 1000), al-Shahrastānī (d. 1153), al-Shahrazūrī (d. ca. 1281), and the fourteenth-century Hebrew mystical works of Elḥanan ben Avraham. Without here worrying about the origin and reception(s) of this Ps. Empedoclean tradition (or traditions),[64] what characterizes these texts is their reporting of a First *'Unṣur,* literally a First Element, which follows directly from the Godhead, and which precedes even the so-called "First Creation," viz. the (Plotinian) Universal Intellect.

In the extant Arabic fragments of the *Fons Vitae,* we can see Gabirol's explicit relation to this textual tradition. There we find that Gabirol's discussion of a spiritual *materia prima* (First Matter) is in fact a somewhat misleading Latin translation of what is in the Arabic a directly Ps. Empedoclean description of a First *'Unṣur—al-'unṣur al-awwal*—literally, a First Element. This First *'Unṣur* (First Matter,[65] if we follow the Latin terminology) is also described by Gabirol—in his Hebrew poetry—in a number of ways, most notably as *Yesōd* (or Foundation). Poetically giving voice to material and formal elements of reality, Gabirol speaks of the Foundation (*Yesōd*) and the Secret (*Sōd*), of the Foundation (*Yesōd*) and the Root, of the Hidden and the Manifest, as well as of the Kernel and its Shell. He also, in what is itself a moment of artistic verbal embroidery, speaks of matter and form as the Essence and its Embroidery.[66]

Here, then, is where I directly root my suggestion of material-as-erotic-presence within Gabirol's textual dynamic. Looking further to at least some versions of the Ps. Empedoclean tradition,[67] we find the Empedoclean ideas of Love (*maḥabba*) and Strife,[68] along with the following series of correlations:

Spirit (*rūḥ*) / Kernel (*lubb*) / Love (*maḥabba*)

vs.

Shell (*qishr*) / Strife

While Gabirol himself does not correlate matter with love directly, I suggest drawing precisely this conceptual link within Gabirol's corpus. For, as we have seen, Gabirol himself correlates Spirit and Kernel with matter, and Shell with manifest form. Given, then, his own text's relation to a tradition at play in his Arabic philosophical milieu that directly links "kernel" with "love," we suggest discerning within Gabirol's discourse on matter—as hidden essence and spark of divine simplicity within each reality—a discourse on the grounding presence of love (here, not a [masculine] love-of-[masculine]-power, but the Neoplatonic desire-to-be-filled) within each existent reality. In the case of a human being, this would suggest that *it is through love that each person encounters his or her own truest, most divine reality, and ultimately, that through which one encounters God himself.*

The transfiguration is complete, and the feminine ground is revealed. Far from a valuation of masculine-as-power at the ground of human subjectivity, Gabirol's "matter-as-love" dynamic frees the "feminine-as-passive" from its bind. For in this turn from "matter-as-evil" to "matter-as-erotic-ground," the feminine-as-loss becomes transfigured to feminine-as-presence. The feminine passive is redeemed in its new role as erotic ground of being itself.

Looking at Gabirol's Ps. Empedoclean matter discourse in this existential way as revealing truths about the very nature of human being, we are far from an Aristotelian analysis of matter. Whereas Aristotle's discourse on Matter and Form aims to demarcate principles needed to explain the workings of physical reality, our reading of Gabirol's own matter/form discourse suggests, on the contrary, a philosophical exploration of the very nature of human existence itself. For Gabirol, as we have argued, the matter discourse explores and rehearses the proper stance for we, who are thrown into this existence. And, as we have argued, for Gabirol this stance is a stance of love—an erotic (feminine) receptivity to the presence of the divine in oneself and in the face of the other. Gabirol's discourse on matter, hence, is no mere chapter in natural science; *it is, on the contrary, at once an existential, theological, and ethical exploration of the very grounds of being and living in and through erotic {feminine} receptivity.* In this regard, we may note Freud's own understanding of the philosophical scope of the historical Empedocles's own discourses on Love and Strife; far from some "natural science" project, Empedocles's project too, according to Freud, must be seen as an existential investigation of the deepest human truths.[69]

🏵 *Conclusion*

We have uncovered in Gabirol's matter discourse the emergence of matter over form, the correlation of matter with the Divine Essence, and, furthermore, the link between matter—as the hidden kernel at the core of existence—and love, a stance of erotic [feminine] receptivity, that passive, expectant longing-to-be-completed that replaces (or transfigures) the masculine longing for active, completing power. It is in this manifold way that we may discover in Gabirol a ground for the feminine voice. Not only does Gabirol's work give us grounds for heralding the material passivity of the feminine over the active masculine force, with the feminine passive emerging now as the very vestige in the world of the hidden Divine Essence itself, but, as we have shown, this hidden passivity may, in light of Gabirol's Ps. Empedoclean context, be explicitly described as a foundational *erotic* (and precisely feminine) kernel at the core of human being—no longer a masculine love-of-power, but rather, an expectant desire-to-be-filled which, following Hadot on Plotinus, we have described as an erotic receptivity and presence. In this way, through an encounter with Gabirol's matter discourse, the feminine passive may be transformed from its historical role as signal-of-loss to a fresh new role as signal-of-presence—it may be valued now as that most divine, because most receptive, aspect of all human being. In our encounter with Gabirol's text, the passivity and receptivity of the feminine stance may be given new voice; she may be allowed finally to sing the song of life itself.

In light of this turn, it is interesting to return for but a moment to the Greek *theilu* (for "feminine"), and to reflect on its conceptual root in the notion of nurturing. Taking a lead from the Greek term itself, note how the Greek adjectives *theilos, theila, theilu* (for "feminine") can be used not only (as mentioned earlier) in the sense of "weak," but also in the sense of "fresh" or "refreshing" (as in the case of dew),[70] as well as in the sense of "tender, delicate, gentle." Whereas "weak" marks the devaluation of the feminine in its subordination to the masculine longing for active power, in our new dynamic—one in which the longing is itself a receptive desire not to overtake but to become—we may speak now instead of the nurturing, refreshing, delicate *theilu*, the *"theilu*-as-presence." Here, then, the *theilu* marks the very ground of living subjectivity—the erotic kernel of the man, and of the woman, and of the Divine Essence itself.

NOTES

I would like to thank Hava Tirosh-Samuelson for providing useful comments and suggestions for the paper. I am grateful also to Rick Furtak and Elliot Wolfson for many engaging
philosophical conversations on these and related themes.

1. [This poem is by the essay's author—Ed.]

2. John Dillon, "Female Principles in Platonism," in John Dillon, *The Golden Chain*
(Aldershot: Variorum, 1990), IV, 123.

3. Aristotle, Metaphysics 986a22–26, in *The Basic Works of Aristotle,* ed. Richard
McKeon (New York: Random House, 1941), 698. For Greek text, see W. D. Ross, *Aristotle: Metaphysics,* vol. I (Oxford, 1924).

4. Plato, *Timaeus* 49a.

5. Of course, the point is that within Plato's Greek context (as we will see in the case
of Aristotle below), the mother is not really much more than a wet nurse, contributing, as
she does, nothing of any real import to the actual offspring. Mother, nurse, hostess: she is
the "space" in which a life grows, and nothing more. On this point in Plato and other ancient thinkers, see Francis M. Cornford, *Plato's Cosmology: The Timaeus of Plato* (Indianapolis: Hackett Publishing Company, 1997), 187.

6. Interestingly, it might also be noted that in Plato's *Menexenus,* it is once again a female character, Aspasia, to whom Socrates credits a particular discourse in which the actual
procreative role of woman, while receiving some sort of positive praise as an ability to contribute to life, is ultimately (as above, though in a different way) devalued in the claim that
"the woman in her conception and generation is but the imitation of the earth" (*Menexenus,*
238a). Thanks to Rick Furtak for drawing my attention to this particular Platonic passage.

7. In this regard, consider Genevieve Lloyd's exposition: "In the *Symposium,* Plato
elaborates the interconnections between love, in its various forms, and knowledge. . . . [On
Diotima's account] Love's aim is birth in beauty, whether of body or soul. This aim in all
its form expresses mortal nature's longing for immortality; and knowledge is one of these
forms. It is through being a form of love that knowledge is connected with immortality.
The pursuit of wisdom is a spiritual procreation, which shares with physical procreation
the desire for immortality through generation—the desire to leave behind a new and different existence in place of the 'old worn-out mortality.' The pursuit of wisdom thus shares
a common structure with physical procreation; but its aim is a superior form of immortality. Men who are 'pregnant in the body only' betake themselves to women and beget children. But there are men who are 'more creative in their soul than in their bodies, creative
of that which is proper for the soul to conceive and bring forth—wisdom and virtue'"
(Genevieve Lloyd, *The Man of Reason: "Male" and "Female" in Western Philosophy* [Minneap-
olis: University of Minnesota Press, 1984], 21).

8. For a treatment of the relation of Aristotle's embryological theory with his larger
system of physics and metaphysics (as well as further references to relevant sites in Aristotle's *De Generatione Animalium* on this issue), see Alan Code's "Soul as Efficient Cause in
Aristotle's Embryology," *Philosophical Topics* XV, no. 2 (Fall 1987): 51–59. For a feminist
treatment, see also Maryanne Cline Horowitz, "Aristotle and Women," *History of Biology* 9
(1976): 181–233.

9. Aristotle, *De Generatione Animalium,* 729a25–32; cf. McKeon's *The Basic Works of
Aristotle,* 676.

10. Aristotle, *De Generatione Animalium,* 729b10–18; cf. McKeon, ibid., 676.

11. In remarks on *Gen. An.* 775a15 and *Politics 1260a8–14,* Aristotle additionally sug-

gests, as Charlotte Witt puts it, not "that women, or their reproductive organs are matter" (as is Aristotle's idea in the embryological biology that we have been discussing above) but additionally, "that there is something wrong with their forms. There is the vague implication that form is really and fully at home in men . . . and not in women. In these statements Aristotle conveys that there is something compromised about the forms that women have, or about the way that they have forms" (p. 123, in Charlotte Witt, "Form, Normativity, and Gender in Aristotle: A Feminist Perspective," in *Feminist Interpretations of Aristotle,* ed. Cynthia A. Freeland [Philadelphia: The Pennsylvania State University Press, 1998], 118–37).

12. See earlier note on the similarity of a mother and a nurse in this regard, as discussed by Cornford in the context of Plato's *Timaeus* (Cornford, 187). Looking in particular at Aristotle's sense of the mother's rather insignificant contribution to the offspring, Cornford references Frazer's *Totemism and Exogamy* i, 338 for a contemporary vestige of this idea that "children emanate from the father alone and are merely nurtured by the mother" in the doctrines of native S.E. Australians (Cornford, 187, n. 1).

13. Contrary to those who see Aristotle's hylomorphic association of the inferior principle of matter with the female as revealing a confused construction on his part of what is an inherently non-normative metaphysics out of the social gender norms of his day, Witt argues instead that Aristotle's hylomorphism is inherently normative in and of itself, and that his association of matter with the female merely reflects the social values of his day in which females were portrayed as inferior. Cf. Witt, op. cit.

14. But, for a view opposing a gendered reading of matter and form in Aristotle, see Marguerite Deslauriers, "Sex and Essence in Aristotle's *Metaphysics* and Biology," in *Feminist Interpretations of Aristotle,* ed. Cynthia A. Freeland (University Park, Pa.: Pennsylvania State University Press, 1998), 138–67.

15. At *Timaeus* 30a, she is described as a "discordant and unordered motion" (see Cornford, 33). For a further elaboration of this chaos, see *Timaeus* 52d–53c (cf. Cornford, 197–210).

16. And so, for example, at *Timaeus* 50b–c, she is denied any characteristics of her own, taking on, rather, the characteristics of "the things that enter" her (cf. Cornford, 182).

17. Cf. Cornford, 181.

18. Focusing on a somewhat different aspect of the *Timaeus* account, Robin May Schott reveals yet another way in which the feminine is not only inferior to, but defined in terms of, the masculine: "In the *Timaeus,* Plato offers a version of the story of creation that posits male superiority over female nature by virtue of men's ability to control sensations and feelings. In the first act of creation, in which all souls are born without disadvantage, human nature appeared in the form of the 'superior race' that would be called 'man' (*Timaeus* 42a). . . . According to this account, then, primordial human nature is male, and those souls who have conquered bodily passions retain the privileges of this superior race. Women are by definition the embodiment of those souls who have succumbed to temptation and live unrighteously. The creation myth in the *Timaeus* vividly portrays the projection onto woman's nature of man's failure to control his sensations and feelings." Robin May Schott, *Cognition and Eros: A Critique of the Kantian Paradigm* (Philadelphia: Pennsylvania State University Press, 1988), 5.

19. One can additionally find a Platonic subordination of the depravity of the feminine to the reasonableness of the masculine in the *Gorgias*'s treatment of unruly (feminine) rhetoric's subordination to orderly (masculine) reasoning/philosophy/dialectic. For a discussion of this Platonic theme, see Susan E. Shapiro, "A Matter of Discipline: Reading for

SARAH PESSIN

Gender in Jewish Philosophy," in *Judaism since Gender*, ed. Miriam Peskowitz and Laura Levitt (New York: Routledge, 1997), 158–73.

20. Luce Irigaray, *This Sex Which Is Not One*, excerpt cited in *French Feminism Reader*, ed. Kelly Oliver (New York: Rowman & Littlefield Publishers, Inc., 2000), 206–207.

21. For a treatment of the existential implications of this thematic in Maimonides, see my "Matter, Metaphor, and Privative Pointing: Maimonides on the Complexity of Human Being," *American Catholic Philosophical Quarterly* 76, no.1 (2002): 75–88. For an extended illuminating treatment of the hermeneutical implications of Maimonides's use of these and related biblical prooftexts in the construction of his Guide, see James Arthur Diamond, *Maimonides and the Hermeneutics of Concealment: Deciphering Scripture and Midrash in The Guide of the Perplexed* (Albany: State University of New York Press, 2002).

22. Maimonides, *Guide* 3.8, 431. References are to Shlomo Pines's *The Guide of the Perplexed, Moses Maimonides* (Chicago and London: University of Chicago Press, 1963).

23. Maimonides, *Guide* 3.8, 432.

24. Ibid.

25. In her own feminist hermeneutical consideration of Maimonides's discourse of matter-as-married-harlot, Susan Shapiro makes the further point that this metaphorical depiction of matter, predicated as it is on an asymmetrical "man-rules-wife" scenario, has the effect of "fail[ing] to offer corrective resistance to [Maimonides's] understandings of marriage in the *Mishneh Torah* and that it further reinforces, rationalizes, and justifies such violence against wives and women" (Shapiro, 165). In her essay, Shapiro additionally examines Maimonides's matter metaphor in light of Platonic theories of rhetoric (as unruly feminine), exploring the crucial role that the metaphor plays within Maimonides's argument against idolatry. Shapiro offers a "redemptive critique" (166) in which the (secondary, feminine) technique of rhetoric (in this case, the use of a metaphor) actually winds up enabling the very possibility of the (masculine, reason-based) philosophical argument in Maimonides's text.

26. Elliot R. Wolfson, "Eunuchs Who Keep the Sabbath: Becoming Male and the Ascetic Ideal in Thirteenth-Century Jewish Mysticism," in *Becoming Male in the Middle Ages*, ed. Jeffrey Jerome Cohen and Bonnie Wheeler (New York and London: Garland Publishing, 1997), 154.

27. Ibid., 154.

28. Ibid., 169.

29. Ibid, 173–74.

30. I would like to express my gratefulness for having been given the opportunity to preview parts of this project.

31. Elizabeth Grosz, "Histories of the Present and Future: Feminism, Power, Bodies," in *Thinking the Limits of the Body*, ed. Jeffrey J. Cohen and Gail Weiss (Albany: State University of New York Press, 2003), 22 (italics in original).

32. Philo, *Allegorical Interpretation of Genesis*, Book II, section 18.73; Colson and Whitaker, 271.

33. Philo, *Allegorical Interpretation of Genesis*, Book II, section III, 67.6, lines 9–13; cf. *Philo* I, trans. Colson and Whitaker, Loeb Classical Library (no. 226) (Cambridge, Mass.: Harvard University Press, 1929), 229. Square bracketed comments are my own.

34. From *hēgemōn*, a guide, a leader, a commander.

35. See, e.g., *Alleg. Interp.* II, section 19.78, Colson and Whitaker, 273; they translate "*árchon*" of the soul here as "ruling part" of the soul.

36. See, e.g., Philo, *De Opificio Mundi*, section 14.46, Colson and Whitaker, 35.

37. Philo, *Alleg. Interp.* II, section 12.41 [lines 5–7]–12.42 [line 1]; Colson and Whitaker, 250. Translation is my own.

38. Philo, *Alleg. Interp.* II, section 17.70; Colson and Whitaker, 269.

39. Philo, *Alleg. Interp.* II, section 23.93–94; Colson and Whitaker, 283–85.

40. Philo does not suggest that the "offspring" of Sense is a daughter; I am just using that language to stand in for the similar image of irrational offspring. Offspring in general—male or female—are irrational as they are not yet full grown virtuous humans within the Philonic system. It is, hence, conceptually apt to speak, as I am, of offspring in feminine terms.

41. The Greek is *dēmiourgēthēnai,* to make, or to create—but often with the sense of to fabricate or craft (recall Plato's Demiurge craftsman . . .). Colson and Whitaker translate *creation;* this seems conceptually acceptable given that elsewhere, Philo describes the creation of mind and of sense perception with the Greek term *genesis,* or creation (see, e.g., *Allegor. Interpr.* Book I, section I.43 [line 3]; Colson and Whitaker, 146). As such, while the Greek "*dēmiourgeō*" verb can be taken in more of the sense of crafting, conceptually, it would seem that Philo is referring to an act of divine *génesis.*

42. Ibid., 241.

43. Philo, *Alleg. Interpr.* II, section 19.78; Colson and Whitaker, 272.

44. Ibid.; Philo makes this point here in conjunction with the Passions, though I see no reason not to extend the idea at least in a general way to include Sense, the other non-Reason aspect of soul, especially in light of Philo's clear sense (already seen above) in which Reason's moment of ascendancy entails Sense's moment of sublimation.

45. Or, more literally: "whenever we wish to think something out precisely."

46. Greek: *apotattómetha;* middle voice of "*apotáttō,*" "to set apart." And so, "saying good-bye" literally as "setting someone apart from oneself."

47. Ibid., 241, 243.

48. From *phtheirō,* to ruin, waste, spoil, destroy. Furthermore, in its passive form, this verb is used as a curse: "*phtheiresthe!*" meaning "may ye perish!" Also worth noting is a special meaning of the passive form of this Greek verb when used of women in particular; it is the term used to refer to a women's "pining away" (used, e.g., in Sophocles to refer to women's pining away in barrenness).

49. Maimonides, *Guide* 3.8, 431.

50. This text, originally written by Gabirol in the eleventh century in Arabic, is extant in a complete Latin version (trans. into Latin in the twelfth century by the translation team of Dominicus Gundissalinus and John of Spain), as well as in an abbreviated thirteenth-century Hebrew version (trans. and abridged by Shem Tov ibn Falaquera). Some bits of the Arabic original of the work can be found as citations in Moses ibn Ezra's *Arugat ha-Bosem.* As Gabirol's full original Arabic text is non-extant, references in this paper are to the Latin translation of the *Fons Vitae* (FV), which is earlier and more complete than Falaquera's Hebrew translation; cf. Baeumker's edition: *Avencebrolis (ibn Gabirol) Fons Vitae, ex Arabico in Latinum Translatus ab Johanne Hispano et Dominico Gundissalino,* ed. Baeumker (Münster, 1892), in *Beiträge zur Geschichte der Philosophie des Mittelalters, Texte und Untersuchungen,* ed. Baeumker and Hertling (Münster, 1895). For a partial French translation and commentary, see *La source de vie; livre III,* trans. with commentary by Fernand Brunner (Paris: Librairie Philosophique J. Vrin, 1950). For a partial English translation, see *The Fountain of Life* (Book 3), trans. Henry E. Wedeck (New York: Philosophical Library, 1962). For a sometimes idiosyncratic, but complete English translation, see *The Fountain of Life (Fons Vitae) by Solomon Ben Judah Ibn Gabirol (Avicebron),* trans. Alfred B. Jacob (Stanwood: Sabian Publishing Society, 1987). For a

contemporary Hebrew translation of the Latin text, as well as the Hebrew text of Falaquera's thirteenth-century abridged translation from the Arabic, see *Rabbi Shlomo ben Gabirol, Sefer Meqōr Hayyīm,* trans. [into Hebrew] by Yaakov Blovstein, in *Ōtsar Ha-Maḥshavah shel Ha-Yahadūt,* ed. Abraham Sifroni (Israel: Mosad Ha-Rav Kuk, n.d.), or *Extraits de la source de vie de Salomon Ibn Gebirol,* in Solomon Munk's, *Mélanges de philosophie juive et arabe* (Paris: Chez A. Franck, Libraire, 1859) for Falaquera's Hebrew text with Munk's French translation and commentary. For the Arabic fragments of the original text as found in Moses ibn Ezra, see Shlomo Pines, "Sefer 'Arugat ha-Bosem': ha-Qetaim mi-tokh Sefer 'Meqor Hayyim'," *Tarbiẓ* 27 (1957–58) reprinted in *Shlomo Pines, Bein Maḥshevet Yisroel le-Maḥshevet ha-'Amim* (Jerusalem: Bialik, 1977), 44–60; see also Paul Fenton's "Gleanings from Moses Ibn Ezra's *Maqalat al-Hadiqa, Sefarad* 36 (1976): 285–98.

51. Gabirol, *Fons Vitae* 5.42, 333, 4–5.

52. Turning to the surrounding Kalām debates in Gabirol's context, "Essence"—or *al-Dhāt*—is one of the most characteristic terms used to talk about God, and in particular, as part of a debate about the nature or absence of divine Attributes that most vigorously stresses God's complete unity and utter Transcendence. Also, Michael Sells notes that in Sufism "the first mode of the real is the *dhāt* (identity), the absolute unity beyond the dualistic structures of language and thought, beyond all relation" (Michael A. Sells, *Mystical Languages of Unsaying* [Chicago: University of Chicago Press, 1994], 64). Sells also speaks of *al-Dhāt* in terms of "the Plotinian One and Echkart's Godhead (*Gottheit*) in the sense that it is beyond all dualism, all name, and all quiddity" (Sells, 244, n. 7).

53. For a relevantly similar notion of positively valenced Matter in Neoplatonism, though, see John Dillon, "Solomon Ibn Gabirol's Doctrine of Intelligible Matter," in *Neoplatonism and Jewish Thought,* ed. Lenn Goodman (Albany: SUNY Press, 1992); see also Jean Trouillard, "*La genèse de l'hylémorphisme selon Proclos,*" in *Dialogue (Canadian Philosophical Review)* VI (June 1967), 1–17.

54. Wolfson refers in this regard to the deep "ontological" esotericism of Kabbalah (in contrast to an "epistemic esoterism") as addressing "the secret that cannot be kept"; cf. Elliot R. Wolfson, *Abraham Abulafia—Kabbalist and Prophet: Hermeneutics, Theosophy, Theurgy* (Los Angeles: Cherub Press, 2000), 52. See also *Through a Speculum that Shines* (Trenton: Princeton University Press, 1994), and for an engagement with this theme in Derrida, cf. "Assaulting the Border: Kabbalistic Traces in the Margins of Derrida," *JAAR* 70, no. 3, 2002.

55. Matter is *"occulta"* (*Fons Vitae* 5.23, p. 299, 17); Matter is the *"summum occultum"* (*Fons Vitae* 1.15, p. 19, 19; 4.8, p. 230, 12.13); Matter is the *"essentia occulta"* (*Fons Vitae* 1.12, p. 15, 22); Matter is the *"finis occultus"* (*Fons Vitae* 1.11, p. 14, 23–26).

56. Gabirol, *Fons Vitae,* 4. 8, p. 230, 8.

57. For text of the poem in Hebrew, see *Shirei Shlomo ben Yehudah Ibn Gevirol* (*Shirei qodesh*), vol. 2, ed. Bialik and Ravnitsky (Tel Aviv and Berlin: Dwir-Verlags-Gesellschaft, 1925), or *Shirei ha-ḥol le-Rabbi Shlomo Ibn Gevirol,* ed. Dov Yarden (Jerusalem: Kiryat Noar, 1975), or *ha-Shirah ha-Ivrit be-Sefarad u-be-Provence,* vol. 1, ed. Jefim (Hayyim) Shirmann (Jerusalem: Bialik, 1954), 257–85. For English translations, see Bernard Lewis, *Solomon ibn Gabirol: The Kingly Crown* (London: Vallentine Mitchell, 1961); Peter Cole, *Selected Poems of Solomon Ibn Gabirol* (Princeton, N.J.: Princeton University Press, 2000); Raphael Loewe, *Ibn Gabirol* (London: Peter Halban, 1989).

58. In reading in Gabirol this positive valuation of feminine passivity, my project can be seen in a conceptual kinship with Daniel Boyarin's own project, one which he has described as "reclaiming the eroticized Jewish male sissy" (p. 135 in Daniel Boyarin, "Justify

My Love," in *Judaism since Gender*, ed. Miriam Peskowitz and Laura Levitt [New York: Routledge, 1997], 131–37).

59. In this regard, one might consider the infinite responsibility of a Levinasian ethics; I hope to explore the relevance of Levinas for my reading of Gabirol elsewhere. Of interest to note here too is Sabina Lovibond's analysis of the "Hebraic" (by which she means Judeo-Christian, in contrast to Graeco-Roman) ethics of obedience [to an infinite God] as an ethics of limitlessness—an ethics of, as Nietzsche puts it in *Beyond Good and Evil*, "infinite demands." Lovibond usefully correlates this Hebraic ethics of infinite obedience with an "ethics of care" (as opposed to one "of justice"). See Sabina Lovibond, "Feminism in ancient philosophy: The feminist stake in Greek rationalism" in *The Cambridge Companion to Feminism*, ed. Miranda Fricker and Jennifer Hornsby (Cambridge: Cambridge University Press, 2000), 10–28. Inclined myself towards Levinas in my own interpretation of Gabirol's limitless ground of being, I additionally see a link between my own reading of Gabirol's erotic receptivity and this "ethics of care." It is worth noting, though, that Lovibond herself is critical of associating this notion of care with feminine virtue, wary, as she is, of making women "'hostage' to the needs (or demands) of others" (Lovibond, 23). In my own treatment of Gabirol, I would see a completely positive valence to such an infinite ethics of care, where in the Gabirol context, of course, it would represent the "feminine core" of all humans, and as such, the demand for infinite receptivity and responsiveness would be made of men and women alike.

60. Pierre Hadot, *Plotinus, or The Simplicity of Vision,* trans. Michael Chase (Chicago: University of Chicago Press, 1993).

61. Ibid., 40.

62. Ibid., 56.

63. For a moving treatment of this theme in Plotinus, see also Frederic M. Schroeder, *Form and Transformation: A Study in the Philosophy of Plotinus* (McGill-Queen's University Press, 2001).

64. For some discussion of this tradition, see the "Anbaduklis" entry by S.M. Stern in *Encyclopaedia of Islam*, volume I, new edition (Leiden: E. J. Brill), 483–84, as well as the "Empedocles" entry in *Encyclopaedia Judaica*. See also David Kaufmann, *Studien über Salomon Ibn Gabirol*, (*Jahresbericht der Landes-Rabbinerschule in Budapest für das Schuljahr 1898–1889*) (Budapest, 1899), in David Kaufmann, *Die Spuren Al-Batlajusi's, Studien über Salomon ibn Gabirol and Die Sinne* (with an Introduction by Louis Jacobs) ([London, (?)]: Gregg International Publishers, 1972), and his essay "*Ha-Pseudo Empedocles ka-Mekor le-R' Shlomo ibn Gabirol,*" *Mehkarim ba-Sifrut ha-Ivrit*, 78–164. For a possible link between this so-called Empedoclean philosophy and the mystical tradition of ibn Masarra, but also for helpful elaborations (including some translations) of the relevant doctrines, see Miguel Asín Palacios, *The Mystical Philosophy of Ibn Masarra and his Followers,* trans. Elmer H. Douglas and Howard W. Yoder, (Leiden: E. J. Brill, 1978).

65. For various different occurrences of terms for Matter in Islamicate thought, and their implications, see L. Gardet, "Hayūlā," in *Encyclopaedia of Islam.*

66. Hence the title of my forthcoming study of *apophasis* and *eros* in Gabirol, *Embroidering the Hidden.*

67. I am working here in particular with al-Shahrastānī's Arabic text, *Kitāb al-Milal wal-Nihal (Book of Religious and Philosophical Sects),* Part II, ed. W. Cureton (Leipzig, 1923), 260–65.

68. The Arabic in the Ps. Empedoclean source (as recounted by Shahrastani) has the word "*ghalaba.*" Literally, this does not mean *strife,* but *victory* (or also: *idle talk, chatter*). I

am not sure what to make of this, but am simply translating *strife* for now since the actual Arabic root in question ("*ghalaba*" = to subdue, to conquer) is indeed the *root* for the Arabic word *strife*, just under a different construction (*strife* = "*ghilāb*"). This, together with the fact that the Arabic source invokes the name of Empedocles and opposes this "*ghalaba*" to the principle of Love ("*mahabba*"), leads me to translate *strife*, at least for the present time.

69. See Freud's "Analysis Terminable and Interminable" (1937).

70. Here it is interesting to note that the root of *male* ("*árren*" relates also to the Greek "*hē ersē*," meaning *dew*, with "*erseieis,—essa, -en*" for *dewy* as well as *fresh* (though here in the metaphorical sense to describe a "fresh corpse").

Thinking Desire in Gersonides and Spinoza

🌀 Apologos: Philosophy as a Political Act

My preliminary remarks seek to articulate both the immediate and the mediated background for the following essay. These comments seek to clarify, first, the manner in which the essay should and should not be read, and second, what I understand by feminist Jewish philosophy. Before I begin with the substantive provisos, I wish to outline a very brief personal, purportedly less philosophical, background to the essay.

When I was first asked to participate in a conference as well as contribute to a volume on "feminist Jewish philosophy," explicitly as an historian of philosophy, I was simultaneously attracted and repelled by the prospect of participating in this endeavor. The reasons for my ambivalent, affective response were the same: namely, there were some fine (very few) women working specifically on (or out of) the history of Jewish philosophy, some of whom were also political feminists; there were some first-rate, contemporary feminist philosophers, who happened to be Jewish but whose work, deliberately or not, ignored the history of Jewish philosophy. To my knowledge, however, there were no contemporary philosophers who reflected on any dimension of the uncanny relations between their various belongings/commitments: Jewish, philosopher, historian of philosophy, feminist, let alone who thematically explored them.

I deploy the language of relations, or belonging/commitments deliberately. For, above all, I question the implicit assumption that the practice of the history of philosophy (let alone philosophy) is a-political. Rather, I insist that, and seek to elucidate how, the so-called history of philosophy or the formation of its canon is the result of theological-political repression rather than philosophical necessity. That is, the so-called history of philosophy is the manifestation of a theological philosophy that, even in its secular form, expresses (and confirms) the ideology of the victors. But whence my ambivalence?

For at least two decades, my academic compulsion has been motivated by a shadow or spectral dialectic between the historical disappearance/repression of a Judeo-Arabic (i.e., Averroist) philosophical tradition and the theologico-political expulsion of materiality/body/woman/jew/other, from access to the philosophical logos. Therefore, I doubted that I either could contribute to or benefit from participation in this conference. Were it not for the fact that I was specifically asked to contribute to the historical part of the project, I may not have experienced the same deep ambivalence. For my entire project puts into question the division between the history of philosophy and the practice of philosophy. Differently stated, since I have long been engaged in dialogues with philosophical texts written by dead male philosophers who, when they are read at all, are suspect to feminist philosophers, on the one hand, and with contemporary feminist philosophers, who do not read them but trace their provenance, inter alia, to Marx, Nietzsche, Freud, and the Frankfurt school, on the other (as if their thinking occurred ex nihilo), since these dialogues are motivated by a single compulsion and form a single inquiry, I could not disengage one aspect of the study from the other without distortion or repression. Loath to renege on a commitment, however, I decided to explicitly bring the apparent tension between historical and contemporary feminist philosophy into relief in order to indicate ways in which such engagements make possible thinking "otherwise."

In order to underline the importance of reading history otherwise, of wrenching it out of the necessary, homogenous continuum (to paraphrase Walter Benjamin),[1] I must be explicit about what I regard as the task of a philosopher, especially a feminist Jewish philosopher today. All too briefly, if the metaphorical shadow of Socrates's trial and death hung over the thinking of Maimonides, Averroes, Gersonides, Spinoza, and others, albeit in different ways, it gained its embodied compelling force from the experiences of concrete, material theologico-political oppressions, repressions, and persecutions. Likewise, if philosophy is still possible today, especially feminist Jewish philosophy, it must begin, quite literally, after Auschwitz, which is to say as the concrete material experience of horror, a horror accompanied by the shocking awakening from the narcotic effects of religious and metaphysical illusion/superstition, an illusion grounded on the claims to a universal, that is neutral, history and philosophy—a claim that is ironically a-historical, a-political, and disembodied.

The progenitors of my understanding of the possibility of feminist Jewish philosophy today can be found in the reflections of Walter Benjamin and Theodor W. Adorno about history and metaphysics respectively, as well as in Husserl's *Crisis.* Brief citations from their works frame my general observations on feminist philosophy as a materialist, historical critique of the canon in an idiom that is clearly political.

> There is no document of civilization which is not at the same time a document of barbarism. And just as a document is not free of barbarism, barbarism taints also the manner in which it was transmitted from one owner to another. A historical materialist, therefore, dissociates [her]self from it as far as possible. [She] regards it as [her] task to brush history against the grain. (Benjamin, Theses vii, 256–57)

> We cannot say anymore that the immutable is truth, and that the mobile, transitory is appearance. . . . If negative dialectics calls for the self-reflection of thinking, the tangible implication is that if thinking is to be true—if it is to be true today, in any case—it must also be a thinking against itself. If thought is not to be measured by the extremity that eludes the concept, it is from the outset in the nature of the musical accompaniment with which the SS liked to drown out the screams of its victims.[2]

Lest Benjamin's and Adorno's reflections be dismissed as extra-philosophical or a-philosophical, lest their materialist critique of pure and pure practical reason be viewed as a destructive, pessimistic rejection of philosophy, reason, history, etc., let me supplement them with an example taken from Husserl on the dogmatism of canonical history.

> The Ruling dogma of the separation in principle between epistemological elucidation and historical, even humanistic-psychological explanation, between epistemological and genetic origin, is fundamentally mistaken, unless one inadmissibly limits, in the usual way, the concepts of "history," "historical explanation," and "genesis." Or rather, what is fundamentally mistaken is the limitation through which *precisely the deepest and most genuine of problems of history are concealed.*[3]

I can now return to the "problematic" preface in order to present a concrete, i.e., materialist direction for the *political* need to think philosophy otherwise than canonically.

🕎 *Preface: Gersonides and Spinoza—"Fellow Unbelievers"*

At the end of Chapter IX of *The Future of an Illusion,* Freud indicates his kinship with Spinoza by means of a quotation from Heine. The freedom from the universal illusion of a (decidedly Christian) religious piety that he dares to imagine will be shared with "fellow unbelievers" (*Unglaubensgenossen*) who will be able to say without regret *"we leave Heaven to the angels and the sparrow."*[4]

The following essay is premised on the conviction that Gersonides and Spinoza are the two earliest *Jewish* philosophical predecessors of Heine's and Freud's community of unbelievers, a conviction that I intend to outline briefly in order to retrieve another philosophical approach to the problem of "being human" freed from religion as superstition and thereby return it to its proper embodied place.

It may seem strange to begin an essay that proposes to provide a "feminist" reading of Gersonides and Spinoza with a reference to Heine and Freud. It may appear even stranger, perhaps even scandalous, that this reference should single them out, especially Gersonides, as Heine's and Freud's "fellow unbelievers," whose fellowship or kinship arises from and is articulated as Jewish philosophy. In addition, to claim, as I shall, that the works of these "male" thinkers are a rich philosophical resource for deepening contemporary feminist philosophy may appear as, at best, idiosyncratic, and at worst, merely contentious. Nonetheless, my emphasis on the uncanny here is deliberate. For insofar as the Jewish philosophical tradition in virtue of which these thinkers are kin has been continuously occluded, or more often, violently repressed, its radical difference from the Christo-Platonic tradition, which tradition has become the single, unified philosophical canon, remains invisible and its idiom remains philosophically suspect. And, although the following essay will not mention Heine and Freud further, it is important to point out that the works of these thinkers suffered uncannily similar fates and for similar reasons. Heine's work has been almost entirely ignored by the literary canon, Freud has been expelled from the philosophical canon, Gersonides's work is invisible to the philosophical canon, and to the extent that Spinoza's works are read (or taught) at all, his thought has been distorted by its incorporation into the one Christo-Platonic, philosophical canon, by Descartes's and Kant's heirs alike. All too succinctly and obliquely stated, the body/materiality of these works either had to become invisible and uncitable or had to assume an alien form by incorporation into its opposite. Viewed in this light, the disappearance of these works from the canonical body mirrors the disappearance of body from the philosophical canon, and for similar reason, as I hope will become evident.

It is important to emphasize, at the outset, that by naming Gersonides and especially Spinoza as "fellow unbelievers," I in no way intend to displace or estrange them from a proper belonging to Jewish philosophy, on the contrary. Moreover, to do so, would, at best, be superfluous since such a displacement has already been accomplished twice. For, in addition to an expulsion or estrangement from the Christo-Platonic *philosophical* tradition, Gersonides's and Spinoza's works, or at least the most important philosophical ones, have generally been either ignored or repressed by the Jewish tradition. If it is the case that *habent sua fata libelli,* then, ironically, the fate of Gersonides's and Spinoza's works marks a duplicitous tragedy, in which the "character flaw" of the heroes is a projection of religious intolerance, and of which the two diametrically opposed paths, paradoxically, make visible the sameness (or mutual origin) of religious and metaphysical dogma.

It should be recalled that both Gersonides and Spinoza have been declared heterodox by the self-proclaimed authorities about Jewish belief, who sought to exile them (or in the case of Gersonides suppress some of his works) from the Jewish community and its canon. With respect to Spinoza, suffice it to recall the ban in order to substantiate my claim. With respect to Gersonides, I must limit myself to two examples: (1) with the exception of some of the logical works, his supercommentaries on Averroes's commentaries on Aristotle have been almost entirely ignored and, apart from a partial edition and translation of the *Supercommentary on the de Anima* as a Ph.D. thesis,[5] they are still in manuscript form; (2) Whereas the commentaries on the Bible began to appear in print in 1477, the books of the *Wars of the Lord*[6] were condemned as "Wars against the Lord" and were not published until December 1560. The greatest irony is that, with the exception of a handful of contemporary Jewish philosophers, the reception of the works of Gersonides in the contemporary religious Jewish milieu mirrors the situation in the late middle ages so that it is extremely difficult, if not impossible, to find an edited copy of the *Wars* in Israel today!

Again, given the complicit, continuous, and duplicitous expulsion of these "fellow unbelievers" from their respective canons, rather than seeking to further estrange them from either the purportedly univocal contemporary philosophical or Jewish canons, I seek to unveil a Jewish philosophical tradition strange to the canonical understanding of philosophy, in general, and modern Jewish philosophy, in particular. To emphasize, then, a kinship in virtue of unbelief is to emphasize the antinomian/heterodox nature of philosophical thinking and Jewish practice.[7]

Now, whereas the works of Gersonides disappeared almost entirely from the Western philosophical canon, Jewish or otherwise, and to that extent were ironically shielded from violent misappropriations, Spinoza's works suffered the opposite philosophical fate, so that to the extent that they were or are read at all by modern philosophers, Jewish or Christian, they are distorted so as to "fit" the Western, Christo-Platonic, philosophical canon, whose basic assumptions are dualist and at odds with Spinoza's.

Since it is my claim that Gersonides's and Spinoza's works have become philosophically inaccessible, either by occlusion/repression or by misappropriation, and that they present an occluded, materialist Aristotelian tradition that can provide an invaluable resource to the feminist critique of the philosophical canon, the remainder of this essay will be divided into three unequal parts, of which the first two will be brief and diagnostic. The order of presentation, following Aristotle's advice, will be from the more to the less known; in the represent context, from the "present" to the "past."

In Part One of this essay, I argue and briefly justify my conviction that what is common to some contemporary feminist philosophers—especially those whose work is motivated by Freudian psychoanalysis—and the occluded Aristotelian tradition exemplified by Gersonides and Spinoza, is a commitment to a non-metaphysical, i.e., concretely historical materialism that precludes mind/body dualism. The immediate consequences of this claim are as follows: (1) a continuity between sensibility and intelligibility, (2) a concurrence between passion and action, and (3) a concurrence between necessity and freedom. Insofar as contemporary feminist philosophy is articulated as a response to the modern *dualist* philosophical canon, it offers a powerful critique that (for obvious historical reasons) cannot be undertaken by a simple return to the works of Gersonides and Spinoza.

However, I shall further argue that, precisely insofar as contemporary feminist philosophers have been formed by the modern canon, their critique is still implicated in some of its presuppositions, as is ironically evident in the assumption that the philosophical canon is a single canon. I shall, therefore, claim that through a return to, or more precisely, a genealogical discovery of the thought of Gersonides and Spinoza, feminist philosophy can be transformed from an abstract critique of dualism, or anti-dualism, to a concrete mode of a-dualist philosophizing.

In Part Two, I lay the groundwork for such a feminist Jewish philosophy by examining one of the most striking aspects of Aristotelian philosophy occluded by the modern canon that is both amply evident in and motivates Gersonides's and Spinoza's philosophical writings, namely, Aristotle's definition of the human being as a desiring intellect in the *Nicomachean Ethics*.[8] I demonstrate that, in contrast to the Latin commentators, who deliberately ignore the continuity between the "natural human desire for knowledge" and all other human desires and hence read the *de Anima*[9] independently of the *Nicomachean Ethics,* both Gersonides and Spinoza read the two works in tandem. Whereas Part Two analyses some of Gersonides's discussions of desire and appetition in the *Supercommentary on de Anima,* Part Three is devoted to Spinoza's radicalization of these notions in *The Ethics,* the *TTP,* and the *TP.*[10]

My aim is to demonstrate that these works provide concrete examples for a critique of the modern universal (male) subject whose disembodied knowledge implicitly underlies all modern ethics and political philosophy. Rather than speak about contemporary feminist philosophy, then, let alone justify the need for a feminist perspective, Parts Two and Three provide brief feminist readings of historical texts in order to retrieve their oc-cluded/repressed, revolutionary, or antinomian potential that is always vul-nerable and hence must be sustained through continuous 'repetitive' readings of the history of philosophy "against the grain" (Benjamin). In the *epilogos,* I will clarify the political implications of my analysis.

🌢 *I. Feminist Critique and Its Blindness*

> *And there you have it, Gentlemen, that is why your daughters are dumb. Even if they chatter, proliferate pythically in works that only signify their aphasia, or the mimetic underside of your desire. And interpreting them only where they exhibit their muteness means subjecting them to a language that exiles them at an ever increasing distance from what perhaps they would have said to you, were already whispering to you. If only.*[11]

Despite her "awkward" syntax and disregard for conventional grammati-cal rules, or perhaps precisely because of these, Luce Irigaray's mimetic appropriation of Socrates' *Apology* simultaneously marks her desire to partici-pate in the Socratic legacy and her exclusion from it by the self-proclaimed male heirs of that legacy. By situating the question of the desire for legibility and intelligibility in the context of the right to inherit Socrates's legacy, a legacy bequeathed to Socrates by Apollo's female oracle but inaccessible to his potential women heirs, Irigaray brilliantly marks the violent misappro-priation involved in the construction of a univocal, unilinear philosophical tradition that is sustained by its progressive reduction to categories, rules, or laws. No serious reader of Plato, let alone of the *Apology,* can ignore the poign-ant irony of Irigaray's mimetic strategy. For, at the core of Socrates's major "fault," the fault that compels him to present an *apo-logos* to the "Gentlemen of the Athenian Jury," or guardians of the conventional (doxatic) Athenian *logos,* was the accusation of deliberate attempts to subvert conventional meaning, to undermine categorical judgments, and in short, to resort to the unintelligible. Differently stated, from a Socratic (and some feminist) perspective, the normative structures imposed upon *logos* by convention are not only hindrances to listening but, above all, to experiencing and thinking otherwise.

Now, irrespective of my (or your) judgment about Irigaray's philosophical merits, the legibility of her works, or those of other feminist philosophers who are formed and informed by Freudian psychoanalysis, and irrespective of some profound disagreements among them, what all share and what I consider as the most important insights of their respective works is a radical critique of categorical, essentialist, or universal language. Moreover, unlike most of their male counterparts, who address the question of philosophical foundation(s) as a critique or deconstruction of metaphysics and/or epistemology, thinkers such as Irigaray and, especially, Judith Butler, insist that the question of universal categories, metaphysics and/or foundations is first and foremost, a political question.

Despite the different strategies they adopt when they interrogate the male canon, those feminist philosophers who engage the philosophical tradition from a psychoanalytic perspective, i.e., those who question the purportedly unified philosophical tradition from the perspective of *psyche*, implicitly or explicitly bring into relief the theological origins of the received philosophical canon.[12]

Nonetheless, it is both striking and surprising that, rather than question the reception of the Socratic canon, e.g., especially in light of texts such as the *Symposium*, Irigaray shies away from severing Socrates's and Plato's philosophical endeavors from their Christo-Platonic (metaphysical) and often violent appropriations.[13] Moreover, in stark contrast to "traditional" appropriations of Greek philosophy (e.g., Ficino's stunningly violent appropriation of the *Symposium*,[14] or even Aquinas's "gentle," but nonetheless Christianizing appropriation of Aristotle's *de Anima, Nicomachean Ethics,* and *Metaphysics,*[15] there exist texts (as well as traces of prohibited readings) that offer radically different readings of the Socratic inheritance. These readings belie the claim to a unitary philosophical canon and, hence, offer concrete evidence as well as opportunities for a critique of the authoritative (i.e., doxatic) readings of significant "founders" of philosophy.

Now, even if feminist philosophers fail to mention, let alone utilize available, but suppressed, alternatives to the authoritative modern canon for strategic reasons,[16] I am convinced that this failure as well as strategy exhibit a blindness at the heart of their work. This blindness ironically demarcates their formation by/acceptance of the canonical authority which they question and the fathers whose recognition they seek. But, insofar as this is the case, and insofar as contemporary feminist philosophers formulate their questions in terms of the received canon, they remain bound to its determination of what are or are not the proper subject as well as idioms of philosophy, albeit negatively. For, however radical the current feminist critique of philosophy is, by addressing the philosophical canon as a unified whole, feminists grant and ground its historically authoritative status.[17]

Ironically, despite their emphasis upon the "political" nature of the formation of the philosophical and other literary canons, feminist philosophers have ignored the extent and effect of theologico-political repressions of extant alternative readings by real powers over beliefs. Differently stated, even the most strident and astute feminist political philosophers have conflated an "enforced" theologico-political *Weltanchauung* with concrete material/historical necessity.[18]

Hence, rather than attempt to trace the genealogies of repression historically, in their attempts (1) to provide critical feminist alternative readings of the canon in order to (2) liberate philosophy, let alone concrete women, from the homogenous and hegemonic tyranny of the "concept" (which confined philosophy to the technical "scientific" rational refinement, women to embodied, passionate silence or philosophical irrelevance), even those feminist philosophers who focus upon repression do so strictly on the basis of the ontological assumptions that underlie traditional political and psychoanalytic theories a-historically.

Let me illustrate the reticence characteristic of feminist readings of the canon and the concrete consequence of such reticence:

(1) Of all her readings in the history of philosophy, Irigaray's reading of Plato's *Symposium* is the most sensitive and least subject to a programmatic agenda. Yet, even here, even as she provides a stunningly sensitive reading of Diotima's speech, she fails to follow her own insights; in fact, she recoils from them. One brief but exemplary quotation should suffice: "What seems to me to be original in Diotima's method has disappeared once again. This intermediary milieu of love, which is irreducible, is resplit between a 'subject' (an inadequate word in Plato) and a 'beloved reality.'"[19]

It is astonishing that, despite her parenthetical recognition of the "inadequacy" of the "subject" to Plato's *Symposium*, Irigaray fails to follow her own insight, perhaps because this very insight would undermine her reading of Plato as the origin of modern metaphysics and epistemology, central to which is the split between "subject" and "object" (beloved reality). For the separation between subject and object as well as immanence and transcendence (which she introduces later) is a mark of the Christian appropriation

of Plato's philosophy, which appropriation Irigaray either deliberately ignores or to which she is blind, perhaps because she is formed by it.

(2) Unlike Irigaray, Judith Butler does not offer any sustained reading
of the philosophical canon preceding Hegel. However, her passing remarks
on Spinoza in *The Psychic Life of Power* simultaneously disclose her indebtedness to the canonical reading of Spinoza and her insightful recognition that
another reading is called for, which reading she does not provide.[20] Thus, although she recognizes the liberating power of Spinoza's *conatus* and endorses
as well as follows his insistence that "desire is always the desire to persist in
one's own being," she proposes "to recast the metaphysical substance that
forms the ideal for desire as a more pliable notion of social being" (p. 28, my
emphasis). But, her own reading of Spinoza's legacy puts in question the canonical reading of the *Ethics* as a metaphysical text and demands that it be
reconsidered in relation to the *TTP* and *TP*. As she states, "If desire has as
its final aim the continuation of itself—and here one *might* link Hegel,
Freud, and Foucault all back to Spinoza's conatus—then the capacity of desire to be withdrawn and to reattach will constitute something like the vulnerability of every strategy of subjection." (Butler, 62; first emphasis is
mine.) But, then, if one links Freud and Foucault to Spinoza, Spinoza's conatus cannot be understood in terms of "an ideal for desire."

In contrast to Butler, who recoils from pursuing the genealogy that her
own insights demand, I want to insist that not only *might* one, but one *must*
trace the understanding of desire as a striving for self-preservation to
Spinoza, a tracing that requires a materialist genealogy. Moreover, I want to
suggest that doing so would alter Butler's stated lineage in a manner such
that Hegel will be replaced by Marx (and perhaps Nietzsche) and Foucault
would be either replaced or supplemented by Freud, Benjamin, and Adorno.

(3) Finally, Cathy Carruth's *Unclaimed Experience: Trauma, Narratives,
and History*[21] makes manifest the manner in which psychoanalytical and/or
philosophical critiques that interrogate canons without exhibiting their op-
tionality, i.e., lack of necessity, remain bound by their categories. Again, one
example must suffice to substantiate my claim. In her introductory description of trauma (which trauma would later be understood both individually
and historically), Carruth presents what she takes to be Freud's understanding of the enigma of trauma as follows:

> [T]he term *trauma* is understood as a wound inflicted **not upon the body
> but upon the mind**. But, what seems to be suggested by Freud in *Beyond
> the Pleasure Principle* is that the wound of the mind—the breach in the
> mind's experience of time, **self**, and the **world**—is not, **like the wound of
> the body**, a simple healable event. (Carruth, 3–4; bold emphases mine)

Now, it is not merely the use of dualist language in Carruth's description of trauma that I find problematic but rather and, above all, the fact that the language implicitly or explicitly reflects a thoroughly Cartesian real (metaphysical) separation between body and mind. Moreover, and even if I overlook the questionable attribution of mind/body dualism to Freud, Carruth's distinction between self and world entails that the mind is the subject-self whose wound renders it incapable of representing itself to itself and hence healing itself as object. In contrast, the body is merely an object (external) whose wound is simple and healable. It is not surprising, therefore, that from this metaphysical dualism Carruth draws an epistemological conclusion that entails that all bodily events/experiences are fully representable and "knowable," whereas trauma marks a *separate* mental experience that, insofar as it cannot be represented, cannot be known. In short, for Carruth, there are mental experiences that are absolutely independent from embodiment.

Rather than Carruth's (implicit?) assumption that some experiences do not depend upon embodiment, in the third part of the essay I shall offer an alternative understanding of experience and knowledge, of which the briefest, albeit enigmatic, expression is found in Spinoza's repeated claim that "[the] mind is *nothing but* [the] idea of the body," of which the origins, in my view is Gersonides, especially his reading of Aristotle.[22] Since it is my claim that another Aristotelian tradition was suppressed owing to ecclesiatico-political, rather than philosophical concerns, namely concerns with individual immortality, allow me briefly to outline what, in the context of the present essay, I consider as the most significant and disclosive differences between what I designate as the Christo-Platonic and Judaeo-Arabic, more specifically, the Averroist-Aristotelian traditions and simply gesture to their consequences.

First, whereas in the Latin, Christian tradition, especially after Augustine, memory is a part of the self-subsistent soul, in the Averroist-Aristotelian tradition memory is an extension of sensation and imagination or a storehouse of common sensibles and images arising from them, and thus does not pre-exist, nor exists independently of them.

Although the re-articulation of Aristotelian psychology whereby memory is understood as a power independent of sensation and imagination, a power whose *proper* objects are disembodied or immaterial, makes possible a plausible defense of individual immortality, it also renders impossible *real* knowledge of the sensible world.

Second, likewise, the Christo-Platonic tradition posits the will as a part of the self-subsistent soul and understands the upright will as a distinctly intellectual, and therefore strictly active faculty, or as an efficient cause of distinctly human action, including the act of affirming, that is conforming to "the true," which is the "good." Indeed, will as an affect, passion, or desire is a mark of the human depravity consequent upon original sin. Thus understood, the separation between two wills mirrors a more fundamental separation between body and soul or human sensible animality and human rationality.

In contrast, from the perspective of Aristotelian psychology, in which moral categories are conventional rather than natural, the dual concepts of *original* sin and *free* will are unintelligible. Hence, rather than assert an originary identity between the "true" and the "good," Averroist-Aristotelian, Jewish philosophers emphasized and dialectically investigated the irreducible differences between concrete/historical religio-political conventions and natural/rational experience-based conclusion.

The most important consequence of understanding the will as an independent active faculty, especially when it is combined with memory as a source of knowledge independent of sensation, is the progressive separation of embodied, hence irrational, desire and disembodied "intellectual love," nature, and freedom so that freedom become essentially freedom from passion/nature rather than being concurrent with them. I am convinced that Descartes's substance dualism and Spinoza's materialism represent the most explicit historical culmination of the radical alternatives provided by these two traditions.

✤ II. Gersonides's Materialism

> It is not thought (dianoia) *as such that can move anything, but* thought *which is for the same of something and is practical, for this is* the principle (arche) *of productive* thought *also; for he who produces does so for the sake of something, though a product* (poieton) *is not an end without qualification but is relative to something else and is a qualified end. But, an object of* action (prakton) *is an end {without qualification}, for a good* action (eupraxia) *is {such} an end* (telos), *and this is what we desire* (orexsis). *Hence intention* (prohairesis) *is either a desiring intellect* (orektikos nous) *or a* thinking *desire (or-*exsis dianoetike), *and such a principle* (arche) *is a {human being}.* (Nicomachean Ethics *1139a35–1139b5*)

In light of the fact that the primary focus of feminist philosophy is a critique of the Cartesian subject and in light of my claim that, precisely for this reason, feminist critiques are not radical enough, the remaining discussion will focus on an alternative understanding of "the subject" as a continuous, indefinite movement of becoming that precludes a subject–object dualism as well as teleology. Because his work has been almost entirely preserved from misappropriation by repression/ignorance, the primary focus of the remaining discussion will be Gersonides's *Supercommentary,* engaging Spinoza's radicalization primarily in the notes or in parenthetical remarks. Subsequently, the "theologico-political" implications of Spinoza's radicalization will be briefly addressed through his critique of metaphysical and religious prejudice/superstition. For the sake of clarity, it should be noted at the outset that the various idioms for motion, appetition, desire, and power (*ko'ah*) in Gersonides should be "translated" into the idioms of force, affection, *conatus,* etc. in Spinoza.[23]

It is important to note, since this is often forgotten, that, insofar as Aristotle's *de Anima* as well as commentaries on it are concerned with living entities, they are concerned with principles (*archai*) of motion, principles of being moved (affected) as well as self-moving (affecting), one of which is the *arche anthropos,* named the desiring intellect.[24]

As principle's of motion, these are determinate, natural possibilities of undergoing, of being affected, as well as of acting or affecting; that is, Aristotle's *de Anima* is a *physis of psyche.* Insofar as principles of motion, in particular the locomotion characteristic of modes of existence that are capable of some degree of self-motion, are the primary motives of the text, the question of knowledge, for Aristotle as well as for Gersonides, is either a subsidiary one, or one that can be understood only after a clarification of the complex motions characteristic of sensible, temporal finite entities. That is, insofar as the natural motion belonging to individual moved and moving, living entities is a complex web of motions, including the motions peculiar to diverse modes of learning and knowing from determinate powers to their actualization, completed or full actuality is a termination or elimination of motion and time/as temporalities, and, hence, of finite life. For, even if we take the "agent intellect," or "*nous poeitikos,*" to be an actualized a-temporal, infinite entity, and if its a-temporality and infinity is unrelated to sensibility as it is in the Christo-Platonic tradition, in fact, especially if we do, its relation to finite motion, especially finite self-motion, remains entirely opaque. From an Aristotelian perspective all motion from power (*dunamis*) to act is appetitive, and appetition cannot come about without sensation, sensibly based memory, and imagination. In the absence of a Christo-Platonic dualist ontology, the God who is the transcendent Logos, and memory as an equiprimordial source of intelligibles, the compelling question underlying the *de Anima,* even in its most constricted sense of the conditions of human knowing, is the source(s) of modes of appetition, their sameness as well as difference. Differently stated, in the absence of an ontological/substantial source of knowledge independent of sensibility, in the absence of a distinct, self-subsistent *faculty* of memory, the pressing question is that of the sameness and difference among processes belonging to different species of animate motions as well as to relations among human sensation, imagination, and modes of cognition. Consequently, long before the question of knowledge simpliciter (i.e., demonstrative knowledge) can be addressed, and before I address Gersonides's discussion of the distinctive desire named by those aspects of *nous* and *dianoia,* intellect and thinking, that are and must remain strictly bound to embodiment/materiality, I must address the multivalent aspects of appetition/desire distinctive of different modes of human motions, affected as well as affecting, that is, retentive as well as constructive.

After glossing and significantly modifying Averroes's claim that "the appetitive power is moved by way of apprehension," and stating that Averroes must or should have meant the apprehension of an imaginative notion, Gersonides explicitly states that appetitive motion can originate *only* from the imagination, rather than from the intellect. Although the intellectual soul is also the cause of appetition, it cannot be the cause of motion,

> [f]or the intelligible does not have a particular thing toward which one might move, except insofar as the imagination imagines a particular thing, whose universal [*kholelo*] the intellect judges to be good. (Mashbaum, 182)

Three aspects of this brief statement are crucial for our following analysis. First, were memory really distinct from the common sense and imagination, especially were it a source of knowledge independent of sensibility, like intellect, it would have no particular "thing" toward which a human being might move. Second, and for similar reasons, the proximity of imagination and intellect cannot be overemphasized, for this proximity is not limited to an extrinsic, i.e., mechanical motion, nor to practical reason, nor is it determined by a real distinction between imagination and intellect so that their activities are ever separable, on the contrary. Third, and lest "good" be taken here as an ontologically grounded moral category, I must note that, almost as if in anticipation of this mis-understanding, Gersonides adds: "for the imaginative form exists in an animal only for the purpose of motion, since that is the *benefit* it *provides* the animal" (Mashbaum, 183). As will become evident, the benefit(s) attained by the *natural* motions that constitute provision (i.e., providence) are judged to be "good" insofar as they enhance the animal's preservation, which preservation is entirely independent of moral/ conventional categories, whencesoever they may originate. The implicit problem, then, for the philosopher in this other "tradition" would not be so much, perhaps not at all, the grounding of moral categories, but rather, that of the possible tension, even opposition, between always, already-given moral categories (social, political, or religion conventions) when these are at odds with desires for what is judged to enhance preservation. Thus understood, the question of *ethics* (and *ethos*) often takes the form of the questioning of conventional moral categories, "rationally" or "dogmatically" construed, returning the inquiry to the relations between sensibly based imagination and appetition. Such a return requires a new beginning at the end of the *Supercommentary,* the very end of the discussion of appetition, as well as the *Supercommentary on the de Anima.*

> Then, when there are an imaginative form and appetition which are not followed by motion, this must necessarily be due to the absence of that concord between the imaginative form and the appetitive one by which movement is perfected. "The failure of the appetitive soul to receive movement from the imaginative form is called paralysis." (Mashbaum, 183; quotation modified)

There is a performative dimension to this ending, an ending in paralysis that enacts what is essential about the soul as a principle of motion whose cession, a cessation of appetition, is the termination of life.

In a word, then, in light of the end of Gersonides's *Supercommentary* (and of Averroes's commentary) in the absence of an imaginatively represented sensible individual that can be desired, there is no life. And, clearly, where there is no desirative life, there can be no knowing. For, although knowledge or understanding/intelligibility may not itself lead to motion, from an Aristotelian perspective (of whatever kind) knowledge or intelligibility depend upon sensibility, imagination, and appetition. It is not surprising, therefore, that throughout the *Supercommentary* Gersonides repeats numerous times in numerous ways the claim that in the absence of sensation, there can be no knowledge whatsoever. In fact, he claims that the intellect is aroused, i.e., comes into being and is moved by sensation, memory, and imagination and, hence, that "whoever lacks one of the senses lacks some intelligible" (Mashbaum, 104). In this light, it is not surprising that Gersonides rejects his predecessor's account of emanation, which rejection necessarily entails a radical rethinking of the ontological status of the agent intellect, especially in relation to human knowledge, including the form of knowledge unique to emanation from the agent intellect, namely, the prophetic.[25]

Given the intimate relation between sensibility, i.e., singular embodi-edness, appetition, and knowledge, and given that intelligibility, or univer-sality cannot be the cause of the motion that renders intelligibility possible in the first place, the question of the relation between sensibility, appetition, and any mode of knowledge, real or apparent, is always investigated in terms of the relation between imagination, or imaginative forms and intel-ligible ones.[26]

From beginning to conclusion, Gersonides's *Supercommentary* attempts to provide a natural account of the relation and distinction between differ-ent powers of the soul such that it makes manifest the continuity not only among different processes within the human soul but also between the human animal and other animals. It is an articulation of the complex natural motions from potencies/powers to actualities that regards both intra- and inter-psychical motions as continuous processes of realization so that an ac-tualized "lower" or, more precisely, "prior" power becomes the substratum/determinate power of a subsequent one. Furthermore, the becoming actual of a natural power generates a new, "higher," in the sense of greater power. Now, it cannot be overemphasized that the relation of "lower" to "higher" signifies, first and foremost, a temporal anteriority and posteriority deter-mined by the "for the sake of" which "fluid," continuously changing *telos* is motivated by the desire for greater power of self-motion, action, and preser-vation.[27] It is in this sense that memory exists for the sake of the imagina-tion, and both exist for the sake of appetition or desire for what enhances the well-being of an animal and repulsion by what is harmful to it. That is, the actualized sensible perceptions in memory or as memory become the possi-bility/powers of representation, construction, and creativity.

In the discussion of the imagination, Gersonides assigns both memory and imagination to animals claiming that, even in the presence of a sensed object, the animal is not moved or is not attracted and repelled by the par-ticular sensible, but rather its motion originates in its imagination. "It is obvious that the animal does not move toward the food because it is white or black or *fragrant,* which is what the animal perceives, but rather because of the *imagined pleasure* of eating it" (Mashbaum, 21). For Gersonides, the perceived sensible is a potential sensible only; the appetitive motion toward it is what can render it an actual sensible. Differently stated, while the "ex-ternal" perceptible sensible is a fully *actual,* real individual, and can, there-fore, show itself from itself, its actual existence is also its possibility of being perceived by another for whom it is a potential sensible only. That is, the in-trinsic motions from potency to act of an entity or its determinate powers for self-motion/action are simultaneously distinct from and closely related to its capacities for being moved or affected by the motions originating in the perceptible entity. Natural motion is double-structured so that the intrinsic movements from determinate possibilities to actualities, which in turn become greater possibilities, are continuously determined by and can determine extrinsic motions. Thus, the power to be extrinsically affected is determinate precisely in the sense that it is a capacity to receive a determining action in a manner such that the affection increases (or decreases) the power of self-motion in the same *respect*. Consequently, the determinate powers to be moved by an extrinsic sensible can both enhance and harm an animal's preservation. The more sensible perceptions are undergone and retained in the common-sense/retentive power of the imagination or memory (all of which name the same actualized, psychic power), the more the animal can both represent and desire, or shun, that is, move itself toward or away from an extrinsic sensible.

In light of his materialist psychology, Gersonides concludes that were the perceivable or perceived external "object" identical to the retained perception, rather than aspectivally related to it, the animal would possess a form in act preventing its desiderative self-movement toward either the immediate or the represented sensible. Consequently, (1) the animal will desire the "object" only in its presence in which case the animal will be moved/determined by the "object" rather than be simultaneously moved and self-moving, and (2) the animal will be unable to desire and move itself toward what is necessary for its self-preservation in the absence of the external sensible, in this case the food necessary for self-preservation. As will become evident shortly, the same intricate distinction and relation of doubled motion, intrinsic and extrinsic, will characterize all motions from potency to act, imaginative as well as intellective.

Ironically, whereas appetitive differences among animals are explained by degrees of strength and weaknesses of the retentive capacity of imagination, i.e., memory, so that some animals move toward the pleasant in the absence of a sensible while others do not, the differences among the more perfect animals and the human animal pertain to the representational capacity of imagination. More precisely, with respect to memory, the human animal does not differ from the other animals. The special human difference is its capacity to err, i.e., to represent and *desire* non-existents as existing, which can clearly be harmful. Thus, were it the case that the human animal did not have a "higher" power than its imagination, its capacity for self-preservation would be inferior to that of other animals. For while all animals capable of self-motion in the absence of an immediate sensible, including the human, are equally affected by, and hence actually possess intrinsic perceptions the possession of which is nothing other than their actual memory, and while all animals are able to recall and represent intrinsic perception, either by choice (i.e., self-motion) [28] or by necessity (i.e., by being moved), only the human animal can manipulate its distinct perceptions so as to distinguish and combine them without regard for what can really exist and hence, what is actually rather than imaginatively beneficial or harmful. And it must be noted that it is precisely this capacity to invent without regard to what is actually rather than imaginatively or merely rationally possible, which is both determined by and determines human convention, ethical and political.

Given the human imaginative deficiency, the practical rational power serves to perfect the deficient imagination. Viewed strictly from the perspective of nature, however strange or uncanny this may appear to us, practical rationality is, properly speaking, not really different in kind than animal imagination. It is the cause of human love and hate as well as all other appetitive motions. The real difference between animal and human desire and its regulation for the sake of self-preservation, is that the former occurs by nature, the latter by convention, or imaginative construction.

Let me again emphasize that were it not for a faculty naturally/temporally anterior to the imaginative one, the desire for knowledge would be a vain desire for the impossible, both in terms of knowledge of the real and in terms of the possible. Likewise, were memory independent of sensibility, practical reason would have no access to a non-constructed/invented sensible individual and could not form judgments about individuals, except either equivocally or in their presence. Quoting Averroes, Gersonides states:

> In general, the moral qualities are a product of it, because these qualities are nothing but the imaginings due to which activities are performed as equitably as possible. Thus one is courageous . . . in the proper place and in the proper degree. Such animal qualities like courage in the lion . . . do not necessitate the presence of the rational faculty. For it is predicated as a kind of amphibolous expression with respect to human moral qualities, because they arise in man by invention. (Mashbaum, 59–60)[29]

Despite its great intricacy and nuance, to which I cannot do justice here, Gersonides's discussion of the relation between the imagination and material intellect follows the same natural development as that found in the preceding discussions of the relation between sensibility and imagination whereby all motions are natural movements from potency to act with each actuality *becoming* the substratum (i.e., *potentiality, power*) or subject of the subsequent one. And it cannot be overemphasized that all natural movement is desirative—i.e., originates in some desired "object" that is perceived, imagined, or believed to be good—and hence appears as a *telos*. The problem, then, is the status of the *telos* and/or its origin. Since, however, desire is, first and foremost, a desire for self-preservation, i.e., since it is always already "grounded" in the concrete material desire for self-preservation, the question of desire is always already praxical.

The *Supercommentary* makes amply manifest that all modes of practical knowing concern preservation and pertain to the order where free human action, i.e., self-motion, can take place. Insofar as human choice concerns the pursuit of what is (*imaginatively*) perceived as good and bad, beneficial or harmful to preservation, it occurs, first and foremost, in the order of the affects/desires, for there is no choice with respect to truth and falsity. More precisely, good and bad are not by nature, or necessity. However, insofar as the natural order is necessary, since no individual knower can understand the order as a unified order, unless some form of knowledge of concrete, material individuals were possible, and unless some "provision" for its persistent regularity were a determinate possibility of the natural order, human affairs will be governed by chance and the natural desire for preservation will be futile, which to Gersonides is absurd. This is precisely the reason why necessity and choice, the material and agent intellect, must be aspectivally related, with the material intellect, qua both material and intellect coming into being through the sameness and difference between memory and imagination, respectively signifying sensible, necessary affect, and creative freedom.

III. *Spinoza and the Liberation from Prejudice*

Although Gersonides's *Supercommentary* makes amply evident the inseparability between Aristotle's discussion of the soul's power and human action, and hence the inseparability of desire/appetition and knowledge, it does not *directly* address the question of ethics/politics in this context. Likewise, although Gersonides explicitly underlines the fact that the moral qualities are products of the relations between the imagination and convention, he does not *directly* address the affective force of convention, let alone the fact that such force can repel contradictory evidence. In lieu of a conclusion, I offer a very brief outline of specific elements of Gersonides's psychology rejected by Spinoza precisely because they can compromise a materialist (i.e., embodied) philosophy, and present Spinoza's account of prejudices, which account undergirds his ethical/political philosophy as a sober critique of the claims of human reason.

Spinoza's rejection of faculty psychology eliminates the major difficulty for, and possible inconsistency in, the material becoming of knowledge, namely, the difficulty of accounting for the sameness and difference between imagination and intellect. For, as a consequence of ascribing really different activities to each power, Gersonides's distinction among the powers runs the risk of reifying them in a manner that undermines his painstaking attempt to explain how one power becomes another while remaining itself or performing its actions, that is, without being sublated. For on his own account, Gersonides cannot simultaneously claim that the intellect comes into being from the repetitive experience of images and that it actively abstracts their forms, unless the intellect were somehow ontologically real prior to its becoming and unless the forms were somehow really distinct from their matter. From a Spinozist perspective, Gersonides's account is too unilinear or teleological so that the perfection of one faculty appears to be its overcoming, which overcoming successively distances subsequent activities from their material origins.

Let me turn directly to Spinoza's radical critique of teleology, a teleology that (together with the belief in the will of God) is singled out as the primary and most powerful prejudice/superstition throughout Spinoza's writing.[30]

> I have taken care, wherever the occasion arose, to remove prejudices that could prevent my demonstrations from being perceived. But because prejudices remain that could and can be a great obstacle to men's understanding the connection of things in the way I have explained it, I consider it worthwhile to submit them here to the scrutiny of reason. All the prejudices I here undertake to expose depend on this one: that men commonly suppose that all natural things act, as men do, on account of an end; indeed they maintain as certain that God himself directs all things to some certain end, for they say that God made all things for me, and man that he may worship God. (*E* 1 Appendix)

What is immediately evident from the citation is that Spinoza does not consider demonstration, even in the *Ethics,* to be co-extensive with reason. In fact, Spinoza's concern with prejudice clearly indicates that no method could suffice to overturn prejudice, let alone bring about understanding. For were demonstrations to have real/rational power over prejudice, the latter would be no more than a passive bodily affect/passion over which the mind would have active dominion, which Spinoza denies.

More precisely, prejudices constitute "great obstacles" precisely and only insofar as they are very powerful affects. Thus, the more a prejudice is held to be certain, the more powerful it is. For, as Spinoza states numerous times in numerous ways, "the mind is nothing but the idea of the body." That is, the mind does not have ideas but *is* the ideas, which ideas arise from the affects. Hence, the more passionate the belief in teleology, the more extensive will be its power and the greater its resistance to the *force* of a demonstration that undermines teleology and the beliefs to which it gives rise, e.g. good and evil, beauty and ugliness, merit and sin, and so on.

As Spinoza's analysis of prejudice makes evident, the origin of the belief in teleology (as well as the normative categories consequent upon it) and its originary force is the natural desire for self-preservation in virtue of which this belief can overpower all contradictory experience. Rather than change their long-held (and inherited) beliefs, humans construct elaborate explanations/mythologies to justify as well as shield them, which mythologies require the insistence of ignorance, i.e., unknowability of causes of events that repeatedly undermine these constructions. And, for Spinoza, all the qualities commonly attributed to God, especially the will, are the cornerstones of such constructions. As a conclusion to the genealogy of teleology (in a classically Aristotelian dialectical manner), Spinoza offers a contradictory thesis: God is Nature or a certain eternal necessity of nature, on which basis he subsequently claims that the belief in teleology "turns nature completely upside down."

The brief genealogy of religious prejudice makes evident that, for Spinoza, all the traditional ethical concepts and the proscriptions and laws based upon them arise from a primary ignorance and its occlusion by subsequent conceptual constructions, be they theological or metaphysical. Now, were Spinoza's analysis of prejudice motivated by metaphysical or epistemological concerns, then few philosophers could stoically avoid the ignorant many who celebrate their bondage to superstition as freedom. Since, however, irrespective of its origin, prejudice has become the official doctrine/truth whose enforcement grounds real, concrete power, at the very least the power of prohibition and exclusion by the force of law, the question of prejudice is, first and foremost, a political question. Hence, following an analysis of wonder at unknown causes of what appears to be ordered, a wonder that results in the attribution of all unknown natural events to the will of God, he briefly alludes to the political dimension of religious prejudice. Describing the will of God as "the sanctuary of ignorance," Spinoza writes:

> Hence it happens that one who seeks the true causes of miracles, and is eager, like an educated man, to understand natural things, not to wonder at them, like a fool, is generally considered and denounced as an impious heretic by those whom the people honor as interpreters of nature and the Gods. For they know that if ignorance is taken away, then foolish wonder, the only means they have of arguing and defending their authority, is also taken away. But, I leave these things . . . (*E* 1 Appendix, 443–44)

which he does or at least postpones their explicit genealogical critique to
the *TTP*. By bringing into relief the real threat of denunciation as heretical
of any attempt to destroy the "sanctuary of ignorance," Spinoza simultaneously makes evident the real power of critique and its limits.

Since my current concern with the power of prejudice/superstition is
specifically political, and since the present discussion of Spinoza is only intended to supplement Gersonides's apparent silence on the political, let me
turn all too briefly to the *TTP* and the *TP* where the political dimensions of
the above discussion are clearly articulated, of which I shall highlight only one.

It is especially ironic that the continuity between Spinoza's *Ethics* and
the political writings is not only ignored, but also, insofar as the *Ethics* is
read as a modern metaphysics rather than (Aristotelian) ethics/politics,[31]
such a reading clearly implies a separation between ethics and politics that
presupposes the separation between the private and public realms or, more
precisely, that subscribes to an understanding of the political as an escape
from nature, which for Spinoza is utopian and absurd. This irony is especially poignant in view of the fact that Spinoza's *TTP* begins, returns to, and
ends with discussions of superstitions and their pervasive political danger.
Now, it is precisely because *by nature* reason cannot overpower the passions,
it is precisely because the passions are natural, as is the human need for my-
thologies/religion to alleviate the pervasive ones, i.e., fear and hope that
Spinoza is at pains to demonstrate throughout the *Ethics,* and because of
their overwhelming power, that Spinoza's political philosophy returns to
them. That is, Spinoza's politics is thoroughly informed by his natural philosophy or materialism and is incomprehensible without it. For Spinoza's
repeated attempts to argue for freedom of judgment and belief, i.e., for the
separation or religion and politics as well as his advocacy of democracy, are
based on his understanding of the indefinitely many ways in which bodies
are affected, hence on the irreducibly many ways in which beliefs/minds
come to be, to have, and to exercise force. That is why in his political writings Spinoza attempts to demonstrate both the absurdity of basing politics
on an abstract ideal of the human being, as an escape from nature that
neither has nor could exist—why his critique of teleology is also a thorough
critique of linear temporality (read progress)—and the inefficacy (disadvantage) of a political regime that attempts to repress the passions by fear, persecution or execution. In short, Spinoza's political philosophy is a radical
alternative not only to Locke and his Enlightened followers but also to
Hobbes's *Leviathan.* And it is my claim that this is the only alternative that
argues for a materially concrete human freedom and attempts to demonstrate the inefficacy of both dualist and reductive materialist constructions

of sovereignty and freedom and tyrannical rule. For, insofar as both attempt to eliminate "how" human beings are by nature, the first by a mythological construction of a real separation between body/animality/passion and mind/humanity/reason, i.e., by a covert repression, the second, by an overt repression, insofar as such repressions are intended to eliminate the indefinitely many ways in which human passions/human beings come to be affected and be, they are inefficacious as well as disadvantageous, even to the rulers.

Three sets of quotations must suffice to exemplify my claims:

(1) On the duality of human nature and the absurdity of Utopia:

> Philosophers look upon the passions by which we are assailed as vices, into which men fall through their own fault. So it is their custom to deride, bewail, berate them, or if their purpose is to appear more zealous than others, to execrate them. They believe that they are thus performing a sacred duty, and that they are attaining the summit of wisdom when they have learned how to shower extravagant praise on a *human nature* that nowhere exists and to revile that which exists in actuality. (*TP* 36; my emphasis)

(2) On the inefficacy of tyranny:

> If the strongest dominion were held by those who are most feared, then it would assuredly be held by the tyrant's subjects, for they are most feared by their tyrants. . . . It is impossible for the mind to be under another's control; for not one is able to transfer to another his natural right [read power] or faculty to reason freely and to form his own judgment on any matters whatsoever, nor can he be compelled to do so. . . . What cannot be prohibited, must necessarily be allowed. (*TTP,* 192; 230; 234)

(3) On the advantages of democracy:

> [It] is imperative to grant freedom of judgment and to govern men in such a way that the different conflicting views they openly proclaim do not debar them from living together in peace. This system of government is undoubtedly the best and its disadvantages are few because it is in closest accord with human nature. For we have shown that in a democracy (which comes closest to the natural state) all citizens undertake to act but not to reason and to judge, by decision made in common. (*TTP,* 236)

Epilogos: Jewish Philosophy and Its (Concrete) Political Implications

In conclusion, let me reflect on the concrete political implications of my philosophical analysis in light of the explicitly stated goals of this volume. Rather than being concerned with the manner in which past Jewish philosophers understood the differences between women and men, or employed gender categories, which concern I consider to be anachronistic, I focus on the challenges that they pose to Western philosophy in general, feminist philosophy in particular, or more precisely, on the possibilities they present for thinking the philosophical canon "against the grain." In an analogous manner, I am not concerned with nor consider relevant religious affiliation and/or practice for inclusion in or exclusion from the practice of Jewish *philosophy;* on the contrary. Although in an *epilogos* I cannot adequately address the boundaries of either feminist or Jewish philosophy, let alone argue against any fixed boundaries, I can briefly indicate how and why preconceived boundaries are philosophically suspect.

First, both in this essay and in numerous others I demonstrate extensively how and why, if he is to be read at all, Spinoza can only be read as heir to Jewish philosophy, albeit one that is occluded by ecclesiastico-political powers. Second, reading Spinoza as a Jewish philosopher is far from idiosyncratic. In fact, it has a long and respected lineage within (and almost exclusively within) the Jewish philosophical tradition. Third, I consider myself to be a Jewish philosopher, despite the fact that I stopped participating in *religious* Jewish practice as soon as I was sufficiently mature to encounter the horrors of Auschwitz. Fourth, the latter identification is no different in kind from my "self"-identification as a feminist philosopher, despite the fact that much of my work focuses on the work of dead men, whose opinion of women, if it could have had the force of law, would have prevented me from the practice of philosophy, *at that time.*

Although I am convinced that this essay explores the impact (actual or potential) of feminist readings of the history of philosophy on the orientation and practice of Jewish philosophy, many readers may be dismayed that I do not, nor wish to, propose *models* for thinking philosophically about Judaism that take the category of gender seriously. To do so would, at best, amount to subscribing to sexual difference as the originary difference, relegating other differences, such as race and sexual orientation, to lesser or secondary attributes of an essentially sexed Jewish subject, a metaphysical rather than concrete, historically situated, political subject. In contrast, in light of the complicity between religion and concrete political oppression, I consider the critique of religious superstition (and metaphysical prejudice/dogmata, e.g., "the subject") to have overwhelming implications for contemporary "Judaism" of whatever sort. For qua philosophers, rather than subordinate philosophical inquiry to an ideal model, *Jewish* philosophers were and remain fully engaged with the scientific problems and idioms of their time and place. In so doing, they neither cease nor can cease to be philosophers or Jews.

Rather than either despair about or offer idealist or pragmatist solutions to philosophy's inefficacy to bring about change in the material conditions of concrete human beings, following Spinoza, I am thoroughly sober about reason's powerlessness in relation to passion/superstition. I insist, however, that the expectations thus placed on reason (be they idealist or pragmatic) make evident its modern reduction to instrumental efficacy.

It is precisely because I am deeply concerned with political practice that I engage the practice of the history of philosophy with a hefty suspicion that it may be a self-legitimating way of avoiding an engagement with the historically specific material conditions of concrete individual human beings. Hence, unlike many American academic Marxists or Freudians, I eschew all forms of scientific positivism/utopianism. Rather than long to restore the Enlightenment idea/ideal of Humanity, even if it is constrained by an Habermasian linguist pragmatism (as Jean Cahan does in this volume), I read Marx to be keenly attuned to Spinoza's materialist philosophy. Consequently, whereas Spinoza focused his philosophical striving on a radical critique of religion and metaphysics, the dogmata which had the force of law in the seventeenth century, Marx focused his on the critique of idealist metaphysics and political economy, the reigning dogmata and oppressive forces of the nineteenth century.

Finally, it is precisely because I am concerned with the concrete implications of science for human freedom and political practice, and because I do not consider any science, let alone the sciences that investigate the human psyche, to be neutral, that I consider the materialism of Freudian psychoanalysis to offer richer critical tools for philosophical inquiry than neurophysiology. For reductive materialisms, political (Hobbesian) or natural (neurophysiological) can no more explain away the natural human need for religion/mythology or the oppressive/repressive concrete power of superstition-borne passions (fear and hope) than a pill can eliminate them, without eliminating the specific desire that renders the human animal a desiring intellect.

NOTES

1. Walter Benjamin, "Theses on the Philosophy of History," in *Illuminations,* ed. Hannah Arendt (New York: Schocken Books, 1969), xvii, 262–63.

2. Theodor Adorno, *Negative Dialectics,* trans. E. B. Ashton (New York: Seabury Press, 1979), "Meditation on Metaphysics," 1, "After Auschwitz," 361–65.

3. Edmund Husserl, *The Crisis of European Sciences and Transcendental Phenomenology,* trans. David Carr (Evanston, Ill.: Northwestern University Press, 1979), Appendix VI, "The Origin of Geometry," 270. My emphasis.

4. Sigmund Freud, *The Future of an Illusion,* trans. James Starchey (New York and London: Norton, 1961), 63. N.B. footnote 4.

5. Jesse Stephen Mashbaum, "Chapters 9–12 of Gersonides' *Supercommentary on Averroes' Epitome of the De Anima:* The Internal Senses" (Ph.D. diss., Brandeis University, 1981; University of Michigan Dissertation # 8126886).

6. Levi ben Gershom (Gersonides), *The Wars of the Lord,* 3 vols., trans. Seymour Feldman (Philadelphia: Jewish Publications Society of America, 1984–99).

7. It must be emphasized that my claim is not that there is not normative Jewish practice. Rather, it is my claim that, for Jewish Aristotelians, *dogmata* and *nomoi* are the greatest hindrances to philosophical thinking and the ethos that informs its practice.

8. Aristotle, *Aristotle's Nicomachean Ethics,* trans. Hippocrates Apostle (Grinnell, Iowa: Peripatetic Press, 1984).

9. Aristotle, *Aristotle on the Soul,* trans. Hippocrates Apostle (Grinnell, Iowa: Peripatetic Press, 1981).

10. The following English references will be used: *Ethics (E),* in *The Collected Works of Spinoza,* vol. 1, trans. Edwin Curley (Princeton, N.J.: Princeton University Press, 1985); *Theologico-Political Treatise (TTP),* Samuel Shirley (Indianapolis and Cambridge: Hackett, 1998); *Political Treatise (TP),* Samuel Shirley (Indianapolis and Cambridge: Hackett, 2000).

11. Luce Irigaray," The Mechanics of Fluids," in *This Sex Which Is Not One,* trans. Catherine Porter with Carolyn Burke (Ithaca, N.Y.: Cornell University Press, 1985), 112–13.

12. Irigaray's texts are the only ones explicit about the theological underpinning of the philosophical canon and, in fact, she most often engages theology and philosophy in and as a single discourse. Although this approach becomes deeply problematic in some of her works, nonetheless, insofar as she explicitly thematizes the question of the male canon in terms of the identity of the Son with the Logos, her work clearly discloses the Christo-Platonic determination of the unified philosophical canon.

13. Luce Irigaray, "Sorcerer Love: A Reading of Plato, *Symposium,* Diotima's Speech," in *An Ethics of Secular Difference,* trans. Carolyn Burke and Gillian C. Gill (Ithaca, N.Y.: Cornell University Press, 1993), 20–33. I shall briefly demonstrate this tension in the conclusion to Part I.

14. Marsilio Ficino, *Commentary on Plato's Symposium on Love,* trans. Sears Jayne (Dallas: Spring Publication, 1985). In particular, Speech 4, C. 3; Speech 5, C. 11; Speech 6, C. 15.

15. Of Aquinas's commentaries on Aristotle's works, the following are exemplary: In *duodecim libros Metaphysicorum Aristotelis Expositio* (Rome: Marietti, 1964), and *Opera Omnia: Sententia Libri Ethicorum,* vol. 47, 1–2, ed. Rene-A. Gauthier (Rome: Commissio Leonina, 1969).

16. And here, Spinoza's work offer the exemplary opportunity, which opportunity both Irigaray and Butler fail to exploit, even when they address his work either in a sustained (Irigaray) or incidental (Butler) manner.

17. It should be noted that this view also implies the materially dialectical necessity of the formation of the philosophical canon, whose historical unfolding accords with a single, progressive teleology, i.e., whose presentation of history is abstract and markedly a-historical.

18. The most astute and poignant observation concerning the prevalence of this "blindness," in my view, is found in Benjamin, Thesis 1, 253.

19. Luce Irigaray, *An Ethics of Sexual Difference,* 29.

20. Judith Butler, *The Psychic Life of Power: Theories of Subjection* (Stanford, Calif.: Stanford University Press, 1997).

21. Cathy Carruth, *Unclaimed Experience: Trauma, Narratives, and History* (Baltimore: Johns Hopkins University Press, 1996).

22. On Spinoza's debt to Gersonides, see Idit Dobbs-Weinstein, "Gersonides' Radically Modern Understanding of the Agent Intellect," in *Meeting of the Minds: The Relations between Medieval and Classical Modern European Philosophy,* ed. Stephen F. Brown (Turnhout, Belgium: Brepols, 1998), 191–213, esp. 205–206.

23. The justification of these "translations" will become evident as the argument unfolds. It should be noted, however, that the English terms fail to capture the rich and nuanced use of either Gersonides's or Spinoza's vocabulary.

24. Or the sameness of the two aspects expressing Spinoza's *conatus.*

25. Although the discussion of prophetic knowledge is beyond the scope of this essay, it must be pointed out that the discussion of dreams, divinations, and prophecy in the *Wars* is consistent with the discussion of practical knowledge in the *Supercommentary,* with one exception. In my view, the *Wars* claims that prophecy is different in kind from dreams and divination, but nonetheless natural rather than miraculous, is internally consistent.

26. Despite the fact that the "imagination" is the images and the "intellect" is the intelligibles, Gersonides retains the Aristotelian vocabulary of which the ones that threaten the consistency of his own account are "forms" and "abstraction." This vocabulary is rejected by Spinoza for reasons that will be evident below.

27. Again, it cannot be overemphasized that the English term *power* fails to capture the full range of the Hebrew "*ko'ah*" and the Arabic "*ku'ah,*" which translate Greek "*dunamis,*" the determinate power to undergo so as to become. The natural contrary of "*ko'ah*" is "*po'al,*" which denotes actuality, activity, creativity, that is, the ability to generate or bring into being in another a determinate power to become in the same respect. "*Po'al*" translates the Greek terms "*energeia*" and "*entelechia.*"

28. It must be noted that Spinoza rejects the ability to recall by choice, a rejection consistent with a materialism more radical than Gersonides's. Likewise, his account of the imagination eliminates an ambiguity (or inconsistency) in the representation of "non-existents" as existing, if it is understood as consequent upon choice.

29. The expression used by Gersonides is "*hotsa'ah mi-libo,*" which literally translates "brings forth from his heart." By making amply evident the appetitive/desirative, rather than theoretical origin of "morality" Gersonides also underscores the desirative origin of reason.

30. It should be noted that teleology is the cause of hope and fear, the passions that nurture superstition.

31. And here suffice it to recall that, for Aristotle, the *Nicomachean Ethics* is the first part of political science and that its separation from the *Politics* is artificial and exemplifies the strange destiny of any book's afterlife.

THREE

HEIDI MIRIAM RAVVEN

Spinoza's Ethics of the Liberation of Desire

 Preliminary Thoughts: On Being a Feminist Jewish Philosopher

In bringing together Jewish feminist philosophers, this volume makes us consider what, if anything, Judaism, feminism, and philosophy have to do with each other besides residing uneasily in the authors of these collected essays. I wear these monikers with some fear and trembling. I have written feminist reflections on Judaism and Jewish identity and also offered a feminist reading of Hegel. So here I turn to Spinoza. Who could better deserve a feminist reading than that great radical and source of radicalisms, Spinoza?

Does this essay contribute to Jewish philosophy? If one narrows Jewish philosophy to consist only in theoretical articulations of Judaism, its values, practices, major modes of signifying and transmitting a specific culture, then the answer may be no. And if one narrows the definition of the Jewish philosopher to one who reflects upon Judaism using the resources of one or more schools of philosophy, then again my answer might be no. But these definitions are too narrow and perhaps even unphilosophical, and they may deracinate our enterprise both from the wider concerns of philosophy per se and from the tradition of Jewish philosophy in particular. For historically, Jewish philosophers have taken seriously the wider concerns of philosophy—ethical, epistemological, political and legal, ontological, cosmological, linguistic, etc.—refusing to regard the Jews as a separate species but in our full humanity.[1] Let us not confuse the task of the philosopher with that of the theologian.

If we think of Jewish philosophers historically as those who studied philosophy, were educated in Jewish texts, philosophical and otherwise, and engaged in a conversation with their Jewish philosophical predecessors, then Spinoza counts. For even a dissenting voice is still engaged in the conversation. Another criterion of who is a Jewish philosopher fits some of us in the academy. For we bring and interpret great Jewish philosophical works to the next generation of both Jews and non-Jews, making these works part of the culture. These books thus become part of what being an educated person knows or ought to know. We bring them alive and show why they live on. Thus many of us are perceptive and even original readers, i.e., *commentators.* We are neither innovators out of whole cloth (the purported task of the constructive philosopher) nor articulators of second-order reflections upon praxis and law (theologians). What could be more Jewish than seeing ourselves as latter-day commentators, neither completing the work nor allowing ourselves to desist from it?

My goals in both teaching and writing are not primarily antiquarian, constrained to presenting texts in the light of their original historical contexts and meanings. For great books are ever generative of new *true* interpretations that are not impositions. The sharp dichotomy between constructive philosophy and the history of philosophy is, I think, misguided.[2] We should be no more antiquarian in reading a Maimonides or a Spinoza than a scholar of Shakespeare or Plato ought to be. For at best, reading is a creative as well as an analytical act. The difference between the more restrictively historical and the more creative treatment I think hangs on the greatness of the thinkers we address. Great thinkers ever demand and deserve our creative engagement anew. So my purpose is both feminist and Jewish in bringing Spinoza into this contemporary philosophical conversation.

Introduction: Feminist Reflections on Spinoza

We are necessarily passive only in so far as we have inadequate ideas, and only in so far as we have inadequate ideas are we passive.[3]

Spinoza envisioned the philosophic life, which was also the consummate ethical life, as aiming at the liberation from all forms of oppression and, particularly, internalized oppression. He termed the latter "passivity." This liberation could be gained, he said, only through developing independence of mind by embracing the pleasures of the broadest human and natural connectedness. I offer here a liberationist reading of Spinoza's ethics and argue that feminists ought to take it seriously. We discover that Spinoza was inspired by Jewish conceptions of ethics and of politics in developing his liberationist theory.

Although Spinoza was not himself a proto-feminist—yet neither was he anti-feminist—he understood the plight of the marginalized and oppressed. He was recognized in his time as having cast his lot with political radicalism. One of his mentors was the radical democrat Franciscus Van den Ende, his Latin teacher. Spinoza also displayed *ideological* (not Christian) affinity with the Quakers and other radical Protestants. Spinoza captured in the *Ethics*—albeit in a highly formal and technical philosophic language—the plight of the powerless in society and proposed a remedy for the internal emotional and cognitive effects of such powerlessness. I suggest here that *Spinoza's greatest concern was with the psychological effects of social oppression.* Thus he was perhaps the first to recognize, articulate, and try to develop a remedy for what we feminists have called the personal effects of the political. Nor did he limit his remedy to an internal cure but also went on to propose a politics that would eliminate as much as possible the social hierarchy and political authoritarianism at their base.

Spinoza recognized the political and social construction of belief. All thinking, he held, is driven by desires, by interests rooted in one's body and in one's social and natural contexts. This insight follows from his claim of the identity of mind and body, theory and praxis. Knowledge is always and necessarily of the body's interconnectedness in the web of its life.[4] Knowledge captures and furthers the ever-expanding relations of our body in the world.[5] Thus it is never neutral with respect to our own interests and purposes. But belief need not be, nor is it in our interest that it be, private and subjectively distorted.

Spinoza never thinks of ethics as having to do with rational choice or any kind of choice. His determinism precludes the possibility of choice as a self-serving fiction. We are left with the determination of our minds by our desires expressive of our body's relations, material and social.[6] The individual is never, for Spinoza, the Hobbesian atomic individual. The individual in the Spinozist sense includes and encompasses its bodily and mental interactions with the world. Andrew Collier proposes in his paper on Spinoza's materiality of morals that the transpersonal nature of the individual is the cornerstone of his moral philosophy. Spinoza relies on a "conception of interests transcending 'ego boundaries.'" Collier suggests that most contemporary philosophical ethicists would regard Spinoza as an "anti-moralist." For Spinoza holds that "we will not make people more moral by telling them to be moral; we will not even make ourselves more moral by trying to be more moral."

Better morals in the conventional sense come about only from understanding how all our interests are interconnected and stand or fall together.

Thus Spinoza engages in a different kind of discourse, one incommensurable with contemporary Anglo-American discussions of almost any variety because his metaphysics and psychology differ so markedly from those originating in the Cartesian or Kantian traditions, to which most discussions, even feminist ones, are heir.[7] The various versions of the feminist ethics of caring, ironically perhaps, share more assumptions with the Cartesian and Kantian models of mind which many feminists in other respects eschew, than with the Spinozist. For these are still wedded to a notion of ethics that considers how we make choices and find reasons for our choices,[8] presupposing minds that are separable from our desires (and hence bodies and situatedness) in ways that Spinoza thinks are pure fantasy and self-deception. Some feminists go so far as to denigrate theoretical understanding as an enterprise[9] as a result of tearing scientific explanation and reflections from a rootedness in self and body. By privileging ethical praxis over rational theory, these thinkers thereby reinstate the mind–body dualism from which the false dichotomy arises and merely choose the other side. Spinoza, instead, aims his scathing critique at the false dichotomy itself. The feminist approaches of Virginia Held, Sarah Ruddick, and others thus seem to have more in common with, e.g., the modified classical liberalism of Martha Nussbaum[10] than either has with a Spinozist approach. The critique of Cartesianism even by feminist ethical theorists of the anti-liberal school has not gone as far as Spinoza's critique and rethinking had in the seventeenth century. Susan James, in her work on seventeenth-century philosophical theories of the emotions, points out that too much feminist philosophic ink has been spilled on caricaturing and demonizing earlier philosophers, at the cost not only of honesty but, ironically, of repetition. Many feminists philosophers have not broken with Descartes and the aftermath deeply enough because their critique has been too crude, too simplistic.[11]

Spinoza's ethical goal of freedom breaks with liberal individualism in that its hallmark is a deeper belonging in larger and larger contexts and webs of relation. We come to see these relations as constitutive of self. Thus Spinoza's understanding of the self is in direct opposition to Descartes's willed subjectivity and all liberal accounts of atomic individualism. His independence of mind is positively correlated with extended interrelations rather than with the transcendence of relations. Instead, the polar extremes are between selves—that is, our desires and hence our ideas—as constituted by the widest web of social and natural relations or instead by the narrowest, most parochial, and most coercive ones.

Spinoza recognized that at times the survival and furtherance of narrow group needs must take precedence over the psychological and intellectual openness necessary for personal liberation and social reconstruction. Sometimes we must use the enemy's weapons in the immediate interest of survival. There are times for battening down the hatches. Virginia Held, Sarah Ruddick, Eva Feder Kittay, and Carol Gilligan all propose variants of an ethic of nurturance, of care, as a feminist model for social relations and for society at large. This parochialism is understandable but regrettable. To expose the constrictedness of an ethic of caring, let us turn for a moment to data, in this case to experience, a proposal in keeping with Held's own approach.[12] I will speak personally for a moment.

Nurturance describes my relationship to my daughter as an infant and my present relation to my cats. Nurturance is a hierarchical relation if there ever was one. No matter how kind one hopes to be, the inarticulate child has no say in this relation. Analysts' couches are filled with the victims of the often well-meaning tyranny of nurturance. My present relation with my daughter, by contrast, is more like that of the mentoring relationship I have with my students. An ethic of care, the ideal of nurturance, is simply not true to my experience of myself as a scholar, a teacher, and, most telling, as a mother. For while the mind engaged in discovery is not selfless and disinterested, neither is it confined to articulating theoretically and to justifying a narrow group praxis. Spinoza's discovery that the mind monitors the body, *its* body, at every stage from the simplest sensations of cold and hot, for example, to the discovery of quantum mechanics, ever delving into both its own connections and origins, legitimates and eroticizes all our endeavors. If true, opportunities for broadening our attachments are always before us, as is openness to new ways of life. For we follow the infinite trajectory of erotic attachment from our center outward. We see here Spinoza's famed collapsing of the theoretical and the practical intellect. Thus there is no thinking for Spinoza that is not practical, embodied, and impassioned. But neither is the practical thereby reduced to finding means to ends derived either from some purportedly detached and pure Beyond or alternatively from some irreducible, natural quarter.

There is this advantage to our experience as women from a Spinozist point of view: rather than confining us to normative stereotypes, our experience ought to prepare us better than men are prepared for gaining an ever wider perspective expressive of our wider webs of relation. Knowledge at best reflects and grasps our ever-expanding practical activities and engagements in the world. Hence, knowledge in the Spinozist sense—and that not only includes but is exemplified by philosophy and science—are empathic endeavors, extending our identifications. Since we cannot constrain the world from affecting us or control how it affects us, there should be no constraint on either our engagement with it or on deepening and broadening our understanding of those interactions. Mortality and the practical demands of living are constraints enough.

Spinoza argues that an ethic that falls short of Intellectual Love, what we today call intellectual passion and wide-ranging curiosity—like feminist nurturance and the various versions of the ethics of care—are simply not in our ultimate interest. They offer neither liberation from oppression nor the attainment of the widest interrelations. Such an ethic may serve a pressing need to overcome the effects of being devalued as women, but our vision for ourselves, our engagement with the world, Spinoza warns, would in following it suffer painful constriction. Some feminist ethical theorists thus recommend what would be classified in Spinoza's schema as an intermediate stage of group life and group-think. Such a solution falls short of full liberation, and hence, ultimately of ethics, for Spinoza identifies the aim of the ethical project as Freedom.[13] Stereotypes—in our case, e.g., the nurturing mother, the supportive wife—he warns us,[14] can be either negative or positive, denigrating or valorizing. But as social constructions that we passively adopt or even embrace, they are always personally constricting and oppressive to others. In this paper I write at some length about Spinoza's use of a normative model of human being as an intermediate ethical strategy but never as ethics' ultimate form. This is a warning we feminists ought especially to heed. We are far too quick to valorize and romanticize the stereotype of the Nurturant Mother—no doubt an important temporary corrective after decades of the vilification of mothers. I suspect that this is more likely than not a generational temptation. Virginia Held acknowledges this possibility,[15] but still recognizes nothing beyond or between the dichotomy of a liberal atomic individualist ethics of impartial rational principles versus an ethics that "sees the world and society and everything in it from the points of view of women"[16] and our stereotypic endeavors, values, and engagements. Spinoza offers us a way out of the horns of this dilemma both theoretically and practically.

While we find that Spinoza's political theory, and the ethics of *ratio* on which it depends, aim to mitigate the structures of oppression as much as possible for a society as a whole, the philosophic ethic of the *Ethics* aims to extend the scope of freedom. Thus I argue that the intermediate rational ethical life, the one in pursuit of what Spinoza calls a "model" of the good human person, initiates but does not fulfill the promise of freedom. While it does so to the greatest extent possible *for society as a whole,* a deeper and wider freedom is possible for some and desirable for as many as possible. So a second ethical possibility emerges from the limitations of the socio-political solutions of the ethical life of *ratio*. It is to replace a socially, culturally, and theologically constructed and politically instituted and enforced rational sociality with the full scope of the liberation of desire.

🌐 I. Ethics as the Transition from Passivity to Activity

Susan James's *Passion and Action: The Emotions in Seventeenth Century Philosophy* (Oxford, 1997) traces the dichotomy of activity/passivity to its origins in Aristotle's causal model of an active formal principle and a passive matter or material principle. Then she delineates the ways seventeenth-century philosophers broke with Aristotelian metaphysics and physics—in particular jettisoning the theories of formal substantial essences and of final causality. Nevertheless, they retained the passive/active dichotomy, transforming it in the light of the new mechanistic science, especially in theories of the emotions.

The Aristotelian tradition located the emotions in the "sensitive" part of the soul, the part devoted to perception and appetite. These represented two types of receptive posture toward the external world. The Aristotelian tradition, unlike the Stoic and unlike that of the seventeenth-century philosophers who in this sense followed the Stoics, theorized discrete parts or faculties of the soul, each with its separate function. In the Aristotelian account, emotions were thought to span body and soul. They were states of body and soul as a composite, precisely consisting of bodily changes with accompanying feelings.[17] The Aristotelian psycho-physical account of the emotions was retained by seventeenth-century mechanical theorists along with the distinction between active and passive, now divested of many of its Aristotelian metaphysical assumptions. Active and passive were reinterpreted as expressive not of Aristotelian formal, final, and material causality but instead of aspects of the new mechanical account of causality, its reduction of all causes to (what in the Aristotelian taxonomy were) efficient causes of motion.[18]

DESCARTES'S ACCOUNT OF ACTIVITY AND PASSIVITY

For Descartes, passive and active characterized the poles of relation of a unified soul to its body. All the functions of the soul were thought to be aspects of its conscious thinking—understanding, willing, imagining, remembering, sensing, and emotional feelings. The union of body and mind is a relation of agent and patient, or patient and agent—and complex permutations thereof. Thus, passivity and activity identify the direction of causality between body and mind in any given behavior. The passivity of one is necessarily inversely proportional to the activity of the other, since it indicates both the source of the impetus of the given motion and its recipient. Descartes held that willing and understanding occur in the soul alone and thus represent its activity, whereas some other modes of thinking—sense perception, the passions, some memories and imaginings—result from interactions of mind and body.[19] Thoughts are either passions or actions, depending on whether they originate in the soul and are initiated by it—these are the "volitions"—or originate outside it and are thus passively received and represented by it—these are the "passions."[20] Thus, for Descartes—and for Spinoza who follows his lead in this—passion and action designate internal psychic states of relative mental weakness or strength in initiating thoughts. For Descartes (but not for Spinoza), when the body affects the soul, the soul is passive, and vice versa.

Spinoza followed Descartes in holding that cognitive passivity consists in the mind's determination in part by its own past experiences. It is that aspect of it that is open to modification. Passions, Descartes says, move us to consent to those things that help us survive and thrive as a union of body and mind—such passions serve to strengthen the link.[21] Even the most abstract thinking initiates emotions. Thus for Descartes all thinking is affective and not tangentially so—an insight that is also the basis of Spinoza's account of the remedies for the passions. Descartes, like Spinoza, never regards the Stoic *apatheia*—passionlessness—as an ideal.[22]

Descartes's theory of the passions draws a line between our passive perceptions and our active volitions. Our perceptual passivity and our passions thus expose part of us as, in a sense, exterior to what is the "true" locus of self. The activity/passivity dichotomy redraws the boundary between self and other, self and world, and relocates it within the customary bounds of the person—the skin. Since only volitions are identified by Descartes as truly "our own," or ourselves, what counts as the self is radically narrowed—a solution with Stoic echoes. For it is the will alone, according to Descartes, that makes us able to have some control over the often unsettling waves of emotion that arise. The will is the movement that the mind's judgment initiates. It reverses the direction of passivity from the mind's pervasion by painful passions to its mastery of them. Volition is the activity of the mind, par excellence, for Descartes. Virtue thus consists in judging what is best and then acting with complete resolve on those judgments. Our virtue is our strength of will. The rewards of such virtue are our pleasure in our capacity for self-control and our satisfaction and ease in knowing that the passions emerging from the winds of fortune cannot move us.[23] Such joy Descartes regards as not itself a passion because it is strictly interior to the mind, involving no passivity to the body[24] while moving the body to emotional expression. Active emotions, that is emotions that originate strictly within the soul as if the soul were without connection to the body, are the ideal for Descartes.[25] Susan James remarks that Descartes envisions a rather narcissistic pleasure.[26] Descartes's active virtue suggests a kind of psychological independence from external circumstance—a Stoic virtue—that will also characterize Spinoza's account of virtue as activity. Yet for Spinoza activity does not, of course, originate in the freedom of the will.

SPINOZA'S ACCOUNT OF ACTIVITY AND PASSIVITY

While Spinoza, like Descartes, identified "activity" with virtue, he parted company with Descartes over the latter's identification of virtue with the active exercise of mental will over an unruly body and environment. He astutely recognized the moralism and theological orthodoxy implicit in Descartes's voluntarism and rejected them both.[27] Spinoza sought to follow what he regarded as the narrow path of scientific psychological explanation devoid of veiled condemnation and praise, also rejecting the Cartesian dualism of mind and body locked in a struggle for dominance.[28]

Spinoza replaced Descartes's theory of an active mental capacity to exercise will power over a passive body (and thereby over the external world) with a theory of an active striving toward psycho-physical self-organization and self-coherence in all organic beings. He linked his account to both the necessary self-causality of God and also to a doctrine of the conatus. The latter notion was adapted in part from Hobbes's materialist conception of a basic human striving for power, the power to maintain bodily stability in the face of external onslaught.[29] In this, Spinoza was influenced by both Hobbes's and Descartes's understanding of an inertial power[30] inherent in things to resist being destroyed by external forces.[31] Spinoza's notion of activity also includes the new seventeenth-century characteristic of internal coherence or equilibrium (his ratio of motion and rest).[32]

He identifies the conatus as each individual thing's essence,[33] glossing it as desire,[34] the desire of the organism as a whole, manifested in both physical and mental expressions, to resist the external forces of disintegration. It is at once a self-organizing principle and an erotic self–self and self–other relation. (In articulating the erotic in this way, we note that Spinoza does not fall into the trap of reifying the body and dichotomizing it as male or female, but instead extends its freedom to any version of its organic integrity without deracinating it from its biological reality.) Desire expresses itself in thought with the same causal necessity and order it does in extension. When functioning optimally, the mind progressively integrates inputs into an expanding and self-correcting unified account of causes. The body at the same time experiences itself as a continuous part of the natural order. I have written about Spinoza's account as a "systems theory of organism."[35] (Antonio Damasio, the neurobiologist of the emotions, has recently called Spinoza a "protobiologist" in his book *Looking for Spinoza: Joy, Sorrow, and the Feeling Brain.*)

Spinoza breaks with the Cartesian theory in that for him active and passive are attributable to body and mind as one entity. They are active or passive as the relative condition of a single thing in relation to its environment and not as a composite entity in a never-ending internal and external struggle.[36] Spinoza defines the mind as the consciousness of the body. We register in awareness the changes in the body as it is affected by or affects the external world.[37] Our emotions span body and mind, registering cognitive and affective awareness of an increase or decrease in the self-integrating power (activity) of the conatus as either pleasure or pain.[38] In this, the emotions, as Susan James puts it, "cater [to] the whole self."[39] When the mind is considered by itself, its passivity is found in its very thinking, in the ordering of its thoughts, in its mental organization or "method."[40] "The active states of the mind arise only from adequate ideas"; Spinoza writes, whereas "the passive states depend solely on inadequate ideas."[41] In *imaginatio,* Spinoza's First Kind of Knowledge, the mind is the incomplete cause of its own ideas,[42] and hence is passive. Reason and Intuition (the Second and Third Kinds of Knowledge), by contrast, always give rise to adequate ideas.[43] Spinoza makes an important distinction between Imagination (*imaginatio*), the most primitive kind of thinking, and the imaginative component (the reformed images) of the two higher levels of knowledge. For all thinking is affective and accompanied by images. In *imaginatio,* thinking is not creative and original, as we might expect, but a product of its local environment, personal experience, and cultural milieu.[44] This kind of mental organization represents a passive psycho-physical posture toward the immediate world. The immediate world shapes both our beliefs and desires.

Imaginative thinking is passive and inadequate because it is associative. It creates ongoing mental links among things that we happen to encounter at the same time and place,[45] or that exhibit some similarity. It thereby creates patterns of mental association and constructs explanations on the basis of the arbitrary correlations that we find around us in the common order of nature—and, as the *TTP* shows, in the common order of culture as well. *Imaginatio* is driven by these remembered associations. Imagination is both our uncritical introjection of what surrounds us and also our helplessness in the face of how past experiences exercise a continuing dominion over the present. We cannot control either how those memories are formed or when and how they recur. For as Spinoza writes, "it is not within the free power of the mind to remember or to forget anything."[46] The imagination is, essentially, a historical kind of thinking, in contrast to the timeless truths of philosophy and science.

> We conceive things as actual in two ways: either in so far as we conceive them as related to a fixed time and place, or in so far as we conceive them to be contained in God and to follow from the necessity of the divine nature. (EVP29S)[47]

That *imaginatio* introjects a context that is cultural and social and even political is borne out in that the great institutions of the Imagination are, according to Spinoza, Language and Religion. Causal explanation, the second and third kinds of knowledge, by contrast, are our mind's reconstruction of its experience and memories according to a rigorous, internally generated order.

The passivity of association as a mental operation—its simple introjection of the arbitrary correlations of external happenstance, circumstance, and preference—makes these passions passive responses to the world. In the passions, we associate contemporaneous (and other imaginatively associated) external objects with our affective experiences of pain and pleasure, naively and mistakenly assigning to these objects a false causal efficacy, and hence power over ourselves.[48] Nevertheless, the imaginative associative component of the passions is open to modification. For Descartes, a given physical state and mental association could be willfully disconnected from each other and the former reconnected to a different thought, thereby reforming the passion. For Spinoza, since a given physical state cannot but be expressed mentally (insofar as the mind minds the body), it is the entire complex that must be modified. The remedy for our domination by the passions will be to enable the mind to express a different physical order, namely, the global causal order. To do that, one must replace passive mental associations with active, that is, self-generated and ever expansive causal explanations. Causal explanation redefines the source and object of a passion as a combination of the internal order of ideas, that is, our own active thinking process, and the global order of causes. It is thus a different extensional state that will be expressed mentally: the new object–subject expressed in a given affect is both internalized and globalized.

🌀 *II. The Ethics of Ratio*[49]

Spinoza turns the Cartesian analysis on its head, deriving his moral categories from what his version of the new science could expose about organic homeodynamic stability as well as about emotional health and contentment rather than falling back on moral judgments clothed in scientific garb. This is Spinoza's famed—to some, notorious—ethical naturalism. The active emotions are good qua active. That is to say, Spinoza redefines the 'good' in terms of the psycho-physical internal organization captured in the designation 'activity'; so, too, the passive redefines the 'bad.'

Spinoza's doctrine has important political implications. He believes it has the power to set us free. He proposes that if we turn to causal self-explanation, then the withholding or bestowal of external rewards by authoritative individuals or social or political institutions can no longer hold such sway over us psychologically. For in seeing social rewards and punishments as only the last link in a chain of necessary causes whose inevitability we now understand to be the outcome of both nature itself and of our own thinking, they lose their tyranny over us. They will not be capable of inducing in us desires and beliefs that serve powerful interests and cultural norms. Here we begin to see how Spinoza's Passivity incorporates a social dimension.[50] The great danger of the passions is political: namely, that they will, as Spinoza so succinctly puts it in the Preface to the *Tractatus,* lead us to "fight for [our] servitude as if for salvation." Thus passivity is less our moral weakness than our tragedy.

THE MODEL OF HUMAN NATURE

As early as the *TdIE* Spinoza had enjoined us to pursue the "true good," by conceiving "a human nature much stronger and more enduring than our own" and to work toward acquiring it. He said there that we ought to do this in preparation for achieving the "highest good," namely, "the knowledge of the union that the mind has with the whole of Nature." In the Preface to *Ethics* IV Spinoza subjects ethical terms to critical analysis as he had earlier done in the Appendix to Part I. He points out the falsity and subjective interestedness of our universal terms and of our ethical standards as products of merely the imagination rather than of reason.[51] He repeats his familiar argument for the conventionality of moral terms—*good, bad, perfection, praise* and *blame,* are, he says, mere "modes of imagining." Nevertheless, immediately afterward Spinoza goes on to recommend the retention of ethical terms. "However, although this is so," he says, "these terms ought to be retained" since they are "useful" in our construction of a *"model of human nature."* He continues:

> For since we desire to form the idea of a man which we may look to as a model of human nature, we shall find it *useful to keep these terms in the sense I have indicated.* So in what follows I shall mean by "good" that which we certainly know to be the means for our approaching nearer to the model of human nature that we set before ourselves, and by "bad" that which we certainly know prevents us from reproducing the said model. Again, we shall say that men are more perfect or less perfect in so far as they are nearer to or further from this model. For it is important to note that when I say that somebody passes from a state of less perfection to a state of greater perfection, and vice versa, . . . that we conceive *his power of activity, in so far as this is understood through his nature, to be increased or diminished.*[52] (My emphases)

Following the Preface, Spinoza sets out the definitions for Part IV. The first two redefine *good* and *bad* and the last redefines *virtue.* Virtue is redefined as "activity," and good and bad as what contributes to, or stands in the way of, that activity. Activity is defined as the human "power" and "essence," what a person does that can be attributed to internal causes rather than to the direct effect of outside forces. Spinoza glosses *activity* as the *laws of human nature.*

> Def. 8. By *virtue* and *power* I mean the same thing; that is (Pr. 7, III), virtue, in so far as it is related to man, is *man's very essence, or nature,* in so far as he has power to bring about that which can be understood solely through *the laws of his own nature.*[53] (My emphases)

Thus human virtue and essential well-being, *human nature,* is to be understood on a scale ranging from passive to active. The passive–active scale is not, however, exclusively applicable to human beings but to all things,[54] both to the whole and the parts of nature. The "model of human nature" would seem to be, at best, a proper common notion, i.e., an imaginative universal derived from the mind's merger of many individuals that is nevertheless adequate because it identifies something which is uniformly in the parts and the whole; a version of it is in all human individuals. A common notion is an imaginative universal that, because of its ubiquity, grasps a rational truth and cannot distort it. (The ideas of motion and rest are Spinoza's paradigmatic examples of common notions.) Spinoza illustrates what he means by *common notions* with a mathematical rule. Rather than a single concept or an abstraction, a common notion is a principle that operates in every case of a given phenomenon and explains it.[55] Thus common notions are concrete rather than abstract imaginative universals.[56] In EIIP38, Spinoza offers a more detailed account of common notions:

> P38: Those things that are common to all things and are equally in the part as in the whole, can be conceived only adequately. . . .

> Cor.: Hence it follows that *there are certain ideas or notions common to all men. For (by Lemma 2) all bodies agree in certain respects, which must be (preceding Pr.) conceived by all adequately, or clearly and distinctly.* (My emphases)

The Common Notions, Spinoza explains (IIP40S2), "are the basis of our reasoning processes." Moreover, Spinoza argues that there are not only universal common notions but also subordinate common notions of a more limited scope and range of knowability. Martial Gueroult designates these the Proper Common Notions to distinguish them from the Universal Common Notions of the previous proposition.

> P39: Of that which is common and proper to the human body and to any external bodies by which the human body is customarily affected, and which is equally in the part as in the whole of any of these bodies, the idea also is in the mind will be adequate.

> P39 Cor.: Hence it follows that the mind is more capable of perceiving more things adequately in proportion as its body has more things in common with other bodies.[57]

Human nature defined in terms of the active–passive scale fits the definition of a Proper Common Notion. It rises to the level of *ratio* because it augments the common notion with an adequate idea of the property of a thing (Spinoza's definition of *ratio* in E II P40S2). That is to say, human nature, defined as activity, identifies precisely the common notion that is its proximate cause. Hence *ratio*, through knowing the proximate cause, which is the essence in created things (by *TdIE* §§ 19, 92, and 95), renders active the passive (yet true) imaginative universal (or true belief, as Spinoza calls it in *KV* II, Chapter 1), which is to say it renders active the common notion.[58]

Thus the imaginative and regulative universal, human nature, when it is reformed in the way that Spinoza proposes so that it captures not the idiosyncratic and culturally biased composite image of many arbitrary individuals but instead grasps the concrete ubiquity of the defining property, namely, the scale of activity/passivity (that is to say, the degree of freedom) of each of us, rises to become the basis of a rational account of the human. Yet Spinoza has exposed here an irony at the center of the ethical life, namely, that the regulative and normative model of human nature that he proposes measures each person's degree of freedom, a freedom defined by the eschewing of all external standards, even and especially internalized ones! In claiming that the ethical model and terms ought to be used to indicate an increase or decrease in a person's "power of activity," any regulative general ethical standard would seem to be precluded. For such a claim is paradoxical in two ways: first, insofar as a person's power of activity is a measure of the condition of *her unique individual essence,* activity cannot in fact recommend standard norms of behavior (i.e., serve as an ethical model), except very roughly and in a necessarily overgeneralized way! Second, since the submission to an *external* authoritative standard (i.e., the kind of ethical model suggested here) would by definition decrease the very power of activity (i.e., of internal origination) that it aims to measure, such a model would be precluded. So it is not surprising that Spinoza designates the regulative model of human nature provisional and thus maintains that it is to be transcended in the end.[59]

The irony also extends to politics, and upon this irony Spinoza builds the very possibility of a politics of freedom. For Spinoza's politics claims to institute *coercively,* via both force and also religious suasion, a rational ethics of *freedom. Thus the very nature of some passive imaginative universals—the common notions—as originating in the passivity of the imagination but capable of being transformed—but not thereby altered in content—via the mind's own active thought processes, is what makes possible not only learning, as Spinoza emphasizes, but also an implicitly liberating politics culminating in his ethics of freedom.*

Spinoza's redefinition of ethical terms and his ethical model are fraught with even more difficulties than those already mentioned. For "activity" is really not a specifically *human* property at all but is by definition inherent in and defining (qua conatus)[60] of all individuals from rocks to God. The capacity to act from the laws of its own nature and not succumb passively to external forces is both ubiquitous but also completely true only of God as *causa sui.* Thus Spinoza's definition of human nature in fact *deconstructs* the very concept! While activity is everywhere, a version of it can be identified as distinctly human, the capacity for enhancing one's activity through Reason and Intuition. Yet individuals and individual essences[61] are what are clearly ontologically fundamental, whereas commonalities or similarities across such individuals are not. For the various universal laws derivative of the divine attributes and also the less universal laws that are specifications of the more universal find their expressions only in individuals. Spinoza writes in the *Tractatus Politicus* that Nature creates only individuals, not groups. The individuals are related to each other by being unique expressions of the same natural forces. Thus natural forces operate from the top down. And they also operate horizontally in the cause-and-effect relations obtaining among singular things or finite modes. But they do not operate in the way an Aristotelian species essence or a Platonic form is said to, that is by generic instantiation, formal causality.

Activity as the definition of the human does not justify the use of that notion as a "model" or normative ethical standard. The justification for its normativity, Spinoza says, comes not from any regulative truth but instead from its utility and its imaginative as well as rational status. The utility in question turns out to be precisely its *social* utility and its *political* necessity. The ethical model is thus at best provisional and its authority is tied to and expressive of a social context. In EIVP37S2 Spinoza introduces his account of the state of nature in contrast with the state of political society, arguing that only in society do moral judgments arise. Moral standards, normative claims, are a product of society and cannot exist apart from it. Not only are they not enforceable except in a social context, but they are not even *conceivable,* he says, apart from it.

> A society, strengthened by law and by the capacity to preserve itself, is called a State (*civitas*): and those who are protected by its rights are called Citizens (*cives*). From this it can readily be understood that in a state of nature there is nothing that is universally agreed upon as good or evil. . . . *Thus in a state of nature wrong-doing cannot be **conceived**, but it can be in a civil state where good and bad are decided upon by common agreement* and everyone is bound to obey the state. *Wrong-doing is therefore nothing other than disobedience,* which is therefore punishable only by the sovereign right of the state. . . .
>
> *In a state of nature nothing can be said to be just or unjust:* this is so only in a civil state, where it is decided by common agreement what belongs to this or that man. From this it is clear that *justice and injustice, wrong-doing and merit, are extrinsic notions, not attributes that explicate the nature of the mind.*[62]
> (My emphases)

Here Spinoza echoes the Maimonidean position on the conventionality of morals. Maimonides had written, "with regard to what is of necessity, there is no good and evil at all, but only the false and the true."[63] Spinoza augments his Maimonidean genealogy of morals with a social psychology. Morals arise, he says, in what we today call the socialization process rather than through any regulative power in ethics or in the mind itself. Standards of behavior are constructed by society and depend on both its culture and its means of enforcement, its rewards and punishments. What we experience as moral conscience is simply the internalization of these social mores. "Our upbringing," Spinoza writes, "is chiefly responsible" for "our actions that are customarily called wrong" being "followed by pain, and those which are said to be right, by pleasure."

Hence the arena of the ethics of *ratio* is the polity. The coercive and suasive forces of socialization can be mustered to implement the principles of a rational ethics. The imposed norms can and ought, paradoxically, to encourage an increase in activity and conduce to the pleasure of self-contentment, *acquiescentia*. Although self-contentment is not the same as Intellectual Love, joy accompanies the exercise of *ratio* and not just Intuition. Spinoza reminds us in IVP63Dem that "all emotions that are related to the mind in so far as it is active, that is (pr.3, iii), emotions that are related to reason, are emotions of pleasure and desire only (pr.59, iii)." The Corollary is that *ratio* eschews the external social motivations of Fear and Hope. Hence the dependence of the Ethics of *Ratio* upon social embodiment in conventional definitions and upon political implementation rooted in Fear and Hope flies in the face of the freedom it promises and that is logically its own. *Ratio* turns out to be the first stage of a two-stage process that can be completed only in Intuition. We now understand Spinoza's repeated insistence that Intuition emerges only from *ratio*. For the accomplishment of *ratio* is Intuition, both intellectually and ethically. Yet Spinoza initially intends in *ratio* to hold the two conceptions, both the imaginative common notion and also the rational defining property, both the regulative ethical model and also his notion of activity, in an uneasy tension. This tension cannot be consistently maintained and pushes beyond *ratio* for resolution in Intuition. But that is the province of the few, never of the many nor of society as a whole.

🌀 III. From the Halakhic Ethics of Ratio to the Feminist Promise of Freedom

Spinoza develops his rational ethical model in Part IV and also in the beginning of Part V by teasing out a set of general ethical principles and more specific prescriptive rules. The notion of human activity is now imaginatively instantiated and enforced in a set of rules and principles to be memorized and applied. Spinoza distinguishes between the second and third kinds of knowledge in his famous Rule of Proportion in EIIP40S2. *Ratio* is knowledge of things via common notion plus adequate ideas of their properties. Intuition is knowledge of the essences of things as they follow from the attribute, or as *TdIE* §99 puts it, within the order and unity of the attribute. I think that Alexandre Matheron is on the right track when he argues that Spinoza's example of the fourth proportional implies that the difference between the penultimate and ultimate stages of knowledge is the degree to which one must make recourse to knowledge that has been already established.[64] *Ratio* has recourse to *imaginatio,* to inherited true beliefs. For a thinker at the level of *ratio* can use *imaginatio* to fill in the gaps in her knowledge by bringing to bear prior proven knowledge as dogmatic rules that are drawn on authority. Rather than deriving the whole proof again from its foundations, *ratio* depends on invoking imaginative strategies, common notions, that have been memorized. It is not that *ratio* itself includes passive knowledge on authority but that it uses knowledge on authority, true beliefs. *Ratio* as such is active knowledge—but it is not complete in its causal analysis. Matheron is, I believe, on the right track when he proposes that understanding something down to its very foundations, not relying on memorized principles that one knows to be true but cannot at the moment derive from their foundations, is what Spinoza means by Intuition.[65] But I would suggest that the invoking of *imaginatio* is not actually a component of *ratio*—which is as such fully active, although not complete, knowledge or explanation—but instead an imaginative strategy in the service of *ratio*. Matheron concludes that the significant characteristic of Intuition is not the instantaneousness of its grasp—for that he says is merely contingently linked to it[66]—but rather its foundationalism. Thus it is not only Intuition, as Matheron maintains, but *ratio*, too, that is knowledge that we ourselves generate. In *ratio* we rethink inherited beliefs whereas in Intuition we take each step back to its foundations, as Matheron suggests, and I would add, in the unity of the attribute. Matheron is correct, I think, in suggesting that this is the way God knows real physical entities in their infinite web of causal relations.[67] Thus intuitive understanding extends the scope of the self-initiation of the mind.[68]

Let us now return to the ethical problem. Initially, for the Ethics of *Ratio* active emotional causal self-understanding would seem to suffice. But Spinoza indicated that it is to be augmented by some recourse to *imaginatio* in a sort of cognitive therapy regime of self-habituation to the right thoughts and actions. The active state of one's mind is apparently too fragile to be relied upon by itself. In the Scholium to Part V P10 Spinoza proposes *precepts* of the rational ethical life and also offers more specific *Rules of Living.* Thus Spinoza implicitly acknowledges that this rational psychotherapeutic praxis of re-associating thoughts and images, although in principle a successful strategy for the management of the emotional life, is nevertheless too fragile to be depended upon given the great vicissitudes of life that strike us all too often and overwhelmingly. Thus a more forceful praxis involving the recourse to *imaginatio* for the implementation of *ratio* is necessary: that of self-imposed authoritative rules of conduct and precepts of reason, a right method of living.

> The best course we can adopt as long as we do not have perfect knowledge of our emotions, is to *conceive a right method of living, or fixed rules of life, and to commit them to memory and continually apply them to particular situations* that are frequently encountered in life, so that casual thinking is thoroughly permeated by them and they are always ready to hand. For example, among our *practical rules,* we laid down (Pr. 46, IV and Sch.) that hatred should be conquered by love or nobility, and not repaid with reciprocal hatred. Now in order that we may have this *precept of reason* always ready to hand in time of need we should think about and frequently reflect on the wrongs that are commonly committed by mankind, and the best way and method of warding them off by nobility of character. For thus we shall associate the image of a wrong with the presentation of this rule of conduct, and it will always be at hand for us (Pr. 18, II) when we suffer a wrong. Again, if we always have in readiness consideration of our true advantage and also of the good that follows from mutual friendship and social relations, and also remember that supreme contentment [*acquiescentia*] of spirit follows from *the right way of life* (Pr.52, IV), and that men, like everything else, act from the necessity of their nature, then the wrong, or the hatred that is wont to arise from it, will occupy just a small part of our imagination and will easily be overcome. . . . We ought, in the same way, to reflect on courage to banish fear; we should enumerate and often picture the everyday dangers of life, and how they can best be avoided and overcome by resourcefulness and strength of mind.
>
> But it should be noted that in arranging our thoughts and images we should *always concentrate on that which is good in every single thing* (Cor. Pr.63, IV and Pr.59, III) so that in so doing we may be determined to act always from the emotion of pleasure. . . . Therefore he who aims solely from the love of freedom to control his emotions and appetites will strive the best to familiarise himself with virtues and their causes and to fill his mind with the joy that arises from the true knowledge of them, while refraining from dwelling on men's faults and abusing mankind and deriving pleasure from a false show of freedom. *He who diligently follows these precepts and practises them (for they are not difficult) will surely within a short space of time be able to direct his actions for the most part according to reason's behest.*[69]

Here we find some resonance of the Deuteronomic and liturgical language of the Sh'ma and in VP41S Spinoza calls his precepts of reason, the Commandments of the Divine Law. In society, at best, people both train themselves and are also compelled to do what agrees with reason, namely to live "according to the Commandments of the Divine Law."[70]

So we find that in spelling out what the model of human nature enjoins, Spinoza elaborates on the ethical implications of *ratio* as self-imposed rules and socially instantiated and instituted norms. *Ratio* thus uses *imaginatio* bidirectionally: we pick up its imaginative, already culturally available common notions, rendering them active through causal self-understanding. That is what we expect from the three-fold schema. But implicitly Spinoza also maintains that we who are at the level of *ratio* immediately go on to instantiate our understanding imaginatively in a self-regulative and socially embodied praxis. He does it again and again in the *Ethics* (as well as the *TTP,* of course), completing Part IV with a ready-to-hand catalogue of the Rules of Right Living, a Spinozist Halakhah of Thirty-Two Mitzvot. The imposed norms can and ought, paradoxically, of course to encourage an increase in activity and conduce to the pleasure of self-contentment, *acquiescentia*—just as according to Maimonides, halakhah both embodied the rational ethical mean and also offered a glimpse and a taste of intellectual truths and the higher salvific life emergent from the pursuit of those truths. Clearly, Spinoza maintains that the coercive and suasive forces of socialization and personal habituation must be mustered to implement the principles of a rational ethics. We not only raise common notions from their imaginative origin, but we also deliberately make those origins our own, even reshaping them in the service of our own path to freedom. For in the Ethics of *Ratio* we glimpse freedom.

Moreover, Spinoza indicates that these rules do not in fact stand on their own but presuppose a cultural, social, and political context in order to come into being and for their implementation. Spinoza makes the same point, in the beginning propositions of Book IV, after delineating the causes of both emotional irrationality and the sources of rational control over the emotions. After offering "a brief survey of the dictates of reason," in the Scholium to IV P18 Spinoza remarks that "we can never bring it about that we should need nothing outside ourselves to preserve our own being and that we should live a life quite unrelated to things outside ourselves." The human rational ethical life demands social expression and political community.

> Therefore nothing is more advantageous to man than man. Men, I repeat, can wish for nothing more excellent for preserving their own being than that they should all be in such harmony in all respects that their minds and bodies should compose, as it were, one mind and one body, and that all together should endeavor as best they can to preserve their own being, and

all together they should aim at the common advantage of all. From this it follows that men who are governed by reason, that is men, who aim at their own advantage under the guidance of reason, seek nothing for themselves they would not desire for the rest of mankind; and so are just, faithful and honourable.

These are the dictates of reason.[71] (My emphasis)

In principle, the Ethics of *Ratio*, like *ratio* itself, is active, appealing to internal incentives—to the mind's self-organizing power and its joy in self-understanding, its contentment (*acquiescentia*)[72] consequent upon observing its own increased activity. And in principle, the Ethics of *Ratio* brings us to Freedom for only insofar as we have inadequate ideas are we passive and *ratio's* ideas, we are told, are adequate. But, in fact, for each learner at the level of *ratio,* there is an appeal to *imaginatio,* to external authority, in both the initially dogmatic and rote dimensions to the learning and also in the dependence upon a socio-cultural context for the acquisition and practice of these truths. *Ratio* begins with true imaginative universals, the common notions, that we both accept on authority and also habituate ourselves to. They are then made active by our causal self-understanding when we augment the common notion with knowledge of its proximate cause or essence and thus know it to be true. However, even then we do not yet conceive the truths in question as a product of our conatus expressing in and through us the divine *causa sui.*[73] That is accomplished only in *scientia inuitiva.* In cognitive terms, our knowledge is neither foundational enough nor yet unified. In affective terms, we have not yet experienced the decenteredness of the self, of the conatus; that its weight is outside us and beyond us as well as in us; that we are an *expression* of the divine; that our internal, active thinking and integration are much larger than ourselves and we extrude ourselves, as it were, into them and not only discover the divine within ourselves but also ourselves within the divine. Some have called this the moment of transformation or transvaluation. It is the discovery of ethical freedom.

This is how *ratio* works: The society whose ethical foundations are derived from reason embodies those principles in conventional rules and institutions and backs them up with its legitimate authority. The person growing up in that society passively picks up those principles as Common Notions, namely, as they appear in the culture, accepting them and obeying them on authority. Hence, that person's imagination passively conforms to rational truths as do the conventions and institutions of that society. The members of that society pick up true beliefs passively and imaginatively and they enact an ethic implicitly promoting activity or freedom. Spinoza's point is that the Ethics of *Ratio,* like the mathematics of *ratio,* does not emerge from *ratio* alone but depends upon the careful use of external authority, of imagination, in the service of activity in mind and in praxis. And that is possible because of *ratio*'s origination in true imaginative universals, the common notions. And it is necessary because of the fragility of Reason. The possibility of raising common notions to activity is the basis of education, and also of society as a moral educator.

Like Maimonides's conception of the nature of halakhah, Spinoza's Rules of Right Living render the rational conventionally, authoritatively, and politically. But for the true intellectual, the pleasures of the intellect trump all ethical coercion, even of the kind that conforms to rational freedom. "If men were born free," Spinoza writes, adopting Maimonides's precise position, "they would form no conception of good and evil so long as they were free."[74] Ethics as activity sets our hopes on gaining independence from the tyranny of external circumstances and from the uncritical embrace of unexamined (cultural and social) influences. *Ratio*'s ethical model is paradoxical in that it has to be imposed authoritatively and coercively. For it envisions a society whose rules and values encourage a greater independence in thought and practice than their initial imposition and authoritative transmission would suggest. In fact, we live in a society whose commitment to freedom of conscience and other freedoms is passed down authoritatively from generation to generation and whose laws enforce it coercively. Spinoza proposed the Jewish biblical community as the paradigm of the just and free society that modern polities should emulate. For the original Mosaic state, the Ancient Hebrew Commonwealth,[75] was, in his estimation, in principle, an egalitarian,[76] federalist,[77] and even partially socialist,[78] direct democracy[79] with extensive checks and balances and a wide division of power (especially between the religious and political authorities),[80] and with an independent judiciary,[81] legal transparency,[82] and a citizen army.[83] This ancient society, Spinoza held, also promoted and defended freedom of conscience.[84]

Thus Spinoza proposed that our modern social ethics and our politics ought to follow the Jewish model: a halakhah that imaginatively conventionalizes and enforces a rational ethics promoting enhanced freedom of thought, independence of mind, and action. From Spinoza we can also derive our (human and feminist) hope for liberation. For as social beings, and particularly as women, we are situated in ongoing conditions of internalized conventions that are at best fair but nonetheless necessarily construct us via internalized subordination. We ought to learn our Spinozist lessons well: both to embrace the necessarily political starting point of ethics but also to heed its social construction and constrictions of aspects of ourselves that we must, in turn, transcend. And we must learn to turn both to inner pleasures and also to the largest possible perspective, a global perspective, on ourselves so that we can come to stake our lives on our interconnectedness with all human beings and with all nature. For only then, Spinoza says, do we finally embrace the scope of the free exercise of our individuality within God.[85]

NOTES

1. On one occasion (*Tractatus Politicus,* chap. xi) Spinoza called into question women's full humanity—a lapse he never had regarding Jews. Yet on most occasions Spinoza presumes women's full humanity in recommending marriage as at its best a friendship between equals devoted to mutual independence. (See, e.g., EIV68S on Eve.)

2. See my "Observations on Jewish Philosophy and Feminist Thought," *JUDAISM: A Quarterly Journal of Jewish Life & Thought* 46 (Fall 1997): 422–38.

3. EIIIP56Dem (Shirley, 138).

4. EIIP23 (Shirley, 81): "The mind does not know itself except in so far as it perceives ideas of affections of the body."

5. EIIP25 (Shirley, 82–83): "The human mind does not perceive any external body as actually existing except through the ideas of affections of its own body."

6. Andrew Collier, in his paper "The Materiality of Morals: Mind, Body and Interests in Spinoza's *Ethics*" (in *Studia Spinozana* 7 [1991], devoted to "The Ethics in the Ethics," 69–93), has argued that the bounds of the individual person whose survival and flourishing are the object of ethics are never atomic. He holds that "we must consider the body as extendible, in the sense that the more the body in the narrow sense interacts with the world about it, the more the world is to be counted as part of the person's 'inorganic body'" (76). In my paper "Spinoza's Individualism Reconsidered: Some Lessons from the *Short Treatise on God, Man, and His Well-Being,*" *Iyyun: Jerusalem Philosophical Quarterly* 47 (1998): 265–92, I agree in substance with Collier's position and suggest some modifications and extensions of his account.

7. As Lee Rice puts it, "Freedom, conceived in a spinozistic sense, is neither the exercise of desire divorced form its empirical conditions (Descartes) nor the exercise of will displaced into a world outside space and time (Kant)." Lee C. Rice, "Reflections on Spinozist Therapy," unpublished manuscript, p. 10.

8. See, e.g., Held's *Feminist Morality: Transforming Culture, Society, and Politics* (Chicago: University of Chicago Press, 1993), 24: "*Moral* experience is the experience of consciously choosing to act, or to refrain from acting, on grounds by which we are trying conscientiously to be guided. Moral experience is the experience of accepting or rejecting moral positions for what we take to be good moral reasons or well-founded moral intuitions or on the basis of what we take to be justifiable moral feelings."

9. See, e.g., ibid., 8, where Held attacks causal explanation as inappropriate to authentic feminist epistemology. The feminist rejection of science suffers from the worst kind of caricature of not only the rational but of women! My paper argues that feminists ought not to eschew science but do better science—as embodied, relational human beings.

10. See, e.g., Nussbaum's Presidential Address, "The Future of Feminist Liberalism," *Proceeding and Addresses of the American Philosophical Association* 72, no. 2 (November 2000).

11. Some feminist interpretations, James writes in *Passion and Action: The Emotions in Seventeenth Century Philosophy* (Oxford: Oxford University Press, 1997), 19, "belong . . . to a not-yet-completed stage in which the patriarchal face of philosophy as it has traditionally been practiced has been boldly, if sometimes crudely, outlined. . . . But feminist research has now reached a point at which the insights yielded by the demonizing approach have been absorbed, and it is safe—and indeed necessary—to muddy the picture by looking more critically at the strategy of vilification." James (18, and footnote 68) identifies Susan Bordo, Genevieve Lloyd, N. Scheman, N. Tuana. E. Fox Keller, Jane Flax, Elizabeth Grosz, and Selya Benhabib as among those with a tendency to vilify as philosophic strategy.

12. See, e.g., Held, Chapter 2, "Feminist Moral Inquiry: Methods and Prospects," esp. pp. 25–28.

13. Lee C. Rice, in an unpublished paper, "Spinoza's Ethical Project," holds, as I do, that Spinoza envisioned two stages of the ethical life, a rule-bound one, the "Servitude" of E IV, and the ultimate "Freedom" of E V.

14. EIIIP46. Lee C. Rice (private communication) pointed out to me that Spinoza's account of stereotypes includes a critique of the group-think applicable to many of those who propose solutions.

15. Held, 168.

16. Ibid.

17. *Passion and Action,* 65.

18. Ibid., 75–76: "Advocates of the mechanical philosophy construe the actions and passions of bodies as motions. A body acts when it transfers its motion to a second; and the second body is acted on when the direction and force of its motion are changed. Equally, the standing capacities or powers of bodies to move and be moved in particular ways are also explained by their motions, in conjunction with their geometrical properties such as size and shape."

19. Ibid., 91.

20. Descartes, *Passions of the Soul,* 17, quoted in *Passion and Action,* 91.

21. *Passion and Action,* 101.

22. So, too, Beyssade, in "De l'émotion intérieure chez Descartes à l'affect actif Spinoziste," in E. M. Curley and P. F. Moreau, eds., *Spinoza: Issues and Directions* (Leiden, New York, Copenhagen, and Cologne: E. J. Brill, 1990), 180.

23. *Passion and Action,* 199.

24. Ibid., 204.

25. Beyssade, 181.

26. *Passion and Action,* 204. In "Mind and Its Relation to the Psyche-Soma," *British Journal of Medical Psychology* 27 (1954), D. W. Winnicott argues (207–208) that the localization of the mind in the head is a sign of mental illness. Psychotherapeutic cure results in the mind being experienced as an unlocalized pervasive consciousness and awareness of the body. Winnicott would seem to bear out the normativity of the Spinozist account of the mind as the consciousness of the body and call into question the Cartesian account as representing psychological abnormality.

27. *Passion and Action,* 124–25.

28. Ibid., 152: "There is . . . a further crucial connotation of the opposition between activity and passivity which is all but obliterated in Spinoza's philosophy: the association of mind with activity and passivity with body. . . . [T]his remained influential among those mechanical philosophers who conceived bodies, including human ones, as passive because they have no power to move themselves, and who contrasted this feature of the

material world with the capacity of human minds to will. For Spinoza, however, there can be no such asymmetry. The body and mind are one thing viewed under two attributes. Moreover, the *conatus* is a single power manifested in both attributes; whatever bodily events constitute the body's striving to persevere in its being are matched by ideas that constitute the same striving in the mind."

29. *Passion and Action,* 134; and 77, where James writes: "Hobbes . . . identifies endeavour with the motion of the internal parts of a body."

30. Lee Rice comments (private communication) that the "conatus was widely used in 17th century physics for what we now call inertial mass (it was used by Huyghens). And Spinoza's sense of conatus, or so Gueroult argues, is closer to Huyghens than to Hobbes. The general law of conatus ('every being tends. . . .') is just the mental equivalent of the physical law of inertia given following E2P13."

31. See *Passion and Action,* 77–78: "Both philosophers are suggesting that the internal motions of bodies conform to comparatively stable patterns of motion which are not necessarily destroyed by impact, so that a body's capacity to resist change survives many of its interactions."

32. EIIP13 Lemma3 Ax. 2Def. and Lemma5.

33. EIII P7. Lee Rice comments that Spinoza's claim of the identity of the conatus with an individual's essence is "what Einstein calls the central claim. When reworked by Einstein, it becomes the principle of equivalence (gravitational and inertial mass are identical) in general relativity. It was the ultimate vindication of Leibniz/Spinoza over Newton (for whom the two concepts are only equal in force, but not equivalent)."

34. EIII Defs. of the Emotions #1.

35. "Notes on Spinoza's Critique of Aristotle's Ethics: From Teleology to Process Theory," *Philosophy and Theology* IV, no. 1 (Fall 1989): 3–32.

36. EIIIP11. Susan James's reading agrees with mine here. See *Passion and Action,* 155: "Because mind and body are the same thing described under different attributes, they can only act or be acted on together."

37. EIIP11, P12, & P13.

38. EIII Definition 3 (Shirley, 104):

> By emotions (affectus) I understand the affections of the body by which the body's power of activity is increased or diminished, assisted or checked, together with the ideas of these affections.
>
> Thus if we can be the adequate cause of one of these affections, then by emotion understand activity, otherwise passivity.

See also General Definition of the Emotions (Shirley, 151–52):

> The emotion called a passive experience is a confused idea whereby the mind affirms a greater or less force of existence of its body, or part of its body, than was previously the case, and by the occurrence of which the mind is determined to think of one thing rather than another.

Explication

> I say in the first place that an emotion, or passivity of the mind, is a "confused idea." For we have demonstrated (Pr.3, III) that the mind is passive only to the extent that it has inadequate or confused ideas. Next, I say 'whereby the mind affirms a greater of less force of existence of its body than was previously the case.' For all ideas that we have of bodies indicate the actual physical state of our body

rather than the nature of the external body (Cor.2, Pr.16, II). Now the idea that constitutes the specific reality of emotion must indicate or express the state of the body or some part of it, which the body of some part of it possesses from the fact that its power of activity or force of existence (vis existendi) is increased or diminished, assisted or checked, etc.

39. *Passion and Action*, 147.

40. For an excellent article on what Spinoza's method is and how it operates, see Vance Maxwell's "The Philosophical Method of Spinoza," in *Dialogue* XVIII (1988): 89–110.

41. EIIIP3 (Shirley, 108).

42. EIIP29S.

43. EIIP41.

44. Spinoza insists that the imagination functions passively (E3P1; Van Vloten and Land, vol. 1: 122), "for it is not within the free power of the mind to remember or forget anything" (E3P2S; Van Vloten and Land, vol. 1, 125–26; Shirley, 108).

45. Lee Rice comments (private communication), "Spinoza follows Descartes in part and [anticipates] Skinner completely. The connexions/association of affects are guided by TEMPORAL laws. Skinner claims this as one of behaviorism's "revolutionary" aspects."

46. EIIIP2S (Shirley, 108).

47. Van Vloten and Land, vol. 1, 264; Shirley, 218.

48. See my chapter, "Spinoza's Rupture with Tradition—His Hints of a Jewish Modernity," in H. M. Ravven and L. E. Goodman, eds., *Jewish Themes in Spinoza's Philosophy* (Albany: State University of New York Press, 2002). I write there: "It is the nature of the passive emotions to be occasioned by the presence—or the imagined presence—of objects *imaginatively associated* with the changes in the affections of the body. All emotions are directed at objects and include the implicit judgment that the object of the emotion is its cause. In the passions, the causal judgments are false or incomplete, insofar as they are determined by imaginative associations to which the mind is passive."

49. Lee Rice points out (private communication) that Spinoza distinguishes between "morality" (*Ethics* IV) and "ethics" (*Ethics* V) for what I call here the Ethics of *Ratio* versus the Intuitive Ethics.

50. I argue in "Spinoza's Rupture with Tradition" that there are three principles of social conformity that Spinoza identifies in *Ethics* III in his discussion of the passive emotions. Spinoza's account of the passive emotions is, I argue, more a social psychology than an individual psychology. The *Ethics* focuses primarily on social conformity whereas *TTP* focuses more on obedience to authority, that other great social force.

51. Shirley, 153–54:

> When men began to form general ideas and to devise ideal types of houses, buildings, towers and so on, and to prefer some models to others, it came about that each called "perfect" what he saw to be in agreement with the general idea he had formed of the said thing and "imperfect" that which he saw at variance with his own preconceived ideal. . . . For men are wont to form general ideas both of natural phenomena and of artifacts, and these ideas they regard as models, and they believe that Nature (which they consider does nothing without an end in view) looks to these ideas and holds them before herself as models.
>
> . . . So perfection and imperfection are in reality only modes of thinking, notions which we are wont to invent from comparing individuals of the same species or kind. . . .

As for the terms "good" and" bad, " they likewise indicate nothing positive in things considered in themselves, and are nothing but modes of thinking, or notions which we form from comparing things with one another. For one and the same thing can at the same time be good and bad, and also indifferent.

52. Shirley, 155.

53. Ibid., 136.

54. Lee Rice comments (private communication) that "nothing but nature/god is completely active, and nothing but nothing is completely passive (last prop of E1)."

55. Lee Rice points out (private communication) that common notions on this account are "quite similar to what Quine and modern logicians call 'mass terms,' water being an example. One logical feature of mass terms which accords well with what Spinoza says about common notions is they have no plural."

56. David Savan argues (105) that the common notions are ideas of "those features which are universal and necessary to [an] attribute." They are ideas of the "modes which flow from the absolute nature of the attribute" and hence share its infinity and eternity.

57. I note here in passing Spinoza's profound commitment to the material basis of cognition. This flies in the face of those who view Spinoza as the quintessential rationalist for whom reason is divorced from body and world. Nothing could be further from the truth. Susan James (205) remarks: "Turning to the claim that reasoning is divorced from everything bodily, we have seen that this is as far as possible from Spinoza's view."

58. I wish to thank Vance Maxwell for working with me repeatedly to help me gain some understanding of this process and these texts.

59. Hence Lee Rice's position that Part IV Preface's model of human nature insofar as it is to be used for "normative purposes" is nothing but a "construct," is, I think, well taken (Rice, 301).

60. EIIIP9Schol.

61. See my "Spinoza's Individualism Reconsidered."

62. EIVP37S2 (Shirley, 176–77).

63. *Guide* I, 2 (Pines: 25/*Moreh* vol. 1: 16b).

64. See "Spinoza and Euclidean Geometry: The Example of the Fourth Proportional," in *Spinoza and the Sciences,* ed. Marjorie Grene and Debra Nails, Vol. 91 of *Boston Studies in the Philosophy of Science* under the general editorship of Robert S. Cohen and Marx Wartofsky. (Dordrecht/Boston/Lancaster/Tokyo: D. Reidel, 1986). For a different account, see Vance Maxwell, "Spinoza's Doctrine of the *Amor Dei Intellectualis,* IV," unpublished paper, p. 3.

65. Matheron, 131–32.

66. Ibid., 137.

67. Ibid., 142.

68. In "The Philosophical Method of Spinoza," *Dialogue* XVII (1988): 89–110, p. 108, Vance Maxwell proposes that Spinoza's method works like this: "In good method, the mind begins by producing a true idea or definition of a particular thing, which idea, being deduced or reflected from the idea of the cause of that thing, directs the mind at once to an order of ideas. Furthermore, in his *Ethics,* Spinoza asserts that 'Each idea of each body, or of each singular thing which actually exists, necessarily involved the eternal and infinite essence of God' (*E*2P45). In the case of our adequate ideas, this involvement means that God Himself thinks these ideas insofar as he constitutes the essence of our minds (*E*3P1Dem.). Therefore, what is 'given' immediately about the idea of the most perfect being is this 'in-

volvement' of God in our true ideas of particular things. And this involvement grows with the evolving order of true ideas constituting the development of deductive method."

69. EVP10Schol (Shirley, 209–11).

70. Shirley, 224.

71. Ibid., 165.

72. In EVP32Dem & Cor, Spinoza shows how *Ratio*'s self-contentment (*acquiescentia*) becomes transformed into the intellectual love of God of Intuition. See also, VP27&Dem.

73. I wish to thank Vance Maxwell for pointing this out to me in a private communication.

74. IVP68 (Shirley, 193).

75. The following is a description taken from my essay, "Spinoza's Rupture with Tradition—His Hints of a Jewish Modernity," in Ravven and Goodman, eds., *Jewish Themes in Spinoza's Philosophy* (Albany: State University of New York Press, 2002).

76. TTP xvii, Van Vloten and Land, vol. 2, 283; Shirley, 265.

77. TTP xvii, Van Vloten and Land, vol. 2, 278; Shirley, 259.

78. TTP xvii, Van Vloten and Land, vol. 2, 283; Shirley, 265.

79. TTP xvii, Van Vloten and Land, vol. 2, 274; Shirley, 255–56.

80. TTP xvii, Van Vloten and Land, vol. 2, 280; Shirley, 262.

81. Ibid.

82. Ibid.

83. TTP xvii, Van Vloten and Land, vol. 2, 280–81; Shirley, 262.

84. TTP xvii, Van Vloten and Land, vol. 2, 274; Shirley, 256.

85. EVP36S (Shirley, 221): "I have thought this worth noting here in order to show by this example the superiority of the knowledge of particular things which I have called 'intuitive' or 'of the third kind,' and its preferability to that abstract knowledge which I have called 'knowledge of the second kind.' For although I demonstrated in a general way in Part I that everything (and consequently the human mind, too) is dependent on God in respect of its essence and of its existence, that proof, although legitimate and exempt from any shadow of doubt, does not strike the mind as when it is inferred from the essence of each particular thing which we assert to be dependent on God."

FOUR

Jean Axelrad Cahan

The Lonely Woman of Faith under Late Capitalism; or, Jewish Feminism in Marxist Perspective

Introduction

It is difficult to decide whether to characterize the current condition of Jewish philosophy generally as one that is optimal or one that is an instance of Brodskyian boredom.[1] In either case, the field seems to be marked by complete agnosticism as to what to expect of itself, not to mention what is to be expected of theology or God; indecision as to whether it is or is not possible to "stand outside" one's own identity in order to contemplate it; and the occasional tone of moral indignation notwithstanding, no discernible concern with the extreme needs of populations who do not share in the economic well-being of American academia.[2] It seems to me that while it is possible that we may thus inadvertently have arrived at a Rawlsian "original position" from which to devise new philosophical principles, an "unencumbered self" that is the better suited to undertaking new commitments and projects in a new, globalized society, what we are really experiencing is an abandonment of the project of philosophy altogether. In my opinion, this would be a bad thing. And so the general view of this paper will be one of nostalgia for Western Marxism, understood in a particular way, in lieu of the "nomadic" mood of much recent writing in Jewish feminist thought, especially that which has joined in postmodern ambitions.[3]

Of course, since for Marxism "the critique of religion is the beginning of all critique," at first glance it is difficult to see how Marxist philosophy could have anything valuable to contribute either to Jewish philosophy generally or to Jewish feminism in either its theoretical or practical concerns. The Jewish conceptions of divine being, historical redemption, and many other topics are simply not reconcilable with Marxism's analysis of the same. To Marx, Judaism was both the source and the culmination of alienated thought in Western civilization; it was the most egregious form of religious consciousness, first correctly analyzed by Ludwig Feuerbach in *The Essence of Christianity;* and Jewish ideas most completely represented the distortions of the capitalist mode of production.[4]

Nonetheless, I shall maintain that certain aspects of Western Marxism— its engagement with Western philosophy, especially German Idealism; its mode of critique of history and politics as exemplified in English and French Marxist historiography; its retention of universal concepts and capacity for abstraction in the course of its analysis of the concrete; its analyses of commodification and of daily life; and its overall critical and oppositional stance toward the dominant forces and powers of a given epoch— can serve as a useful foil, if not a significant corrective, in Jewish feminist thought. Contemporary Jewish feminist philosophy, building on the work of Foucault and other postmodern thinkers, intends to dissolve the categories and methods of Western philosophy, arguing that the rationality that is the supreme value of that tradition is a specially male type of rationality serving largely male intellectual and social interests.[5] But this criticism of Western philosophy weakens more than it liberates; it denies what men and women have in common, namely, the capacity to reason, to form and reflect on their friendships, as well as to think about the far greater economic divisions between nations, regions, and hemispheres. The insistence on a universal capacity to reason does not imply that there will be or need be universal agreement on what values and norms ought to be pursued. It only means that the vocabulary of philosophy can serve as a universal means of dialogue on great questions. Let me explain a bit further what I mean by this.

I. Marxism, Feminism, and Jewish Philosophy

As is well known, at least since the time of Kant, philosophers have hesitated and argued about whether distinctively philosophical reasoning exists, and, if it does, what useful or edifying purpose it serves. This is not the place to rehearse the case for each side of this issue. I will only point to the model of philosophy represented in Jürgen Habermas's theory of communicative action. For Habermas, given the prevalence of disagreements about values, practical requirements of the moral life, and so on, the task of philosophy is to participate in discourse about these problems, without regarding itself as the final decisor.[6] Again, universal agreement may not be reached, nor does this view of philosophy exclude the viability of other means of universal communication such as science. But the discourse of Western philosophy, with its logic, ontologies, concepts of causation, knowledge and belief, justice and right, and other features, has proved beneficial in clarifying many important dimensions of human endeavor, even though, I would add, it has frequently fallen into abstruse, self-referential language and has often been very distant from social and political realities.

While Habermas conceives of philosophy/discourse ethics as differing fundamentally from "material" ethics, which are based on perspectives and types of rationality confined to a particular individual or form of life, it is not immediately obvious that this conception is incompatible with a materialist approach to mental life, which Marxism requires. Habermas defines philosophy and discourse ethics as being concerned only with questions and values that have universal application; such questions strictly relate to normative justice, not practical norms of actual individual and social behavior. While it would seem that questions about normative justice are abstract, that would not for Habermas preclude the capacity for reasoning about normative justice to be based in neurophysiology, as materialism would require.

There is no need to pursue this topic further here. The important point for our purposes is that while Marxism insisted on material bases of both individual and social thought and behavior—see especially *The German Ideology,* 1846—the material individual was immediately and inevitably linked to other individuals and groups; the isolated individual in the state of nature never existed and has no function in historical, political, or cultural explanations. Thus to "place the gendered body first," as some feminist theorists would like to do, is to remain in a particular life form, as Habermas would put it; to foreclose on explanation, from the Marxist perspective. Marx stood in the intellectual tradition, deriving from Aristotle, which holds that the whole is prior to the part, metaphysically, politically, and heuristically. To concentrate on the experiences and perspectives of the gendered body, even on the domination relations of sexual acts involving more than one person, is to limit the explanatory project; for Marxism, the gender-neutral need for subsistence, and for cooperation in deriving the means of subsistence from a generally intractable natural environment, is of primary importance. This is not to deny that the labor process by which subsistence is acquired may rapidly become divided along gender lines, but it is to emphasize that social systems for producing the means of subsistence should constitute the starting point for historical and cultural explanation.

Although Marxism sought to invert the traditional methods and concepts of Western philosophy, it did not seek to eliminate them altogether. This is evident in the main philosophical text of classical Marxism, Marx's 1844 *Manuscripts,* and it is even more apparent in Western Marxist writing of the second half of the twentieth century. The work of such figures as Lukacs, Bloch, Adorno, and Sartre is largely devoted to analyses of social ontology and of cultural superstructures, utilizing the vocabulary and methods of pre-Marxist Western philosophy. Thus within the Western Marxist world-view, in a world in which economic objects and relations are the ultimate determinants of other spheres of life, philosophy is not merely an otiose by-product of economic processes but also a critical tool in theorizing economic, social, and political life and therefore an important instrument of reform or revolution (depending on the theoretician).

By contrast, the postmodern efforts of Jewish feminist thought so heavily emphasize the bodily dimensions of existence that the possibilities of abstraction are lost from sight/site altogether. And so we end up with philosophical myopia, a focus so restricted to the mundane that justifications and possibilities for political change are actually obscured rather than enhanced. Tamar El-Or has noted the lack of abstract thinking among some Orthodox women,[7] but it is difficult to see how postmodern feminism would lead to a different result. It is noteworthy that Foucault himself did not go this far. In *The Order of Things* he speaks of man as an "empirico-transcendental doublet," able to recover "his integrity on the basis of what eludes him."[8]

Thus although Marxism was from its inception largely indifferent to the question of women's liberation—even the writings of its pre-eminent female theoretician, Rosa Luxemburg, systematically blocked out special consideration of issues of concern to feminists (and Jews)[9]—and was hostile to Jewish emancipation outside of the context of a world-wide emancipation of the proletariat, its retention of an idea of humanity as the unit of analysis, and of universal rationality, the quintessence of the currently much-despised modernism, left open conceptual possibilities and perhaps political possibilities that I think contemporary Jewish feminism closes off. We can see this in the contrast between the current generation of Jewish feminists (to be discussed in some detail in the next section of this paper) and an earlier generation represented in the collection *On Being a Jewish Feminist,* edited by Susannah Heschel and published in 1983. While not explicitly Marx-inspired, some of the essays display contradictions between "consciousness and society," between the universal idea of equality as against pressing material needs, that only appear in greatly attenuated form in more recent writings. Similarly, certain writings by (male) philosophers from the 1950s and 1960s, which contain strong echoes of Marx, constituted attempts to take an oppositional stance over against the vast tide of commodification, consumerism, and other aspects of late capitalism. Abraham Joshua Heschel analyzed at length the material and epistemological blocks to knowledge of freedom and of God.[10] In *The Lonely Man of Faith,* Joseph Soloveitchik eloquently articulated deep anxieties about the seemingly relentless pursuit of profit and power over nature. As he saw it, even the pious are occupied in a certain spiritual productivity that is to be distinguished from genuine faith, which does not seek control, competition or success, but is humble, and powerless and prefers that condition.

> I am mainly interested in contemporary man of faith who is, due to his peculiar position in our secular society, lonely in a special way. . . . He looks upon himself as a stranger in modern society, which is technically-minded, self-centered and self-loving, . . . scoring honor upon honor, piling up victory upon victory, reaching for the distant galaxies, and seeing in the here-and-now sensible world the only manifestation of being. What can a man of faith like myself, living by a doctrine which has no technical potential, by a law which cannot be tested in the laboratory . . . what can such a man say to a functional, utilitarian society which is saeculum-oriented and whose practical reasons of the mind have long ago supplanted the sensitive reasons of the heart?[11]

The title of this essay is intended to evoke Soloveitchik's description of the individual alienated from modern capitalist society and some aspects of institutionalized religion, while intimating that the condition of women ought to be a major focus of critique. But while Jewish feminism has attended to some problems of institutionalized religion, it has completely neglected the other topic Soloveitchik was pointing to, namely the effects of industrial, scientific, capitalist modernity. Though Soloveithchik was preoccupied mainly by the spiritual and emotional effects, a starting point for Jewish feminists might well be the considerable literature on women in the global economy, calling attention to the effects on family life and on other types of political relations.[12] The relevance of this literature to the lives of contemporary Jewish women throughout the world ought to be explored.

A general acquaintance with Marxism would also lead one to identify the state as an important focus for critique. Feminists, both Marxist and non-Marxist, have indeed begun this work.[13] The ideal of weakness as it appears in Jewish thought and philosophy has recently become important in arguments over the definition of the Jewish state: to what extent were European notions of manliness (the opposite of weakness) imported and utilized by Jewish groups colonizing Palestine and striving to form a Jewish state there?[14] And might it not have been preferable, as Martin Buber, among others, held, for Jews to remain powerless in the military and political senses rather than to perpetrate crimes against Palestinian Arabs? Here we may see that Marxist responses have been uncertain: on the one hand, Marxists would and did hold to a universal notion of equality and the insistence that this can only be realized in a secular, democratic socialist state; on the other hand there has also been a reluctance to draw the conclusion that this entails an end to Israel as a Zionist state.[15] David Roskies has recently drawn an interesting comparison between Zionism and Marxism as ideologies that lay bare the tensions underlying modern societies.[16]

Since the "first wave" of Jewish feminism and certainly since the days of Soloveitchik and Heschel, the problems associated with late, global capitalism have only deepened. For this reason, Marxists today on the whole take the view, which I share, that feminism, while raising extremely important issues from which there is no turning away, or going back, nonetheless has preoccupations best understood in a larger context of economic globalization. While the effects of women's oppression ought not to be underestimated— the effects on self-worth, on family, on memory, on civil rights obviously— the *economic* origins of many of these forms of oppression ought to be kept in the forefront of analysis.[17] In Jewish thought and philosophy today, feminist or otherwise, the Marxist idea of the predominance of production, and the rectification of injustice that this entails, finds very little "resonance" (despite some remnants of the vocabulary, which carry little actual analytical weight, as we shall see), except perhaps in the thought of Emmanuel Levinas ("Marxism invites humanity to demand what it is my duty to give it").[18] Nevertheless, I shall use it as a foil against which to discuss some recent work. In doing so, I shall adhere to the general position that, as I have already indicated, the mode of critique of Western Marxism, with its universal aims of justice and equality, its heavy reliance on social science and German idealist philosophy, and therefore on abstract concepts, can remain useful to Jewish philosophy. But this position requires some elaboration.

(i.) I hold that, while Marx's critique of religion (relying as it does on the notions of projection, alienation, "*Entfremdung,*" is not acceptable as an explanation of religious belief, the uses to which this notion is put in Marx's critiques of political economy, of history, of capitalism, are still deserving of intellectual consideration (though the practical political uses to which these ideas were put in the twentieth century—the entire "harvest of sorrow" in the former Soviet Union, dictatorship and mass murder in many other parts of the world—must be utterly repudiated by any decent person). Thus the concepts of reification, of fetishism of commodities, of transitions between modes of production, relations of production, class conflict, and so on, may still be use-ful and illuminating in our time, even though Marxist analyses of religious consciousness are unconvincing. I am therefore inclined to agree with those commentators on Marx who wish to mark an "epistemological break" be-tween the early and the late Marx, though for a different reason.[19] While those commentators wish to avoid "contamination" of the later "scientific" analysis of capitalism through the philosophico-anthropological analysis of religion, I seek to preserve the philosophico-theological sphere from the political and ideological depredations of the sphere of human life and history, the sphere in where we do things to ourselves. That is, I want to keep separate our most ab-stract, universal ideas about God, being, and truth—philosophical theol-ogy—and at the very least leave open the possibility that these are not or not only, as Marxism would have it, social constructs. Of course, I cannot go very far in defending this goal within the confines of this paper, but it is a guiding thought in my reading of contemporary Jewish feminist work.

(ii.) Following this train of thought, I would add that the tendency of Jewish philosophy to borrow from Western philosophy is a good thing, if handled carefully. The aspirations of Aristotelians, Neoplatonists, Kantians, Hegelians, and democratic Marxists to arrive at universal truths, prin-ciples—though all are finally in some sense unsuccessful—have nonethe-less been in a way admirable and comparable to religious aspirations. They can become "totalizing" and oppressive when combined with the desire for domination, but in my opinion they are not inherently or necessarily op-pressive. On the contrary, such philosophical aspirations have often proved liberating and democratizing. In both metaphysics and ethics—from Neo-platonist emanationist schemes, to Mendelssohn, Hermann Cohen, Rosen-zweig, and Buber, to name only some—the influence of Western philosophy has proved enriching and illuminating. The wholesale rejec-tion of Western philosophy and Enlightenment thought by much of con-temporary Jewish feminism would be a considerable theoretical loss.

On a practical level, this rejection is also deleterious. If there is no philo-sophical vocabulary and method of reasoning that aspires to be universal, then our ability to communicate with others is curtailed; we are limited to exchanges of sympathy and metaphor, as opposed to thorough-going politi-cal and moral analysis and possibilities for change based on that. An ex-ample from Jewish history: the Arab-Israeli conflict. As Zeev Sternhell has argued, the idea of workers' liberation pursued by Labor Zionism in the prestate phase of Israel's history was a very limited one, bearing no real connection to the universal ideas of justice and equality expressed by European democratic Socialism and avoiding its theoretical analysis; what has resulted from this, among other things, is an inability (not merely an unwillingness) to form an adequate conception of the needs and interests of Palestinian Arabs, which has of course greatly influenced the development of the State of Israel.[20] Another way of putting this would be to say that the ideas of justice and equality of European democratic Socialism, formed in part through engagement with Western philosophy as well as through historical and political struggle, not only provided a standard by which to judge events elsewhere, but also a means through which the needs, interests, and political circumstances of two cultures and societies could be rationally discussed.

I agree with Cynthia Ozick, therefore, that ultimately the right question about the situation of women is not philosophical or theological, but rather political, legal, and, I emphasize, economic.[21] Of course there remains the fundamental question of how, both in general and in the case of Judaism, philosophy and theology relate to history and political economy. Both Western and Jewish philosophy contain numerous attempts to answer this question, to construct religious and philosophical theories of history, to prove or disprove the presence of divine providence in human affairs. Neoplatonist emanationist ontology, Spinoza's system of attributes and modes, Maimonides's theory of providence, and Jewish historiography from Josephus through Krochmal, Dubnow, and Leo Baeck are all attempts to address this topic. One could even characterize Marxism as a type of response, namely one that holds that the concept of God should be removed from the theory and practice of history and politics. Despite the fundamental contradiction between Judaism and Marxism on God and the meaning of history, Western Marxism can still provide insights on such matters, including the causes of poverty; the nature of authoritarian political regimes; and the character and limits of political consciousness. Obviously these are important both within and beyond Jewish communities. Western Marxism cannot construct a philosophical theology, nor a theodicy of any kind, but it can illuminate what I (paraphrasing Maimonides) above called the sphere in which we human beings do things to ourselves. Jewish thinkers can make use of what has been learned about social institutions in recent centuries, whatever the conjectures or conclusions about God's relation to history and particular events in Jewish history. An example of this would be analysis of the Holocaust: might we not consider this the result of Germany's transition from feudalism to capitalism, or of imperialist competition between European nations, even if we also ultimately identify a special religious meaning for this catastrophe? Moreover, insofar as Western Marxism represents an oppositional stance to late capitalism, it supports rather than conflicts with Judaism. Judaism, in the form of the commandments "I am the Lord thy God" and "Thou shalt make no graven image," is the ultimate oppositional stance, the ultimate critique. The practice of abstract thought, through philosophy as well as through other forms of study, brings both women and men to a better acquaintance with oppositional stances, with the ultimate other, and not only the otherness of gender, ethnicity, and class.

I now turn to a more detailed consideration of three texts of Jewish feminist thought. Although the purpose of this volume is to discuss Jewish feminist philosophy, there is in fact relatively little work containing Jewish feminist ideas that philosophers trained in either the Anglo-American analytic tradition or in Continental philosophy would recognize as "philosophy proper." But to refuse to consider ideas or methods that are not strictly part of the two traditions mentioned might be to neglect important insights. Moreover, Marxism itself is a questionable example of these traditional conceptions of philosophy proper, with their millennia-old preoccupations and modes of argumentation. One could argue that while Marx's theory of history and his socio-economic work proved very rich, from a metaphysical and epistemological standpoint they were quite limited and even unoriginal. Nonetheless, Western Marxism—including such figures as Lukacs, Korsch, Gramsci, Benjamin, and Adorno, among many others—was articulated mainly through the vocabulary and methods of traditional Western philosophy, and in this way it remains a useful foil against which to assess other modes of social and intellectual critique.[22] I have selected certain texts, then, because broadly speaking they concern three different areas of intellectual activity—history, rabbinic literature, and philosophy, though they share the assumption that feminism benefits from alliance with postmodernism, with its rejection of Enlightenment rationality and values, its preoccupation with difference, and its fragmentary rather than systematic method. It will be my position that, seen in Marxist perspective, the "parodic playfulness" of postmodern feminism is more likely a symptom of than a solution to the problems of late capitalism.

II. Engaging Jewish Feminist Thought

HISTORY

One of the most vehement expressions of concern with the otherness of women is the work *Spinning Fantasies,* by Miriam Peskowitz. This work deals with the occupation of spinning, and its representations, in Roman Palestine.[23] Though sprinkled with the remnants of Marxian terminology and apparently driven by the supreme value of "ordinariness"—a value itself largely shaped by Marxism[24]—it actively avoids any notion that material base and cultural superstructure might be distinct and causally related. The two are so fully "imbricated" that neither work, gender, nor everyday life as a category "is prior to the other, and all were sites for early rabbinic imagination."[25] We are told that "work is a mode of production of culture," which has a good Marxist ring to it, but also that "like gender, work itself is constituted in part through stories told and retold." But this "in part" leaves out precisely what a materialist conception of history would hold to be of primary importance: how work itself originates in the appropriation of something external to the individual; how it involves particular kinds of tools and methods; *how* gender relations, relations of productions and cultural activity are both produced by and modulate the labor process. Surely explanation of any kind, materialist or otherwise, requires an heuristic process of ordering, assigning primacy, secondariness, and so forth, to concepts, objects, causes. Nothing is *explained* by the refusal to assign priority, and Peskowitz's inconclusive treatment of gender and work, though deliberate, is unsatisfying to those of us stuck in modern, as opposed to postmodern, epistemologies.

In a reading of Mishnah Ketubot 8.1, Peskowitz seeks to analyze relations between property and gender, to display their imbrication, but the result of this exercise is unclear. To show such an imbrication would not be new or surprising, given what historians have already written about the rabbinic period. Nor does the conclusion—that in this passage R. Gamliel revealed a conscious need to find a legal foundation for a legal innovation concerning betrothed women and wives—seem startlingly original. Isn't it a well-known feature of talmudic discussions that they sought foundations and authority for the standpoints and interpretations offered?[26] Nor does the result seem to be to have discovered in R. Gamliel an ally, a precedent, for contemporary feminist struggles; Peskowitz is unwilling to make a direct connection between a past standpoint and a contemporary effort. While it is an historical and philosophical question of considerable complexity whether such a connection can ever legitimately be made, whether there are "lessons" from history for present political purposes, Peskowitz's hesitation here reveals a weakness of the postmodern agenda generally: in its effort to be exquisitely sensitive to local texts and topics, and avoid any "totalizing" thinking, it cuts the ground out from under any more general effort for change, and for broad historical conceptions or theories that might be called in to assist in that change. Thus a talmudic reading that begins by raising the expectation of radical innovation simply flatlines, epistemologically and politically.

Although acknowledging the writings of other scholars on the so-called external realities of Roman Palestine and of rabbinic culture, *in a footnote* Peskowitz declares that all this work participates in "the problem of masculinizing the category 'worker,'" so that women are always excluded from considerations of work and production, domains that become masculine at their inception.[27] Here Peskowitz may be attempting to apply to Roman Palestine the more general idea put forward by some Socialist feminists that systems of political economy have always been inextricably bound up with patriarchy and gender. In this view, capitalism, for example, "[identifies] men as 'primary' workforce material and women as 'secondary' workforce material."[28] Further, the structure and functioning of the male-dominated nuclear family reinforce the male-dominated societal economy. While this is an important conjecture, worth exploring further, Peskowitz's study does not explain *how* the concept of *worker* is to be understood as inherently or instantly masculine. What does it even mean to say that the concept of *worker* is inherently masculine? One thing it manifestly cannot mean is that historically all workers have been men. Peskowitz's own study, relying on the work of Zeev Safrai[29] and others, shows that both women and men were engaged in the occupations of spinning and weaving, even though writers and artists expressed the view that spinning was pre-eminently an occupation of females.

By way of an answer to this, we again encounter Peskowitz's desire to eliminate causal sequences, to vitiate any distinction between subjective and objective reality: "The tasks of textile production were transformed into a range of human traits," such that "the weaving of yarn into cloth would indicate men who were neither sexually trustworthy nor respectable as men."[30] Here one wants to say: the tasks *were associated with* certain character traits, but were not themselves transformed. But Peskowitz does not want to look at it this way. Rather,

> In common language, fantasy often seems linked inextricably to sex. . . . There is an ethos, a set of operative assumptions, in which work is presumed to be material and physical, and in which things that are material and physical are seen as more truthful and real. I want to break down this habit of imagining the ancient world. Used as a critical term, "fantasy" . . . calls into question the more pedestrian ways in which words about work are usually understood.[31]

Thus not only the materialist assumption that external, material reality exists and is ultimate, but any distinction between reality and (sexualized) fantasy is to be "broken down." The task of the historian is to fantasize, not chase after "evidence." Again in a footnote, the rather substantial scholarly effort on Roman Palestine that uses conventional historical methodology is dismissed with an undeveloped, unargued-for remark: "Undoing the distinction between truthful description and imaginative fantasy calls into question all of the existing handbooks and publications on work, labor and textile production in Roman Palestine, the Talmud etc., which precede [*sic*] as if these are references to real physical practices."[32] But in what way is this scholarly work called into question by removing the distinction between truthful description and imaginative fantasy? While on the one hand wishing to argue that the distinction between reality and fantasy leads to a misogynist history/past, in which only men do "real," waged work, and women are merely consumers, Peskowitz also wishes to maintain that "wage-producing labor" was also "part of Jewish women's lives" in that they engaged in it.[33] While one might agree with Peskowitz that this had the effect of blurring gender differences and therefore posed a problem for rabbis who envisioned a greater separation of the sexes and gendered identities, it does not show that work or the conceptual category of *worker* was or is inherently masculine. And the blurring of distinctions between reality and fantasy is also at odds with Peskowitz's language of "showing how material conditions matter," of "sites of production" and "modes of production," which gives the impression that a materialist, indeed Marxist, approach to history has value. But this language in her work is probably only cosmetic.[34]

To the extent that there is an organizing theme in Peskowitz's work, it is that of ordinariness. In early rabbinic Judaism, in her view, halakhah, work, and gender were "integral parts" of ordinariness.[35] They were all rolled up into one, in a way that modern thought cannot appreciate.[36] Western European thought imposed a false unity on Jewish history—not this unity that Peskowitz has sought to articulate—and it excluded women, and later Arabs. This false history had real political consequences, she hints, in the formation of the state of Israel. I would maintain, on the contrary, that Peskowitz's reluctance to make conceptual distinctions between physical reality and fantasy (sexual or otherwise), itself imposes a meaningless unity on Jewish history, a glorification of "ordinariness" that in Marxist terms is nothing but the recognition of the centrality of material production and reproduction of the means of subsistence in human life, and that in Jewish religious terms requires sanctification at certain points and in certain ways.

LITERATURE

In *Carnal Israel,* Daniel Boyarin also seeks a "new thinking" to replace "traditional positivistic historiographical approaches" to rabbinic literature. Again there is no interest in "[imagining] any outside to the text," but rather a Foucauldian understanding of literature as "a process rather than simply a set of products," in which texts and objects of various kinds are related in a discourse, seen as permeated by certain social processes.[37] Thus texts of various genres that have been constructed can be related, contrasted with one another, and the production of social meanings studied. But texts of various kinds, especially in early rabbinic culture, should be regarded as all being "of the same epistemological status."[38] That is, there is no way and no point in making the distinctions that historians use between primary and secondary sources, between documents and fictions. Boyarin sees his method as similar to Stephen Greenblatt's "cultural poetics," frequently regarded as one of the first essays in the New Historicist approach to literary studies. Though there is little agreement as to what exactly the New Historicism amounts to, minimally one could say that it is an approach that seeks, in contrast to formalist methods, to show that some sort of relation exists between literary texts and the context of social institutions and non-discursive practices in which they originate.[39]

Boyarin's approach seeks to avoid claiming that literary texts directly "reflect" their contexts. If the relation is not one of mere reflection, what is it for Boyarin? Rabbinic literature produces *analogues* to social practice, but it should not be put more strongly than that.[40] Rabbinic texts are expressions of attempts to conceal/propose utopian solutions to tensions, strains, and pressures in culture and society. By reading them using a "hermeneutics of suspicion," the underlying social tensions can therefore be exposed. Such a hermeneutics will also reveal literary practices as "forms of resistance or accommodation or accommodating resistance and resistant accommodation to the dominant practices of the colonizing culture [pagan and Christian Rome]."[41] Moreover, it will be seen that the discourse of rabbinic culture was quite fractured; a plurality of voices emerged on a variety of questions relating to women, sex, and gender, and in this way dissent became not merely acceptable but "canonized."[42]

Nonetheless, beneath the diversity of opinions of the Talmud is an underlying unity, a unity that consists in "the interpretation of human beings as fundamentally, essentially corporeal. This idea, *which itself grows out of its own material causes,* becomes the spring that drives multifarious aspects of socio-cultural practice within formations of rabbinic Jews in Palestine and Babylonia from the second century until the Arab conquest" (emphasis added).[43] The definition of "material causes" is perhaps what distinguishes Boyarin's conception of culture and history from other materialist, especially Marxist, conceptions. Although he does not give examples of how this idea (that human beings are essentially corporeal as opposed to essentially

constituted by a soul) or any other emerges from material causes, we can surmise that the causes are either (a) human bodies themselves, or (b) the process of satisfaction of bodily needs through interaction with other bodies,
and the conflicts or associative acts that are part of this process. Boyarin's
readings of rabbinic texts suggest that he has the latter in mind. For example, the need for sexual intercourse on the part of both women and men
leads to elaborate thinking about what is owed to whom in the marriage relation, and on the "unresolvability of the cultural problem of tension between marriage and Torah-study within the Babylonian rabbinic system."[44]

Boyarin's contribution to feminist thought would seem, then, to be
two-fold. First, by pointing to the plurality of voices and the practice of dissent in the Talmud Boyarin's method emphasizes the non-authoritarian, democratizing tendencies of Jewish thought and further "destabilizes"
traditional attitudes toward authority in the sphere of both family life and,
by implication, national politics.[45] Second, by assigning theoretical primacy
to the gendered body and to sexuality, Boyarin strengthens those feminist
approaches that see sexuality and not socio-economic life as the main locus
of male power and domination.[46] The question for anyone writing from a
Marxist perspective would then be: does Boyarin's materialist feminist reading of the Talmud lead, as he expressly hopes, to a "usable past"; and does
this form of cultural critique change the world?

The Marxist literary theorist Fredric Jameson has argued that the most
remarkable feature of the New Historicism is its avoidance of thinking
"time and history," the social transformations that have occurred over time.
It is a tendency to project onto *space*—place, landscape and, above all, the
human body—relations that have evolved over time.[47] In refusing to set priorities, to recognize historically developed structures, it displays a "disenchanted and uninhibited superficiality." Even if Jameson is too harsh, it
seems to me that this mode of cultural critique is too tentative to serve as a
tool in understanding the current social conjuncture and in recommending
concrete solutions. While an acknowledgment that deep social tensions existed in medieval Jewish communities might be *a step in arguing* for new,
halakhically acceptable solutions to problems in Jewish life now, I maintain
that changes in the role and status of women in Judaism have come and will
continue to come through overwhelming pressure from "the outside world."
Did the decision of the Conservative movement to ordain women rabbis, for
example, arise from the recognition, through textual readings, that "things
were not always like this," i.e., male-controlled? No, the change in policy
arose from the social fact that Jewish women brought up in the context of
American history (during an age in which two world wars and the Depres-

sion required their skills and education, and during which time a wider civil rights movement took hold) agitated for equality wherever they could: in the organization of the household and family life, and in the composition of synagogue boards, charitable offices, and other places. Postmodernists, New Historicists, and Jewish feminists who were strongly influenced by these factors seem to me to have abandoned any real conceptual or political hope and to have "become for [themselves] the objects of a hermeneutics of suspicion."[48] While their cultural critique might aim to be a "sensibility" toward difference and is not oppressive, neither is it clearly emancipatory—it leaves everything largely as it is, even if somewhat less stable.

Philosophy

An interesting attempt has been made in Susan Shapiro's essay, "A Matter of Discipline: Reading for Gender in Jewish Philosophy," to return to the idea that the "right question is theological," or at least philosophical.[49] Shapiro argues that gendered concepts are at the foundation of Jewish philosophy and its Greek and Islamic buttresses. The concepts of matter and form, basic to any premodern metaphysic, are so closely associated with femaleness and maleness respectively, that the latter are virtually constitutive of the former. Thus, metaphors such as that of the married harlot are not merely addenda that can be contextualized and then dismissed, but are central to the philosophical project within Jewish and other cultures.

> These figures and tropes perform intellectual and cultural labor that is necessary if the so-called properly philosophical work of these texts is to be done.[50]

But what exactly is the intellectual and cultural labor that needs to be done, prior to the "properly philosophical work"? And what is properly philosophical? It would seem that the answer to the first question is that Maimonides's metaphor of the married harlot "connects Greek and Jewish thinking about matter." Greek thought reinforces the aim of medieval Jewish philosophy, in this case as reflected in Maimonides, to bring unethical, degrading "feminine" matter under formal control. Philosophy is to rhetoric what masculinity is to femininity, what order and discipline are to irrationality, disruption, or corruption. The answer to the second question is not clear; no further explication of "properly philosophical work" is given, beyond the notion that it is a mode of thinking that seeks to discipline and govern.

Shapiro's reading of Maimonides is subtle and obliges any holder of a traditional conception of philosophy to think again about its fundamental categories. But two responses can be made at this point.

First, it is just as plausible to understand Maimonides's conception of matter by equating it with class rather than gender, though there are no memorable metaphors associated with this idea. By *class* I mean here a person's position in the economy, together with habits formed through education. Maimonides holds that there are so many variables and circumstances that determine whether or not a given individual will be able to apprehend truth, and arrive at a stage of being able to experience spiritual as opposed to material pleasure, that it is likely that only a small elite and not the multitude will achieve these goals. Thus the people of the desert grew accustomed to their disorderly and hardscrabble lives and could not be detached from a belief in God's corporeality. Further, says Maimonides, most men are so occupied with vital material needs, and also tend to become so preoccupied with superfluities, that their theoretical interests get buried, as it were.

> In view of these causes, these matters [the search for truth and wisdom] are only for a few solitary individuals of a very special sort, not for the multitude.[51]

Thus errors of the imagination, and misleading rhetoric, as opposed to purity of intellect, are characteristic of the masses in contrast to that of a small elite; these errors are not the weakness of women only. While it is highly unlikely that Maimonides would admit that a woman could be among the intellectual elite, he does not, as far as I can tell, explicitly preclude this. The physiological and economic hindrances to women's achieving this status would no doubt be even greater than it is for most men, but the emphasis on the role of social circumstances suggests that there is at least a conceptual possibility of rearranging things socially so as to allow females to improve their capacities for study and the apprehension of truth.

A second response to Shapiro is that "properly philosophical work" *ought to be* an enterprise and a *carrière ouverte aux talents* (to use an Enlightenment expression), that is, a universal project. An inversion of the functions and status of logic and rhetoric would make this difficult, if not impossible, and would not be a desirable thing for women or anyone. While Shapiro's essay might be intended to illustrate how traditional philosophy, both Western and Jewish, participates in a patriarchal cultural hegemony and the domination of women, its effect is to destroy philosophy while purporting to save it. That is, I think that the "very disciplinarity" of philosophy, and along with it of philosophical theology, ought to be conserved as exactly that sphere which aspires to think without metaphors, through universal reason. As we readily see in the histories of philosophies, this aspiration frequently falls short, but that does not mean it is an unworthy or even wholly unsuccessful project. When human beings debate the enormous questions that they pose to themselves—why is there sickness, death, and crime in the world; why is virtue fragile; what makes a state just, and so on—do they not seek a truthful answer rather than a persuasive one? The thought that metaphors help to explain truths, but are not themselves truths, and that therefore rhetoric is ancillary, is an expression of an underlying aspiration to arrive at truths in as pure a form as possible, abstracted from individual physiology, self-interest, greed, grief, and power distributions. This does not require us to avoid noticing that oppression and exploitation exist, even within the institutions and practices of philosophy, but it does require an aspiration to transcend these through the use of reason. This is not to deny any role to metaphor and imagination, but to insist that these roles are different and less general in their effects. While metaphors in philosophy and science have frequently moved thinkers to develop their thought in a certain direction, until now no one has claimed that metaphors are themselves "theory-constitutive." To put forward a metaphor is not to construct a detailed, coherent theory about something.[52] Women should seek to participate in Western philosophy, Jewish philosophy, and Torah–Talmud study, just as they do in science and mathematics, not by redefining the discipline but by insisting on social, economic, and educational arrangements that make increased participation possible. In this way, they would share in, not undermine, what Hegel called the aspiration to "find the region in which all riddles of the world, all contradictions of thought are resolved, all griefs are healed."

🌼 Conclusion

Western Marxism provides a way of thinking about the socio-economic conjuncture and the vast culture of commodification and consumption in which we find ourselves, as well as with how these relate to other parts of the world. The condition of women is largely shaped by these objective circumstances, as are decisions about innumerable ethical and political issues, such as public health, education, and international criminal justice. What Jewish thinkers have to say that is distinctive about these questions to an extent still remains to be seen. But modern Jewish philosophy's engagement with German Idealism, and more indirectly with Marxism, has been, in my opinion, more politically creative than that with postmodernism and the New Historicism. The efforts of Hermann Cohen, Rosenzweig, and Buber, to name only the most prominent, to rethink the meaning of Jewish history, the relations of the Jews to modern nation-states and to the adherents of other religions, seem to me much more coherent and rich than what we are seeing now. And I would add that those who are interested in the traditional questions of philosophy as well as the concerns of women can still usefully read the critiques of subjective consciousness and experience, of philosophy and of the whole cultural superstructure by Lukacs, Adorno, Bloch, and English Marxists such as Raymond Williams, to name only a few. They have the virtue of seeking to adhere to universal concepts and reasoning, and of pursuing the project of universal freedom and justice, whatever that may amount to. And that is the point: it is the aspiration to think about what universal justice would amount to that is philosophically and politically important, even if the actualization of it is impractical and very remote indeed.

> If material reality is called the world of exchange value, and any culture whatever refuses to accept the domination of that world, then it is true that such refusal is illusory as long as the existent exists. . . . [Yet] in the face of the lie of the commodity world, even the lie that denounces it becomes a corrective. That culture has so far failed is no justification for furthering its failure.[53]

Philosophy, including Jewish philosophy and its particular concerns, has and perhaps will continue to provide a vocabulary and mode of discussion about everything under and above the sun, including the situations of women. It is neither a substitute for a religious way of life nor a substitute for political, social, and legal action to improve women's lives. But through its concepts, rules of reasoning, and aims of universality it constitutes an important means of human communication and action.

The theoretical and practical problematics surfaced by feminist thought in recent decades greatly complicates an already difficult contest between religion and materialist philosophies. In my opinion, that contest is far from over, despite the apparent pervasiveness of the "culture of unbelief." One of the tasks of Jewish philosophers is to put forward arguments and ideas as to why we remain Jews, in the face of both history and materialist philosophies of history. But in order to retain any plausibility as interpreters of reality, we must address feminist criticisms of Jewish thought and praxis, whether traditional or contemporary. I have tried to suggest that, apart from its wrongheadedness on the nature of religion, Western Marxism remains a useful source of conceptual tools with which to carry on a critique of the contemporary world order. The scale of problems facing the world requires a primary emphasis on the phenomena of competition, exploitation, alienation, class relations, and so on, all of which affect men as well as women. Psychoanalytic or other subjectivist theories of patriarchy, while very insightful, seem to me to be of secondary usefulness. Relations between the sexes and the gendered division of labor should be seen in the larger context of humanity's relations with nature and the struggle for subsistence. While it might be argued that this simply plays along with male interpretations of history and male values like rationality, it is not clear that patriarchy and political economy are necessarily linked. Indeed, it would seem more likely that the capitalist economy is a *solvent* of patriarchy rather than a consolidating factor. The history of American Jewry, with its emphatic shifts away from tradition, reflects this.

Philosophical concern with poverty and exploitation comports well with Jewish ideals, as is well known. Concern with internal family dynamics, the place of women in the family and the role of the family more generally are all obviously also important questions for Jews, but are best analyzed within a wider historical context. These political and practical concerns leave untouched whatever inner relatedness an individual Jew may feel to her or his God, but that is a subject for another occasion.

NOTES

1. Joseph Brodsky, *On Grief and Reason: Essays* (New York: Farrar, Straus and Giroux, 1995).

2. An example of recent discussion of the future of Jewish philosophy would be Steven Kepnes, Peter Ochs, and Robert Gibbs, eds., *Reasoning After Revelation: Dialogues in Postmodern Jewish Philosophy* (Boulder: Westview Press, 1998).

3. The characterization of postmodern thought as "nomadic" comes from Fredric Jameson, *Postmodernism, or, The Cultural Logic of Late Capitalism* (Durham, N.C.: Duke University Press, 1991), passim.

4. Karl Marx, "Zur Judenfrage" in Karl Marx and Friedrich Engels, *Werke*. Band 1 (Berlin: Dietz Verlag, 1981); Karl Marx, "Theses on Feuerbach," in Robert C. Tucker, ed., *The Marx-Engels Reader* (New York: W. W. Norton & Company, 1978).

5. This will become evident below. It is a critique that closely follows non-Jewish or more general feminist thought. A good overview of this topic is to be found in Catharine A. MacKinnon, *Toward a Feminist Theory of the State* (Cambridge, Mass.: Harvard University Press, 1989), Chapter 5 and the extensive bibliographic references there. See also Susan J. Hekman, *Gender and Knowledge: Elements of a Postmodern Feminism* (Cambridge: Polity Press, 1990).

6. Jurgen Habermas, *Moralbewusstsein und kommunikatives Handeln* (Frankfurt am Main: Suhrkamp Verlag, 1983).

7. Tamar El-Or, "Power/Knowledge/Gender," in *Judaism since Gender,* ed. Miriam Peskowitz and Laura Levitt (New York: Routledge, 1997).

8. Michel Foucault, *The Order of Things: An Archaeology of the Human Sciences* (New York: Vintage Books, 1973), 323.

9. Rosa Luxemburg, "Women's Suffrage and Class Struggle," in Rosa Luxemburg, *Se-*

lected Political Writings, ed. Dick Howard (New York: Monthly Review Press, 1971); *The Woman Question: Selections from the Writings of Marx, Engels, Lenin, and Stalin* (New York: International Publishers, 1951).

10. Abraham Joshua Heschel, *Between God and Man: An Interpretation of Judaism,* ed. Fritz A. Rothschild (New York: Free Press, 1959).

11. Joseph B. Soloveitchik, *The Lonely Man of Faith* (Northvale, N.J.: Jason Aronson, 1997), 6, 14ff, 93ff.

12. A sophisticated introduction to this topic is to be found in Saskia Sassen, "Toward a Feminist Analytics of the Global Economy," in *Globalization and Its Discontents* (New York: The New Press, 1998).

13. See, for example, a much-cited article by Jean Elshtain, "Sovereign State, Sovereign God, Sovereign Self," *Notre Dame Law Review* 66 (1991): 1355–78; MacKinnon, *Toward a Feminist Theory;* Ellen Meiksins Wood, *Democracy against Capitalism: Renewing Historical Materialism* (Cambridge: Cambridge University Press, 1995).

14. Yoram Hazony, *The Jewish State: The Struggle for Israel's Soul* (New York: Basic Books, 2000); Laurence J. Silberstein, *The Postzionism Debates: Knowledge and Power in Israeli Culture* (New York: Routledge, 1999).

15. Silberstein, *The Postzionism Debates,* Chapter 3; Zeev Sternhell, *The Founding Myths of Israel: Nationalism, Socialism, and the Making of the Jewish State,* trans. David Maisel (Princeton, N.J.: Princeton University Press, 1998).

16. David G. Roskies, *The Jewish Search for a Usable Past* (Bloomington: Indiana University Press, 1998), 161.

17. See, for example, Ellen Meiksins Wood and John Bellamy Foster, eds., *In Defense of History: Marxism and the Postmodern Agenda* (New York: Monthly Review Press, 1997). Marx's own view of the destructive effects of capitalism on the family are to be found in Karl Marx, *Das Kapital: Kritik der Politischen Okonomie,* Erster Band (Berlin: Dietz Verlag, 1982), 417ff.

18. Emmanuel Levinas, *Entre Nous: On Thinking-of-the-Other,* trans. Michael B. Smith and Barbara Harshav (New York: Columbia University Press, 1998), 119.

19. Louis Althusser and Etienne Balibar, *Lire le Capital I* (Paris: Francois Maspero, 1978).

20. Sternhell, *The Founding Myths of Israel,* Epilogue.

21. Cynthia Ozick, "Notes toward Finding the Right Question," in *On Being a Jewish Feminist: A Reader,* ed. Susannah Heschel (New York: Schocken Books, 1983).

22. Cf. Perry Anderson, *Considerations on Western Marxism* (London: New Left Books, 1978).

23. Miriam Peskowitz, *Spinning Fantasies: Rabbis, Gender and History* (Berkeley: University of California Press, 1997).

24. See Charles Taylor, *Sources of the Self: The Making of the Modern Identity* (Cambridge, Mass.: Harvard University Press, 1989).

25. Peskowitz, *Spinning Fantasies,* 23.

26. Cf. Jacob Neusner, *Invitation to the Talmud* (New York: Harper Collins, 1989).

27. Peskowitz, *Spinning Fantasies,* 185, n.11.

28. Cf. Iris Young, cited in Rosemarie Tong, *Feminist Thought: A More Comprehensive Introduction,* 2nd ed., 122–23.

29. Zeev Safrai, *The Economy of Roman Palestine* (London: Routledge, 1994).

30. Peskowitz, *Spinning Fantasies,* 50.

31. Ibid., 63.

32. Ibid., 185, n.9.

33. Ibid., 64.

34. Ibid., 15.

35. Ibid., 76.

36. Ibid.

37. Daniel Boyarin, *Carnal Israel: Reading Sex in Talmudic Culture* (Berkeley: University of California Press, 1993), 13.

38. Ibid.

39. Cf. Hayden White, "New Historicism: A Comment," in *The New Historicism,* ed. H. Aram Veeser (New York: Routledge, 1989).

40. Boyarin, *Carnal Israel,* 18.

41. Ibid., 16–17.

42. Ibid., 29.

43. Ibid.

44. Ibid., 143.

45. I owe this phrase to Prof. Aryeh Cohen, in conversation.

46. MacKinnon, *Toward a Feminist Theory of State,* Chapter 7.

47. Jameson, *Postmodernism,* 174.

48. Cf. Catherine Gallagher, "Marxism and the New Historicism," in *The New Historicism,* ed. H. Aram Veeser (New York: Routledge, 1989).

49. Susan Shapiro, "A Matter of Discipline: Reading for Gender in Jewish Philosophy," in *Judaism since Gender,* ed. Miriam Peskowitz and Laura Levitt (New York: Routledge, 1997).

50. Ibid., 166.

51. Maimonides, *Guide for the Perplexed,* in *A Maimonides Reader,* ed. I. Twersky (New York: Behrman House, 1972), 264.

52. Cf. Susan Haack, "Dry Truth and Real Knowledge: Epistemology of Metaphor and Metaphors of Epistemology," in *Aspects of Metaphor,* ed. Jaako Hintikka (Dordrecht: Kluwer Academic Publishers, 1994).

53. Theodor Adorno, *Minima Moralia,* cited in Fredric Jameson, *Late Marxism: Adorno; or, The Persistence of the Dialectic* (London: Verso, 1990), 47.

FIVE

LEORA BATNITZKY

Dependency and Vulnerability: Jewish and Feminist Existentialist Constructions of the Human

Martin Buber, Franz Rosenzweig, and Emmanuel Levinas describe the human being as dependent and vulnerable. Significantly, each of these philosophers uses gendered terms to make his arguments. This essay describes the ways in which their Jewish existentialist accounts of what it means to be human have a number of important affinities with contemporary "women-centered" feminist philosophies, and feminist philosophies of care more specifically.

Within feminist circles, "women-centered" arguments are diverse and contested. Some feminist thinkers argue that "woman" is wholly separate from "man," while others are more inclusive. Particularly controversial is a strand of contemporary "women-centered" thought that associates "women" and "the feminine" with "mothering." Some feminists claim that this line of thought is reactionary, relegating women to the very roles from which the women's movement hoped to emancipate them. Feminist philosophers arguing in favor of "mothering"—to whom I will refer for the sake of brevity as "feminist philosophers of care"—respond by maintaining that such a conception of "women" and "the feminine" has critical if not transformative value not only for feminist thought but also for moral and political theory at large.[1]

Unlike feminist philosophers of care, Buber, Rosenzweig, and Levinas use the terms *feminine, women, mother, maternity,* and *pregnancy,* with few, if any, qualifications.[2] While they make it clear that these terms could to varying degrees be applied to men as well as to women, they do not engage critically with the meanings of these terms for the purposes of feminist thought. Nonetheless, these Jewish philosophers share some important philosophical arguments with feminist philosophers of care. Like contemporary feminist philosophers of care, Buber, Rosenzweig, and Levinas seek to elucidate a notion of the self who is not wholly autonomous but who is dependent on others and responsive to the vulnerability of others. Like feminist philosophers of care, Buber, Rosenzweig, and Levinas suggest that ethics and responsibility emerge from human dependence and vulnerability. And like feminist philosophers of care, Buber, Rosenzweig, and Levinas describe human dependence and response to vulnerability as "feminine" in character, and in fact as a kind of "mothering."

In the first two parts of this essay, I argue that contemporary feminist philosophy can help us to understand better both the philosophical functions of and historical reasons for the use of gendered terms in modern Jewish philosophy. In the third part of the essay, I contend that the account of the human as dependent and vulnerable is philosophically and politically valuable. However, I suggest that, perhaps ironically, the notion of "the feminine"[3] attached to Jewish existentialist and feminist views of the human as dependent and vulnerable undermines the critical value of this construction of the human, for historical, philosophical, and political reasons. In the conclusion, I consider a number of alternatives to considering dependency and vulnerability as fundamental to what it means to be human, without calling these characteristics "feminine."

I. Receptivity and Subjectivity: Judaism, Ethics, and "the Feminine"

The "existentialism" of Jean Paul Sartre and Simone de Beauvoir is predicated on a philosophical affirmation of a human subject that bestows meaning onto the world. Applying existentialist philosophy to feminist thought, de Beauvoir criticized in particular the notion that woman is man's *other.*[4] It is a rethinking if not a rejection of de Beauvoir's radically individualist and voluntaristic outlook of the human subject, or indeed the very view that de Beauvoir advocates such an individualist and voluntaristic view, that mark important if contested trends in recent feminist philosophy.[5] Many recent feminist philosophers both in the European continent and in the United States have insisted instead that *woman* is truly other and that an elucidation of her otherness should orient not only feminist theory but moral and political philosophy as well. These "women-centered" feminist philosophies are themselves rather diverse—some of them call for a separation between men and women, some of them are inclusive and less essentialist—but what they have in common is the notion that there is a distinctively "women's" experience that calls into question "male" accounts of experience, accounts that contrast with the "male" project of self-constitution.[6]

While these diverse "women-centered" feminist theories take as their starting point the rejection of a certain type of existentialist subjectivity, the premises of this line of thought nonetheless share in another strand of philosophical existentialism, which emphasizes the fundamentally receptive nature of human being.[7] Jewish existentialist thinkers such as Buber, Rosenzweig, and Levinas focus on the philosophical import of the particularities and vulnerabilities of human existence. These Jewish existentialist thinkers have a greater affinity with contemporary "women-centered" feminist philosophies and with feminist philosophies of care more particularly than they do with either Sartre's or de Beauvoir's existentialism, which focus on the process of self-constitution. Indeed, Buber, Rosenzweig, and Levinas maintain, like a number of rather diverse "women-centered" feminist philosophies, that the process of self-constitution is inherently "male." Most basically, these Jewish philosophers and contemporary feminist philosophers of care agree that the fundamental experience of relationality grounds existence. As Levinas puts it:

> Contemporary philosophy denounces as an abstraction the subject closed in upon itself and metaphysically the origin of the world. The consistency of the self is dissolved in relations: intentionality in Husserl, being-in-the-world or *Miteinandersein* in Heidegger, or continual renewal of *durée* in Bergson. Concrete reality is man always already in relation with the world, or always already projected beyond his instant. These relations cannot be reduced to theoretical representation. The latter would only confirm the autonomy of the thinking subject. In order to demolish the idea of the subject closed in upon itself, one must uncover, beneath objectification very different relations that sustain it: man in situation before situating himself.[8]

Levinas emphasizes here a view of the human subject who is both active and passive. As we will see in greater detail, Levinas argues that it is in the passive capacity of the human being that we find our ethical relation to others. Levinas, following Rosenzweig and Buber, suggests that this passive capacity, the locus of ethics, is fundamentally "feminine" in nature. Many contemporary American feminist philosophers of care have emphasized this same connection between receptivity, care, and "the feminine." Drawing on the philosophy of Martin Buber throughout her work, Nel Noddings, one of the most articulate proponents of what she calls "a feminine ethics of care," puts it this way:

> The receptive mode is at the heart of human existence. By "existence" or "existing," I mean more than merely living or subsisting. When existentialist philosophers refer to "existence," they mean to include an awareness of and commitment to what we are doing, what we are living. . . . Existence involves, then, living with heightened awareness.[9]

In the philosophies of Buber, Rosenzweig, and Levinas, the receptivity of the human being gives meaning not only to ethics but also to the relationship between the Jewish people and God. Each in his own way argues that the receptive capacity of this relationship is what defines Judaism, making it relevant not only for Jewish people but for all philosophical and ethical thinking. Significantly, Buber, Rosenzweig, and Levinas all use notions of "the feminine" to make their respective cases for defining the human as receptive, dependent, and vulnerable to the encounter with other people and God.

Buber is probably best known for his dialogical philosophy. Simply put, Buber maintains that there are two fundamental types of relation: the I-It which is purely instrumental and objectifies the other as object and the I-Thou which treats the other as subject to which the I responds and by which the I is transformed. Perhaps more profoundly, Buber regards the I-Thou relation as the true meaning of being (*Wesen*).[10] As Buber puts it in *I and Thou*, "In the beginning is the relation—as the category of being, as readiness, as a form that reaches out to be filled, as a model of the soul; the *a priori* of relation; *the innate You.*"[11] Significantly, Buber describes this fundamental relationality with reference to "the womb of the great mother":

> Every developing human child rests, like all developing beings, in the womb of the great mother [*im Schoß des großen Mutter*]—the undifferentiated, not yet formed primal world. From this it detaches itself to enter a personal life, and it is only in dark hours when we slip out of this again (as happens even to the healthy, night after night) that we are close to her again.[12]

For Buber, however, this primal relation to the womb of the great mother is nonetheless immature and differs from the mature I-Thou relation that comes only after the separation from the great mother and the formation of I-It relations. The I-Thou relation thus involves freedom and commitment, which are not present in the immature relation. Significantly, when Buber writes of the mature I-Thou relation, he does so as a male speaker:

> When a man loves a woman so that her life is present in his own, the You of her eyes allows him to gaze into a ray of the eternal You. But if a man lusts after the "ever repeated triumph"—you want to dangle before his lust a phantom of the eternal?[13]

The primal relation to the womb of the great mother thus makes possible first the separation from the mother into the I-It world and then the free male's mature confirmation of the Thou.

Yet Buber's I-Thou relation is not so one-sided. As he describes at great length, the I-Thou relation is one of mutuality and reciprocity: "Relation is reciprocity. My You acts on me as I act on it. . . . Inscrutably involved, we live in the currents of universal reciprocity."[14] It is for the lack of reciprocity that Buber criticizes Heidegger's notion of *Fürsorge,* care for others:

> In mere solicitude [*Fürsorge*] man remains essentially with himself, even if he is moved with extreme pity; in action and help he inclines towards the other . . . he [does not] accept any real mutuality, in fact he probably shuns it; he is "concerned with the other," but he is not anxious for the other to be concerned with him.[15]

In order to appreciate Levinas's more radical notion of the dialogical situation and its implications for his understanding of "the feminine," we must appreciate his criticism of Buber precisely on this point. Levinas criticizes Buber for his insistence on mutuality, maintaining that the dialogical relation is fundamentally asymmetrical in character. Ethics, for Levinas, is not about mutuality but about a one-sided responsibility. In Levinas's now well-known words paraphrasing Dostoevsky, "the I always has one responsibility more than all others."[16]

Prefacing his remarks with the qualification that "It is not, surely, to Heidegger that one should turn to for instruction in the love of man or social justice," Levinas defends Heidegger against Buber on the issue of care and mutuality:

> But *Fürsorge,* as response to essential destitution, is a mode of access to the otherness of the Other. . . . But Buber allows himself to say "All dialogue draws its authenticity from consciousness of the element of *Umfassung* [embracing]." [Yet] Consciousness reappears behind *Umfassung.* . . . Relation itself, apart from its goal, differs from knowledge.[17]

Levinas's point here is important for an appreciation of the fundamental direction of his own thought as well as for understanding his relation to contemporary feminist philosophies of care. The dialogical relation, Levinas maintains, is both non-cognitive and not reciprocal. Here Levinas is in agreement with Noddings's feminine ethic of care, which maintains that "an ethic of caring locates morality primarily in the pre-act of consciousness of the one-caring."[18] Moreover, Levinas is in agreement with Noddings's statement that "To demand such responsiveness is both futile and inconsistent with caring. The one-caring is motivated in the direction of the cared-for and she must, therefore, respect his freedom. She meets him as subject—not as object to be manipulated nor as a data source."[19]

It is precisely a notion of "the feminine" that Levinas uses to describe this non-cognitive and non-reciprocal relation. Levinas's constructions of Judaism and "the feminine" serve as fundamental components of his effort to offer an ethical critique of what he argues are modernity's totalizing tendencies. Just as Levinas claims that Judaism (or Hebrew) destroys philosophy's (or the Greek) quest for totality, so too he argues that "the feminine" resists the logos quest for the universal: "To overcome an alienation which, fundamentally, arises from the very virility of the universal and conquering logos, and which stalks even the shadows that could have sheltered it—such would be the ontological function of the feminine."[20] Levinas makes two claims about the "feminine." The first is in his first major philosophical work *Totality and Infinity* (1961) in which he describes the role of "the feminine" in what we might call the economy of morality. The second claim is in his second major work, *Otherwise than Being or Beyond Existence* (1974), in which he describes, I shall argue, "the feminine" as ethics itself.

Levinas's first description of "the feminine" is in keeping with Buber's notion of the womb of the great mother as the source of an independent person who is capable of responding to the other. In Part Two of *Totality and Infinity*, Levinas suggests that "the feminine" is the condition for ethics: "The woman is the condition for recollection, the interiority of the Home, the inhabitation."[21] "The feminine" creates the home so that the pre-ethical, independent man can leave it and become ethical. In this sense, "the feminine" functions as the pre-condition of the condition of ethics (the independent "man" who is capable of becoming ethical). In Part Four of *Totality and Infinity*, "the feminine" is not the pre-condition of the condition of ethics but is now the condition itself. Levinas argues that the erotic encounter with the feminine other is a necessary prerequisite for ethics:

> [T]he encounter with the Other as feminine is required in order that the future of the child come to pass from beyond the possible, beyond projects.

> The relationship resembles that which was described for the idea of infinity: I cannot account for it by myself, as I do account for the luminous world by myself. . . . The relation with such a future, irreducible to the power over possibles, we shall call fecundity.[22]

Though Levinas calls voluptuosity the "future in the present," the encounter with the feminine other remains "an irresponsible animality which does not speak true words."[23] Nonetheless, this irresponsible animality literally produces an ethics of responsibility, which is embodied in the relationship between parent and child. Significantly, this relationship is not a gender neutral one. Levinas writes: "This alteration and identification in fecundity—beyond the possible and the face—constitutes paternity. In paternity desire maintained as insatiate desire, that is, as goodness, is accomplished."[24] Once again, the feminine other makes ethics possible but does not participate in the realm which she literally creates. Here Levinas's analysis of "the feminine" parallels aspects of the psychologist Carol Gilligan's description of the way women and men understand "women's morality":

> [W]omen not only define themselves in a context of human relationship but also judge themselves in terms of their ability to care. Women's place in man's life cycle has been that of nurturer, caretaker, and helpmate, the weaver of those networks of relationships on which she in turn relies.[25]

Perhaps in response to feminist criticisms of his view of "the feminine" in *Totality and Infinity,* most notably from Simone de Beauvoir,[26] Levinas seems to change the direction of his argument in *Otherwise than Being,* arguing there, as I will detail below, that "the feminine" is not merely the basis for ethics but ethics itself. Yet attention to contemporary feminist philosophies of care shows, I think, that the direction of his argument does not actually change but rather intensifies. The progression of Levinas's thought about "the feminine" shares in the general direction of feminist philosophers of care who have argued that the care of mothers is and should be the basis of all ethics. Indeed, Levinas's complex phenomenological formulations of "the feminine" and "maternity" find more colloquial expression in, for example, the feminist philosopher Virginia Held's arguments about the ethics of maternity:

> The feelings characteristic of mothering—that there are too many demands on us, that we cannot do everything we ought to do—are highly instructive. They give rise to problems different from those of universal rule vs. self-interest. They require us to weigh the claims of one self-other relationship against the claims of other self-other relationships, to try to bring about

some harmony between them, to see the issues in an actual temporal context, and to act rather than merely reflect.[27]

We will see that Levinas's arguments share three important features with Held's characterization of mothering. First, Levinas uses "maternity" to show that ethics is an infinite task ("that we cannot do everything we ought to do"). Second, he uses "maternity" to refigure the relation between the self and other. And third, and most basically, Levinas uses "maternity" to highlight the priority of praxis over theory within philosophy.

We have seen already that Levinas's ethical theory describes ethics as a kind of "natural" relation that become ethical. The "natural" relation to "the feminine," first in the home and then between lovers, provides the basis for ethics. Levinas's argument about the "natural feminine" precondition for ethics is intensified in *Otherwise than Being*. Levinas's arguments about "the feminine" and "maternity" are in accord with Noddings's statement that "Ethical caring, the relation in which we do meet the other morally, will be described as arising out of natural caring—that relation in which we respond as one caring out of love or natural inclination."[28]

Catherine Chalier has commented on the highly significant role that "the feminine" plays in *Otherwise than Being or Beyond Essence,* and I follow her in asserting that in *Otherwise than Being,* "the feminine" is not merely a condition for ethics, but ethics itself.[29] *Otherwise than Being* turns directly to questions of material existence in order to describe the phenomenality of ethics as first philosophy, as Levinas states that "Signification, the-one-for-the-other, has meaning only among beings of flesh and blood."[30] It is by way of the attempt to think deeply about questions of materiality that we find some of Levinas's most provocative and perplexing statements about what it means to exist as a being oriented by ethics. Ethics, Levinas suggests, must be understood in material terms. Ethics is "to give to the Other . . . a gift of my own skin." Responsibility is "a denuding, an exposure to being affected, a pure susceptiveness."[31] Reference to "maternity" is a fundamental component of Levinas's attempt at articulating the materiality of the ethical, human task.

Again, Levinas argues that "the I always has one responsibility more than all others."[32] Responsibility is excessive and, as Levinas argues in *Otherwise than Being,* each "I" must "bear the wretchedness and bankruptcy of the Other, and even the responsibility that the Other can have for me."[33] In one of his most provocative statements, Levinas suggests that to bear the "wretchedness and bankruptcy of the Other" is to "bear responsibility for the persecuting by the persecutor." It is maternity that gives material meaning to this perplexing statement. Levinas writes:

Is not the restlessness of someone persecuted but a modification of maternity, the groaning of the wounded entrails by those it will bear or has borne? In maternity what signifies is a responsibility for others, to the point of substitution for others and suffering both from the effect of persecution and from the persecuting itself in which the persecutor sinks. Maternity, which is bearing par excellence, bears even responsibility for the persecuting by the persecutor.[34]

Maternity, for Levinas, is the flesh and blood of the one-for-the-other. It is in fact maternity that gives meaning to Levinas's at times equally perplexing references to "incarnation":

Incarnation is not a transcendental operation of a subject that is situated in the midst of the world it represents to itself; the sensible experience of the body is already and from the start incarnate. The sensible—maternity, vulnerability, apprehension—binds the node of incarnation into a plot larger than the apperception of self. In this plot I am bound to others before being tied to my body.[35]

In maternity, the body exists for the sake of the other. Of course, the body being referred to here is not just any body; it is a female body. The embodied disembodiment of maternity *is,* for Levinas, the flesh and blood of the one-for-the-other. Here, in *Otherwise than Being,* "the feminine" is no longer a condition of ethics, but ethics itself. In maternity, the natural becomes ethical.

On the one hand, Levinas's philosophical formulation of maternity is in keeping with Sara Ruddick's comment that "Maternal practice begins with a double vision—seeing the fact of biological vulnerability as socially significant and as demanding care."[36] Yet Ruddick differs from Levinas in maintaining that she "deliberately stress[es] the optional character first of perceiving 'vulnerability' and then of responding with care. Maternal responses are complicated acts that social beings make to biological beings whose existence is inseparable from social interpretations."[37] Levinas's difference from Ruddick is also broadly speaking his difference from Buber. Levinas argues that maternal caring is not an option, nor is it reciprocal. I cannot (ethically) choose to turn away from the vulnerability of the other, nor can I expect any response from the other. Where Ruddick deliberately emphasizes that maternal caring is "one kind of disciplined reflection . . . with identifying questions, methods, and aims," Levinas is emphatic that what he describes as "maternity" is non-reflective in character. "Maternity" is concerned neither with identifying questions, nor with methods and aims. Rather, "maternity" is an unchosen responsibility that chooses me.

While Levinas goes to great lengths, especially in some of his later essays, to emphasize that what he calls "ethics" not only requires but grounds justice, he maintains nonetheless that caring for the other is and must be the primary ethical orientation of the human being.[38] Indeed, Levinas's description of ethics shares with Noddings's the general suspicion that ethics of principle are, to use Noddings's words, "ambiguous and unstable" and that "when we must use violence or strategies on the other, we are already diminished ethically. Our efforts must, then, be directed to the maintenance of conditions that permit caring to flourish."[39] Levinas and Noddings do not reject instrumental thinking in ethics outright. Their argument, instead, is that ethics (or caring) orients principles. When principles are said to orient ethics, ethics is destroyed. In Noddings's words, "Instrumental thinking may, of course enhance caring; that is, I may use my reasoning powers to figure out what to do once I have committed myself to doing something. But clearly, rationality (in its objective form) does not of necessity mark either the initial impulse or the action that is undertaken."[40] In Levinas's words, "Every love or every hatred of a neighbor as a reflected attitude presupposes this prior vulnerability, this mercy, this 'groaning of the entrails.'"[41] Significantly, Levinas notes that his use of the term *mercy* in the above quotation is in keeping with the rabbinic term *rahamin*, which also means "womb": "[I]t is a mercy that is like an emotion of maternal entrails."[42] Once again, we see the intimate connection between Levinas's arguments about the nature of vulnerability, "mothering," and ethics, arguments that we have seen resonate with much of Noddings's writings. It is important to note that other feminist philosophers of care, such as Ruddick and Joan Tronto, have criticized Noddings for this very position that she shares with Levinas that denies the fundamentally reflective character of "mothering." We will return to some of these arguments in the conclusion of this essay.

II. Articulating Philosophy's "Other" in Gendered Terms: Why?

We have seen that Buber and Levinas use notions of "the feminine" to articulate their dialogical philosophies that also purport to criticize aspects of the Western philosophical tradition that deny the fundamental ethical relation between people. Some recent discussions amongst feminist philosophers can help us to begin to think about why Jewish philosophers use "the feminine" in this way. Let me begin by saying that I don't think Levinas uses "the feminine" because he is any way concerned about articulating a "women's morality" or because he is concerned with actual women.[43] He is not. As we have seen, he is concerned with articulating a notion of ethics that is pre-cognitive and that cannot be subordinated to consciousness. As a number of feminist philosophers, including Annette Baier, Selya Benhabib, and Joan Tronto have pointed out, modern philosophical articulations of ethics after Kant focus on the rationality of ethics.[44] These feminist thinkers have John Rawls's *Theory of Justice* at the forefront of their arguments, but their criticism of a notion of morality limited to rational agents is one that has an important affinity with what Levinas maintains is Western philosophy's totalizing tendency to deny care for the other. Indeed, Levinas's contrast between "Hebrew" and "Greek" is premised on his argument that philosophy ("Greek") silences the cries of the stranger, orphan, and the widow, whose cares are the primary orientation of Judaism ("Hebrew").

As Benhabib, along with Carole Pateman, Marilyn Friedman, and Lorraine Code, have argued, the focus on moral agents in the history of modern moral and political philosophy has the effect of *privatizing* women's experience.[45] In Benhabib's words:

> [T]he definition of moral autonomy . . . in universalistic, contractarian theories from Hobbes to Rawls, lead to a *privatization* of women's experience and to the exclusion of its consideration from a moral point of view. In this tradition, the moral self is viewed as a *disembedded* and *disembodied* being.[46]

It is important to see that the privatization of women's experience begins historically with the privatization of religion and notions of the good. This double privatization has the effect of placing concerns about the good and caring into the private realm while leaving only discussion of justice in the realm of public discourse.[47] As Benhabib puts it, "Justice alone becomes the center of moral theory when bourgeois individuals in a disenchanted universe face the task of creating the legitimate basis of the social order for themselves."[48] The contours of Jewish modernity and its relation to the privatization of religion and women's experience deserve special consideration, which are obviously beyond the scope of this essay.[49] Nevertheless, I think we can fairly say in the context of Benhabib's analysis that it should not be surprising that when a modern Jewish philosopher such as Levinas attempts to bring a philosophical account of Judaism ("Hebrew") into philosophical discourse, then he should do so by reference to "the feminine"—for both "Judaism" and "the feminine" have come to represent spheres of morality that have been silenced by philosophy's modern concern with rationality and calculable justice.

In the next section, I turn to the problem of Levinas's as well as Rosenzweig's and Buber's uncritical use of gendered terms (such as *the feminine,* and *maternity*). For now I would like to continue to focus on how Benhabib's analysis helps us not only to account for Levinas's use of "the feminine" in his account of ethics but also for the theological background of his arguments. Here I suggest that we look at the theological use to which a notion of "the feminine" is put to use in the philosophy of Franz Rosenzweig, Levinas's self-acknowledged most important influence.[50] Attention to two aspects of the analysis of care in recent feminist philosophy helps us appreciate the ways in which Levinas's use of "the feminine" is a de-theologized and de-politicized version of Rosenzweig's arguments about the relation between Judaism and Christianity.

First, as Gilligan and a number of feminist philosophers of care have noted, the care orientation of women is, in developmental psychology, political theory and indeed Western philosophy, subordinated to "male" moral reasoning.[51] Feminist philosophers of care attempt to argue that care is not an immature relation but the primary relation that itself grounds morality. I suggest that Rosenzweig uses a similar strategy in arguing against Christian supersessionism. Using "feminine" metaphors to describe Judaism, Rosenzweig maintains that Judaism, contrary to Christian opinion, is the complete revelation, to which Christian revelation is eternally trying to catch up.

Second, Rosenzweig's arguments about Jewish eternity as opposed to Christian worldliness are similarly couched in gendered terms. Here, too, Rosenzweig relies on a notion of "the feminine" to describe what he argues is the Jewish experience of "eternity in time." As Benhabib puts it, "The private sphere, the sphere of care and intimacy, is unchanging and timeless. . . . The dehistoricization of the private realm signifies that, as the male ego celebrates his passage from nature to culture, from conflict to consensus, women remain in a timeless universe, condemned to repeat the cycles of life."[52] My suggestion is that in the post-Holocaust era, Levinas relies on Rosenzweig's explicitly theological thought and turns his notions of Judaism and "the feminine" into an interpersonal ethic. Levinas represents the ethical obligation to the other as the eternal mark of humanity while Rosenzweig describes the Jewish people as themselves living this timeless ethic for the sake of others.

Rosenzweig's use of gender is perhaps most blatant in Book Two of Part Two of the *Star,* in the section on revelation in which his analysis of the Song of Songs also appears. Rosenzweig begins this section with an argument not only about an abstract feminine element but also with an argument about real women. He begins by quoting the Song of Songs:

> Love is as strong as death [Song of Songs 8:6]. Strong in the same way as death? But against whom does death display its strength? Against him

whom it seizes. . . . The beloved is seized, her love is already a response to being seized. . . . Initially it is for the beloved that love is strong as death, even as nature has decreed that woman alone, not man, may die of love. What has been said of the twofold encounter of man and his self applies strictly and universally only to the male. As for woman, and precisely the most feminine woman above all, even Thanatos can approach her in the sweet guise of Eros. Her life is simpler than that of man by reason of this missing contradiction. Already in the tremors of love her heart has become firm. It no longer needs the tremor of death. A young woman can be as ready for eternity as a man only becomes when his threshold is crossed by Thanatos. . . . Once touched by Eros, a woman is what man only becomes at the Faustian age of a hundred: ready for the final encounter—strong as death.[53]

Before offering an interpretation of this very strange passage, I want to point out that even within the *Star*'s own context, this reference to real women, and to "the most feminine women above all," is deeply perplexing. A bit further on, Rosenzweig seems to contradict his own statement. He writes:

Between man and woman the roles of giver and receiver of love pass back and forth, the higher the blossoms which the plant of love generates between them, the more that it rises above itself and its subterranean roots like a veritable palm-tree, although the roots of sexuality ever restore the unambiguous relationship to nature.[54]

Though maintaining a reference to an "unambiguous relationship to nature," Rosenzweig suggests here, in seeming contradiction to his comments at the beginning of Part Two, Book Two, that the roles of masculine lover and feminine beloved are not literally confined to men and women. Here, as opposed to the earlier passage, the implication seems to be that "male and female," "masculine and feminine," are being used metaphorically.

The only way to resolve this contradiction, in my view, is to recognize the connection between the argument for revelation in Part Two of the *Star* and Rosenzweig's construction of Judaism in Part Three. While Rosenzweig does use "feminine" and "masculine" metaphorically to suggest the give and take of a romantic encounter, it is no accident that he also uses "feminine" and "masculine," and indeed "woman" and "man," in a consciously literal way. For Rosenzweig, while all people are capable of participating in a dialogical relation, and while "masculine" and "feminine" can apply to both men and women, the Jewish people, like real women, have a special, ontological share in revelation. The argument about real women that he makes in Part Two of the *Star* is intimately connected to the argument that Rosenzweig makes in Part Three, about the reality of the Jewish people. Real women, who are not reducible to a metaphorical "feminine," function for Rosenzweig in this text as a foil for real Jews.

Recall Rosenzweig's statement: "Once touched by Eros, a woman is what man only becomes at the Faustian age of a hundred: ready for the final encounter—strong as death." What does it mean for a woman to be ready for eternity in a way that a man is not? And how might this readiness for eternity relate to being "strong as death"?

For Rosenzweig, a woman is a priori ready for eternity just as the Jewish people are a priori eternal. Just as Rosenzweig argues that a woman has already reached the goal towards which a man is always striving—again, " a woman is what a man only becomes at the Faustian age of a hundred: ready for the final encounter—strong as death"—so too does Rosenzweig argue against Christian supersessionist arguments that "The Jewish people has already reached the goal toward which the nations are still moving."[55] The Jewish people, like the "most feminine woman," are naturally disposed to revelation. I use the word *naturally* because Rosenzweig's argument about the Jewish people, as is well known, is an argument about the "true nature" of the Jewish people, which is found, he argues, in the natural substance of Jewish blood. In the *Star,* Rosenzweig suggests that just as her sexual nature prepares a woman for the final encounter with the other, so too the blood running through Jewish veins prepares the way for the Jews' eternity. In the case of both actual women and actual Jewish people, Rosenzweig argues that the "natural" provides a kind of transcendental condition for the supernatural. A woman embodies a natural openness to the supernatural realm of love, just as Jews embody in their blood God's revelation to them.

Rosenzweig's constructions of "the feminine" woman and the Jewish people are even more intimately connected. In fact, though he does not use the word *maternity*, Rosenzweig's understanding of Judaism is expressed precisely through an explicit reference to pregnancy. He writes as follows:

> For it [the Jewish community] alone the future is not something alien but something of its own, something it carries in its womb [*Schoße*] and which might be born any day. While every other community that lays claim to eternity must take measures to pass the torch of the present on to the future, the blood-community does not have to resort to such measures. It does not have to hire the services of the spirit; the natural propagation of the body guarantees it eternity.[56]

As in Levinas, pregnancy, or maternity, is used by Rosenzweig as *the* expression of the natural moving beyond the realm of being. And as for Levinas, for Rosenzweig pregnancy, or maternity, is so powerful because of the particular sense of embodied disembodiment that it represents.

Rosenzweig's claim that Judaism is a blood community is in necessary conjunction with his claim that Judaism is *not* a community oriented by land. Recall the famous words from the *Star:* "To the eternal people, home never is home in the sense of land, as it is to the peoples of the world who plough the land and live and thrive on it, until they have all but forgotten that being a people (*Volk*) means something besides being rooted in a land."[57] For Rosenzweig, the eternal people are a people in exile. Rooted not in land but in blood, the Jewish people exist in a state of embodied disembodiment. The natural propagation of the Jewish body guarantees it eternity, but the Jewish people remain physically dispersed in exile.

Though Rosenzweig is more explicit about the theological dimension of Judaism's embodied disembodiment, his claims also have—to be anachronistic for a moment—a Levinasian ethical dimension to them. For Rosenzweig, the meaning of the eternal people's embodied disembodiment is found in Israel's role as witness to the nations. He writes "Israel intercedes with him [God] in behalf of the sinning peoples of the world and he afflicts Israel with disease so that those other peoples may be healed. Both stand before God: Israel, his servant, and the kings of the peoples; . . . so inextricably twined that human hands cannot untangle them."[58] For the sake of the nations, Jews literally bear the burden of homelessness. For Rosenzweig, Judaism disembodies itself in order to propel the nations toward redemption, in order to make the world a better place.

The similarity between this claim and Levinas's claim that responsibility is bearing responsibility even for the persecutor is striking. Indeed, Levinas makes the explicit link between an ethics of embodied disembodiment and martyrdom when he states "Signification is witness or martyrdom."[59] For both Levinas and Rosenzweig, it is the construction of "the feminine," and the explicit references to maternity and pregnancy, that allow for the development of an ethics or theology of embodied disembodiment, of the natural becoming supernatural, of the natural becoming ethical.

We have already seen that Rosenzweig uses a notion of "the feminine" in order to argue against Christian supersessionism. His gendering of the Jewish–Christian relation goes even deeper. Rosenzweig contrasts Judaism as the feminized, rootless other that has contributed to the creation of Christian masculine culture:

> Christian life leads the Christian into the outside. The rays radiate evermore, till all the outside shall be irradiated. Jewish life is just the opposite. Birth, the whole natural Here, the natural individuality, the impartible participation in the world—already exists here. . . . The Christian way

becomes expression and expropriation and irradiation of the outmost, while Jewish life becomes memory and internalization of the innermost.[60]

Judaism is not just "feminine," but in remaining homeless "she" makes Christianity and the nations of the world more "feminine." By not allowing Christianity to become totalitarian, Judaism forces Christianity to remain somewhat rootless and thereby more "feminine," Jewish, and ethical. Again, my suggestion is that in the post-Holocaust era, Levinas relies on Rosenzweig's explicitly theological thought and turns his notions of Judaism and "the feminine" into an interpersonal ethic. Instead of producing a blatant critique of Zionism and an argument for Jewish homelessness, Levinas presents an interpersonal ethic of homelessness, and feminine metaphors are again used to describe this condition. In the same way that, for Rosenzweig, Judaism exposes itself for the sake of the nations, each "I," for Levinas, exposes itself, to the point of disembodiment, for the sake of the other.

🏵 III. What to Say about "the Feminine"?

What should we say about the use of "the feminine" in the philosophies of the Jewish thinkers examined here? We have already seen that contemporary feminist theory helps us to understand better the ways in which "the feminine" functions within the philosophies of the Jewish thinkers considered in this essay. But can we say that their notions of "the feminine" have any critical value? In my reading, Buber's, Rosenzweig's, and Levinas's use of "the feminine" does much of the same moral work as it does in feminist philosophies of care. The broad, shared claim of these two sets of thinkers is that something characterized by "the feminine" represents an ethic of caring in which responsibility is excessive, not contractual, and, at least at its most basic level, profoundly non-cognitive in nature. It is no doubt significant that Buber, Rosenzweig, and Levinas offer no account of their use of their gendered terms—a significance to which I turn below. And while feminist philosophers are no doubt more sophisticated in their use of these gendered terms, I would like to suggest that the equations of Judaism and "the feminine" *and* of women and "the feminine" are historically problematic and therefore philosophically problematic.

To begin with, both of these equations obscure the ways in which differences are really different. Ironically, the equations of women and "the feminine" and of Judaism and "the feminine" both undermine the broader shared philosophical goal of the Jewish philosophers under consideration here as well as feminist philosophies of care, which is to take philosophically seriously the particularities of existence. In the case of feminist philosophy, the goal of this philosophical approach is both positive and negative: to appreciate philosophically the forms of life particular to women but also to appreciate the ways in which these same forms of life have contributed to women's oppression. In the case of Jewish "existentialist" philosophy, the goal of this philosophical approach is to appreciate the nature of praxis for philosophical reflection and the ways in which a de-emphasis on praxis obscures the vitality of the Jewish tradition. The conception of the human as dependent and vulnerable offered in both of these analyses is philosophically valuable and important for ethics, but this importance is undermined by the use of "the feminine."

Sandra Harding has commented on the strangeness of the comparison between what are called "feminine" and "African" moralities.[61] As Harding notes, both African morality and feminine morality are said to be primarily relational as opposed to rule-oriented, and significantly both "world views" link "nature" with morality. Harding argues that this strange confluence ought to give us pause in two ways. First, we should be wary of the kind of a-historical reductionism that posits essentialized views of "the feminine" or "the African," for such reductionism obscures the differences within both "the feminine" and "the African." Second, the fact that what is claimed to be essentially "feminine" is also claimed to be essentially "African" should give us pause in attempting to link biology to philosophical world views.[62] The seeming confluence between "Jewish" and "feminine" world views should equally give us pause, even more so than the comparison between "African" and "feminine" world views, because in the former case, as opposed to the latter, the claim is that "the Jewish" *is* "the feminine." The historical and therefore philosophical absurdity created by this double identification should make us very wary indeed.

Yet despite this very profound problem, I suggest nonetheless that engaging Jewish existentialist philosophical constructions of "the feminine" is philosophically useful for feminist philosophy and moral philosophy more broadly. Harding points to what she calls "the problem of metaphoric explanation—what the anthropologist Judith Shapiro has happily called gender totemism."[63] By this Harding means the dichotomies that are created by white European men and that are then perpetuated by the "others" of these dichotomies. Harding's point is to caution feminist and Africanist philosophers against internalizing and reifying white, Eurocentric views.[64]

Levinas and Rosenzweig were surely "white bourgeois men," but they were also Jewish men trying to articulate an alternate conception of philosophy and ethics from within the Western philosophical tradition that was historically largely Christian and hence in important ways anti-Jewish. We have already seen some of the ways in which much of Rosenzweig's argument about "the feminine" is an argument against Christian supersessionism. This Jewish philosophical appropriation of "the feminine" does have the constructive effect of calling into question the category of "white bourgeois men." Nonetheless, it would be too easy to conclude simply that the category of "white bourgeois men" is more complex than we might think. The reality to which the category refers is surely more complex than the category, as reality always is. What we see in regard to Levinas's, Rosenzweig's, and Buber's use of "the feminine" are some of the ways in which oppressed communities knowingly and unknowingly reproduce majority prejudices. Indeed, Sander Gilman has made precisely this point in regard to Freud's arguments about women. In an effort to dispel racial prejudice against Jews, Freud displaced these very biological and cultural arguments onto women.[65]

There is of course an important difference between Freud on the one hand, and Buber, Rosenzweig, and Levinas, on the other. Where Freud sought to displace everything negative onto "woman," Buber, Rosenzweig, and Levinas displace everything positive onto "her." Nonetheless, what these four have in common is their use of "the feminine" to define men. Without excusing Freud, Buber, Rosenzweig, and Levinas, we see that their use of gendered categories adds to our understanding of the complexity of the ways in which identities are constructed philosophically. At the very least, we must recognize that the uncritical use of gendered categories serves to obscure rather than illuminate this complexity. And part of task of feminist philosophy, it seems to me, is to shed light on the complex interplay of identity. In this sense, then, an engagement with the role of "the feminine" in Jewish philosophy is constructive for feminist philosophy.

But are these points generic—that categories themselves are always more complicated than they present themselves and that oppressed groups internalize the categories of their oppressors, often oppressing members of their own groups with these very categories? Or is there something to Jewish philosophy itself that may aid feminist theory and moral theory more broadly? I would like to suggest briefly that there is also a particular critical contribution of Jewish philosophy to feminist and moral philosophy.

As we saw in our brief discussion of Benhabib above, the privatization of women's life into a sphere of care was also historically a privatization of religious life. As the French feminist Julia Kristeva has put it, feminism is "situated within the very framework of the religious crisis of civilization."[66] Marilyn Chapin Massey expands Kristeva's point, arguing that "women-centered" feminists are saying that if Western woman, along with man, gave up a divinizing mirror, she would be left with man's science. She would be left hoping that someday she would be an equal partner in his projects of transcendence. . . . But women-centered feminists do not want to be left with man's science or his secular project of transcendence. . . . Not at home with their new identity as equals with men . . . women who have entered into the project of transcendence do not experience the joy of being free, autonomous subjects of history, but the pain of being split, divided subjects. . . . What they hope to discover . . . is not merely the virtues of nurture and intimacy as the necessary complements of man's ethics of transcendence and his definitions of justice and equality but a completely new, transformative ethic.[67]

Massey's description could well describe the Jewish philosophers under consideration here. They, too, are involved in the attempt to develop a "new, transformative ethic" that questions precisely the notions of autonomy, "man's science," and the "secular project of transcendence." It is in the particular contours of this transformative ethic that I believe something of value lies for the critical projects of feminist philosophy as well as moral philosophy. But while Massey's analysis is very useful, it nonetheless assumes and advances a Christian subtext. Her notion of "religion" to which "women-centered" philosophies respond and transform is, as she acknowledges, the Christian religion. I want merely to suggest that some aspects of "women-centered" philosophies remain entrenched (often unconsciously) in a kind of post-Christian rhetoric that aspects of Jewish philosophy can call into question.[68]

✿ IV. Conclusion: On Trying to Do without "the Feminine"

I have argued that, despite profound problems, an engagement with Jewish existentialist uses of "the feminine" contributes to discussions that concern feminist and moral philosophy. Nonetheless, I suggest, by way of conclusion, that Jewish philosophy and feminist philosophy would do better without the use of "the feminine." It is worth mentioning again that whatever shortcomings there are to feminist constructions of "woman" and "the feminine," these constructions arise at least within the context of an attempt to engage critically the complex social and political systems that constitute real women. No such disclaimer can be attributed to the Jewish existentialist philosophers under discussion here. Nonetheless, in a broad sense, the question for the Jewish and feminist philosophers under consideration here is the same: when does the notion of "the feminine" do more damage than it does critical work?

Joan Tronto has argued perhaps most persuasively that "we need to stop talking about 'women's morality' and start talking instead about a care ethic that includes the values traditionally associated with women."[69] Tronto rightly points out that, among other things, a notion of "women's morality" obscures the class divisions within contemporary American society that relegate the work of care to low-income groups and minorities. Moreover, Tronto points out that an exclusive emphasis on care leads to two major dangers: paternalism/maternalism and parochialism.[70] Nonetheless, she maintains that "Care is not a parochial concern of women, a type of secondary moral question, or the work of the least well off in society. Care is a central concern of human life. It is time that we began to change our political and social institutions to reflect this truth."[71] That we are all dependent and vulnerable means that ethics must be based upon this recognition.

As Tronto, Ruddick, and most recently Eva Feder Kittay argue, care as practice involves not only an acknowledgment of our mutual dependency and vulnerability, but also the recognition of the necessary social structures that allow for the cultivation of the moral possibilities and virtues of others.[72] "Mothering" does not end with the (albeit infinite) response to a crying child but with the raising of the child to independence. In different ways, Ruddick, Tronto, Kittay, and most recently drawing on the work of these feminist philosophers of care, Alasdair MacIntyre, have all advocated what might loosely be called a virtue ethic based on recognizing that the human being is fundamentally dependent and vulnerable.[73] These arguments are admirable on a number of counts. First, they seek to show that we are all dependent and vulnerable. Second, they maintain that the cultivation of virtue is necessary if members of a society are to care for those who are dependent and vulnerable. And third, they suggest that a virtuous society must strive to secure for all of its members precisely the possibilities for independence. While we are all at one time or another dependent and vulnerable, each of us should be given the opportunity and means to become an independent reasoner. A virtue approach to "maternity" saves "maternity" from essentialism. In so doing, feminist and Jewish philosophers do not confine women (and, as Tronto rightly points out, minorities and low-income groups) to positions of care, allowing these groups the possibilities of independence to which all citizens should be entitled.

We must return, though, to the question feminists often ask about feminist philosophers of care. Does a philosophy of care relegate women to the very roles from which the women's movement wants to provide potential freedom? And here we see the most basic consequence of Buber's, Rosenzweig's, and Levinas's uncritical use of "the feminine." In the end, these thinkers relegate women to the roles of mother and keeper of the home. Rosenzweig's and Levinas's traditionalism is particularly apt in this regard. It is not a coincidence that these two philosophers (and Rosenzweig more particularly) are considered more theologically "Jewish" than some of their more rationalist predecessors. Their view of the human being is post-liberal in questioning the most basic liberal assumption that human beings are naturally free and equal. We have seen that Rosenzweig and Levinas do not put equality among persons first but argue, as feminist philosophers of care do, that notions of equality are secondary to ethics. While there are profound if not essential differences between Jewish and feminist philosophy, they currently share the same underlying problem, which is to elucidate their respective relations to political liberalism. Undeniably, Jews and women alike have benefited enormously from political liberalism, but as we have seen throughout this essay, Jewish and feminist thinkers argue also that a philosophically liberal framework depletes something vital about Jewish and women's experience respectively. From a Jewish philosophical perspective, is it possible to hold onto the very valuable view of the human as dependent and vulnerable in a more egalitarian manner?

To begin to address these issues, let us turn to the more nuanced discussions of "the feminine" in feminist philosophies of care. In the first part, I referred briefly to Sara Ruddick's argument that what she calls maternal thinking is a "disciplined reflection . . . with identifying questions, methods, and aims." Ruddick goes a long way in making the case for "maternal thinking" as a kind of reasoned practice. Ruddick's criticism of Noddings should be applied in equal if not greater measure to Levinas. Seeing Levinas's "maternity" as "maternal thinking" allows for the re-emergence of the elements of critique and volition that are missing (purposively) in Levinas's analysis. Indeed, though Levinas and Rosenzweig have enjoyed more philosophical popularity than Buber has in recent years, when we consider these Jewish philosophers in light of feminist philosophy, Buber's stress on reciprocity and on consciousness as an essential mode of relation is a welcome antidote to Levinas and Rosenzweig's more Heideggerian emphasis on the primacy of non-cognitive praxis.

Yet the quest for an analysis of an ethic of care as a kind of practice requires more, I think, than Buber's philosophy. For Buber, as for Rosenzweig and Levinas, a notion of justice follows from the account of the phenomenality of relation. We must remember in this context that the phenomenological, existential account of relation, as opposed to the calculability of reason and justice, is historically an attempt to emphasize an aspect of human experience that had been de-emphasized by overly rationalistic accounts of the human. Recognizing the historical give and take of philosophical positions opens the door to rethinking aspects of the Jewish rationalist tradition that had been de-emphasized in the attempt to compensate for what was left out. I suggest that it is Hermann Cohen's thought that can potentially supplement Jewish existentialist accounts of the human on the question of "the feminine."

The interdependent and vulnerable human being is a conception that is very much in keeping with Cohen's ethical Socialism and the philosophical specifics of his position, but it is a view of the human that is often overshadowed by Cohen's neo-Kantian framework that emphasizes, often with profound tensions, the priority of consciousness, a priority that is rejected by Jewish existentialists. Still, it is Cohen's concept of compassion (*Mitleid*) that serves as a source for Buber's, Rosenzweig's, and Levinas's notion of the interdependent human being. Buber, Rosenzweig, and Levinas take these ideas out of Cohen's neo-Kantian framework and make them the center of also much that is lost. To begin with, Cohen is the one modern Jewish philosopher who focuses on the virtues, both for philosophical reasons and for what we might call socio-political reasons. Indeed, in one of his last essays before his death, Cohen argued that the renewal of Judaism in the modern world should be based on the renewal of the virtues of truthfulness and humility.[74] One of the central virtues that Cohen explicates (drawing on Avodah Zarah 20b) in his posthumous *Religion of Reason Out of the Sources of Judaism* is the virtue of pious loving-kindness (*liebestätige Frömmigkeit; hasidut*) that could provide the basis for a virtue approach to the existential ethic derived from the notion of the human as dependent and vulnerable. Indeed, Cohen's rationalized account of virtue provides the possibility of viewing pious loving-kindness not only as the "natural" response to human dependence and vulnerability but as importantly as disciplined reflection. Just as contemporary feminist philosophers of care are attempting to balance their arguments with stronger accounts of justice, so too could Jewish existentialist approaches benefit from reconsideration and a re-appropriation of these aspects of Cohen's thought.

NOTES

1. Feminist literature on mothering is, of course, diverse and complex. For an alternative view of mothering and the institution of mothering, see Adrienne Rich, *Of Woman Born: Motherhood as Experience and Institution* (New York: W.W. Norton & Company, 1995).

2. Levinas expresses his most extended disclaimer about his use of "the feminine" in

his early work *Time and the Other,* published in 1947. See in particular *Time and the Other,* trans. Richard Cohen (Pittsburgh: Duquesne University Press, 1987), 86–87.

3. I will use the term "the feminine" for the sake of brevity to designate the multiple female-gendered terms used by these thinkers.

4. See in particular *The Second Sex,* trans. and ed. H. M. Parshley (New York: Random House, 1974), xxxiii–xxxiv.

5. For more nuanced views of de Beauvoir, see Judith Butler, *Gender Trouble: Feminism and the Subversion of Identity* (New York: Routledge, 1992). See also Sonia Kruks, *Retrieving Experience: Subjectivity and Recognition in Feminist Politics* (Ithaca, N.Y., and London: Cornell University Press, 2001).

6. What I am calling "women-centered" thought is itself rather diverse and includes the rather disparate voices of, in the American context, Mary Daly, Eva Feder Kittay, Nel Noddings, Adrienne Rich, Sarah Ruddick, the many feminist philosophers who have responded with mixed reactions to Carol Gilligan's pioneering work in developmental psychology (such as Annette Baier, Selya Benhabib, Virginia Held, Joan Tronto and others), as well as French feminist thinkers, including perhaps most prominently Hélène Cixous and Luce Irigaray. All of these thinkers approach the problem of "the feminine" critically, yet all to varying degrees maintain nonetheless that the concept is a critical one, not only for feminist philosophy but for moral and political philosophy more broadly.

7. As I detail below, this strand of existentialism takes its bearings from Heidegger's reading of Husserl.

8. "Martin Buber in the Theory of Knowledge," in *Proper Names,* trans. Michael B. Smith (Stanford, Calif.: Stanford University Press, 1996), 19.

9. *Caring: A Feminine Approach to Ethics and Moral Education* (Berkeley: University of California Press, 1984), 35.

10. "Every word must falsify; but look, these beings live around you, and no matter which one you approach you always reach Being" [*die Wesen* (creatures) *leben um dich herum . . . du kommst immer zum Wesen* (essence)]," *I and Thou,* trans. Walter Kaufman (New York: Charles Scribner's Sons, 1970), 67.

11. Ibid., 78.

12. Ibid., 76–77. Buber's relationship to his own mother was quite complex as she left him before he was three. For Buber's account of this abandonment and its effect on his thought, see his autobiographical statement "My Mother" in *The Philosophy of Martin Buber,* ed. Paul Arthur Schlipp and Maurice Friedman (La Salle, Ill.: Open Court, 1967), 3. See also Buber's early essay, "Das Zion der jüdischen Frau," *Die Welt* 5, no. 17 (April 26, 1901): 3–5, now translated in *The First Buber: Youthful Zionist Writings of Martin Buber,* ed. and trans. Gilya G. Schmidt (Syracuse: Syracuse University Press, 1999), 112–18.

13. *I and Thou,* 154. The German actually uses the indefinite pronoun "*wer*" (whoever) and not, as the English translation indicates, "a man": "*Wer ein Weib, ihr Leben im eigen vergegenwärtigend, liebt: das Du ihrer Augen läßt ihn in einen Strahl des ewigen Du schauen*" (*Ich und Du,* p. 150, in *Werke*).

14. *I and Thou,* 67.

15. *Between Man and Man,* trans. R. G. Smith (New York: Macmillan, 1965), 170, translation altered.

16. *Ethics and Infinity,* trans. Richard Cohen (Pittsburgh: Duquesne University Press, 1985), 99.

17. "Martin Buber and the Theory of Knowledge," pp. 33–34, translation altered slightly.

18. *Caring,* 28–29. Noddings defends Buber's view of reciprocity, maintaining that it is not a matter of consciousness but of receiving something back from the one who is cared for. Her point is well taken, but, as I will suggest briefly below, Levinas is right to recognize that there is an element of consciousness in Buber's notion of reciprocity. On this point, I believe Buber's is actually the stronger position (as opposed to both Levinas and Noddings).

19. Ibid., 72.

20.*Difficile liberté,* 2nd ed. (Paris: Vrin, 1982), 53, trans. E. Wyschogrod; "Judaism and the Feminine Element," *Judaism* 18, no. 1 (1969): 33.

21. *Totalité et infini,* 4th ed. (The Hague: Martinus Nijhoff, 1971). Trans. Alphonso Lingis as *Totality and Infinity* (Pittsburgh: Duquesne University Press, 1969), 115.

22. *Totality and Infinity,* 267.

23. Ibid., 263.

24. Ibid., 272.

25. Carol Gilligan, "Women's Place in Man's Life Cycle," *Harvard Educational Review* 49 (1979): 440.

26. *The Second Sex,* xix; de Beauvoir maintains that Levinas disregards the consciousness of woman. She refers here not to *Totality and Infinity* but to Levinas's earlier *Time and the Other.* A consideration of this text is beyond the scope of this essay, but Levinas's arguments about "the feminine" are similar to the ones he makes in *Totality and Infinity.* De Beauvoir maintains that Levinas is incapable of understanding reciprocity between the sexes, a charge also leveled by Luce Irigaray (see "Questions to Emmanuel Levinas: On the Divinity of Love," in *Re-Reading Levinas,* 109–18).

27. "Feminism and Moral Theory," in *Women and Moral Theory,* ed. Eva Feder Kittay and Diana T. Meyers (Savage, Md.: Rowman & Littlefield, 1987), 119.

28. *Caring,* 4–5.

29. *Autrement qu'être ou Au-delà de l'essence* (The Hague: Martinus Nijhoff, 1974); *Otherwise than Being or Beyond Essence,* trans. Alphonso Lingis (The Hague: Martinus Nijhoff, 1981). See Catherine Chalier, "Ethics and the Feminine," in *Re-Reading Levinas,* ed. Robert Bernasconi and Simon Critchley (Bloomington: Indiana University Press, 1991), 119–29.

30. *Otherwise than Being,* 74.

31. Ibid., 117.

32. *Ethics and Infinity,* 99.

33. *Otherwise than Being,* 117.

34. Ibid., 74.

35. Ibid., 76.

36. *Maternal Thinking* (Boston: Beacon Press, 1989), 18.

37. Ibid.

38. See in particular Levinas's discussion of justice in *Otherwise than Being,* 158–59.

39. *Caring,* 5.

40. Ibid., 35–36

41. "Identity," in *Collected Philosophical Papers,* trans. Alphonso Lingis (The Hague: Martinus Nijhoff Publishers), 146–47.

42. Ibid., 147. Levinas writes "biblical," but the biblical term would be *"rahamim"* from which the Aramaic *"rahamin"* is derived. I have described the term *"rahamin"* as rabbinic to avoid confusion.

43. See note 1 above.

44. See Annette Baier, *Moral Prejudices* (Cambridge, Mass.: Harvard University Press, 1994); Selya Benhabib, "The Generalized and the Concrete Other: The Kohlberg-Gilligan

Controversy and Moral Theory," in *Women and Moral Theory,* 154–77; and Joan Tronto, *Moral Boundaries* (New York and London: Routledge, 1993). These are all discussed below.

45. See Carole Pateman, *The Sexual Contract* (Stanford, Calif.: Stanford University Press, 1998); Lorraine Code, *What Can She Know? Feminist Theory and the Construction of Knowledge* (Ithaca, N.Y., and London: Cornell University Press, 1991); and Marilyn Friedman, *What Are Friends For? Feminist Perspectives on Personal Relationships and Moral Theory* (Ithaca, N.Y., and London: Cornell University Press, 1993).

46. "The Generalized and the Concrete Other," 158.

47. Benhabib mentions the role of religion in this process only briefly (159–60).

48. "The Generalized and the Concrete Other," 160.

49. David Sorkin's *The Transformation of German Jewry, 1780–1840* (New York: Oxford University Press, 1987) and Marion Kaplan's *The Making of the Jewish Middle Class: Women, Family, and Identity in Imperial Germany* (New York: Oxford University Press, 1991) each describes the privatization of Judaism and, in Kaplan's study in particular, the role of women in this privatization.

50. Levinas's indebtedness to Rosenzweig has been remarked upon at length by both Robert Gibbs and Richard Cohen. See Robert Gibbs, *Correlations in Rosenzweig and Levinas* (Princeton, N.J.: Princeton University Press, 1992), and Richard Cohen, *Elevations: The Height of the Good in Rosenzweig and Levinas* (Chicago: University of Chicago Press, 1994).

51. Kohlberg himself privatizes the care orientation, claiming that it is a lower, if not immature, stage of moral reasoning ("Synopses and Detailed Replies to Critics," with Charles Levine and Alexandra Hewer, in L. Kohlberg, *Essays on Moral Development,* vol. II: *The Psychology of Moral Development* [San Francisco: Harper & Row, 1984], 360).

52. "The Generalized and The Concrete Other," 162–63.

53. *Der Stern der Erlösung* (The Hague and Boston: Martinus Nijhoff, 1976). Trans. William W. Hallo as *The Star of Redemption* (Notre Dame, Ind.: University of Notre Dame Press, 1985), 156.

54. *Star,* 169.

55. Ibid., 331.

56. Ibid., 299.

57. Ibid., 300.

58. Ibid., 306–307

59. *Otherwise than Being,* 77–78.

60. *Star,* 397.

61. "Feminine and African Moralities," in *Women and Moral Theory,* particularly 299.

62. Ibid., 307.

63. Ibid., 304.

64. Ibid., 305.

65. *Freud, Race, and Gender* (Princeton, N.J.: Princeton University Press, 1993).

66. Julia Kristeva, "Women's Time," *Signs* 7, no. 1 (Autumn 1981): 32, as cited in Marilyn Chapin Massey, *The Feminine Soul* (Boston: Beacon Press, 1985), 181.

67. *The Feminine Soul,* 181–83.

68. For example, while engaged in an effort to rethink the primacy of unchosen obligations for moral theory, Annette Baier nonetheless concludes "an obligation to love, in the strong sense needed, would be an embarrassment to the theorist, given most accepted versions of 'ought implies can.'" (*Moral Prejudices,* 5). From a Jewish philosophical perspective, however, this is not the case and in fact reflects a deep Christian, if not Pauline, prejudice in the history of philosophy, which has consequences for modern conceptions of

law (religious and secular alike). See, for example, Hermann Cohen, *Ethik des reinen Willen in Werke,* (Hildesheim: G. Olms, 1984), 267–68.

69. Joan Tronto, *Moral Boundaries,* 3.

70. Ibid., 170–72.

71. Ibid., 180.

72. See ibid.; Ruddick, *Maternal Thinking;* Eva Feder Kittay, *Love's Labor: Essays on Women, Equality, and Dependency* (New York and London: Routledge, 1999).

73. Alasdair MacIntyre, *Dependent Rational Animals* (Chicago: Open Court, 1999).

74. "Mahnung des Alters," in Hermann Cohen, *Jüdische Schriften* (Berlin: C.A. Schwetschke & Sohn, 1924), bd. II, 177–80. This essay was originally published in December 1917.

SIX

CLAIRE ELISE KATZ

From Eros to Maternity: Love, Death, and "the Feminine" in the Philosophy of Emmanuel Levinas

Plato's *Phaedo* is often read as an "ode to death," with the philosopher's task being to live his (or her, but in this case his) life such that death will be welcome. The soul will be liberated and the body will no longer be a hindrance to the knowledge the soul desires. This view, though transformed in a variety of ways, culminates in Martin Heidegger's philosophy (especially in *Sein und Zeit*), where being-toward-death (namely, my own death) is the anxiety that shapes my life.

In addition to this view of death, Plato's *Phaedo* also has an underlying current that is often overlooked. At the beginning of this poem about death, Socrates expels his wife, Xanthippe, from the room. She leaves, beating her chest in an emotional outburst that appears to make the rest of the men uncomfortable. The excess of the emotive is suppressed and quite literally sent away. It is clear in this dialogue that "womanly" behavior will not be tolerated.

The explicit theme of death and knowledge that permeates the Western philosophical tradition is accompanied by an implicit masculine tenor. From Plato to Heidegger, we have a view of death, life, and philosophy that still has not gotten us any closer to the other person. Human subjectivity has been defined in terms of freedom, independence, and knowledge.[1] Western philosophy is stuck, running in place and gnashing at the same tired view it has had for over two thousand years.

Emmanuel Levinas concedes Heidegger's point that we cannot know the other person's death and that our deaths are our own. But Levinas does not concede that the dialectic of death can only be understood in terms of being and nothingness, nor does he concede that death is only about knowing what death is. He replaces the concern for my own death with the concern for the other's death, thus subjectivity is transformed from one who is free to one who is always already obligated. In so doing, human subjectivity is always already inter-subjective and always already ethically accountable.

It should come as no surprise, then, that in his endeavor to shift the focus of philosophy from my own death and my quest for knowledge to the death of the other and the responsibility for the other, Levinas also inverts the tenor of the discussion from the masculine to the feminine. The relationship between ethics and ontology that characterizes his project can also be cast as a tension between the "feminine" and the "masculine," between passivity and virility. According to Levinas, philosophy's history as a discipline gave priority to the ontological over the ethical, and the relationship we have to our own death had priority over the ethical relationship we have to the other. This oversight parallels his work insofar as the work of the "feminine" in his project has been underestimated. As a result, commentators either condemned him for the sexism in his use of the "feminine," or they overlooked the "feminine" as an insignificant, if unfortunate, trope.[2] Ultimately, the significance of this inversion for how we understand philosophy and what it means to be human is also overlooked.

But Levinas's conception of the other needs to be distinguished from the conception of the other found in the Western philosophical tradition. On his account, unlike Hegel's and those who follow him, e.g., Sartre, the "other" is not the antagonistic other, nor is the other the non-subject to my subjectivity. Rather, for Levinas, the other is the one to whom I am most responsible. Thus, contrary to the tradition, which has often cast woman as "Other," and that other was to be disparaged, the other in Levinas's philosophy is privileged. For example, Simone de Beauvoir's criticism of Levinas's conception of the "feminine" other in a footnote to the introduction of *The Second Sex* suggests that she is unaware of the priority the "other" holds in Levinas's philosophy.

But even when the priority of the "other" is recognized, Levinas's philosophy does not escape additional concerns. In "Questions to Emmanuel Levinas," Irigaray asks, "[w]ho is the other, the Other [*l'autre, autrui*], etc.? How can the other be defined? Levinas speaks of "the Other" [*autrui*], of "respect for the Other" [*respect d'autrui*], of the "face of the Other" [*visage d'autrui*], etc. . . . Who is the other, if sexual difference is not recognized or known?"[3]

And in "Choreographies," Jacques Derrida's interview with Christine Mc-Donald, Derrida asks, "What kind of an ethics would there be if belonging to one sex or another became its law or privilege? What if the universality of moral laws were modeled on or limited according to the sexes? What if their universality were not unconditional, without sexual condition in particular?"[4] The questions posed by both Derrida and Irigaray are directed at what is problematic in Levinas's ethical analysis. Both questioners point to what would be disturbing in an ethics that discriminates on the basis of sexual difference—either by an exclusion of it or an emphasis on it. Although both signal what is problematic in Levinas's analysis, a broader understanding of his work may nonetheless help us reconcile an ethics marked by sexual difference.[5]

Throughout Levinas's writings, we see the way sexual difference plays a fundamental role in his project. In *Time and the Other,* Levinas characterized "the feminine" as *Eros;* in *Totality and Infinity,* he characterized it as the dwelling; and finally, in *Otherwise than Being,* he characterized it as maternity. If we believe Levinas's characterizations simply revitalize traditional views of women that reinforce dangerous stereotypes, then each of these characterizations can be understood negatively. This essay demonstrates that Levinas's characterization of "the feminine" can be viewed as positively inflected. My view is that Levinas's characterization of "the feminine" can be set against the glorification of both masculinity and virility (terms that are synonymous for Levinas) that is all too common in the history of Western philosophy.

"The feminine," characterized in Levinas's writings, demonstrates a shift from the priority of death to the priority of life, where life is linked to responsibility for the other. Levinas's use of sexual difference in his project is tied to his wish that we shift our focus away from the virile. Thus, my aim in this essay is to demonstrate that Levinas's project, either in spite of or because of his characterization of "the feminine," has value for feminist concerns. In the first part of this paper I address the issue of sexual difference and the role it plays in Levinas's project. I then turn to Levinas's discussion of erotic love in *Totality and Infinity.* And finally, I turn to the mature characterization of "the feminine" as maternity in order to examine the implications that this view of "the feminine" has for women.[6]

🌸 *Alterity in the Garden of Eden*

In his talmudic reading, "And God Created Woman," Levinas examines the two stories of creation in the Hebrew Bible: the first is Genesis 1:27, which reads, "He created him; male and female. He created them"; and the second is Genesis 2:21–23, which describes the creation of Adam and Eve.[7]

Levinas begins his discussion of the passage from Genesis 1:27 with a question about the Hebrew. In the Hebrew text, the word *vayitzer* ["made"] is written with two *yod*s, but when it is used to indicate the creation of other things, for example, animals, it is written with only one *yod*. One rabbi speculates that this discrepancy designates the difference in the types of creations: man is not the same creation as other things God made. Another interpretation suggests that *yetzer* indicates inclination; thus, man was created with two inclinations so as to demonstrate that man was created with both good and evil. According to Levinas, this interpretation cannot be correct since *yetzer* means *creature*, not *inclination*.[8] And he cites Isaiah 29:16 as his evidence. But it is Levinas's final interpretation that concerns me presently.[9]

This interpretation suggests that the two *yod*s indicate the dual sexual dimension of humanity itself. Midrash indicates that "even Adam's physical creation was twofold, male and female in one body. In front "Adam" was a man, but attached to "Adam" in back was a woman."[10] Rabbi Jeremiah b. Leazar tells us that "When the Holy One blessed be He, created Adam, He created him an hermaphrodite [bi-sexual]."[11] And Rabbi Samuel b. Nahman said, "When the Lord created Adam he created him double faced."[12] Here Levinas indicates a possible explanation of the odd spelling with two *yod*s. For Levinas, this line suggests a creation with two faces, a being who is open and exposed, a being who indicates the end of interiority, the end of the subject (GCW 167/DCF 132). This passage also suggests to Levinas that woman is not yet an issue. The "feminine" face does not appear until later, and, contrary to how this verse is normally understood, woman is not created from man. Rather, woman and man are created from what is human (GCW 168/DCF 132). Thus, according to Levinas, who thinks of sexual difference as secondary to the primary status of merely being human, the face is not marked, even by sexed characteristics.

Derrida focuses on this point, since it is this claim that Levinas gives as his defense against the problem of an ethics marked by sexual difference. Derrida correctly reminds us that that there are now "two" created from what is/ was "one."[13] There are two beings created from what was/is already human. In spite of the force of the arguments offered for this position, I disagree that this interpretation demonstrates that sexual difference is secondary to what is human. And I challenge Levinas's notion that the distinction between the creation of humanity and the creation of sexual difference that emerges from humanity are signs of Levinas's own equity with regard to the sexes.

With consideration to the first point, that sexual difference emerged out of the creation of humanity, the conclusion actually appears to be precisely the opposite. The phrase reads, "[God] created him; male and female." Both the phrase and the midrashim on this phrase indicate that the birth of sexual differences occurred *at the same moment* as the creation of what is human. If what is human is created simultaneously with male and female, how can we distinguish priority, ontological or otherwise? Thus, if humanity is created as male *and* female, humanity is *always already* marked by sexual difference. Does this not undermine any attempt Levinas might make to claim that it is the relationship to woman as woman that is secondary? This concept of sexual difference views our sexuality as if it were merely an accident of our existence rather than an inextricable feature of who we are.

The second version of the creation of woman from man, the fashioning of the "man's" rib into woman, projects a more complex understanding of this act than traditionally thought. According to Levinas, the contribution of the rib to the creation of the face of another exemplifies the "for the other" since it indicates the loss of one's skin to another. I would add that it is a "for the not-yet" other, since it is in the giving of the skin/rib that the other first comes into existence. Further, the commentary on this story emphasizes that God creates the woman from man's rib and not vice versa. The relationship is not interchangeable. And so Levinas asks, does this non-interchangeable relation not mark the difference between the sexes? (GCW 168/DCF 133). Nonetheless, Levinas wants to insist that while woman is not herself secondary, the relationship to woman, as woman, is secondary. And he underscores this point when he tells us that "[f]undamental are the tasks that man accomplishes as a human being and that woman accomplishes as a human being. They have other things to do besides cooing, and, moreover, something else to do and more, than to limit themselves to the relations that are established because of the differences in sex" (GCW 169/DCF 135). The sexual relation is incidental to the human: "culture is not determined by the libido" (GCW 172/DCF 140). And yet, even here, Levinas reiterates comments he makes in both "Judaism and the Feminine" and *Totality and Infinity.* These comments do not simply align the woman with home life and the man with his role in civil society. They also underscore the indispensability of the role of the woman.

Thus, in spite of Levinas's insistence that we should understand sexual difference as secondary to what is human, he nonetheless acknowledges and favors the position of the male in the order of creation of sexual difference. So on the one hand, Levinas wishes to claim that the presence of the creature prior to sexual difference indicates that there is a priority to what is human in the relationship between the sexes. Yet, on the other hand, the fact that woman is *created from* man's rib indicates, in the order of the creation of the sexes, that woman is created second. And Levinas not only does not dispute this point, but he also offers a justification for it (GCW 174–177/DCF 143–148).

Thus, Derrida's worry that there is still a privileging of male over female has warrant. Derrida claims that Levinas implicitly assumes male neutrality in the story of the creation of humanity. But this implicit privilege results from the attempt to whitewash the secondariness of woman: rather than simply say that woman is secondary to man, Levinas rephrases the point so that we understand him to be saying that sexual difference is secondary to what is human. And Levinas cites Rav Abbahu, who claims that God originally wanted two beings, two equal beings—not man issuing from woman or woman issuing from man. He wanted two separate, equal beings. But this equality could not be possible, for in his opinion there would be war. He suggests that two equalities would fight to establish a hierarchy. To create a world that would not self-destruct, he had to subordinate them one to the other. There had to be a difference that did not compromise equity and did not affect justice as it related to human beings. Sexual difference, then, where one sex has privilege over the other, was created in order to prevent a war.[14] Of course we can ask how men's power over women does not affect the justice of human beings. Thus, in spite of this attempt to "save" equity, the hierarchy that resulted from the division between the sexes, and the interpretation of the order of the creation of man [male] and woman [female], i.e., the "fact" that woman is created from man, left open the possibility of reading this relationship as a priority of male over female, even if this priority was "created" for political reasons in the narrative.

In *Time and the Other,* we see Levinas's illustration of the need for "the feminine" as distinct from the male, in order to provide the first experience of alterity and possibility of a relationship to another. In this book, Levinas tells us that "the feminine"—radical alterity—accomplishes the break in Parmenidean unity; it breaks the totality. Sexual difference provides the condition for the possibility of reality as multiple. In contrast to Aristophanes's speech in Plato's *Symposium,* Levinas insists that sexual difference is not the result of a duality of two complementary terms, "for two complementary terms presuppose a preexisting whole" (TO 86/TA 78). Love, according to Levinas, is not to be posited as a previously existing fusion.[15] Levinas reaffirms this point in "Judaism and the Feminine,"[16] when he says that "if woman completes man, she does not complete him as a part completes another into a whole but, as it were, as two totalities complete one another—which is, after all, the miracle of social relations" (DF 35/DL 58). Rather than seeing the separation of the two as a punishment, as is the case in Plato's Aristophanes's speech, Levinas sees the separation as "worth more than the initial union."[17] So Levinas takes issue with Aristophanes's view that the initial fusion is better than the separation that results from it. Aristophanes's view holds that love is the result of a lack that can be, or could have been, sated merely by finding, or having been joined to, one's complementary part. For Levinas, love is both need and desire, but neither of these can be simply fulfilled. There is always an alterity in the other that eludes me. It can never be completely joined with me. And it is only in a relation of separation that I can have a relation with absolute alterity.

So if we return to the biblical verse, "he created him, male and female; he created them," we can observe how two beings might always have been present. There was not a previously existing whole or a fusion. Instead, there were always two beings who were attached as one; two beings who from the beginning were marked by their relation to sexuality.

Levinas on Love, or Why Eros Is Not Ethics

Recalling the earlier discussion from *Time and the Other*, we see that Levinas underscores this same theme of Eros and the "feminine" in *Existence and Existents* when he says, "the plane of *Eros* allows us to see that the other par excellence is the feminine" (EE 85). The same two themes are reinforced in both writings: (1) separation and individuation are not punishments, but instead are the very means by which we can have a relationship to and with the other; and (2) "the feminine" is the first experience of alterity, one that makes possible the experience of any other. What, then, is the connection between eros and love? Levinas does not state the relationship explicitly. But one can grasp the connection by reading his books and essays with the theme of "the feminine" in mind. As I mentioned earlier, Levinas initially characterizes "the feminine" as *eros*. When we see "the feminine" fifteen years later in the first part of *Totality and Infinity*, he has characterized "the feminine" in terms of the dwelling—with the qualities of hospitality, welcoming, and generosity.[18] But towards the end of the book, "the feminine" reappears in a discussion of love in the section titled, "The Phenomenology of Eros."

Levinas returns to the reading of the Aristophanes myth he gives in *Time and the Other*. Although he still disagrees with the implication of fusion signaled by the myth, Levinas does find compelling the ambiguous notion of love as a relation in which there is a return to the self, but he also views love as a relation in which the self is transcended. The face of the other, of the beloved, reveals within it what is not yet. The ambiguity of love lies, finally, in the possibility of the other appearing as an object of need, and yet, still retaining its alterity. Levinas sees the love relation as ambiguous precisely because the ethical does not disappear. Rather, the face of the other is *hidden* by the erotic moment in love.

Levinas's discussion in the "Phenomenology of the Eros" follows Rosenzweig's discussion of love found in *The Star of Redemption*.[19] Both of these discussions are derivative of the biblical poem *The Song of Songs*. In Rosenzweig and Levinas, one important detail should not be overlooked: the two people in the relationship alternate positions between lover and beloved. In his discussion, Levinas alternates pronouns, and the "feminine" is not the only one to occupy the position of the beloved. Finally, if one looks closely at Rosenzweig's reading, one begins to see why it is important that the "masculine," or the male, embody the position of lover. It is not, as some might think, for the purposes of being active and remaining in control. Rather, it is precisely the opposite. To be in the position of the lover is, according to Rosenzweig, precisely to be able to show vulnerability and dependence. The lover must approach the beloved and lay himself out to her without knowing if she will return those feelings. For Rosenzweig, this act is precisely an act that counters the view of subjectivity as autonomous and independent, a view found in the history of Western philosophy. Because Levinas's stance on subjectivity counters this tradition as well, it is not surprising that he would adopt Rosenzweig's position specifically on this point.

Levinas's view of love has been criticized by many commentators, most notably by Luce Irigaray.[20] Though indebted to Levinas for the way his ethics influenced her own work, Irigaray claims that Levinas's ethics, as radical as it may be, remains blind to its faults.[21] Irigaray's critique takes into account two primary points: (1) She reads Levinas as saying that voluptuosity can only be fulfilled in the marriage bed where sexuality would be "purified" by the intent to produce a child, and (2) she claims that Levinas has excluded women from any relation to God.[22] Irigaray's critique is both insightful and significant, but I also think she misses some important elements of Levinas's discussion, elements that would alter the way Levinas's discussion of love appears.

Irigaray is correct, in my view, to claim that the other cannot be regarded outside of terms of sexual difference.[23] However, I am less inclined than Irigaray is to say that Levinas is unsuspecting of what he is doing, even though he does claim to want an ethics that will be neutral with regard to sexual difference. The problematic account of the "feminine" and its relation to ethics arises precisely because Levinas does take account of sexual difference. Moreover, Irigaray is mistaken when she assumes the Beloved is always the woman.

If one takes seriously this relationship between Levinas and Rosen-zweig, some of Irigaray's worries should begin to dissipate. Envisioning an apparent absence of the ethical from the erotic does not represent an accurate reading. Levinas states that the erotic covers over the face of the other, not that the face of the other is absent. The point Levinas appears to be making is that the erotic relation, when one is engaged in eros itself, is different from the ethical relation. The erotic is not asymmetrical or serious; rather it is fun-loving, consuming, and light. It is precisely this blur between the two that makes love so complex, so interesting, and potentially so dangerous. If we understand Levinas's ethics as asymmetrical, and if we see the merits of defining ethics as such, then we need to be very careful if we want the erotic to be ethical *in Levinas's terms.* I argue that Levinas sees precisely what is at stake in both eros and ethics, and it is for this reason that Levinas is not an ascetic thinker. I do not mean to imply that Levinas's philosophical thought holds that lovers have no responsibility to each other. Rather, Levinas is de-scribing the erotic experience—not the relationship itself. In eros, reciproc-ity is—and should be—expected. Love is consuming and silly, and often wild and animal-like. It is precisely in love that we forget ourselves, not our-selves as the ego, but the converse. We forget ourselves as the ethical *I.*

The future of love, understood as fecundity, is not meant to redeem love or sexuality. According to Levinas, whose view is similar to Rosenzweig's, love aims at a future. But this claim is meant to be descriptive of love; it is not meant to be normative. Thus, on the one hand, love seeks to be in the moment, to make one live life to the fullest now. And on the other hand, it also seeks to be eternal; it wishes to exist forever in the other. So in Levinas's account, the birth of the child is the outcome of the eternity that is sought. But Levinas's connection between love and fecundity should not be inter-preted to mean that he thinks every sexual act *ought* to *end* necessarily in ma-ternity, or even be *intended* to *end* in maternity. We must be careful to avoid a logic that reverses the necessary relation between sexuality and birth. Factu-ally, the birth of a child—or pregnancy—requires sexuality (traditionally), while sexuality does not require birth. In terms of his ethical analysis, how-ever, Levinas does give priority to sexual activity that ends in fecundity. Thus, we have two views of sexuality in Levinas's writings: (1) the one that gives priority to an erotic love that produces a child, and (2) the one in which he acknowledges and affirms a sexuality that intends pleasure for its own sake. Additionally, his remarks about the sexuality that we find in Judaism further complicate the relationship sexuality has to fecundity. And finally, the various ways in which fecundity happens, for example through adoption and teaching, introduce possible paths to go beyond Levinas's own analysis.

Fecundity—in all its manifestations—is how love achieves a victory over death; it extends beyond death. But if one accepts the relationship loosely, then one realizes that the outcome does not have to be the physical birth of a child. The responsibility to the future and the way one makes oneself immortal can occur through adoption, teaching, and caring for the next generation.[24] The family may provide the initial model for Levinas, but certainly one can see teachers as the cornerstone to any community—a point not lost on Judaism itself. Finally, Levinas's view of love is intended to be something contra Christian *agapē* in which one loves everyone and therefore no one, and which is not bodily, sexual, or of the material world. In light of this point, it would make sense that Levinas sees the next generation as an outcome of love. Not so that sex is redeemed, but because sex and birth are part of the bodily processes that he is trying to underscore. Thus, Levinas begins his discussion of the "feminine" in *Totality and Infinity* by using terms such as *welcoming, hospitality,* and *generosity.* At the beginning of this book, the "feminine" provides the transcendental condition for the partner in the dwelling to enter the ethical relation. The discussion of love, which comes after the discussion of the ethical relation, emphasizes the materiality of being human, in this case seen in love, sexuality, and children. These two discussions together demonstrate why his discussion of maternity and the materiality of the body found in *Otherwise than Being* would follow the discussion found in *Totality and Infinity.*

🕎 *Maternal Responsibility*

In Genesis 21:12, God says to Abraham, "Whatever Sarah tells you, do as she says." This statement is made with reference to Sarah's wish that Hagar and Ishmael, Hagar's child by Abraham, be cast out into the wilderness. At first glance, Sarah does not appear to be particularly sympathetic to the other woman and her child. In fact, her decision to expel them from her house appears to be cold and callous. However, when we take a closer look at the events leading up to Sarah's choice, what appears to be an unsympathetic reaction turns out to be an exemplary response by a mother who sees what others cannot see.

Avivah Zornberg illuminates what Sarah sees and what we do not see.[25] We may be initially sympathetic to the plight of Hagar and Ishmael. However, according to Zornberg, Sarah senses that Abel's fate—the outcome of two brothers whose relationship ends in the murder of one by the other— will fall to Isaac. In this case, it is Isaac who is vulnerable to the games of Ishmael. According to Zornberg, "Rashi cites the midrash that presents the game the boys are playing as a kind of William Tell game, with Ishmael shooting arrows at Isaac and then claiming, 'But I am only playing.'"[26] Ishmael's injured innocence does not fool Sarah, and she foresees that there will be a struggle to the death. Regardless of Ishmael's own motivations—for example, choice or non-choice in the matter of his character and actions—Sarah's responsibility is to protect her only son. She sees what Abraham cannot. Rashi traces her ability to see this threat not simply to the fact that she is a woman, but also because she is his mother.

Although Zornberg's reliance on Rashi is compelling, Sarah's choice is not unproblematic. Sarah's decision to expel Hagar and Ishmael from the house is, to say the least, troubling. It certainly undermines any claims that women naturally treat others better than men do. Zornberg's and Rashi's need to justify Sarah's actions within the context of motherhood demonstrates their own uneasiness with Sarah's dilemma and the choice that she makes. But the problematic nature of her choice is precisely what makes it noteworthy in the context of Levinas's discussion of maternity. Sarah's choice raises questions about a mother's love for her child and the choices she may have to make to protect that child. She exemplifies Levinas's description of the relationship of ethics to politics because her actions raise questions about who counts as the Other and when.

In a note to his essay "No Identity," Levinas confides, "we are thinking of the Biblical term '*Rakhamin,*' which is translated as mercy, but contains a reference to the word 'Rekhem,' uterus; it is a mercy that is like an emotion of the maternal entrails."[27] And in the talmudic reading "Damages Due to Fire,"[28] Levinas elaborates on this discussion of mercy. He asks, "What is the meaning of the word Merciful (*Rakhmana*)"? And he answers,

> It means the Torah itself or the Eternal One who is defined by Mercy. But this translation is altogether inadequate. *Rakhamim* (Mercy), which the Aramaic term *Rakhmana* evokes, goes back to the word *Rekhem,* which means uterus. *Rakhamim* is the relation of the uterus to the *other,* whose gestation takes place within it. *Rakhamim* is maternity itself. God as merciful is God defined by maternity. A feminine element is stirred in the depth of this mercy. This maternal element in divine paternity is very remarkable, as is in Judaism the notion of a "virility" to which limits must be set and whose partial renouncement may be symbolized by circumcision. (DDF 183/DCPF 158)

For Levinas, maternity is not simply a metaphor derived from physical proximity between mother and child, though certainly he does not overlook the immediacy of the relationship. For Levinas, mercy [*rahamim*] is the ethical response to the other and it derives from the Hebrew word for uterus [*rekhem*]. Thus we see a similarity between this derivation and the central themes of *Otherwise than Being*—namely, the gestation of the other in the same. And we see an implied contrast with the Greek word for *uterus*—*hyster*—from which we [English-speaking people] derive our word for *hysterectomy*. By the Greeks, and similarly by us until very recently, the uterus was believed to be the site of the emotions. Thus, if a woman was thought to be "crazy" (excessively emotional), the solution was to remove her uterus. But as indicated by the conclusion to the passage above, Levinas suggests a tempering of virility—both literally and metaphorically—through circumcision. Not only does Levinas believe that mercy in the form of the womb—"the feminine"—is good, but he also suggests by his comments that men should temper their own virile inclinations. In fact, it is significant that when he talks about the responsibility and the maternal body he uses the French word *comme* [as, or like]—responsibility is *like* the maternal body. Thus, while Levinas's focus on the womb leaves little doubt that he means maternity as it applies to women—gestation and birth—the image is nonetheless meant to be instructive.

But even this mature characterization of "the feminine" does not escape its critics. In her essay "Masculine Mothers? Maternity in Levinas and Plato,"[29] Stella Sanford explores the following two questions regarding Levinas's conception of maternity: (1) What is the maternity of which Levinas makes use and is this conception metaphorical? and (2) What are the implications of his conception of maternity, regardless of what we decide about its meaning? Sandford rehearses a few of the common perspectives on Levinas's use of this term. For example, Monique Schneider sees Levinas's use of maternity as a welcome reversal of the "matricidal impulses of Western thought visible already in Aeschylus's *Oresteia* and in Athena's avowal of her purely masculine parentage,"[30] while Tina Chanter and Catherine Chalier remain critical of Levinas's introduction of maternity.[31] Although these perspectives concern Sandford, it is John Llewelyn's reading of maternity that most interests her.

Llewelyn advances the interpretation that maternity is a corrective to the discussions of "the feminine" and the emphasis on paternity found in Levinas's earlier books. For Llewelyn, offering a corrective is not contingent on whether Levinas was aware he was characterizing "the feminine" negatively. If Levinas is criticizing virility, then maybe the emphasis on the father at the end of *Totality and Infinity* is not helpful to his project. Maternity might be more effective for a number of reasons, but among them, it can signify for both male and female. Sandford summarizes the discussion of maternity in two points: First, the maternal is not intended to designate something exclusively female. Although we have biological understanding of maternity, maternity can also refer to the aspect of nurturance and care involved in the biological process. This aspect of maternity need not remain exclusively female. Second, in spite of the previous point that states how the care aspect of maternity exceeds the biological necessity of the female body, the commentators whom she discusses share the belief that maternity does in fact refer only to "the feminine."

Thus, Sandford wants to know if there can be a different genealogy that "gives birth" to a different possibility concerning maternity. Can a conception of maternity yield something that includes men and also allows women to be something other than mothers? Because Sandford assumes that Levinas's view of eros has its roots in a Platonic conception of eros, she compares his view of maternity to the one found in Plato's *Symposium*. Sandford's reminder of a question that emerges from this Platonic dialogue is helpful: Who is giving birth and to what? Citing Adriana Cavarero, Sandford writes, "The pregnant birth-giving male, like the male who practices midwifery, stands as the emblematic figure of true philosophy."[32] When men give birth, it is to the abstraction of ideas.

Notwithstanding whatever similarity or debt Levinas's view of eros might have to Plato's, it is apparent that his conception of maternity is not indebted to Plato. Although Levinas certainly does not want to dispense with philosophy, he is nonetheless critical of that which philosophy has traditionally offered in the realm of ethics. Thus even if maternity is employed as a metaphor, the image Levinas has in mind, contrary to what others have argued, is not Greek. In fact, Levinas's own references to Isaiah indicate that he draws the image of maternity from the Hebrew Bible.

Throughout Isaiah, the narrator refers to the image of the womb and the experience of birth—the most intimate bond between mother and child. In Isaiah 49:15, for example, the prophet asks, "Can a woman forget her baby, forget to have compassion [*merachem*] on the child of her womb? Can a woman forget her sucking child?" Isaiah answers, "Though she might forget, I never could forget you." Isaiah's answer indicates that there is a bond stronger than the mother–child bond, namely the bond between God and God's people. However, the strength of the bond between God and God's people is described in terms of the bond between a mother and a child. His question and its answer derive their force precisely from the image of the mother–child relation. Isaiah's question is intended to present this bond as the strongest one possible between two humans. And this bond is surpassed only by a relationship with God. Thus, Levinas develops his notion of maternity as the ethical relation *par excellence* in light of this image of the mother–child bond. A woman could conceivably abandon her child, and certainly this happens. But when it happens, it nonetheless jars our sensibility—precisely because we also understand the bond as Isaiah does. The image of maternity, when used as a metaphor, derives its meaning and its power as a metaphor precisely because of how we understand the relationship in its empirical instantiation.

Concerned about the relationship between the figure of "the feminine" and ethics in Levinas's work, Catherine Chalier argues that "maternity is the very pattern of substitution. . . . It has not chosen the Good but the Good has elected it. It is the very contrary of the *conatus.*"[33] In a similar way to which Levinas views maternity, Chalier believes that "maternity is the ultimate meaning of "the feminine," the very metaphor of subjectivity."[34] Finally, Chalier tells us that "we have to encounter this failure in the virility of being in order to understand the meaning of the Other. The maternal body knows in its flesh and blood what subjectivity means."[35] In Chalier's view, the maternal exemplifies that which is held hostage and gives itself over to the other completely. The maternal body is unselfish. The mother has no sooner taken in food than her body transports that food to the fetus inside her. This is why Chalier echoes Levinas's point that the body in maternity "suffers for the other, it is 'the body as passivity and renunciation, a pure undergoing.'" Chalier's essay emphasizes a feminization of the virile, as does Levinas's passage on *rakhamim.* Thus, recalling the description of Abraham's actions in the Binding of Isaac and the recommendation of both Chalier and Levinas, one might say that Abraham needed to be feminized.[36]

In *The Feminine and the Sacred,*[37] Julia Kristeva refers to the experience of the "face-to-face with [the] emergence of the other" as "alchemy."[38] She claims that outside motherhood, no situations exist in human experience that so radically and so simply bring us to that experience. She continues by adding that "the father, in his own, less immediate way, is led to the same alchemy; but to get there he must identify with the process of delivery and birth, hence with the maternal experience, that is, the father must himself become maternal and feminine, before adding his own role as indispensable and radical distance."[39] Because the psychoanalytic tradition influences Kristeva's thought, she concludes that the father figures as the third who brings the mother and child into the phallic world. This is how the call of language is generated.

Much can be made of her last claim, and certainly one would have to accept the assumptions of psychoanalysis in order to accept her final conclusion.[40] However, I am less interested in disputing issues in psychoanalysis than I am in highlighting Kristeva's sensitivity to the simultaneously singular and peculiar nature of the maternal. Her insight helps to disclose an important shift in Levinas's own thinking in both the description of "the feminine" and the conception of the ethical from *Totality and Infinity* to *Otherwise than Being*. The formulation of the "child who is me, but not me" in *Totality and Infinity* was spoken from the standpoint of Levinas, the father. The father-child is the ethical relation *par excellence*. In *Otherwise than Being*, "the feminine" *and* the ethical are transformed into the figure of maternity, the "gestation of the other in the same." The formulation of the "child who is me, but not me" is now understood in terms of the *mother* and the child. And if we remember that "the feminine" is the interruption of the virile, an insertion of "the feminine" into the virile, we can see Kristeva's point, which is similar to Levinas's: the father, the masculine, can get to the experience of the other, but only by first becoming feminine.

Nonetheless, the image of maternity as the paradigm of the ethical relation is not without its problems. Tina Chanter rightly points out that Levinas's ethics cannot ignore the very real historical events that have demanded and then exploited the sacrifices women make for men;[41] nor can Levinas ignore the very real risk women take in pregnancy and childbirth.[42] Additionally, Chanter raises the concern that the discussion of maternity takes place in the absence of any related discussion of eros.[43] The conception of eros that precedes the discussion of paternity in *Totality and Infinity* drops out of Levinas's analysis, as the discussion of paternity is exchanged for the discussion of maternity. We are thus left with an image of maternity that appears cleansed of erotic pleasure.[44] Maternity, sanitized of eros, begins to look like the Madonna often desired: not only would childbirth be necessary to redeem any act of sex, but the real desire would be for children to be born without *women* having to have sex at all. And in Chanter's view, this move away from eros indicates a move farther away from "the feminine."[45]

In light of Chanter's concerns, I suggest that the eros of *Totality and Infinity* is not separate from the responsibility of maternity. I realize that Levinas's discussion of fecundity cannot be equated with Levinas's reference to maternity. Nonetheless, there is enough similarity that referring to the two discussions in tandem is not completely unwarranted. In fact, it is precisely because Levinas makes reference to the erotic act that precedes fecundity that we can certainly assume someone had to be pregnant in order for the birth of the son to occur. And Irigaray's concern raised in "The Fecundity of the Caress," that Levinas joins reproduction and eros, supports my assumption.

Like Chanter, I also would worry if Levinas promoted such a position. However, I do not think he is suggesting that eros be absent from maternity. Rather, his discussion of maternity in *Otherwise than Being* centers on the efficacy of the image of maternity to express the ethical relation. We see in *Totality and Infinity* that he wished to separate the experience of the erotic from the ethical. This does not mean that the ethical and the erotic never intersect. In fact, we know that the ethical is an interruption of eros. If we read *Totality and Infinity* and *Otherwise than Being* together, we can see that Levinas has not abandoned eros. In *Totality and Infinity,* the erotic— the play between the lovers—is prior to the ethical—the birth of the child. In *Otherwise than Being,* the discussion of maternity is not a discussion of what led to the maternal body. The discussion focuses on the maternal body as such. And for Levinas, the maternal body illuminates what he means by the ethical relation.

The maternal body is the example of the ethical relation *par excellence.* If this is the case, then Levinas has not moved farther away from "the feminine"; he has moved closer to it. "The feminine" in the earlier writings sat on the margins of the system. Levinas describes "the feminine" as that which provided the first experience of alterity and inaugurated the ethical relation, only to be excluded from participation *in* the ethical relation. But "the feminine," now understood as maternity, is central to the ethical relation. The maternal body is responsibility—a responsibility the *pregnant* woman does not choose. Her body simply responds to the needs and vulnerability of the fetus.

Thus we can see why Tina Chanter asks if "the feminine" understood as maternity is now absent of eros. This question alerts us to the potential problems we face when we cast women in the paradigmatic role of responsibility. Does this now mean that "the feminine," or women, must be endlessly self-sacrificing? Additionally, does this mean that the playfulness and enjoyment of eros is now absent from women's lives? I would pose the question differently. What if responsibility were not the only aspect of maternity? I suggest that maternity also displays a *jouissance* or a *joie de vivre.* We find this other dimension of maternity in the biblical figure of Sarah, just as we see in her earlier the exemplification of maternal responsibility.

🪻 Sarah's Laughter, or Maternity Revisited

Rachel Adler calls attention to Sarah's laughter and tells us that in order to construct a "feminist theology/ethics of sexuality, we should first retrieve the meaning of Sarah's laughter."[46] My concern lies elsewhere, but I would say that in order to address the charge that Levinas's account yields a "sexless mother" and a joyless maternity, we also should turn to the issue of the laughter. What is particularly striking about Sarah's laughter is the context in which we find it. Sarah has just been told that she will give birth to a child, and that the many nations will come from a child to whom she will give birth. Upon hearing this news, Sarah laughs. And her laughter is not just that she, at the age of ninety, will give birth to a child. She also understands what it will mean to give birth to the child: she must first conceive the child. But as Adler observes, to conceive a child, Sarah realizes that at the age of ninety, "[she and] 'the old man are going to do it again!' The picture of their fragile bodies shaken by fierce young pleasures evokes from her a bawdy and delighted guffaw."[47] Sarah's thought moves from having the child to the pleasures involved in conceiving the child. So Sarah laughs and the angel asks why. The angel only understands destiny and cannot relate to the human mechanics by which this destiny is to be accomplished. Sarah's laughter *is* and is about eros. According to Adler, laughter is erotic, spontaneous, and anarchic, a powerful disturber of plans and no respecter of persons.[48]

Thus, laughter interrupts and it does not matter who it is who laughs. The angel who brings the message to Sarah is serious; Sarah, who receives the message, is incredulous, and so she laughs! As Adler comments, the traditional focus on Sarah's laughter in this story centers on the idea that Sarah is incredulous at the possibility of conceiving. These commentaries conveniently overlook Sarah's reference to *ednah*—sexual pleasure. So Sarah gives birth to a son and says, "God has brought me laughter; everyone who hears will laugh with me" (Genesis 21:6). More interesting is the fact that Sarah not only laughs, but even names her child "Isaac" [*Yitzhak*], meaning "one who laughs." Her child becomes the embodiment of the sexual pleasure Sarah experienced with Abraham. Zornberg adds to this discussion by commenting that Abraham and Sarah "represent the dialectics of laughter."[49] With Isaac, the age of laughter begins.[50] And with Isaac, Sarah's motherhood is also tested. She is not aware that her husband has been asked to take her son to Moriah to offer him as a sacrifice.

The biblical story ignores her completely, and the very next chapter, *Chayye Sarah*—Life of Sarah—opens with Sarah's death. We can only surmise what might have happened. Isaac returned and told his mother that Abraham intended to sacrifice him and then stopped. Maybe he was rendered speechless and told his mother nothing.[51]

Rashi's gloss on the midrash has Sarah hearing the news from Isaac: "Sarah's death was consequent to the Binding of Isaac, because upon [hearing] the news of the *Akedah*—that her son had been readied for slaughter and had almost been slaughtered—her soul took flight and she died."[52] In other words, merely hearing the possibility is enough to kill her. We see in this interpretation of Sarah's death a belief that a mother's love is so strong that she would die from the heartbreak of his tragedy.

According to Zornberg,

> [Sarah] dies not simply because she cannot endure to the end of the story: that would constitute a relatively primitive tragic irony. She dies of the truth of *kime'at shelo nishhat*—of that hair's breadth that separates death from life. . . . No one deceives her, Isaac lives and tells his story, she questions him, she screams six *Teki'ah* notes [Shofar notes] and she dies *before she can finish them*. The profundity of her anguish is suggested in every detail. Her perception of moral vertigo is displaced onto Isaac's *kime'at shelo nishhat* experience. Sarah dies because she sees in Isaac's life what might have happened.[53]

Upon hearing what was to transpire on Mt. Moriah, Sarah dies, and her grief does not merely tell us of a mother's love, although it does tell us that. It also tells us about what is not in our control, the sacrifices that are made beyond our control. Sarah dies, one might say, in place of Isaac. But nothing demanded that she die. Rather, her love for Isaac and the incomprehensibility of how fragile life is, of how she almost lost him, is enough to kill her. Her death does not indicate a normative component showing that a mother ought to sacrifice her life. Rather, it indicates the risk one takes precisely when one loves and cares for another.

What we see as a common thread in all of the midrashim on Sarah's life and death is something unique in her relationship to Isaac as his mother. She sees immediately that something was done to him: she knows. She dies from heartbreak. Or she dies from the mere possibility that her son was to have been killed. We thus perhaps can see the connection between these different aspects of mothering: the one who laughs, whose sexual pleasure willingly conceives a child, and the one who would grieve so fiercely she would die. Sarah's very conceiving of Isaac is not divorced from sexual pleasure. It is Sarah's conception of Isaac that inaugurates "the age of laughter."

Returning to the introduction of this paper, we recall that Plato's *Phaedo* is often read as an "ode to death": the philosopher's task is to live life such that one will not fear death. Socrates takes the task one step further. For him, the task is to welcome death. The soul will be liberated and the body will no longer be a hindrance to the knowledge the soul desires. In addition to holding this view of death, Plato's *Phaedo* also expresses an underlying, often overlooked theme. We recall that Socrates expels his wife, Xanthippe, from the room, and as she leaves she beats her chest in an emotional outburst that appears to make the rest of the men uncomfortable. As I mentioned previously, *Chayye Sarah* opens with Sarah's death and in the first few verses we see Abraham not simply mourning her death, but profoundly grieving for her. The image drawn in the Bible is poignant, for it suggests a man who has been weeping with sorrow. It is an even more striking image when we view it in contrast to the dismissal of those who would weep at Socrates's death, those who were too "woman-like." For Levinas, the death of the other, contrary to what Heidegger says, cannot be excluded from the analysis of our relation to death. Should not an analysis of death that does not to allow us to weep for the other be suspect? And should this analysis not be suspect especially if it indicates the feminine element interrupting and transforming the virile?

Levinas's ethics is a response to the extreme violence he sees throughout the history of Western philosophy and which, he thinks, culminates in the *Shoah.* Hence, his ethics takes a strong position on what our responsibility is so that we cannot ignore what it means to be ethical beings, humans in relationship with others. Levinas does not mean to imply that women should become mothers. Rather, Levinas intends to say something more fundamental than that: the initial ethical relation is one we can all understand through the intimacy evoked by the image of mother and child. And the image of maternity disrupts the virile model given to us in the philosophical tradition. If Levinas's philosophy has a specific audience in mind, that audience consists of those who embody virility, those who rationalize, thematize, and totalize. Levinas's use of "the feminine" not only teaches us a great deal about responsibility via the image of maternity. It also teaches us a great deal about maternity, by using this image to express his conception of responsibility. Levinas's image of the ethical—the possibility of "dying for"— reveals the deep and profound unwilled caring for others that subverts the nihilist view of ethics. Profound care for the other is not only possible. It also gives meaning to life. Thus, Levinas's project does offer something of use to feminists, but it will not offer it to us easily and it will not be found by applying a straightforward reading of his work motivated by a typical set of feminist concerns. Levinas's work may offer us the opportunity to see feminist concerns in a different light and to see a wider range of what those concerns might be.

In *Totality and Infinity,* Levinas writes, "Life is *love of life,* a relation with contents that are not my being but more dear than my being: thinking, eating, sleeping, reading, working, warming oneself in the sun" (TI 112/ 84). I would add to that series, experiencing the erotic and having children. Maternity—the ethical relation *par excellence*—unites enjoyment *and* responsibility. Like Rosenzweig, Levinas gives us a philosophy of hope, a philosophy that does not claim that death marks our end, but rather frames the issue of responsibility in terms of a future, a future beyond death, a victory over death.

NOTES

1. Levinas uses *autre* to designate otherness and *autrui* to designate the human other. These have been translated into English as *other* and *Other* respectively. For ease of reading, I do not use the capital letter unless I am quoting directly. Instead, I use the context of the discussion to indicate when I am referring to the other person.

2. The most famous criticisms come from the work of Luce Irigaray. See for example, "Questions to Emmanuel Levinas," in *The Levinas Reader,* ed. Margaret Whitford (Oxford: Blackwell, 1991), 178–89 (hereafter cited as QE followed by the page number), and "The Fecundity of the Caress," in *An Ethics of Sexual Difference,* trans. Carolyn Burke and Gillian Gill (Ithaca, N.Y.: Cornell University Press, 1993). Those who avoid talking about "the feminine" are too numerous to name, since this avoidance encompasses most of Levinas scholarship.

3. Irigaray, "Questions to Emmanuel Levinas." Irigaray is responding to Levinas's work in *Time and the Other* (*Le Temps et l'autre* [Montpellier: Fata Morgana, 1979; first edition 1947], English: *Time and the Other,* trans. Richard Cohen [Pittsburgh: Duquesne University Press, 1987], hereafter cited as TO/TA followed by the respective page numbers), and *Totality and Infinity* (*Totalité et infini: Essai sur l'exteriorité* [The Hague: Martinus Nijohff, 1971; first edition 1961]; English: *Totality and Infinity,* trans. Alphonso Lingis [Pittsburgh: Duquesne University Press, 1969], hereafter cited as TI followed by the English and then the French page numbers).

4. "Choreographies," an interview between Jacques Derrida and Christine V. McDonald, trans. Christine V. McDonald, *Diacritics* (Summer 1982): 73.

5. Derrida's questions arise out of a discussion of "woman's place" and, in particular, the place as defined in the biblical books of Genesis and Job.

6. A longer, expanded version of this argument appears in my book, *Levinas, Judaism, and the Feminine: The Silent Footsteps of Rebecca* (Bloomington: Indiana University Press, 2003). See especially Chapters 3–6 and 9–10.

7. Emmanuel Levinas, "And God Created Woman," in *Nine Talmudic Readings,* trans. Annette Aronowicz (Bloomington: Indiana University Press, 1990), 161–77. Originally published in French as *"Et Dieu créa la femme,"* in *Du sacré au saint: Cinq nouvelles lectures talmudiques* (Paris: Minuit, 1977), 122–48. Hereafter cited as GCW/DCF followed by their respective page numbers.

8. These are Levinas's words. It was noted to me that Levinas may have made a mistake with the Hebrew, since it is *yetzur* not *yetzer* that means creature. Thanks to Hava Tirosh-Samuelson for pointing this out to me.

9. The citation Levinas gives in his text, Isaiah 29:6, appears to be a misprint.

10. *The Midrash Says: The Book of Beraishis,* ed. Rabbi Moshe Weissman (Brooklyn: Benei Yakov Publications, 1980), 33.

11. According to the Rabbis, the interpretation of the duality as hermaphrodite rather than androgyny is significant since it emphasizes the creation of two bodies in one rather than one being with ambiguous or dual genitalia. *Midrash Rabbah,* Genesis, vol. I, trans. Rabbi Dr. H. Freedman (London: Soncino Press, 1983), 54. Although the rabbis also conjecture that the taking of the rib indicates that woman is a separate creation, the taking of the rib could be interpreted as merely the separation of the two bodies. The rabbis use the term *bi-sexual,* but not to indicate dual sexual orientation. Rather, I presume, they wish to indicate the presence of two sexes within one being. However, there is debate as to whether God took a rib or a side. If it had been a side, this would support the position that the bodies

were independent but attached. Finally, another Midrash interprets the creation of woman this way: "While Adam slept, Hashem severed the female body that was attached to Adam's back and replaced the missing part with flesh" (*The Midrash Says,* 38).

12. Ibid.

13. In "Judaism and the Feminine," Levinas cites one interpretation that claims there were "two distinct acts of creation . . . necessary for Adam—the one for the man in Adam, the second for the woman" and that this interpretation affirms a rabbinic text (*Difficult Freedom,* 34).

14. See also Daniel Boyarin's essay. Boyarin cites a passage from Mieke Bal, *Lethal Love: Feminist Readings of Biblical Love Stories* (Bloomington: Indiana University Press, 1987), where she criticizes the explanation Robert Alter gives for this change. Alter claims that the original version, which presents the sexes equally, was altered when the narrators, living in a society where there was no gender equity, had to account for the disparity. Thus, the version that presents the creation of the sexes unequally was introduced.

15. For another detailed discussion of this idea see Edith Wyschogrod, *Emmanuel Levinas: The Problem of Ethical Metaphysics,* 2nd ed. (Boston: Fordham University Press), 116–17.

16. In *Difficult Freedom.*

17. Wyschogrod, *Emmanuel Levinas,* 116–17.

18. I give a full treatment of "the feminine" in *Totality and Infinity* in my article, "Reinhabiting the House of Ruth: The Work of the Feminine in *Totality and Infinity,*" in *Feminist Interpretations of Emmanuel Levinas,* ed. Tina Chanter (University Park: Penn State University Press, 2001).

19. We only need to recall Levinas's note in the Preface to *Totality and Infinity,* where he tells us that Rosenzweig's work is so much a part of this book that it would impossible to reference it.

20. Luce Irigaray, "The Fecundity of the Caress," in *An Ethics of Sexual Difference,* trans. Carolyn Burke and Gillian Gill (Ithaca, N.Y.: Cornell, 1993). Hereafter cited as FC followed by the page number.

21. For a detailed discussion of the relationship with and the debt to Levinas that Irigaray has, see Tina Chanter, *Ethics of Eros: Irigaray's Rewriting of the Philosophers* (New York: London, 1995).

22. One theme in Judaism claims that women are not required to study Torah because they are already ethical; they are already closer to God. See Franz Rosenzweig, *The Star of Redemption,* trans. William Hallo (Notre Dame, Ind.: University of Notre Dame Press, 1970), 326. One can see both the positive and negative in this view. Historically, women have been denied both rights and privileges because they {women} were thought to be more moral. Ironically, women were initially denied the U.S. vote because politics was deemed too dirty for them to touch; women then acquired the vote because it was thought their moral character would improve the lot of politics. Unfortunately, the non-requirement to study Torah was transformed into a prohibition. One cannot help but wonder how the view that holds women to be more ethical than men and closer than men to God informs Levinas's analysis. For a similar claim regarding women and the ethical, see Catherine Chalier, "Exteriority and the 'Feminine' in *Faces and the 'feminine,'*" trans. Bettina Bergo, in *Feminist Interpretations of Emmanuel Levinas,* ed. Tina Chanter (University Park: Penn State University Press, 2001).

23. And Derrida is correct that Levinas left us little choice but to think the other as not woman—or at least not a woman anchored to a home and a man. See Jacques Derrida, "At This Very Moment in This Work Here I Am," in *Re-reading Levinas,* ed. Robert Bernasconi and Simon Critchley (Bloomington: Indiana University Press, 1991), 19–48, an essay

devoted primarily to a discussion of *Otherwise than Being,* although it also comments on this problem in *Totality and Infinity.*

24. See Robert Gibbs, *Correlations in Levinas and Rosenzweig* (Princeton, N.J.: Princeton University Press, 1992), 238.

25. Zornberg, *The Beginning of Desire: Reflections on Genesis* (New York: Image/Doubleday, 1995) 134–35.

26. Zornberg, 135.

27. Levinas, "No Identity," in *Collected Philosophical Papers,* trans. Alphonso Lingis (Dordrecht: Kluwer Academic Publishers, 1993), 147, n. 6.

28. In *Nine Talmudic Readings.*

29. Stella Sandford, "Masculine Mothers? Maternity in Levinas and Plato," in *Feminist Interpretations of Levinas,* 180–201.

30. Ibid., 185.

31. See Chanter's *Ethics of Eros* (London: Routledge, 1995) and most recently *Time, Death, and the Feminine* (Stanford, Calif.: Stanford University Press, 2001). See Chalier, *Figures du féminin* (Paris: La Nuit surveillée, Collection Questions, 1982) and "Ethics and the Feminine," in *Re-reading Levinas,* ed. Bernasconi and Critchley (Bloomington: Indiana University Press, 1991).

32. Sandford, "Masculine Mothers?" 195. See 202, n. 49 and n. 60.

33. Catherine Chalier, "Ethics and the Feminine," in *Re-reading Levinas,* 119–29. Similar to my interpretation of Ruth, Chalier also offers us the biblical character of Rebecca, whose excessive fulfillment of "the feminine" moves her from beyond the ethical to the very example of the ethical itself. Levinas also cites this very story as an example of the ethical at the beginning of his essay, "The Bible and the Greeks," in *In the Time of the Nations.*

34. For an interesting discussion of Chalier's view, see Richard Cohen's comments in *Elevations,* p. 96. As my discussion indicates, I disagree with Cohen's claim that maternity is simply a condition of ethics rather than naming the ethical relationship itself.

35. Chalier, "Ethics and the Feminine," 126–27.

36. See Daniel Boyarin's work, for example his fine essay "Justify My Love," in *Judaism since Gender,* ed. Miriam Peskowitz and Laura Levitt (New York: Routledge, 1997), 131–37. See also Jonathan Boyarin and Daniel Boyarin, *Powers of Diaspora* (Minneapolis: University of Minnesota Press, 2002).

37. Julia Kristeva and Catherine Clément, *The Feminine and the Sacred,* trans. Jane Marie Todd (New York: Columbia University Press, 2001).

38. Ibid., 57.

39. Ibid.

40. For example, if we view Levinas's analysis through Kristeva's lens, it is the father who moves the child *away* from the ethical and toward the political. The maternal, then, is the exemplary paradigm of the ethical.

41. See Chanter's introduction to *Feminist Interpretations of Emmanuel Levinas,* 26 n. 10 and Chanter's discussion in *Time, Death, and the Feminine.*

42. Although we commonly speak of a woman who died in childbirth, people often forget that pregnancy itself produces its own risk to a woman's health and life.

43. It is worth noting the opposing positions with regard to the relationship between eros and "the feminine." On the one hand, Irigaray is concerned that, in *Totality and Infinity,* fecundity is connected to eros, thus claiming that Levinas's analysis implies that the only "good" sexual encounter is one that intends to produce a child. On the other hand, Chanter is concerned that eros drops from the discussion when maternity enters it in *Other-*

wise than Being, suggesting that Levinas offers a conception of maternity that is absent of eros. I do find it interesting that Levinas is unable to give us a relationship between eros and childbearing that is satisfactory to feminist theorists, even when he is thought to be offering opposite accounts of this relationship. Regardless of the outcome to these questions with regard to Levinas's project, these concerns highlight a larger question: "How are we to think of the relationships between motherhood and feminism, sexuality and childbirth, women and responsibility?"

44. See Chanter, *Ethics of Eros,* which is excellent on the topic of "the feminine." In particular, see Chapter 5, 197–207.

45. See Chanter's Preface to *Ethics of Eros.*

46. Adler, *Engendering Judaism,* 107. For another interesting discussion, see the chapter on Sarah, "Du rire à la naissance," in Catherine Chalier, *Les Matriarches: Sarah, Rebecca, Rachel et Léa* (Paris: Cerf, 2000).

47. Adler, *Engendering Judaism,* 105.

48. Adler tells us that "laughter," from the Hebrew root *tzahak,* is sometimes associated with biblical sex. The king of the Philistines sees Isaac *mitzahek,* "playing" with his wife (Gen.8). Potiphar's wife accuses, "That Hebrew slave, whom you brought into our house came to me *l'tzahek bi* [to dally with me]" (Gen. 39:17). Its use in Exodus 32:6 in connection with the feast for the Golden Calf where the people "sat down to eat and drink and then rose *l'tzahek,* to make merry" leads the classical commentators to envision an orgy. Adler, *Engendering Judaism,* 106.

49. Zornberg, *The Beginning of Desire,* 113.

50. Ibid., 112.

51. See *Midrash Genesis Rabbah,* LVIII 5.

52. *Ariel Chumash,* Rashi Chayye Sarah 23:2.

53. Zornberg, *The Beginning of Desire,* 127–28.

RE-THINKING ASPECTS OF JEWISH PHILOSOPHY

Part Two

SEVEN

T. M. RUDAVSKY

To Know What Is:
Feminism, Metaphysics, and
Epistemology

Introduction

The interactions between feminism and philosophy, and feminism and Judaism, have undergone serious challenge in recent decades. Starting with the former, many feminists have argued that Western philosophy has systematically excluded women. More specifically, feminists have argued that what Western male philosophers have presented as "essentially human" is in fact rooted in the male experience and does not reflect women's experiences; that because the (male) ideals of reason were formed completely without female input, the Western philosophical tradition is thus biased; and that many philosophical works, written by men, contain numerous misogynist statements. So, too, many Jewish feminists have argued that Jewish traditions have systematically excluded women's voices; that Jewish institutions have been predominantly male-oriented and reflect male concerns and priorities; and that many traditional Jewish texts, written almost exclusively by men, contain misogynist statements.

In this essay I analyze the implications of feminist critiques of metaphysics and epistemology with respect to the development and self-perception of Jewish philosophy. I begin by stating how I characterize the respective domains of feminist thought, philosophy, and Jewish philosophy. I then turn to a brief synopsis of feminist critiques of metaphysics and epistemology, both of which have long been regarded as the core, the canonical domain, as it were, of modern Anglo-American philosophy. Only then can we turn to the implications of these critiques to the discipline of Jewish philosophy. After a brief characterization of what I take to be the main concerns of Jewish philosophy, I will argue that inasmuch as Jewish philosophy has traditionally *not* concerned itself with "core" metaphysical issues as analyzed by Anglo-American philosophers, many of the criticisms of philosophy adduced by feminists are simply irrelevant when applied to Jewish philosophy. I shall conclude that, in fact, feminist philosophers would be well advised to look for support in Jewish philosophy, and not dismiss it as hopelessly anti-female.

🌼 *Feminism, Philosophy, and Judaism*

Before turning to the implications of these feminist arguments, let me briefly summarize some of the more blatant differences that will emerge between feminism and analytic philosophy. I shall argue that the following ingredients comprise the philosophical method as promulgated by the Anglo-American tradition: a focus on objectivity; an emphasis upon reductivism; an emphasis upon abstract generalization; the importance of logical argument embedded in reason; and the consensus that philosophy should be bias-free. In contradistinction, traditional feminist thought has traditionally emphasized the following characteristics: a rejection of the model of objectivity as a desideratum; the primacy of emotions to the search for truth; the downplaying of logic as an important methodological tool; a concern with practical and political matters, leading to activism; and the validation of biases grounded in feminist values.

These obvious differences lead to several concerns. The first is whether, in light of these differences, feminism and philosophy are capable of accommodation. Susan Sherwin argues it would be against feminist values to say that feminism and philosophy are incompatible. The very admitting of the notion of "incompatibilities" reinforces a male model of thinking rooted in logic, and so feminists should not view feminism and philosophy as unbridgeable. As Sherwin has succinctly stated, "I think it is important for feminists to resist the temptation to pursue dichotomies from our own perspective. . . . I cannot, therefore, conclude that feminist and philosophic methodologies are incompatible. They are, however, made compatible only with significant effort from each end."[1] The recent plethora of anthologies devoted to feminism and philosophy reflect the enormous effort being made on both sides to find common ground.

The second question has to do with the impact of the feminist critique of philosophy upon Jewish philosophy. Hava Tirosh-Rothschild [Samuelson] has pointed out that Jewish feminists have had little to say specifically about Jewish philosophy, nor have Jewish philosophers responded to feminist challenges to philosophy in general. She suggests that this lack of interest is in part a result of ignorance in that neither feminists nor Jewish philosophers have taken the time to familiarize themselves with the terrain outside their own disciplines. According to Tirosh-Rothschild, feminists must prove that "because Jewish philosophy attempts to reconcile Judaism and philosophy, it is doubly androcentric and oppressive to women— namely that Jewish philosophy is a philosophy written by Jewish men, for Jewish men, about androcentric Judaism, by means of masculinist philosophy."[2] Why have Jewish feminists not managed to dispel the "myth of objectivity" embedded in Jewish philosophy? Tirosh-Rothschild suggests that possibly they are not aware of the "blatant contradiction" between their own work and the exclusion of women from scholarly activity in Judaism; or because they accept feminism as a political program but do not believe that it belongs in the academy.[3] In an attempt to open up dialogue, Tirosh-Rothschild suggests that by studying Jewish philosophy, feminists might come to recognize that Jewish philosophy is complex: on the one hand it shares the androcentric biases of Western philosophy, but on the other hand it is critical of many of the tendencies of Western philosophy, replacing some ideas with more "feminist" ideas. So too she suggests that feminists must rethink their critique of reason, for it is reason that "facilitated the liberation of women and the emancipation of the Jews."[4] Jewish philosophers can remind feminists that "an attempt to debunk the ideal of rationality would be self-defeating for both Jews and women."[5] Further, she suggests that Jewish philosophers must address the "anti-foundationalist tendencies of feminist thought, which negate Jewish religious beliefs no less than traditional philosophy."[6]

I agree with Tirosh-Rothschild's assessment that Jewish philosophy has not engaged the feminist critique of philosophy, and further that many Jewish philosophers are uncomfortable with the implications of feminism. But it is important to note that the uneasy tension existing between Jewish philosophy and feminism is not unique; a similar discomfort exists between feminism and "secular" philosophy. Many feminists have pointed to the discomfort, both personal and intellectual, they have felt in trying to reconcile what appear to be contradictory states of being. Sally Haslanger, for example, asks whether academic feminism is an oxymoron: if academic theorizing is an attempt to achieve objectivity, and feminism is a political movement with moral and political agendas, how can there be such a thing as academic feminism? Furthermore, the idea of feminist metaphysics seems absurd: "Reality is what it is, and the metaphysician's goal should be to discover what it is apart from the social and political values we bring to it."[7] And so how could feminism have anything to offer metaphysics? Similarly, Alison Wylie asks whether there can be feminist philosophy of science. Echoing those who have argued that the very idea of feminist philosophy of science is a contradiction, she suggests that feminism, inasmuch as it is representative of a partisan political standpoint, can have no bearing on the practice of science, which is presumed to be value neutral and objective.[8]

On a more personal level, both Marcia Homiak and Linda Martin Alcoff address the reactions of women philosophers to the feminist enterprise. Homiak asks how women can reconcile their commitment to feminism with a scholarly life devoted to the study of philosophers (e.g., Aristotle, Kant, Hume) who explicitly describe women as inferior to men, and who regard women as unfit for the best life available to human beings. Although Homiak herself argues that Aristotle's picture of the rational life "is neither inherently masculine nor inherently exploitative," she agrees that the very project of studying dead white male misogynists is unsettling.[9] Alcoff goes even further, suggesting that senior women working in traditional areas may be threatened by feminist scholars, the suggestion being that their work is not feminist enough or is the product of internalized oppression. A feminist presence can cause alarm, alarm about the projected guilt by association, or irritation at claims made about one that one has no sympathy for, or "fear that the derision of feminist work will cast a general doubt about women's ability to philosophize."[10] In short, as Louise Antony has exclaimed, is it possible to "be a feminist and still do *that* kind of philosophy?" On the one hand, many female philosophers agree that the revealed misogyny of Western philosophy cannot simply be dismissed as accidental; on the other hand, they are committed to reason and objectivity and hence want to pursue the one discipline that purports to value these modes of thought.[11]

In what follows, I shall examine the main lines of attack leveled by feminist theorists against the Western philosophical tradition in general, and the Anglo-American school of analytic philosophy in particular, which has come to dominate much of the philosophical community. By the "analytic" tradition, I refer to those philosophical works that emphasize logical analysis, particularly in the areas of metaphysics, epistemology, and language. I shall focus first upon the feminist attack upon reason; I shall then develop the implications of this attack for epistemology and metaphysics, both of which are rooted in our very conceptions of language. I will then turn to a discussion of the relevance of this feminist critique to Jewish philosophy.

🏵 *The Feminist Critique of Philosophy*

For many feminists, the proper enemy is analytic philosophy, and in particular analytic epistemology, that is, the epistemology that has flourished in Anglo-American circles since the early twentieth century. Some feminists have argued that analytic philosophy, along with formal linguistics, is "inherently male, phallogocentric." Others have argued that analytic philosophy reinforces the theoretical commitments of the Enlightenment with its connections to individualism and political liberalism, with its notions of the self rooted in rationality. Perhaps the most trenchant feminist attack has been directed toward the faculty of reason itself. According to Genevieve Lloyd, maleness has been associated with reason, while the female is associated with what rational knowledge transcends. By reason I mean minimally the method involved in giving arguments and subjecting them to tests of logical validity.[12] Reason took on special associations with the realm of pure thought, a realm from which women were excluded. Alcoff points out that historically the nature of rhetoric and its distinction from philosophy is at the heart of this exclusion. Rhetoric has been associated with seduction, the female, in contradistinction to philosophy which is associated with reason and the discovery of truth (cf. Plato).[13] Furthermore, feminists have repeatedly argued that language itself, which expresses rational propositions, is manmade; even when they use the same words, men and women do not mean the same thing.[14]

The rational method adopted by philosophers assumes what Susan Langston calls the "nonsituated distanced standpoint," namely that things in the world are independent of us, and their behavior is constrained by their natures. We can best discover these natures by looking for their regularities, which are exhibited under "normal circumstances." This position assumes "direction of fit," according to which one's beliefs about the world conform to the world. Now this metaphysical view, and its attendant epistemological structures, have already been subjected to critique from within the history of philosophy: Kant developed the view that reason and knowledge are limited by the intellectual and perceptual attributes of humans; Hegel argued further that knowledge and reason are marked by history in that they are temporally located or indexed; and Nietzsche and Freud rejected the rigid demarcation between abstract reason and body. In this sense, the feminist critique of reason is part of this long tradition within philosophy. Feminists have extended this historical critique by arguing that concepts of reason are reflections of gendered practices passing as universal practices.[15]

But does a rejection of the objective grounding of reason lead necessarily to an embrace of irrationality, and ultimately to relativism? Early feminists like Simone de Beauvoir argued that in order to avoid the inevitable identification of body with the female that results when reason is associated with the male, women should refuse marriage and motherhood, and thus regain ownership of the rational realm. Others, however, have argued that the project to reappropriate mind will never work, and so feminists must "reconfigure the role of bodily experience in the development of knowledge."[16] Alcoff, for example, argues that although misogynist statements do exist in the canon, this does not mean that feminist philosophy should forego the "recourse to reason, objectivity, and truth."[17] To maintain that rationality is essentially historical and socially context-bound does not lead to absolute relativism. What does follow is that reason is not timeless. Hence the feminist critique of reason challenges philosophy's "self-understanding as a discipline of discourse primarily organized by the pursuit of truth."[18]

The feminist attack upon reason has led to a questioning of philosophical models of knowledge. In response to the traditional (male) conception that reason and philosophy provide an objective, universal foundation for knowledge, knowledge for feminist philosophers is seen as "subjective, historically situated, linguistically bound, and politically motivated."[19] Following Kant's espousal of the intellect as an active creator of knowledge, feminists have argued that if the human mind constructs knowledge, then the identity of the knower becomes relevant to the process of knowing. Furthermore, feminists argue that the idea of detached, impartial knowledge is oppressive to women because it plugs into a subjective–objective dichotomy that ultimately provides reasons for the exclusion and oppression of women.

Feminist standpoint theory was introduced by Sandra Harding as an extension of Marxist critiques of epistemology. Harding argued that gender relations necessarily affect our epistemic standpoint and that, in fact, women may often occupy a privileged epistemic standpoint. Feminists emphasize that the identity of the knower, who is socially situated, *must* enter into the production of knowledge. Feelings and emotions are valid sources of knowledge, and knowledge becomes distorted when feelings and emotions are not acknowledged. Feelings must be recognized as a "route to truth." The French feminists (e.g., Hélène Cixous, Luce Irigaray, Julia Kristeva) emphasize that inasmuch as thinking takes place within a human body, "embodied thinking" must be adopted in contradistinction to the male phallocentric thinking models.

In arguing that social identity and power relations influence epistemic access to the world, standpoint theory became associated with the postmodern rejection of epistemology. Take, for example, Jean François Lyotard who, in *The Postmodern Condition,* argued that the rules of language games are strictly "local," and thus undermine epistemology: "there are no translocal norms of rationality and justification."[20] What Lyotard means is that the authority of the rules of a given "language game" resides in a fleeting agreement, which will then be revised—all norms of judgment are local. The problem, of course, is one endemic to all forms of skepticism: the postmodernist is incapable of sustaining ordinary critical judgments, such as the judgment that some models are unjust or false. In other words, who is to say which "language game" should be played? The skepticism associated with postmodernism in general, and standpoint theory in particular, has proved counterproductive and has been rejected by many feminists. If all knowledge is "situated and perspectival," then feminists must accept the thoroughgoing relativism of postmodernism; but if feminists claim that they are "epistemically privileged," then they cannot support their own position. For those who have retained a version of standpoint theory, then, a major question is how to understand the embeddedness of knowledge/science claims, gender included, without resorting to radical relativism.

More recently Louise Antony and others have broached the question of whether we need a feminist epistemology altogether. Of course, this depends on what we mean by feminist epistemology. If we mean that many problems that arise as a result of feminist analysis must be resolved by adopting an adequate epistemology, then feminist epistemology clearly plays an important role. But if we mean that we need a specifically feminist alternative to currently available epistemological frameworks, then Antony disagrees with those feminist philosophers who argue that existing epistemological paradigms are unsuited to the needs of feminist theorizing. She finds, for example, that Willard V. O. Quine's "naturalized epistemology" can offer enormous aid to feminists.[21] Antony argues that Quine's critique of epistemological foundationalism bears many similarities to contemporary feminist attacks on 'modernist' conceptions of objectivity and scientific rationality; further, she argues that his positive views on the holistic nature of justification provide a theoretical basis for feminist epistemological concerns.[22] How is it possible to criticize the partiality of the concept of objectivity, without assuming objectivity? In other words, how do we tell a good bias from a bad bias? This is precisely the problem posed by critics of empiricism such as Quine, Nelson Goodman, Carl Hempel, Hilary Putnam, and others. According to Antony, naturalized epistemology permits "an appropriately realist conception of truth, viz., one that allows a conceptual gap between epistemology and meta-physics, between the world as we see it and the world as it is."[23]

The issue of philosophical bias lies at the heart of the feminist critique of objectivity. It is here that philosophical and scientific methods share a similar fate. What science and philosophy have traditionally had in common is a search for objectivity and truth. The term *objective* has been used in many ways, including for referring to material that is detached, un-biased, impersonal, publicly observable, existing independently of the knower, or "really real" or "the way things are." But feminists have accused both philosophers and scientists of dogmatism in their positing an "objec-tive" domain that is fallacious at best, pernicious at worst. With respect to the more "theoretical" sciences, the feminist claim that science is andocen-tric has forced theoreticians to question the objectivity and rationality that supposedly underlie the scientific enterprise.[24] The traditional workings of contemporary science assume a realist ontology; by realist, I mean that the phenomena of the natural world are fixed in determinate relations with each other, that these relations can be known and formulated in a consis-tent and unified way, and that it is the task of scientists to discover these relations. This realist picture is seen as andocentric and is rejected by femi-nists in favor of a Kuhnian understanding of science as social process. But Evelyn Fox Keller points out that if we view science as pure social product, then science dissolves into ideology and "objectivity loses all intrinsic meaning." Thus truth recedes into the political domain. Some feminists have suggested a return to "female subjectivity" and wish to leave rational-ity and objectivity in the male domain. But here again, we are threatened with total relativism: by rejecting objectivity as a masculine ideal, femi-nism simultaneously lends its voice to an enemy chorus and dooms women to residing outside of the *realpolitik* modern culture; it "exacerbates the very problem it wishes to solve."[25]

This epistemological critique has had enormous impact upon feminist appraisals of Anglo-American metaphysics. Some feminists have argued that traditional metaphysics and language are both male-biased and should be re-placed with less male-biased models. They have argued that the very idea of dualistic metaphysics is andocentric. Feminists have criticized the mind–body distinction, for example, which is reflected in the reason–emotion dis-tinction. Because emotions are associated with the female, the very elevation of reason over emotions is seen as male-biased.[26] Still even more radical femi-nists have argued that feminists should reject metaphysics altogether. The very occupation of trying to understand the world "as it is" is seen as a hope-lessly male enterprise.

A good example of "malestream" metaphysics has to do with the issue of *natural kinds,* i.e. whether there exist groups of things that share a common essence. Realists about objective types or kinds will argue that there is a type of unity independent of us that distinguishes certain groups of individuals from others. For many feminists, realism, which is associated with essentialist metaphysics, is simply not a metaphysical option.[27] Essentialism is the theory that certain properties are ontologically necessary to an object, meaning that an object will not be that very object without these properties. Some feminists (see Charlotte Witt) distinguish further between individual gender essentialism and generic gender essentialism. The thesis of individual gender essentialism holds that there is some property (or properties) necessary to my being a woman, like being nurturing, or being oppressed, or having a uterus. The thesis of generic gender essentialism holds that there is a commonality of experience or a characteristic that unites all women; this core of properties constitutes the generic woman and must be satisfied if someone is to count as a woman.[28] Most feminists, ignoring the distinction between individual and generic gender essentialism, reject essentialism in both its forms. They deny the existence of any single or shared properties that must be satisfied in order to count as a woman. The very notion of essentialism is seen as a sign of "lingering maleness." Feminists have emphasized what Stoljar calls the "diversity argument," which rejects the commitment to the existence of "common identities" among women. Inasmuch as individual women are particular, and there are important differences of race, class, culture, and experience among women, their particularity is incommensurate with claims of universalism that are inherent in essentialist positions.

❦ What Is Jewish Philosophy?

Turning to the implications of this extended feminist critique to Jewish philosophy, we must first address the somewhat thorny issue of what counts as Jewish philosophy. Many scholars have remarked that Jewish philosophy is not a sub-discipline within philosophy, analogous to linguistic philosophy, Greek philosophy or political philosophy. What has traditionally been construed as Jewish philosophy crosses a number of disciplines, incorporating issues in the history of philosophy, ethics, political thought, and to some extent metaphysics. A number of scholars however, have suggested that there is no such thing as Jewish philosophy. Isaac Husik's monumental study, *A History of Mediaeval Jewish Philosophy,* ends with the famous statement that "there are Jews now and there are philosophers, but there are no

Jewish philosophers and there is no Jewish philosophy."[29] Recent scholars have echoed Husik's assessment. Menachem Kellner, for example, claims that "unless one is willing to admit a specifically Jewish mode of reasoning I don't see how one can make any sense of the claim that there can be a Jewish philosophy, where philosophy is construed as a process, not a product."[30] Daniel Frank, however, takes a different angle. Arguing that the very term *Jewish philosophy* is an invention of nineteenth-century *Wissenschaft,* he suggests that pre-nineteenth-century thinkers such as Maimonides, Gersonides, or even Mendelssohn did not think of themselves as "Jewish philosophers." Rather, according to Frank, they saw themselves as providing interpretations of Jewish texts and issues, using certain philosophical methods based on reason; they did not philosophize in a particularly Jewish way.[31] Steven Schwarzschild, on the other hand, not only recognizes an enterprise properly described as Jewish philosophy, but claims that there is a "carefully hidden, Jewish agenda that underlies the issues that are overtly discussed in this area—philosophy of science, aesthetics, and so on. Constructionalisms of many varieties want to say, Jewishly, that God "is" not in the world and that, indeed, reason has to shape, "create" the world."[32] Schwarzschild argues that there is a "Jewish way of doing philosophy. . . . It is not so much a matter of doing Jewish philosophy as doing philosophy Jewishly."[33]

Of course, much of the disagreement has to do with what philosophy *itself* is, and secondarily with how philosophy relates to Judaism. The issue becomes complicated even further when we admit non-standard philosophical texts, such as rabbinic commentaries and mystical texts, into the canon. Consider, for example, recent attempts by Shalom Carmy, David Shatz, and David Novak to locate philosophical reflection in Scripture and talmudic sources.[34] In order to make sense of the status of Jewish philosophy, let me reiterate a standard distinction, drawn by Barry Kogan and others, between philosophy as process and philosophy as systematic content. If we construe philosophy primarily in terms of method, as an activity, then Jewish philosophy can be regarded as an activity applicable to contemporary as well as the medieval period. By "process," Kogan means the "analysis, systematization and critique of descriptive and normative statements."[35] This process is then applied to statements and issues pertaining to Judaism.

Philosophy as process is often juxtaposed against the construction of systematic ontology and cosmology. While I agree with the many critics who have noted the dearth of systematic Jewish philosophy in recent years, this is not to say that Jews have never engaged in systematic philosophy. The enterprise of systematic philosophy has waxed and waned in the secular world as in the Jewish world. Gersonides's works are a prime example of a systematic philosophy that incorporates metaphysics, science, cosmology, epistemology, and philosophical theology. So too are the works of Hermann Cohen. Adopting this distinction, then, I shall suggest that inasmuch as a thinker applies those methods that are grounded in rational analysis to subjects directly germane to Judaism, she or he is engaged in a philosophical analysis of Judaism. One need not be a Jew to engage in this enterprise, but an understanding of the texts, issues, and values central to Jewish belief is critical.

Jewish Philosophy and the Critique of Reason

I noted above three main areas in which feminists argue that analytic philosophy has denigrated or marginalized women's experiences. The first has to do with the primacy of reason—which was upheld as a predominantly male feature—at the expense of emotions and bodily reality. The second concerns the false espousal of objectivity, which ignores the "point of view" of the knower. The third has to do with the postulation of metaphysical essentialism based on a realist view of the world. My view is that Jewish philosophy itself is ambiguous with respect to these three issues. In fact, I shall argue that even a cursory glance at relevant texts and discussions within the history of Jewish philosophy reveals an affinity between contemporary feminist positions and those of Jewish philosophers, past and present, on a number of issues. A consideration of several issues will highlight what I have in mind.

Let me turn first to that area which most interests both feminists and Jewish philosophers, namely the area of *method*. We have examined the grounds upon which feminist theorists have critiqued the primacy of reason: the emphasis upon "dispassionate objectivity" as the sole guarantor of truth has come under trenchant attack. Feminists have argued that the primacy of reason is itself rooted in a male, patriarchal bias, that we must incorporate other strands into our philosophical method without running the risk of total relativism. I suggest that the same concern can be found within Jewish philosophical evaluations of reason as the prime guarantor of truth. Many Jewish philosophers, both medieval and modern, have questioned the efficacy of objectivity as a method for achieving religious truth, arguing that religious truth derives its veridical nature from divine revelation. This is not to say that all Jewish philosophers have rejected the ultimate grounding of reason. But as we peruse the pages of both medieval and modern Jewish texts, we find among many Jewish philosophers a tendency to gravitate toward a form of religious truth based on faith. Just as for feminists the question is to what extent "faith" is compatible with a feminist epistemology, so too for religious thinkers does the issue center around the compatibility of faith and reason.

Even a cursory survey of works from the medieval period reveals a striking congruence among Jewish, Christian, and Islamic thinkers to the extent that all three are engaged in a critical attempt to analyze their own religious traditions in accordance with the ontological and metaphysical constraints of what we may call secular philosophy. I agree with Aviezer Ravitsky that approaching Jewish philosophical texts with the presumption that their authors were completely isolated from their non-Jewish intellectual environment is to misunderstand the underlying tension inherent in these very texts.[36] On the contrary, Jewish philosophers, both medieval and modern, have had to wrestle with the project of reconciling "outside" sources and influences with their understanding of scriptural dicta.

More specifically, throughout Jewish history, a major component of halakhic Judaism has been to stress the importance of Torah study and learning. For the People of the Book, the topics that concern divine revelation—the word of God as reflected in Scripture—enjoy pre-eminence. This picture of Jewish devotion to Jewish texts, attractive as it may appear at first blush, is double-edged, however. I shall not discuss here the gender implications of such a paradigm; I shall only mention that this paradigm has been, until the latter part of the twentieth century, the enclave of male study. Steven Katz argues that "no one can be a fully satisfactory Jewish philosopher if he is not also, at least, a competent Talmudist. The reason is this: such a thinker is out of touch with the most important Jewish spiritual resource next to the Bible."[37] If Katz is right (and I think this point needs to be argued, not assumed), then this phenomenon might account for the paucity of women engaged in the study of Jewish philosophy, given that only in the present century have women had systematic access to study of Talmud.

Thus the problem of reconciling philosophy and Judaism has been a prevailing motif throughout Jewish thought. Whenever Jews have lived surrounded by another culture, they have had to assess the cosmology represented by that culture. Interestingly enough, however, Jewish thinkers have avoided many of the challenges presented by modern philosophy in general, and by contemporary Anglo-American philosophy in particular. Katz, for example, correctly notes that contemporary Jewish thinkers have avoided issues of ontology and metaphysics. "As Jewish philosophers we have to be willing to take a stand on 'what there is,' i.e., on the existence of God, His character and attributes, His relations to Israel."[38] Turning to issues of language and logic, Katz maintains that "modern Jewish philosophers, with the exception of Buber's pronomial approach, have made almost no contributions to the modern debate about religious language and the impact of logical considerations on theological discourse."[39] But in order for theology to be open to rational discussion, the rules of logic and language must be understood and respected by Jewish philosophers; otherwise, Jewish philosophy is "reduced to the making of statements which have little cognitive content."[40]

And so I would suggest, following Katz, that the reluctance of Jewish philosophers in the present generation to address issues posed by feminism is part of an overall reluctance to engage in the analytic enterprise altogether. Perhaps it is the sense that logical analysis is irrelevant to issues of theological concern; perhaps it is a lack of training in the rudiments of logic and philosophy of language. But more important, perhaps, the reluctance of Jewish philosophers mirrors the reluctance on the part of analytic philosophers themselves to tackle issues in cosmology and theology, areas less open to reductive analysis. Only in recent years, for example, have contemporary philosophers of religion engaged in a systematic analysis of topics germane to philosophical theology.

Inasmuch as feminist philosophers are critiquing the very enterprise that is eschewed by Jewish philosophers, it is even more difficult to ascertain whether the feminist critique applies to Jewish philosophy as well as to the analytic tradition. As I suggested above, much of Jewish philosophical method arises outside of the analytic tradition; in fact, it replaces the epistemological quest for reason with a notion of faith that is associated with a non-cognitivist "trust in God" rather than as a propositional affirmation or denial. This move is apparent particularly in the medieval tradition. Until the late fourteenth century, the term *emunah,* a translation of the Arabic term *i'tiqād,* was used to convey the sense of belief or conviction. In fact, it is Maimonides who introduced into Judaism a propositional or cognitivist notion of belief by defining *heresy* as the questioning of any of the thirteen principles of faith articulated in his introduction to the tenth chapter of *Tractate Sanhedrin (Perek Helek).* In this work Maimonides argued that anybody who questions any one of these thirteen principles excludes himself from the community of Israel, and hence forfeits his share in the world to come.[41] According to Maimonides, adherence to these propositional belief states is a necessary condition for assuring immortality of the soul.

Maimonides's conception of belief defined post-Maimonidean philosophy, as Jews tried to respond to a cognitivist theory that tied immortality to intellectual attainment. When scholasticism infiltrates Jewish circles, the term *emunah* takes on the additional meaning of "faith" (*fides*).[42] We find both Jewish philosophers vacillating between a volitional and a non-volitional understanding of belief (*fides, emunah*), which becomes superimposed upon the rationality of belief. Some philosophers collapsed the distinction between true and certain beliefs altogether, arguing that rational knowledge is inferior to the state achieved through *emunah*. Other theories emphasize the primacy of will over that of intellect in the acquisition of beliefs. Many examples of the volitional or non-rational status of belief abound in fourteenth- and fifteenth-century Jewish literature. This fideistic attitude toward faith and reason is reflected in contemporary Jewish thought as well, as exemplified in Soloveitchik's celebrated distinction between Adam I and Adam II.

Many Jewish philosophers thus share with feminists a distrust of reason as the ultimate method for achieving knowledge of reality. While the grounds for distrust differ between the two groups, nevertheless the end-result is the postulation of an alternative epistemology. Feminists have emphasized the primacy of emotions, of bodies, as modes of knowing. Jewish philosophers have emphasized non-cognitivist modes of knowing, which supplement an epistemology that recognizes belief states that transcend reason. Nevertheless this very denigration is itself double-edged, and carries with it enormous implications with respect to philosophers' attitudes towards women.

On Spiritual Perfection and Unseemly Kisses: Is Maimonides a "Feminist"?

Are feminists right to decry that women have been "written out" of philosophical conceptions of perfection; that women, qua female, cannot attain to the very goals espoused and lauded by philosophy? My second example, drawn from the metaphysics of essentialism, highlights the ambivalence toward the ability of women to achieve perfection that can be found in Jewish philosophical texts.

Given the feminist characterization of Western philosophy as phallocentric and anti-female, one might expect Jewish philosophers to equal (if not surpass) their misogynist peers in their denigration of women's ability to achieve ultimate perfection. For not only were many Jewish philosophers influenced by the Greek and Western theological equation of women with unreason and sin, but they were writing as well against the backdrop of rabbinic attitudes and texts that were ambivalent, at best, with respect to the halakhic status of women within Judaism. Even a brief set of examples will express what I have in mind.

Jewish feminist theologians have noted the absence of the female voice in many of the defining halakhic moments of Judaism. The very covenant between God and Abraham, reiterated in the *"brit milah,"* is characterized as a theologically defining event from which women, by virtue of their physical being, are excluded. As Judith Plaskow has so strikingly reminded us, women were conspicuously absent from the moment of revelation: "At the central moment of Jewish history, women are invisible. . . . The Otherness of women finds its way into the very center of Jewish experience."[43] The continual re-enactment of this event reminds women that their radical "otherness" has excluded them from the dramatic interplay between God and the Jewish people. But nowhere is the Rabbinic exclusion of women manifested more clearly than in the discussion of women's exemption from positive time-bound ritual commandments, a discussion in which Maimonides the legalist plays an important role. In the following mishnah, women's and men's obligations are compared with respect to ritual observance.

> And all positive mitzvot that are time-bound (*mitzvot aseh she-ha-zeman gerama*), men are obligated but women are exempt. And all positive mitzvot that are not time-bound, the same holds for men and for women, they are [both] obligated. And all negative mitzvot, whether or not time-bound, the same holds for men and for women, they are obligated.[44]

In this text, both women and men are obligated to three out of four categories: negative time-bound commandments, negative non time-bound commandments, and positive non time-bound commandments. Only in the area of positive time-bound commandments are women exempt from obligation. Examples of positive time-bound commandments are given in the *Tosefta*: "What is an example of a positive time-bound commandment? *Succah, lulav, shofar, tzitzit,* and *tefillin.*"[45] Clearly the rabbis were exempting women from observances that were to be performed at a particular time of day. But what is important to notice about these texts is that the rabbis do not explain *why* it is that women are exempt from these positive time-bound commandments. Why is it, in other words, that the category of time-bound commandments was chosen to delineate women's exemption? Judith Hauptman examines some of the reasons commonly given for this exemption, e.g., that performance of these commandments might interfere with women's domestic responsibilities, and she finds these apologetic reasons inadequate.[46] Her own suggestion is that these exemptions reflect the fact that a woman is owned by another and therefore "cannot be independently obligated to perform them [positive time-bound rituals]."[47] Further, pointing out that the phrase "positive time-bound" is mentioned only in connection with women, Hauptman argues that the very taxonomy exists only to distinguish between a women's ritual obligations and her exemptions; therefore, the essence of the distinction must reside in the meaning of the phrase itself, namely in that these are the "key mitzvot of marking Jewish time."[48] By exempting women from those very ritual acts that mark Jewish time, women are cut off, as it were, from the temporal patterns that define a religious community. If the positive time-bound commandments represent the key commandments involved in marking time, and if the Children of Israel are commanded to sanctify time, then clearly women are excluded from this enterprise. Activities such as reciting the *Shema* three times a day and putting on phylacteries are central public duties that mark the passage of time. By exempting women from these duties, temporality itself has been utilized to erode the relation between women and the Deity.[49]

Given this exclusionary rabbinic tradition, coupled with the anti-feminist biases already noted in Western philosophy, we might expect an even more trenchant anti-female diatribe in Jewish philosophy. Interestingly enough, however, such is not univocally the case. In order to illustrate my point, let me turn to one of the most powerful descriptions of the attainment of spiritual perfection that occurs at the very end of Maimonides's *Guide of the Perplexed.* Based on this text, I shall argue that, because of his cognitivist conception of belief, Maimonides represents a counter-example to feminist descriptions of misogyny.

Describing the ultimate goal of human existence, Maimonides gives the following description of the attainment of ultimate bliss achievable by a mortal:

V.1 The philosophers have already explained that the bodily faculties impede in youth the attainment of most of the moral virtues, and all the more that of pure thought which is achieved through the perfection of the intelligibles that lead to passionate love of Him, may He be exalted . . . when a perfect man is stricken with years and approaches death, this apprehension increases very powerfully, joy over this apprehension and great love for the object of apprehension become stronger, until the soul is separated from the body at that moment in this state of pleasure. . . .

V.2 Because of this the Sages have indicated with reference to the deaths of Moses, Aaron and Miriam that *the three of them died by a kiss.* . . . And they said of Miriam in the same way: *She also died by a kiss.* But with regard to her it is not said, *by the mouth of the Lord; because she was a woman, the use of the figurative expression was not suitable with regard to her.* [My emphasis] Their purpose was to indicate that the three of them died in the pleasure of this apprehension due to the intensity of passionate love.[50]

In V.1, Maimonides describes the state of perfection of one who has achieved the fullness of philosophical study encouraged in this work. Reflecting the Neoplatonic motif that corporeal bodies hinder immaterial perfection, V.1 emphasizes the separation from corporeality as a necessary condition for spiritual perfection. It is important to note that a young person is never capable of achieving this level of perfection. The instant of ultimate perfection is manifested by the divesting of corporeality, a state that is presumably not possible for a youth still subject to passions. In fact, Maimonides tells us that only three individuals have ever reached this level.

V.2 is a truly remarkable passage, for here Maimonides acknowledges that even a woman—Miriam—can in theory achieve the kind of perfection described in V.1. Moses, Aaron, and Miriam all die "in the pleasure of this apprehension." Presumably Miriam, as well as Moses and Aaron, has achieved the final separation of soul from body described in V.1. This separation is consummated by a kiss. But Maimonides is reluctant to admit that God kisses Miriam directly, presumably because to kiss a female is unseemly for the Deity. This reluctance reflects the sentiments of the following rabbinic passage:

> V.3 Our Rabbis taught: there are six [persons] over whom the Angel of Death had no dominion—Abraham, Isaac, and Jacob, Moses, Aaron, and Miriam. With respect to Moses, Aaron, and Miriam, they "died by the mouth of the Lord." [Num. 33:38 and Deut. 34:5] But "by the mouth of the Lord" is not stated in the case of Miriam. . . . And how come Scripture does not say "by the mouth of the Lord" as in the case of Moses? Because saying such a thing would be inappropriate [in the case of a woman].[51]

Why is it inappropriate to have God kiss Miriam directly if presumably she too has shed her corporeality? Reactions to V.2 and V.3 have been surprisingly minimal in the literature. Rawidowicz notes that "even women" are capable of achieving the highest ideals, but does not explore the implications therein. Fishbane has argued that the deaths of Moses, Aaron, and Miriam are "anthropomorphically transfigured in this midrash . . . the very moment of death is itself infused with an erotic element."[52] In these passages, the kiss of God represents the culmination of a spiritual quest, a poetical way of talking about the "consummation of spiritual *eros* as the death of the earthly self."[53] But if, as Maimonides believes, matter represents the manifestation of corporeality and evil, and this matter is identified with the female principle, then in an important sense one might expect that the female in such an ontology can never fully rid herself of the mark of sexuality. And if the female is *by nature* material, then she cannot engage in the same sort of "God-talk" as somebody who can divest himself of corporeality.

Idit Dobbs-Weinstein has pointed to the ambivalence inherent in Maimonides's thinking about the relationship between matter and evil. She suggests that this ambivalence results in part from Maimonides's attempt to accept both an Aristotelian and Neoplatonic ontology.[54] Dobbs-Weinsten emphasizes Maimonides's insistence upon likening matter to the female principle. This insistence is evidenced in the following passage from the *Guide* in which Maimonides clearly identifies matter with sexual license:

> V.4 All bodies subject to generation and corruption are attained by corruption only because of their matter. . . . The nature and true reality of matter are such that it never ceases to be joined to privation; hence no form remains constantly in it, for it perpetually puts off one form and puts on another. How extraordinary is what Solomon said in his wisdom when likening matter to a married harlot (Prov. 6.26), for matter is in no way found without form and is consequently always like a married woman who is never separated from a man, and is never free. However, notwithstanding her being a married woman, she never ceases to seek for another man to substitute for her husband, and she deceives and draws him on in every way until he obtains from her what her husband used to obtain. This is the state of matter.[55]

The implications of this parable are striking when juxtaposed against Maimonides's statement that it is matter that stands in the way of human perfection. Matter acts as a veil, a barrier, to human knowledge of God:[56]

> V.5 Matter is a strong veil preventing the apprehension of that which is separate from matter as it truly is. It does this even if it is the noblest and purest matter, I mean to say even if it is the matter of the heavenly spheres. All the more is this true for the dark and turbid matter that is ours. Hence whenever our intellect aspires to apprehend the deity or one of the intellects, there subsists this great veil interposed between the two. This is alluded to in all the books of the prophets; namely that we are separated by a veil from God and that He is hidden from us by a heavy cloud, or by darkness or by a mist or by an enveloping cloud, and similar allusions to our incapacity to apprehend Him because of matter. . . . And though that great assembly was greater than any vision of prophecy and beyond any analogy, it also indicated a notion; I refer to His manifestation . . . in a thick cloud. For it draws attention to the fact that the apprehension of His true reality is impossible for us because of the dark matter that encompasses us and not Him . . . for He . . . is not a body.[57]

Not only does the female, *qua* matter, stand in the way of male perfection and actualization, but she herself can never rid herself of the matter that constitutes her very essence: the female qua personification of matter veils herself.

The metaphysical basis for the distinction between male and female has been well documented in recent feminist scholarship. We need only to reflect upon the significance of Pythagoras's Table of Opposites that is based upon his theory of number.[58] In this Table of Opposites, the female principle is aligned with what were considered in Greek thought to be negative characteristics: unlimit, plurality, left, moving, darkness and evil, thus emphasizing the overall unsavoriness of the female principle. In general, those characteristics regarded as "better" or aligned with "perfection" are associated with the male principle, whereas those regarded as lower or "worse" are associated with the female.[59] This opposition between the male and female principles, with all its attendant moral and metaphysical implications embedded into Pythagoras's cosmology, reappears throughout the history of Greek philosophy. Consider the many passages in Aristotle that associate the material principle with corporeality, grossness, imperfection, and femaleness, as contrasted with the formal principle that is allied to incorporeality, perfection, and maleness.[60]

This identification of the female principle with matter and corporeality has had enormous implications with respect to the attitude held toward women both in philosophy and theology. As Carol Ochs has so eloquently argued, "God's own nonphysicality makes the physical suspect, if not absolutely evil. If God, the perfect Creator, creates in a non-physical way (by word alone), then our nonphysical creations are more divine than our physical creations. . . . Procreation is certainly not viewed as a central spiritual experience."[61] In a hylomorphic ontology, the female is upheld as the quintessence of materiality; only by overcoming her materiality, in other words by no longer being female, can she attain to a level of spiritual perfection.

In such an ontology, we have the crucial result that the female, qua material being, comes to represent the negative rootedness of substance in a material temporality. "The destroyer of man's primeval timeless innocence is represented as a serpent," suggests James Whitrow in speaking of the loss of Eden.[62] In this statement, notions of gender, corporeality, and moral evil are conflated. It is the woman, personification of materiality, who succumbs to the temptation of the serpent; it is the woman, in her pursuit of that which is forbidden, who introduces evil and transgression into a state of perfection; it is the woman, subject to her desires, who introduces corporeality into an incorporeal sphere.

In the classical rabbinic interpretations of Genesis 3, Eve is endowed with the responsibility for having introduced evil into the emerging human

material essences. And so women are no more or less excluded from the domain of spiritual perfection than are men.

 *Conclusion*

In this essay, I have attempted to unravel the interweaving of several strands within feminist thought and Jewish philosophy: strands connected to philosophical methodology having to do with the role of reason; implications of this methodology with respect to issues in metaphysics and epistemology; and the reverberations of both matter and materiality to issues pertaining to gender and sexuality. In the final part of the essay, I have used Maimonides's *Guide* III.51 to explore the importance of the identification of materiality itself with the female. This identification carries with it implications with respect to theodicy as well. The very existence of evil can be associated with the material substratum, thus accounting for how an omnipotent, omniscient, benevolent Deity can create an imperfect world. For if imperfection is created within materiality itself, then God cannot be blamed for the ontological character of this material. Both the ancient philosophers, starting with Pythagoras, as well as religious thinkers, were quick to associate this material principle with the "female." Thus Eve's sin is quickly associated with sexuality, with matter, and this presumption of evil is then equated with all women.[68] It is this association that has come under such trenchant attack among contemporary feminists.

My argument, however, is that while anti-female biases can certainly be detected in Western philosophy in general, it is a mistake to assume similar bias in Jewish philosophy; such an assumption is both facile and unsubstantiated. Notwithstanding the apparent anti-female biases in rabbinic literature, it turns out, in fact, that Jewish philosophers share with many feminist philosophers a distrust of reason altogether. Feminist philosophers should find themselves much more comfortable with the epistemological non-cognitivism of much of Jewish philosophy. Furthermore, it is not clear that women, and the female in general, are deprecated in Jewish philosophical texts. In Maimonides's work, for example, the image of Miriam can be seen to function as a hermeneutic device that unites divine predication, intellectual union, and spiritual perfection. The "unseemliness" of God's kissing Miriam reinforces the fact that she is ontologically unable to transcend her material being. By acquiescing to midrashic interpretations of Miriam's kiss, Maimonides supports an exoteric reading of intellectual perfection according to which the female is ontologically imperfect when compared to the male. However, on an esoteric reading, the very fact that Miriam receives

God's "kiss" suggests that, like her male compatriots, Miriam has pene-trated the *mysterium* that is defended by negative predicates. With this inter-pretation, Miriam's perfection symbolizes not that she has almost shed her "female" material nature, but rather that Miriam, Moses, and Aaron have overcome their humanness. Being female no longer stands in Miriam's way.

NOTES

1. Susan Sherwin, "Philosophical Methodology and Feminist Methodology: Are They Compatible," in *Women, Knowledge, and Reality: Explorations in Feminist Philosophy,* ed. Ann Garry and Marilyn Pearsall (Boston: Unwin Hyman, 1989), 33.

2. Hava Tirosh-Rothschild, "'Dare to Know': Feminism and the Discipline of Jewish Philosophy," in *Feminist Perspectives on Jewish Studies,* ed. Lynn Davidman and Shelly Tanen-baum (New Haven, Conn.: Yale University Press, 1994), 104.

3. Ibid.

4. Ibid., 105.

5. Ibid., 106.

6. Ibid., 107.

7. Sally Haslanger, "Feminism in Metaphysics: Negotiating the Natural," in *The Cambridge Companion to Feminism in Philosophy,* ed. Miranda Fricker and Jennifer Hornsby (Cambridge: Cambridge University Press, 2000), 107.

8. See Alison Wylie, "Feminism in Philosophy of Science: Making Sense of Contin-gency and Constraint," in *The Cambridge Companion to Feminism in Philosophy,* 166–84.

9. Marcia L. Homiak, "Feminism and Aristotle's Rational Ideal," in *A Mind of One's Own,* ed. Louise M. Antony and Charlotte Witt (Boulder: Westview Press, 1993), 2.

10. Linda Martin Alcoff, "Is the Feminist Critique of Reason Rational?" *Philosophical Topics* 23 (1995): 3.

11. Antony and Witt, eds., *A Mind of One's Own.*

12. See Genevieve Lloyd, *The Man of Reason: "Male" and "Female" in Western Philosophy* (Minneapolis: University of Minnesota Press, 1984).

13. Alcoff, "Is the Feminist Critique of Reason Rational?"

14. Tirosh-Rothschild, "Dare to Know."

15. Alcoff, "Is the Feminist Critique of Reason Rational?" 8.

16. Ibid., 9.

17. Ibid., 14.

18. Ibid., 5.

19. Tirosh-Rothschild, "Dare to Know," 88.

20. Jean François Lyotard, *The Postmodern Condition: A Report on Knowledge,* trans. Geoff Bennington and Brian Massumi (Minneapolis: University of Minnesota Press, 1984).

21. Louise M. Antony, "Quine as Feminist: The Radical Import of Naturalized Episte-mology," in *A Mind of One's Own,* 187.

22. Ibid., 188.

23. Ibid., 190.

24. Evelyn Fox Keller, "Feminism and Science," in *Women, Knowledge, and Reality:*

Explorations in Feminist Philosophy, ed. Ann Garry and Marilyn Pearsall (Boston: Unwin Hyman, 1989), 179.

25. Ibid.

26. Tirosh-Rothschild, "Dare to Know."

27. Haslanger, "Feminism in Metaphysics," 117.

28. Charlotte Witt, "Anti-Essentialism in Feminist Theory," *Philosophical Topics* 23, no. 2 (1995): 322.

29. Isaac Husik, *A History of Medieval Jewish Philosophy* (New York, 1916).

30. Menachem Kellner, "Is Contemporary Jewish Philosophy Possible," in *Studies in Jewish Philosophy,* ed. Norbert Samuelson (Boston: University Press of America, 1987), 27.

31. Daniel H. Frank and Oliver Leaman, eds., *History of Jewish Philosophy* (London: Routledge, 1997), 6.

32. Steven S. Schwarzschild, "Authority and Reason Contra Gadamer," in *Studies in Jewish Philosophy,* 103.

33. Ibid., 105.

34. See, for example, Shalom Carmy and David Shatz, "The Bible as a Source for Philosophical Reflection," in *History of Jewish Philosophy,* 13–37, and David Novak, "The Talmud as a Source for Philosophical Reflection," ibid., 62–80.

35. Barry S. Kogan, "A Response to Professor Kellner," in *Studies in Jewish Philosophy,* 35.

36. See Aviezer Ravitsky, *History and Faith: Studies in Jewish Philosophy* (Amsterdam: J. C. Gieben, 1996) for a penetrating discussion of the status of Jewish philosophers vis à vis their intellectual environment.

37. Steven Katz, "Jewish Philosophy in the 1980's: A Diagnosis and Prescription," in *Studies in Jewish Philosophy,* 89.

38. Ibid., 71.

39. Ibid., 74.

40. Ibid.

41. Maimonides's text can be found in Menachem Kellner, *Dogma in Medieval Jewish Thought* (Oxford: Oxford University Press, 1986), 16.

42. See Manekin's discussion of *emunah* in Charles H. Manekin, "Hebrew Philosophy in the Fourteenth and Fifteenth Centuries: An Overview," in *History of Jewish Philosophy,* 350–78.

43. See Judith Plaskow, *Standing Again at Sinai: Judaism from a Feminist Perspective* (New York: Harper Collins, 1990), 25.

44. Mishnah Kiddushin 1:7b, Judith Hauptman, *Rereading the Rabbis: A Woman's Voice* (Boulder: Westview Press, 1998), 224.

45. Kiddushin 1:10, quoted in Hauptman, *Rereading the Rabbis,* 224.

46. Ibid., 225.

47. Ibid., 226.

48. Ibid., 227.

49. Rochelle L. Millen, unpublished manuscript.

50. Maimonides, *Guide of the Perplexed,* III.51.

51. Baba Bathra 17a.

52. Michael Fishbane, *The Kiss of God* (Seattle: University of Washington Press, 1994), 18.

53. The original eros is transfigured, and "the male-female love of the Song is now read as God (spiritually) kissing men but not women, for that would be a consummate breach of propriety." See Fishbane, *The Kiss of God,* 26.

54. See Idit Dobbs-Weinstein, *Maimonides and St. Thomas on the Limits of Reason* (Albany: State University of New York Press, 1995), 89ff.

55. Maimonides, *Guide* III.8. For her trenchant discussion of this passage, see Susan Shapiro, "A Matter of Discipline: Reading for Gender in Jewish Philosophy," in *Judaism since Gender,* ed. Miriam Peskowitz and Laura Levitt (New York: Routledge, 1997), 158–73.

56. Maimonides, *Guide,* III.9, 436.

57. Maimonides, *Guide* III.9, 436–37.

58. Aristotle, *Metaphysics,* 1.5 986a 22–b2.

59. For a penetrating discussion of the implications of Pythagoreanism in Western culture, see Margaret Wertheim, *Pythagoras' Trousers: God, Physics and the Gender Wars* (New York: W. W. Norton & Co, 1995).

60. For a discussion of the implications of the female principle in religious thought, see Judith Plaskow, "Jewish Theology in Feminist Perspective," in *Feminist Perspectives on Jewish Studies,* 62–84; Susan Shapiro, "A Matter of Discipline"; Hava Tirosh-Rothschild, "Dare to Know."

61. Carol R. Ochs, *Women and Spirituality* (London: Rowman and Littlefield, 1997), 21.

62. See Whitrow, "Time and the Universe," 564.

63. Susan Niditch, "Genesis" in *The Women's Bible Commentary,* ed. C. A. Newsom and S. H. Ringe (Louisville: Westminster/John Knox Press, 1992).

64. For additional discussion of these passages, see Menachem Kellner, "Philosophical Misogyny in Medieval Jewish Philosophy—Gersonides vs. Maimonides," *Jerusalem Studies in Jewish Thought (Sermoneta Jubilee Volume)* (1998): 113–28; and Abraham Melamed, "Maimonides on Women: Formless Matter or Potential Prophet?" in *Perspectives on Jewish Thought and Mysticism,* ed. A. Ivry, E. Wolfson, and A. Arkush (Amsterdam: Harwood Academic Publishers, 1998), 99–134.

65. See Y. Tzvi Langermann, "Science and the Kuzari," *Science in Context* 10 (1997): 495–519.

66. Maimonides, *Guide* III.51, 623.

67. Maimonides, *Guide* III.28.

68. See Daniel Boyarin, *Carnal Israel* (Berkeley: University of California Press, 1993) for a detailed analysis of this identification in Jewish thought.

EIGHT

LAURIE ZOLOTH

Into the Woods:
Killer Mothers, Feminist Ethics,
and the Problem of Evil

Introduction

Several years ago I was invited to give a philosophical presentation on the topic of "Women and Violence," and the presumption of the organizers, which was indeed played out at the event itself, was that the important issue about violence, women, and philosophy concerned the situation of the victim and her rescue. Women were subjects of violence by individual men, or by a society constructed by patriarchy, and it was the structure of the world itself, as prepared and dominated by patriarchy and its manifestations that was the root source of evil and violent deeds. It is a familiar enough theme and it is, of course, in part a correct theme, but I decided to tack off in a different direction to ask another sort of question. I wrote instead about what we think and how we reason as philosophers and as feminists when women are not the victims, but the perpetrators, the evildoers, the enactors of evil. It seemed to me then, that while moral philosophy had a tradition of literature on evil, as of yet feminist moral philosophy had not considered the issue in as robust a way as was needed. I therefore turned to my interest in Jewish ethics for resources. Since a traditional place to begin in philosophy is definitional, I began by trying to define evil. I was well along into this problem when events overtook me, and the news of a child-killing mother, Susan Smith, hit the press.

Into the Woods

Susan Smith was a beautiful, young, white woman, married and raising two little boys and working as a secretary in a small town in rural Appalachia, and she claimed that she and her sons were car-jacked by a black man who abducted her sons when he stole her car. After their loss, Smith was seen for days with piteous appearances on national TV, begging for their release. However, then their bodies were found strapped to the children's car seats, drowned in the car, which was dredged from a nearby lake. It turned out further that there was no black man at all—Smith herself had gunned the car with the children inside into the lake deliberately to kill them so as to be free to pursue her boss's son, who was not interested in an affair with a woman with children. This was an act of such violence, and of such evil that it dominated American attention, and so I wrote with this problem in mind. When the editor of this volume asked for a submission about how feminism and philosophy and Jewish thought inform my discipline of social ethics, I returned to this theme. Once again, events provided a powerful context. It was three years later, in the summer of 2001 as I was writing the final draft that killer mothers were again the subject of national reflection; a Texas mother of five drowned her babies one by one, and placed them neatly on their beds.

But in September of 2001, all previous reflections on evil were reconfigured. Suddenly, the discourse on evil in which I had been an ironic observer consumed us all as surely as the flames in New York and Washington. All Americans were suddenly confronted with not only a new physical vulnerability, but a sense of the paucity of our explanatory systems, and in particular, the explanatory capacities about good and evil. I watched the events unfold on CNN, and since I was working at that moment on this chapter, I had books on evil in my briefcase: Ted Peters, Elaine Pagels, Hannah Arendt, Alain Badiou, and Richard Rorty.

Without a robust theory of evil, without a careful and complex understanding of evil, philosophy, especially feminist philosophy, cannot understand nor interpret the world, and hence cannot begin to do that which ethics must do—apply reason to the storm of history, create an argument for the moral gesture, oppose evil, allow for judgment. Without taking on the problem of evil, there is a terrible lacuna in our theory and hence in our capacity to respond. Without a theory of evil, we turn to psychology, or to the thin accounts of a politics of materialism, as if goodness were something more readily available to the privileged. This chapter represents preliminary notes toward a reconstruction of the moral truth claims we make about our society and toward how a Jewish and feminist ethics might take on the hard tasks and responsibility of judgment. Can we create a feminist ethics, informed by Jewish texts, in which serious judgments of the other can stand, and in which partisan authority can be evoked?

It will not be a simple task to leave the certainty of the first task of feminism: the close reading of the oppression in the status of women, the discourse of the victim herself. Of all the discourses in feminist philosophy, the discourse surrounding the problem of evil is the least developed. Unlike much of Western philosophy, feminist theory has not taken up the classic debates about evil as an independent force or a force of corrupted but essential nature, nor robustly considered theodicy, although this could be extrapolated or implied in much of the early work of feminism. In part, this choice was a methodological privileging of the local, particular narrative over the larger "universal" narrative, a method that wanted to see the political in the personal action overlooked in classic texts and theories. In our search for meaning amidst the details of ordinary life, feminists theorists, with few exceptions, have left such metaphysical speculation and larger definitional tasks to theologians, and in so doing, have ceded much of the discourse to feminists with concerns about the primal biblical narrative of good and evil, a discourse so freighted that reactions to it have been largely uni-dimensional. In point of fact, one of the foundational tenets of feminist religious ethics, found in many of the first feminist works on biblical literature, is a rejection of the narrative of Eve as the culpable source of human befallenness. It has remained a staple of all feminist biblical criticism. Hellenistic and other folk versions of this tale are similarly seen as the imposition of patriarchy and the suppression of female moral impulses for the good. It is this suppression that is named as the simple, nearly essentialist, source of evil. In our construction of both epistemic and normative ethics, feminists have relied on persuasive revelations about power and patriarchy to construct such a narrative. The portraiture of the women as the source of sexual and religious deviance, the associations among evil, female potency, and the evil forces in the natural world have been addressed by Mary Daly, Susan Griffin, and others. In every case, feminist theory rejects the account of Eve as evildoer, and constructs an alternate vision: that women are wrongly accused. In fact, Eve's choices and, hence, all women's essential nurturing "natures," represent a source of deep moral strength and wisdom in a world not of our own making.

In works on war, or rape, or environmental degradation, the refrain is repeated: it is patriarchy, or it is male "energy," or it is "the way men have been socially constructed as oppressors" that is the problem. It is wrong to actually blame women for evil acts. Blaming women, in this argument, is merely a clever way of ignoring their situation, or worse, of suppressing women, or of fearing women's deeper wisdom, or women's intrinsic connection to the world, as mothers, or as persons with a more accurate sort of "knowing," or as people with a truer understanding of the natural world, or the embodied world, or of "care" itself. The ethics of care supposes an intuition for the good, against an ethics of rigid forms of justice, or excessive rule-making, seen as a feature of some patriarchal systems. Consider the framing of the problem by Petra Kelly:

> Women must lose all fear of speaking up and demand what is theirs and their children's. Only if we begin to rediscover our own nature, can we discover new ways of wholeness, balance and decentralization—can we forge a bond with the Earth and the Moon, living with cooperation, gentleness, non-possessiveness and soft energies.[1]

But if Eve's reach for forbidden knowledge or her gesture of disobedience is liberatory and not the source of evil, what of the problem of the definition and etiology of evil? The problem of evil remains a central problem for feminist theory to address, going beyond the narrative of victimization, or the narrative of compassionate response. It is a problem for feminist ethics not only because it is not fully elaborated, or difficult to define—it is a problem for our philosophic stance because the facticity of the matter ought to disrupt our proclamations. For even the accurate portrayals of women as victims, as powerless, and as subjugated do not fully address the occasions of female perpetration of true evil.

Hence, beyond the problem of definition is the problem of cases. What are we to make of the horrific (and well reported) cases of child abuse and murder by women? It might seems to us as though it is the rarity of the event that catches our attention. When women perpetrate violence it is constructed as a double violation: evil that is done by the citizen against the society and evil that is an out(rage) against the normative moral judgments of how a woman ought to mother—after all, the notion of women as inherently nurturing is a fixture of both the most mainstream popular culture and of postmodern feminist theory. The iconographic case of Susan Smith leaped to our attention in part because the specter of race that framed the case (she claimed a "hooded, black man with a gun" had taken her children), but in part because it stood for much more as a social construct—the threat to the pervasive theory of mothers and goodness. When Susan Smith murders her children, the oldest tropes are evoked: dangerous women and vulnerable sons, overlaid with the starkly racist tone of her first defense. Social notions of good mothering not only pervade an American civil discourse, but feminist theory as well.

While feminist theory and a general liberal stance have been eager to identify how a female gender is assembled, and while a robust theory of the good has been established in feminist philosophy by our consideration of caring, of community, of relationally, and of mothering, there has been far less corresponding attention to the philosophical and ethical problem of evil. The works of Kathleen Sands and Nel Noddings have begun to address this, querying how far our ideas of "care" can be extended in social policy, but far more needs to be said about the simple pervasiveness, the ordinariness of wickedness (note the almost hopelessly old-fashioned sound of this language). And in the aftermath of the violence of September 2001, the problem of evil present a challenge to feminist ethics that cannot be avoided.

Let me defend several claims. First, without serious consideration of evil, feminist philosophy is diminished. Second, without a Jewish contribution to the discourse, the powerful theology of Christianity that is assumed by much of Western philosophy will overtake our feminism, and there are important reasons to expand the ethical considerations of evil beyond the Christian ones since it is understanding of the complexities of a response to evil that allows for a more accurate grasp of the phenomena. Finally, a feminist philosophy informed by Jewish texts and arguments creates a richer discourse within feminist thought as well as within philosophy. Hence, when one intends to create a relationship within Jewish philosophy, feminist philosophy, and ethics, one can fruitfully begin with a problem that has both descriptive and normative implications.

🌣 *Murderous/Murderess Methods*

This chapter will address the philosophical issues in our consideration of evil, and locate the debate in the dramatic cases of child murder by mothers. The method itself is important, and because, in earlier drafts of this essay, colleagues became puzzled (even rather alarmed) about why I spent so much time in a sociological, nearly journalist account of this horrible crime, I want to stress my attention to method. It was hard to find a clear case of evildoing that all could define as evildoing—murder of innocents seemed to be the signal case. When I began the research I thought such cases rare, and interesting in their rarity—only later did I come to understand these cases as depressingly common, and hence interesting in their ordinal nature, a claim, I realized, that I had to document. I was curious, at first, whether when such cases arise and are now increasingly well reported in the popular press, if they were reflective of significant alterations in the position of women, if they were contextually based in the historical dynamics of ordinary mothering, or if they were brought to our attention by a popular culture made uneasy by images of female power. The point of beginning in cases, rather than theory, is precisely out of a commitment to both a tenet of feminist thought that calls attention to the mother–child bond as indicative of theory, and a tenet that demands attention to particular, tangible narratives. This practice is also derived from the casuistry of talmudic reasoning; hence we begin in the praxis and in the specific "texts" of the narratives themselves.

Without a robust theory and without a language that explains and contextualizes the capacity for great and small sin, moral theory itself is impoverished. The turn toward the therapeutic rather than the theological is an unfettered trend in liberal theory, but feminism without a theory of evil is boosterism. Beyond the usual normative response lies a deeper question: the ontological one inherent in a reconsideration of evil.

In this chapter, I will look at this problem from several perspectives and a number of different sources. The Smith case and others will be analyzed, and the story as reflected in selected feminist texts will be noted. Finally, I will reflect on the problem of evil from a feminist Jewish perspective and will analyze selected texts from the Jewish tradition that aim toward a reframing of a feminist theory and theology that both accounts for and struggles with evil.

Evildoing

Why do people choose to do evil deeds? Why do women act wickedly? Is there a difference in these two questions? That is, is there particularity in how the experience of evildoing is motivated when women are the moral agents? I mean, as well, that when philosophy asks the former question, is it really asking why it is that *men* act evilly? It was impossible to raise this question in the last half of the twentieth century and the emerging twenty-first century without noting the breathtaking scope of the magnitude of evil itself—the sheer possibilities for harm to innocents, the magnitude of the slaughter. Any serious discussion of evil occurs in the face of the capacity for the enormity of violation that is possible in human sociability.

All talk of evil now has become large, international, formal. It is talk that is set beside the Shoah, the horrific aftermath of the wars in Southeast Asia, Rwanda, and Bosnia, and now, it is talk about the destruction in New York and Washington. But the issue that I want to begin with is the problem of ordinary evil, the acts of terrible wrong that live in the darkest margins of ordinary choices in parenting, relationships with the familiar, dependent other. It is particular, and it is about understanding that all evildoing begins in the turn of one body on to another.

Here we do not have a complex struggle over terms. I want to focus our attention on the problem of evil and responsibility and causality: hence, the case of the unequivocal evil of child murder. It is an act of deep wrongness to inflict harm on the innocent. Child murder is the ultimate end of the continuum in child abuse and neglect that begins in the most ordinary of refusals by parents of the needs of the child, and it is certainly and without argument a bad thing. The consideration of this case in a book about feminist Jewish philosophy is central for two, terrible reasons. First, because such cases recur across class, race, and ethnic divides—a famous example, the Nussbaum case, did in fact involve Jewish parents. The case involved a lawyer father who beat and tortured both his wife and his child, but the mother not only colluded and did not seek medical help, but actively hid the years of abuse and neglect as they both pursued drug habits. Secondly, because although it mostly does not happen that parents kill, but it does happen that parents think about it, walk near to it in the imagination, and then do *not* kill. Evil runs its course alongside daily life—close, but then not quite there. Why is this?

THE FACTS OF THE CASES

Let us begin with fact patterns. In America, most acts of the truest evil, murder, occur within relationships (61 percent of the 22,540 murders in 1992, for example).[2] Of these acts, few reach our national attention because they are so very ordinary, but the case of the murder by Susan Smith was one such act that did make front-page news.

Susan Smith appeared on our TV screens in the late fall of 1994 as a sobbing, desperate mother pleading for the life of her two heartbreakingly beautiful sons, babies that we saw in fuzzy, endearing images so often that they began to seem like children we knew, not from the news, but from our own home movies. The venue was our own, an "Our Town" America for the 1990s, a small city, a small and good life, a small and good young woman, a birthday party, high chairs and cake. Into this sweetness, we were told, had erupted the classic paradigm of the evil and violence of the twentieth century. The monsters in the urban legends do not have faces; they ubiquitously wear ski masks; they are always men; and they are always men of color.[3] For a week, Smith had us convinced of her sincerity, of the commonness of her plight. This could happen to *me,* the story told us, to anyone stopped at a traffic light with her baby boys.[4] The subtext of the demonic man at the edges of ordered white rationality did not seem odd: few commentators noted on the face of it how absurd it would be for a bad black man in his ski cap to emerge out of the shadows and take a car full of white children who needed their diapers changed every few hours and disappear into the American South. (Try, for example, to imagine what would have happened had Smith told police that a white man in a nice business suit had taken her car, and you will see immediately how the class gradient works to reify the truth claim.) Smith's story rested on our oldest tropes of evil: that Satan is everywhere, an intimate enemy; his shrouded witches are the other, come to snatch the babies into the woods if we turn.[5]

But the story doubled in on itself. And when the deeper story emerged, like a pentimento becoming visible under the portraiture, the power in the horror of Susan Smith's confession that it was in fact she herself who had killed her children, she who had strapped them into their car seats (the worst detail), and she who had driven them into the dark lake to their deaths, was its familiarity.

Why familiar? Why resonance and not only dissonance? In part because of the same statistics that led the sheriff of Smith's small town to doubt her—the comparative rarity of stranger abductions, the commonness of parental ones, that the violence against small children is most often at the hand of their parents. In the 196-bed hospital where I consulted as a clinical ethicist, there are an average of 4.5 child abuse referrals called into the child protective services *per day*.[6]

Resonant, too, was the story of the deeply evil stepmother figure from classic folklore (the single divorced mother being the modern equivalent of the "bad" woman). Consider the tale of Hansel and Gretel.[7] Here we have the desperate parents, driven by their hunger to desperate action. The children realize the starkness of their plight, so they will go into the woods with white stones to lead the way home, and when they do, the good but weak father is at first glad, but soon is tempted again, ready to lose the children.

> [T]here was once more great dearth throughout the land, and the children heard their mother saying at night to their father: "Everything is eaten again, we have one half loaf left, and that is the end. The children must go . . . there is no other means of saving ourselves."[8]

This time it works. Note, by the way, how the attempted murder/abandonment is wrapped in a lie. The children are lied to, and when they survive, they are chastised for oversleeping. We follow the children into the woods and we see the darkness at nightfall, how they can be lost in a moment, how the fairytale wife becomes the child's tormentor. In the woods is the old woman witch's house, another doubling: deception at its sweet heart. The children tear the "house" (read body) of the witch apart and stuff it into their hungry mouths: the roof, the windows. Here is food, abundance, but danger. It is the externalized mother we now fear. She will feed the children lavishly; in fact, she will feed them their fantasy treats, but she wants to consume them. Here, too, her own hunger is really at stake. (This is why the birthday videotape of the Smith boys reads to us as so sinister.) Having read the story as children, we understand its power as remembering adults: children are expendable in a marginal economy.

Smith's story as told was resonant in that it exposed how readily racism potentiates a narrative of evil. The notion that the evil that threatens is brought into ordinary (read white) lives by blacks is fundamental to the account of evil as external. The blamed is other, the Beast in the woods. But finally, the most complex mirroring of the Smith case was the reflection of the near miss narratives that millions of witnessing parents were able to find within their own lives. The desperation, the choice for violence, the limitless hatred of the dependent that also wait in us, the razor's edge of passion, the oddly American hunger for freedom and regression—all the wicked choices that are possible, daily available to parents—this too was familiar. We know this town; we live here too; we know the woods at the edge.

As the case progressed, the classic outlines of the tragedy were crystallized. Beneath the image of the brokenhearted mother, the victim, had lain traces of the evil seductress, and beneath this, the victim again—Susan Smith had been abandoned in childhood by a suicidal father, and when her mother remarried, it was to a stepfather who would confess to sexual assault on her as a fourteen-year-old. In an ironic touch, the stepfather was the Republican county chairman, the family the very picture of good family values. But Smith continued the relationship well into her adulthood, and along with concurrent sexual relationships with her ex-husband and her lover had explored this relationship again in the weeks just prior to the murders. (Note how every detail of this woman's sexual life is spread before us; one wants to avert the gaze, but we are called to look again and again, and at worse.) In this sense, the Smith case could meet any metaphorical need. Perhaps evil acts are only the retributive struggles of the abused grown child. Perhaps they are the conscious choices of the moral agent, protection gone awry. Here as well, in the motive for the crime, the contending views had ample evidence for disparate positions. Was Smith poor, a single mother on the verge of desperation? Or was she relatively well off for her town, making $17,000 a year, plus alimony payments and child support, as compared to her ex-husband's $20,000, with a secure white collar job, and a gym membership, whose aerobic class she had attended immediately prior to the killings. Was she driven to desperation by the demands of raising two babies? Or was she frustrated by her lover's dismissal of her and his couching his ambivalence in terms of his reluctance to become involved with her two children? In this case, the measure of what women were expected to be, of how feminism has reconstructed the American landscape, even in Union, South Carolina, was clearly at stake. Writing on women and the problem of evil, Nel Noddings notes that there have long been conflicting, cultural norms about the ontic expression of both pure evil and pure good as female. Noddings adds that Jungians, notably Erich Neumann in *The Great Mother,* have noted the power of this conflicted archetype:

> the Good Mother, the Terrible Mother, the negative anima, or (more simply, the seductive young witch), and the positive anima (or Sophia the goddess or the virgin).[9]

But one does not have to be a Jungian theorist to note the power of the complexly shifting views of the mother/seductress/virgin victim. At issue is the nature and the meaning of the consequence of action and the relationship of the consequences to the motive. And it is here that feminist theory falters. Does the legitimacy of past harm justify any level of evil? Mendacity and murder of the innocent? Are there just limits to the victim defense? And what is the ethical implication of a recourse to this defense?

IS THIS CASE AN ABERRATION?

The Smith case, and our imaginative reconstruction of the case, was not the only Killer Mother story that has surfaced in just this past year. In January 1994, Philadelphia mother Vivian King reported that her seventeen-year-old daughter was missing—a month later her bullet ridden body was found in a nearby park. The community rallied with outraged calls about violence in the neighborhood. King, who had passed out lavender-colored ribbons in her daughter's memory, confessed, recanted, and then was convicted of her death.[10] In March, a Los Angeles mother was arrested for trying to burn her two children to death.[11] In August, a Massachusetts woman murdered her five-year-old stepson. In her statement to the police, she was reportedly "unhappy about the child support her husband paid and resented having to care for the boy while her husband was at work."[12] That same month the *Los Angeles Times* reported the murder suicide of another mother, Teri Lynne Esterak, and her three children. In September, Dora Buenrostro of San Jacinto was arrested after stabbing her three children ages nine, eight, and four, and failing to convince police that her estranged husband had killed them.[13] In October, Pauline Zile, clutching her missing daughter's stuffed animal, gave a gripping account of how her seven-year-old daughter was abducted from a Fort Lauderdale flea market restroom, and pleaded for her return.[14] Pauline Zile and her husband later admitted to beating the child to death "because she would not stop crying." In March 1995, three Orange County newborns were found dead in one four-day period.[15] In May in Los Angeles, Donna Jean Fleming threw her three-year-old and twenty-two-month-old sons into the L.A. river and then jumped in herself. The three-year-old was rescued, but the twenty-two-month-old died.[16] In June, an article appeared that detailed the alimony arrangements that a judge had ordered the ex-husband of a convicted killer mother (she stabbed their three-year-old son with a steak knife). This case only made the news because of the unusual nature of payment while a woman was in prison for murder.[17] The AP wire service carried the report of four mothers who were housed together in jail in "kind of like a little coffee klatch" according to one or their lawyers. Included were Zile; Clover Boykin, who killed her five-month-old son in October after having a nightmare; Joanne Mejia, accused of shaking her baby to death; and Paulette Cole, accused of smashing a crib top on her two-year-old adopted daughter's neck.[18] In July in Dayton, Ohio, the community mobilized in the thousands for searches and prayer vigils after a four-year-old girl, Samantha Radich, was missing and her mother had pleaded for her return on TV. She was later found, bludgeoned by her mother, and thrown into a pit at an abandoned foundry. In November 1994, in Indiana, a mother pushed her sons, aged eight and eleven, from the roof of a Purdue University parking garage before she jumped to her death. Such cases make the press only because of some unusual "angle," which is to say, they are not news; for mothers and fathers kill their children 1,300 times a year, beat their children 45,000 times a year, and abandon their children so regularly that it is only the novelty case that we hear about. Since I wrote the first draft of this paper in 1994, each year there have been more stories. In 2002, for example, the Texas wife of a NASA engineer methodically drowned all five of her children, one after the other.

As I wrote that paragraph, I began to wonder where I was heading with this analysis. What, I wondered, is the scholarly point that I am trying to make? Had I gone too far? Had I created an overblown list, demonstrating yet another example of the popular unease with fundamental alterations in family, power, women's role? The story of abuse and victimization that results in blind but righteous anger is the framing story of feminism itself.

One's anger is not personal, but political, resultant to the creation of patri-archy.[19] Women, we have powerfully noted in two decades of modern fem-inist theory, are silenced, dispossessed, scorned by the culture, culturally constructed as lesser, and told we are hysterical, or weak, or unstable. Such are the veracities of the literature, and their repetition does not make them less valid. Is this surge in the reporting of killer-mother stories part of the anti-feminist backlash against feminist ideology? Let me reset the frame: it is factually correct that women are beaten and killed unjustly, and in very large numbers, in a culture that really and symbolically violates all women. But of the children who are killed each year, more than half are killed by mothers or by female caretakers, because that is who is there both to help and hurt them. "An estimated 650 to 700 mothers kill their children each year. . . . That represents more than half of the . . . children killed by par-ents or caretakers each year since 1976."[20] And while, despite the flurry of publicity, cases of mothers killing their children have declined in the last century, the issue still requires some explaining.[21]

I want to argue that it is in part true that the killer mother–witch story that is popular now is a function of "our" culture continually making mon-sters of women. Part of the construction of a particular ideology, that of the imperiled self besieged by social chaos and external threats on all sides, is that violence is inexorably, epidemically, on the rise:

> Many experts believe newborn homicides are part of the overall pattern of growing violence in the United Sates. "These poor little infants, they are just a small fraction of the whole violence epidemic in America."[22]

Yet this phenomenon is only in part a cultural construct. It is also murder and it is also a choice for evil.

In reflecting theologically on such a moment in a human relationship, we must take into account the horrible evil that child murder in fact represents—and not just in metaphorical terms, but through deep unwar-ranted harm to the innocent persons. It is harm that is potentiated by the fact that the innocent are not bystanders, which would be enough of a moral violation to warrant our attention, but that they are dependent on and powerless before their killer mothers. Let us, then, explore the explan-atory schemes for interpretation.

BUT AREN'T THEY JUST CRAZY?

Of course, in response to the Smith story and others, one could simply claim that at issue is the random insanity of the individuals. I wish to note here that this was one popular first response to the evil of terrorism as well—"they were insane acts of a madman." Here is one way, an extraordinary popular way, for intellectuals to make sense of such action. Therapeutic intervention stresses a non-judgmental attitude. States a therapist who specializes in postpartum depression:

> After talking to so many mothers, I realize that they are so much like me. This could have happened to me. I don't think of myself as being able to kill my children, but I can understand how something could take over my mind so I could do it. . . . All I can tell her is she didn't kill her child, her illness did.[23]

Let me say at the onset of this analysis that, of course, it is a type of insanity for anyone to kill a child. But this insanity conceals more than it reveals about the problem of evil deeds, which have real resonance. And while it is especially descriptive and perhaps useful in the cases of child abuse that have gone too far, in the sudden anger against the little fragile child self, the explanation does not help us in the cases of premeditated murderous acts. The Smith case and others named here are different. Their deeds are the same type of thought-out, carried-out, and in many cases concealed acts that we would not see as explicable by psychology alone if the perpetrators were gendered as men. Here we would think first of punishment for patriarchy taken to its ultimate extension. But the too-many cases of random or drug-induced violence against children, and the particular narrative of homicide then deceptive reframing of the story (especially in ways that invoke racist imagery) raise issues of a different magnitude.

For scholars trained in religious theory, it is of course impossible to hear the explanation of the therapist without being struck by its similarity to the language of Satanic causality: She didn't kill her child, some thing that took over her mind—Satan—did.

But Aren't They Just Oppressed?

Feminist social theorists have other explanations, the leading contender of which is that oppression makes one kill. Here again, as the world regards the acts of evil in terrorist bombings, we are reminded to think of the possibility that poverty itself might cause evil. Such cases of child murder recall, of course, the novel *Beloved,* Toni Morrison's account of the murder of a girl child by a mother desperate, fleeing from slavery, and saving her child from a life of rape and enslavement. Many of the stories that I researched had this feature to them, as they were accounts of women who had killed themselves and/or their child to avoid giving the children to their ex-husbands, whom, in some cases, they had accused of child molestation. Several accounts feature neighbors describing the desperate poverty the families faced. Smith herself spoke about her sense that her children would be finally safe, better off in heaven. This is surely another way to see the problem—as injustice and not evil, or as having the feature that liberation theologians have taught requires a different hermeneutic and response.[24] In this oppression account, it is different when women kill children or husbands, because the act itself is set in a frame of the moral equivalent of war or slavery, a terrain of such constraints that death is seen as protective, and violence seen as a rupture within a far more violent system. Just as the response to the psychological theory is medical therapeutic intervention, so is the response to the social construction the necessary indictment and subsequent development of a responsive community. In a murderous world, we all are culpable. The act of childrearing is unsupported, interstitial, overwhelming, isolating, "crazy-making," impoverishing. Being poor is the root cause for violence—if only the women were freer, or had more resources, such evil could be avoided. This becomes a harder case to make when a murder seems to cut across class and race boundaries, however, or when women kill, though they are fully surrounded by social networks.

But at this juncture the questions arise about how we are to make moral order, meaning, and social reconstruction when we are social witnesses to such evil. Even if one is convinced by the usual argument of feminist philosophy—that evil is done by women only if they are insane or oppressed—the act still demands some normative response and evaluation. It is because I find these two—the psychological or the oppression theory— obvious answers offered by feminism somewhat compelling, and certainly powerfully made, yet essentially inadequate, that I argue that harder questions need to be asked about why these cases raise such a deep response in us, the readers of the actions.

My premise is that our understanding of epistemic, normative, and aspirational ethics ought to begin in the relationship that we experience in the ordinary commerce of a life. The tendency to draw ethical norms from extreme situations that have little to do with real human gestures is an affectation of philosophy and history. Ordinary life is infused with choices taken or not taken, assessments of what can be known, and, given the limits of knowledge, what can be done, and what can be yearned for.[25] Impulses for evil beckon in a familiar sort of way.

We see frequent small meannesses, excesses, indifferences, acts of mendaciousness, and acts of cruelty. We see these in private, and we see them in the public arena (so often that the instances are a mocking feature of American politics, so often that the word *politics* is often a secular stand-in for the word *evil* itself, as in "it was just office politics") and we see them in the family. In part, we know of the power of evil because we are shaken, if we are honest, daily by its temptation and its power, and much of a human life is spent in controlling the impulses toward evil that could consume us. In response, several theorists have turned to the problem of evil in an attempt to offer alternative responses. Can these accounts point the way toward an understanding of women and evil?

The Epistemological Question: A Review of the Literature

Evil, in the terms of classic ethics, rests principally on two accounts: either evil is of a radical nature, a dualistic force in the moral universe that competes with the good, and in which the good needs defense, an argument most clearly associated with Immanuel Kant. Defense includes the protection of negative rights, with one's dignity linked to the ability to live well without the danger of evil. The second account of evil maintains that it is a depravation of the good, an argument associated classically with Augustine. In this account, the world is a good one, with good intent and design, but through sin, or error, evil exists in the breach. Feminist ethicists struggle with the same themes. Martha Nussbaum[26] and Kathleen Sands[27] both direct us to reflect on the idea that human persons operate as moral agents in an essentially tragic universe. In this view, tragic choices are invariably made because human persons are obliged to live in a world of imperfection and loss. Sands reminds us that

> by applying a tragic heuristic, religious feminists can approach evil as a *question* for insight and judgment, not as a legitimizing explanation.[28]

This view offers the necessity of "forc[ing] feminist work from its metaphysical islands, . . . teach[ing] it to breath in the deep waters of tragedy.[29] Our response to the world of tragedy ought to be compassion, pluralistic and attentive community, and a wounded but resilient spirit of continuance in its face. We will be confronted with tragedy because that is our nature. It is our social response to this problem that will allow for healing, compassion, and remembrance that to be flawed is to share the human fate with one another.

In work that challenges the tragic view, John Kekes offers what he calls "a hard reaction." Here he suggests

> that much of the evil that jeopardizes human aspirations to live good lives
> is caused by the characteristics but unchosen action of human beings. . . .
> And people cause evil when they act naturally and spontaneously, without
> much thought or effort, in accordance with the vices that have achieved
> dominance in their characters.[30]

Kekes would have us understand that we face real failure, real loss, but
that it is our task as human persons to develop "the reflective temper" or a
controlling moral intellect to prevent evil action from overtaking us. Faced
with a universe that is not especially tragic, Kekes argues that habits of
character shape us for evil choices. Such habits can be altered, controlled,
and ultimately judged.

> Our best chance of avoiding evil is still to increase our control, including
> control over the feelings that falsify our situation. And this is what those
> who have the reflective temper can do better than those who lack it.[31]

Andrew Delbanco, noting both the pervasiveness of evil actions and
violence that characterize modernity, and the linguistic shifts in American
history that name first the other as Satan and then the other as social disease, reflects on the need to examine the privation in each, and call for the
"miraculous paradox of demanding the best of ourselves."[32] Delbanco's account rests on the problem of externalizing the problem of evil—it is a radical intrusion, it can be avoided, guarded against, and distanced from. He
also notes the American tendency to distance oneself from the evil action.
But the narratives of evil I have noted allow us no such luxury.

Against a theory of radical evil, others posit the idea of evil as depravation, absence, or perversion of the Good, a theme, of course, most fully developed in Augustan philosophy. Alain Badiou, in his argument for evil as
the radical absence of the good and the true, offers us a clear account of the
source and natural history of evil. Badiou argues against a theory of vulnerability in need of protection. It is wrong, in his view, to see the world as
needed protection, as endangered by violence, and needing defense.[33] It is
Badiou's argument that ethics begins with the radical understanding of the
truth. Evil is the betrayal of one's fidelity to this truth—the truth, the
good, can be failed, and this failure to understand and fully apprehend the
good is the root of evil. The betrayal of the true and the good is done by the
renunciation of fidelity, or by delusion (confusion of the real "event of
truth" with a false idea of what is true—here he places Nazism—or by the
imposition of what he calls "terror," the "effort to impose the total and un-
qualified power of a truth.")[34]

"Evil exists," argues Badiou, and

> it must be distinguished from the violence that the human animal employs
> to persevere in its being, to pursue its interests—a violence that is *beneath*
> Good and Evil; nevertheless, there is no radical Evil, which might otherwise
> clarify this distinction; Evil can be considered as distinct from banal preda-
> tion only in as far as we grasp it from the setting of "some-one" by a truthful
> process; that as a result Evil is not a category of the human animal, but of
> the subject; (and) that there is Evil only to the extent that man is capable of
> becoming the Immortal he is.[35]

Against this evil, all that one has is fidelity to the event, or insight of pure
truth, a principle of what Badiou calls "consistency" or the ability to say
"keep going."

> Evil is only possible through an encounter with the Good. The ethics of
> truths—which simply serves to lend consistency to that "someone" that we
> are, and which must manage to sustain with its own animal perseverance,
> the intemporal perseverance of a subject of a truth—is also that which tries
> to ward off Evil, through it effective and tenacious inclusion in the process
> of a truth.[36]

In reflecting on the actual narratives, such philosophy is helpful. This
interpretation does allow us to complete one task of philosophy, that of
defining and naming, allowing us to speak of evil as differentiated within
a typography that acknowledges that the source justification of evil acts is
varied, a continuum along which each point has it own amplitude.

Naming the categories allows us the first step toward ethics: knowing and
having conversation that is shared about the kind of problem we are facing. I
am going to suggest the following. The first kind of evil, *indifference,* is rooted
in the lack of the moral ability to respond adequately to the appeal of the other.
These acts are common, and we live them daily: walking by the one in need,
and showing insensitivity. The next category is rooted in *hunger:* egotistic evil,
greed, passions, and acquisitiveness, a yearning for power. Evil can be rooted
in *affiliation,* heteronymous attentiveness to duties and rules that are harmful
to others, but that seem logical and in fact valorous to the moral agent. Lastly,
there is an evil of *savagery,* in which an agent seems to derive pleasure from
harmfulness.[37] It seems to me that acts of wickedness toward children are complex, having their etiology in various points along this continuum.

Naming and categorizing only begins the theoretical task. However,
this naming raises the obvious question of whether little, ordinary evil is
just big evil that has not had a big chance to develop. This leads us back to

our accounts of real and concrete examples of evil. If women were more robustly in situations in which they could exercise real power, perhaps the theory of the essential nature of women to be nurturing might be less easily substantiated. In other words, are the statistics that would indicate women's relative peacefulness, relationship-directed, consensual-building selves a function of women's social construction rather than evidence of their possession of a clearer vision of virtue? Hence, is the account of men and not women as responsible for world violence merely a description and not an explanation of patriarchy?

I would argue that it is. All theories that avoid this conclusion are merely in error. Child abuse is the central example for this question: "Every year in the United States, abuse by parents leaves 2,000 children brain-damaged, 45,000 hospitalized, and an estimated 5,000 dead."[38] Such statistics of so many are overwhelming. So is just one life: a fifteen-year-old boy who is accused of a fatal shooting in Milwaukee. Let us return to the narrative texts. From the police report:

> The boy's grandmother killed the father of two of her children and possibly three other people. At age 6 the boy watched as his drunken mother shot another woman in the arm and chest. At age 9, the mother shot and killed her boyfriend in front of him and his three siblings. On several occasions the Child Protective Services (who made a total of 290 contacts with this family) reported that he was whipped, thrown down the stairs, and threatened to be killed. The boy's aunt threatened to kill him with rat poison. This aunt sliced her boyfriend's ear with a razor and attacked the grandmother's boyfriend with a bottle (all of this in front of the kids). At age 14 the grandmother held a loaded gun to the boy's head and threatened to kill him and his cousin.[39]

But it is not just child abuse that illustrates the point that women, if given the opportunity, will commit acts of domination at a fierce rate. For example, rates of reported sexual victimization among lesbians is reported to be "significantly higher" than among gay men.[40] Studies of lesbian relationships find the same cycles of escalation of violence from threats to murder, of justification, of abuse, and of denial that characterize heterosexual relationships.[41] Even in heterosexual relationships that end in murder, while white female spouses are likely to be killed in two-thirds of the cases, male spouses are killed in one-third. In 1977, more black husbands were killed than black wives. In 1982, the same pattern prevailed. By 1992 the trend had reversed slightly.

Aggressive evil, while undoubtedly more culturally available to men than to women, is not reliably limited to men.

The debate today about the proper attention to women aggression vis-à-vis women's victimization must be understood in the context of a contradiction created by women's historical circumstance. Gerda Lerner (1986) argued that women's victimization is the result of exclusion from history making as well as other forms of subordination to men, but that "it is a fundamental error to try to conceptualize women primarily as victims," . . . it is only when we look at violence against women [as] female weakness. . . . Other than in intimate relationship . . . men are the targets of murder more than women, yet no one is claiming that these high rates of victimization render an image of men as weak and helpless. . . . The question is not who is more aggressive. In fact available data does not provide a clear answer to this question.[42]

S. I. Benn notes this issue of access to opportunity as moral luck in his work on wickedness.

[W]hat preserves quite many ordinary people from wickedness is the good fortune of their circumstances and that in a Belsen or Auschwitz they might be capable not merely of the desperate meanness of so many of the inmates but also of the wickedness of very nearly all the guards.[43]

In fact, in his discussion of heteronymous wickedness, Barry Clarke does discuss precisely the example of prison camp guards. By acting as good Nazis, guards were in fact following evil norms in a wholehearted way. Here, the evildoer has made initial evil assumptions—Jews are animals, children deserve to be beaten for their violations—and then has acted out the wickedness with passion. What make such acts true evil despite the defense (raised of course by Smith's attorney as well) is that ignoring morally significant appeals[44] transforms the moral constitution. Women guards as well as men in the camps acted with terrible violence: true examples of evil. There is no literature in the extensive documentation of the Shoah that suggests that Nazi women nurses, for example, protected their research subjects, that women guards were more nurturing, or that women resisted the work thrust upon them by National Socialism.

One does not need to take an extreme example such as Nazi prison guards to make the point. In fact, in the ordinary world of work, while there is careful research on how women use language in a more inclusive way,[45] there is no evidence that women actually act in ways different from men if given serious power at the workplace. In fact, competition, secrecy, manipulation, and aggression might be just as common.[46] The moral luck that Benn cites is not random in these cases. In other words, it is precisely in the situations in which women achieve power (in the workplace or in intimate relationships), or attain power by default (as in childrearing) that we see the abuse take fullest form.

Women are as fully capable of evil as men and there is no protection because of their "caring," or "nurturing," or "essential nature." To ignore this is to deny the real enormity of the power of patriarchy. If we all know that unjustified and unilateral exercise of male power denies women participation and creativity in every other field, it ought to come as no surprise that given the chance, women seem to achieve parity in this most terrible way as well.

WHAT DOES THIS MEAN FOR THE PROBLEM OF GOODNESS? FAITH AND MURDER

To speak of such stories and such statistics, even within a hermeneutics of suspicion, is to walk on dangerous ground. It is ground that is abhorrent, perilously close to blaming the victim, or calling for "personal responsibility" as a solution for poverty. In part, it seems to reflect on the most rejected of faith-origin stories, of Eve as hungry temptress, responsible for the argumentation that allowed the first exile.

If the explanatory narrative of Christian texts is of female culpability and untrustworthiness, then feminist theorists have put forward the alternate account of essential caring at the heart of a women's nature either as inherent,[47] secondary to object relations theory,[48] or as a function of their work as mothers or nurses.[49] In writing from a world dominated by external male power, it is hard not to see women's strategies for resistance and solidarity as inherent, and inherently good. And I have written about the insights of nursing experiences, of mothering as a foundational experience of care and indeed of spiritual journey. But to ignore the darker side of motherhood is to ignore the power of freedom itself.

Reading feminist analyses of evil can tend to collapse the problem. The extraordinary account of evil and tragedy in Kathleen Sands, for example, is directed toward the ontic existence of evil in the moral universe. But the question that I am asking is slightly different. When women are the perpetrators, there must be a moment for the theorist that goes beyond the blame of the other to the reflection on the self. For a woman who kills is one of our own stepping forward, though she be out of place in a chilling and negative way.

We need an account of evil that takes both freedom and moral agency with equal seriousness, one in which both social construction, tragic limits, and accountable moral action are equally regarded. If women are not taken seriously as perpetrators of violence, then they lose ground as real subjects, and hence as moral agents in the narrative that we share. Women then become objects: of pity, of disdain, of justification, but not subjects that would direct their own action and hence shape social policy. In this account, what they are is fundamentally unfree, living out a variant of an unchosen life as object of our theory, which remains distinctly partisan rather than feminist and ethical.

My vantage is of a Jewish feminist scholar. Hence, the theoretical way home from the woods that I will suggest is based on three disparate sources. If evil is so pervasive, and if we do not have fully useful explanatory or normative resources in ethics, even feminist ethics to comprehend it, then where can one turn for responses in the creation of a Jewish feminist ethics?

The first argument I will make is from an analysis of the classic rabbinic theology that struggles with the notion of evil as resultant of choices presented to the moral agent by the *Yetzer Hara,* or evil inclination or desire. The second is from a literary account by the writer Ilona Karmel, and the last is from a reclamation of the work of Hannah Arendt, whose life-long struggle in theory and in practice to understand evil took several useful and critically important directions.

🕎 *The* Yetzer Hara

According to Daniel Boyarin,[50] the rabbinic discourse on human good and evil was a "doubled discourse." Characterized on the one hand by internally competing evil and good instincts, it was at the same time simultaneously marked by texts that refer to humans as motivated by only one kind of desire, a passion that has the potential for evil within it. The *Yetzer* is also the desire that enables all creativity, generatively, and human industry.[51] The following section of a talmudic story famously illustrates this point:

> They prayed and [Desire] was committed into their hands. He said to them, be careful, for if you kill (me) the world will end. They imprisoned him for three days, and then they looked for a fresh egg in all the land of Israel, and they did not find one. They said, "What shall we do? If we kill him the world will end. If we pray for half, in heaven they do not answer halfway prayers. Blind him and let him go."[52]

What is happening in this text? Boyarin and others have noted that the concept of evil as externalized, as Satan, as other, is not an uncontested notion in the Jewish textual tradition. When the rabbis capture desire to destroy it, they have imperiled the power that drives fecundity. This doubling, the good that is only possible as a concomitant of evil, is at the heart of the rabbinic irony that the names the *Yetzer Hara* in another text as "very good." But that desire is blinded means that some acts are/ought to be masked to us, opaque to our moral sight. Buber, in his discussion of the entrance of evil into the world,[53] notes that "seeing" is what is acquired by Eve in the Garden, a knowledge of the range of possibilities that include the choices for good, evil, life, and death. In the subsequent account of the first murder, Cain, whose name literally is derived from the word for *acquisitiveness*, is given the choice in actual terms. The first murder is the murder of the first child, and it is a murder within the intimacy of family. Evil begins, says the biblical admonition, at the moment when Cain understands that it is always present, at the door, admitted into the narrative, after all, by the sense that attention is desperately needed, and is worth any price. Violence—and by this I mean the negation of the other for whom you have responsibility— begins with the sense that the other can be obliterated by our need for this attention.

If evil in the Jewish view is rooted and sibling to hunger, to desire, then how is one to live in the world without sin, understood as constant acts of amoral passion. How does one blind but not capture desire?

Here we can turn to the second source text, a literary source. The book is *An Estate of Memory*,[54] a novel by Ilona Karmel that describes in careful detail the lives of four women struggling to survive in a Polish concentration camp. Here, even in the most unfree, restrained place, the worst of human imagination, we still see the complexity of choices of hunger, passion, and love. The central drama of the book is the pregnancy of one of the women, and the bringing to term of her baby, who beyond belief is smuggled out of the camp to freedom. The moral universe is marked by the constancy of the multiple and graded choices for evil or aspirational action, and the characters choose and then see their choices doubled: one becomes a camp guard, but dies saving another; one chooses to be an orderly for the hopelessly ill, but first finds herself becoming harsh with her patients, and then dies because she refuses to abandon them. Choices to protect the baby will be choices to endanger the community of women. Every action one takes is dependent on, and will influence the whole group.

The women negotiate the deal with a Nazi soldier:

> How will you pay him? Tola asked as they walked into the woods.
> Somehow. With my coat; no, it must have been sold; then with my shoes. Come on, how can you think of such trifles? Barbara paused. Very cautiously she took Tola's hand, on it round bruises shining like red metal coins. "Tola. I have never been good to you," she said. And from then on they walked in silence.[55]

Into these woods the way is not so clear; there are not the binary choices that allow for personal responsibility or the lack thereof. Passion and its consequence exist only within an inescapable community. Here the child is not killed to protect her from certain death: in fact, she is redeemed because the community can envision and organize, against the worst of scarcity, and at terrible risk to themselves, a miraculous hope.

🌀 *Hannah Arendt and the Problem of Evil*

Arendt began her academic career with a dissertation about love. Her life, however, was interrupted by what she came to call the "storm of history"—the events that led to and ended with the destruction of European Jewish civilization and the horrific torture murder of nearly all of Europe's Jews. It is critical to the intent of this chapter to understand that Arendt's first job after the completion of her dissertation was to head the rescue efforts of the Youth Aliyah, the organization that took Jewish children from certain death in Europe to Palestine in the late 1930s. Arendt personally accompanied many of these children to Jerusalem, a complex and compromised journey, since it was a transport from danger to danger—Palestine was a British colony, surrounded by hostile Arab, pro-Nazi forces.

Her scholarly consideration of evil, *The Origins of Totalitarianism*, was predicated on a Kantian theory of radical evil. It was her first major scholarly effort to analyze how her beloved German social order could become so quickly and so deeply evil. For German intellectuals, it was a personal, family matter—in Arendt's case, it was more profoundly true, since her first German intellectual and academic mentor (and lover), Heidegger, had been a part of the Nazi movement that sought to eliminate her.[56]

"It is the appearance of some radical evil, previously unknown to us, that puts an end to the notion of developments and transformation of qualities,"[57] Arendt argues at first. Evil is possible, can come into existence, when it "kill(ed) the juridical person in man." Evil is not a part of the normal human condition, but is only possible when conscience is distorted, making the evil action desirable, by "attacking the moral person in man."[58] The evil is employed by "creating conditions under which conscience ceases to be adequate and to do good becomes utterly impossible, the consciously organized complicity of all men in the crimes of totalitarian regimes is extended to the victim and thus made really total."[59] The notion that radical evil could enter a situation and provide for no alternative guided Arendt's subsequent works as well. In these works she turned from philosophy to political theory and focused on the necessity for human activity, for creativity, against totalizing certainties. It was to "labor, work, action" in the name of political theory for states, and not to the inner world of personal ethical choice that she directed her work. One could be tempted away from the capacity for action through fear, or profound instability, a temptation that could be countered with a full engagement with the "political."[60] If one is truly free, then one can make activity, and, by implication, the quest for the good life, the examined and uncertain but discerning life, a possible choice.

But it was Arendt's encounter with Adolf Eichmann at his trial for crimes against humanity that changed her entire assessment of what evil was in human life. In Eichmann, Arendt expected to see the face of radical evil incarnate—but she did not. She saw instead "banality."

> When Arendt did see Eichmann, what struck her most forcefully was the mind-boggling discrepancy between the monstrous horrors in which he had played a role and this petty, mediocre, silly man. "Now that the devil himself was in the dock," as she put it, he seemed appallingly ordinary.[61]

For Arendt, it is the very "quotidian" and "*stinknormal*" quality of Eichmann that was so striking. He organized evil out of a sense of duty only to his own career, to the need for personal power, not for important theories or causes; he was "a common mailman" without language except for the most banal of clichés about his life and work, asking *who am I to judge?* For Arendt, it is precisely this failure to judge that is at the heart of the problem of evil. Evil is not a radical outsider, entering into history—it is the capacity, available to each of us, to fail.

What stands against evil action is the capacity to think, to reason, and to create: the Socratic possibility to create questions:

> [T]o think and to be fully alive are the same, and this implies that thinking must always begin afresh; it is an activity that accompanies living and is concerned with such concepts as justice, happiness, virtue, offered us by language itself, as expressing the meaning of whatever happens in life, and occurs to us while we are alive.[62]

It was this insight from Arendt that allowed her to understand that even under conditions of utter totality (as we see in Karmel), choices were always possible—even for the oppressed, even for those doomed to death. Unlike in her earlier work, she argued that "choicelessness" was never possible. One could always act with responsibility, achieving if not success, then a dignity of outcome. In this, and in later work and commentary in which she declines to embrace those aspects of feminist theory that are based on a narrative of essentialism, Arendt returns to a consistent theme: that the renewal of choice against the possibility, always available, for evil is the core of moral action.

🪻 Normative Questions

Theory, definition, and clarity of the questions that might be raised by Jewish source texts to the problems of feminist philosophy are a decent beginning, but as recent events and the cases of real evil that I have described show, analysis needs a second step if we are to create a credible discourse for *ethics.* Not far from analytic horror in the narrative of child abuse rests a desire to change the ending, if not for those children, then for other children.[63] Much of feminist social policy is shaped by a reliance on women as inherently nurturing. But the cases of murderous mothers raise the problem of the social construction of this reliance. What about justice in our constrained culture, a sociability of limits in which some children will be faced with a mother who cannot mother them? There is a powerfully emerging popular need to punish and to reward such acts, and to begin to question the explanations of psychology, of genetics, of medicine, and of science to account for such action. As a religious theorist, but as a feminist, I greet such reframing of the discourse with wary encouragement. For I believe that ultimately the problem of murder is, as directed in nearly all faith texts, a religious question, an ontic question of the deepest moral accord in a difficult freed journey. After September 11, 2001, there is another reason to take on the facile account of oppression or patriarchy as responsible for evil, and women as victims, outside of the order of evil. And that is that it is too easy to stand aside from the terrible responsibility to work for, and theorize in support of the good. If, as Arendt argues, taking responsibility for one's own choices is the beginning of humanity, and the moral discernment is at all times the work of human activity, and in fact all that we have of humanity, then to leave women aside from this task is a dreadful error.

Taking hunger seriously means that we acknowledge the *Yetzer* of limits, the blinded *Yetzer.* If some choices are not available to us, if we can limit the *Yetzer* by human action, then violation of limits merits social consequence. Limitedness is problematic, judgmental, yet is not compassion without parameters: for Jewish ethicists live within the borders of the halakhah after all, and one of the first commandments after we turn from the direct encounter with God is the direct encounter with the other. It is her vulnerability, what Emmanuel Levinas reminds us, her ability to be killed by us, that compels us not to kill.

Before murder there is exile, from Gan Eden into the woods we must till from chaos into fecundity and satiation. We are expelled into time, and into "seeing," and into freedom: a first exodus. Exile in the world means an exile into choices, consequence and mutability. Living in a world of hunger means that the imperative to consume is at least as compelling as the imperative to protect one's next generation. This is not to argue for a fixed human "nature." Far from it. It is, however, the religious ability of human persons to understand themselves as both obligated and as free, which offers an essential relationally and a terrible loneliness at once.

The second Exodus repeats the themes. We are freed from slavery in Egypt, choicelessness, and sent into the wilderness. A doubling: for the literal translation of Egypt, *mitzrayim,* is the narrow place. We are in exiled into the widest world. That is to say, we live in a world of large and disparate choices, and we choose and choose again. This is what the biblical story reminds us. We are the freed ones, we are the not-Pharaoh, meaning we are not possessive of an inevitably hardened heart; and it is not our "nature," or our genetic destiny, or our entrapped history to be evil. It is our choice, one among many in the wide spiritual place in which we live. This radical freedom and our enormous hungers can lead us to be tempted by ancient terrible decisions. It is not odd that the Department of Justice assures us that child murder is less prevalent than a century ago. A close reading of Grimm would tell us the same data.

Choosing virtue means recognizing vice. Much of what is written in my field of ethics is about virtue theory.[64] Yet to choose to act virtuously means recognizing that one is first a freely discerning agent and second that one is acting with a certain degree of moral courage—often, given the structure of the difficult worlds, a great deal of courage. To choose against heteronomous norms, for example, is to choose to respond to a moral order of one's own making. What holds us together as a human world is thin and tenacious. To be a woman of faith as opposed to cynicism, to worry about the religious implication of this work, to want to see the goodness that is possible loom larger than the evil that is possible—focusing on the reality of evil is difficult.[65] But to deny the depths of the evil that can be—and is—chosen, and deliberately so—is to deny the complexity and power of the choice for goodness, even in the desperate woods that Karmel illuminates.

In thinking about women and evil, it seems important to think both of the nature of freedom and of obligations. This is the meaning of using the same term, the *Yetzer Hara,* to describe all the hungers. The human person, in our essence, is obliged yet free, and in this, feminist theory must take on the largest challenges of both responsibility and freedom. We are obligated because women are born into, and with any luck will die from, the waiting hands of the other, from a complicated series of relationships, family and friends. We are obligated to our children perhaps most of all: by species structure and social norms, we do not normally abandon our young. But the fact exists that it is possible to do just that: to lead them into the world and leave them to die.[66] Such a fact is paradoxically what makes the choice to love them and nurture them so extraordinary, and so valiant. This choice for the good is why it is important not just to understand the acts of Smith and the killer mothers, and not to only have compassion for them, although compassion and recognition is where we must begin. We must name these killings as the worst choice we can imagine: both evil and, finally, as chosen. It is because the acts of evil are possible always that the gesture of considered rejection of evil is so fundamental to what it means to be human.

To name *wrong,* to name *sin,* to call out the missing of the mark, is difficult in this postmodern era. Yet to do less is to trivialize the most human and difficult of our actions, taken in faith, the simplest and hard task of protection of one another in a would in which both great evil and great good waits in the next breath.

NOTES

1. Petra Kelly, "Women and Ecology," in *Women on War: Essential Voices for the Nuclear Age from a Brilliant International Assembly,* ed. Daniela Gioseffi (New York: Simon and Schuster, 1988), 308–12.

2. Bureau of Justice Statistics, *Selected Findings,* Domestic Violence, "Violence between Intimates," November 1994.

3. And nearly always African American. Interestingly enough, in the one large public case in 1994, the Polly Klaus case, in which a real stranger assault took place on a child, the perpetrator, Robert Allan Harris, was a white drifter.

4. I want to contextualize this story. At the time, my own boys were five and three, my daughter eight months old. I was riveted to this case, and believed every word of Smith's story.

5. For the best account of the construction of Satan historically, see Elaine Pagels, *The Origins of Satan* (New York: Random House, 1995).

6. Children's Hospital, Oakland, statistics from the Department of Social Work, 1998.

7. "Hansel and Gretel," in *Grimm's Fairy Tales* (New York: Pantheon Books, 1944), 86–94.

8. *Grimm's Fairy Tales,* 88.

9. Erich Neumann, *The Great Mother* (Princeton, N.J.: Princeton University Press, 1955), 27. See also Nel Noddings, *Women and Evil* (Berkeley: University of California

Press, 1989), 77, from which this quotation of Neumann is drawn. Noddings notes the power of the archetype in her work on evil.

10. Lynn Smith and Elizabeth Mehren, "Why Does a Mother Kill Her Child?" *Los Angeles Times,* 5 November 1994, 1(A).

11. "Mother Charged with Trying to Kill Children," *Los Angeles Times,* 19 March 1994, Metro, 3(B).

12. What made this case noteworthy was that she was pregnant at the time, and her husband sued for custody of their unborn child. "Defendant Cedes Custody of Unborn Child," *Boston Globe,* 14 April 1995.

13. "Why Does a Mother Kill Her Child?" *The Los Angeles Times,* 5 November 1994, 1(A).

14. Associated Press, 4 November 1994.

15. Julie Marquis, "Body of Third Dead Baby Found in O.C.," *Los Angeles Times,* 15 March 1995, 1(A).

16. "Competency Hearing in Toddler's Death," *San Francisco Chronicle,* 9 May 1995, 16(A).

17. "Judge Orders Man to Pay Ex-Wife Who Killed Son," *Salt Lake Tribune,* 2 May 1995 1(D).

18. Associated Press, 8 March 1995.

19. Gerda Lerner, *The Creation of Patriarchy* (New York: Oxford University Press, 1986).

20. Lynn Smith, op cit. Smith quotes this statistic from Richard Gelles, director of the Family Violence Research Project at the University of Rhode Island.

21. Ibid.

22. Ibid., 2.

23. Sarah Pattee, "Maternal Instinct Gone Awry," *Los Angeles Times,* 30 September 1989, View, Part 5, 13.

24. Gustavo Gutierrez, *We Drink from Our Own Wells: The Spiritual Journey of a People* (Maryknoll, N.Y.: Orbis Books, 1984).

25. Alert Kantians will notice that I have paraphrased his three philosophical questions in ethics: What can I know? What ought I to do? and What can I hope? John Kekes notes this in his discussion of true and false hope. John Kekes, *Facing Evil* (Princeton, N.J.: Princeton University Press, 1990), 11.

26. Martha Nussbaum, *The Fragility of Goodness: Moral Luck and Ethics in Greek Tragedy and Philosophy* (Cambridge: Cambridge University Press, 1986).

27. Kathleen Sands, *Escape from Paradise* (Minneapolis: Fortress Press, 1994).

28. Ibid., 67.

29. Ibid., 66.

30. Kekes, *Facing Evil,* 6.

31. Ibid., 221.

32. Andrew Delbanco, *The Death of Satan* (New York: Farrar, Straus and Giroux, 1995). Much more could be said about this book, whose themes echo the much more limited task of this paper, which is to look at one kind of evil, child murder, and one type of person: the mother.

33. Alain Badiou, *Ethics: An Essay on the Understanding of Evil,* trans. Peter Hallward (London: Verso, 2001), xxiii.

34. Ibid., xxii.

35. Ibid., 67.

36. Ibid., 91.

37. S. I. Benn, "Wickedness," in *Ethics and Personality*, ed. John Deich (Chicago: University of Chicago Press, 1972).

38. Leslie Berkman and Lynn Smith, "Behind Perfection, a Broken Life," *Los Angeles Times*, 21 October 1991, 3(A).

39. *The Milwaukee Sentinel*, 26 August 1994. This condensation came from Cathy Young from an Internet discussion group on violent women. My thanks to Armon Brott for this citation.

40. Caroline Waterman et al., "Sexual Coercion in Gay Male and Lesbian Relationships: Predictors and Implications for Support Services," in *Brief Reports* (Albany: University of Albany, State University of New York [paper], 1989).

41. Susan Murrow and Donna M. Hawhurst, "Lesbian Partner Abuse: Implications for Therapists," *Journal of Counseling and Development* 68 (September/October 1969): 58–62.

42. Jacqueline W. White and Robin Kowalski, "Deconstructing the Myth of the Non-aggressive Woman: A Feminist Analysis," *Psychology of Women Quarterly* 18 (1994): 504.

43. Benn, "Wickedness," 210.

44. Ibid.

45. Deborah Tanner, *Talking from 9 to 5: How Women's and Men's Conversational Styles Affect Who Gets Heard, Who Gets Credit, and What Gets Done at Work* (New York: William Morrow and Company, 1995).

46. Perhaps more disturbing is the passive participation in the rewards of systematic or class evil by women. One certainly does not see legions of American women in the top 1 percent of the socioeconomic bracket decrying the plight of the bottom, nor engaging in gender notable amounts of noblesse oblige toward the poor. Women partake of this sort of violence, in fact one could almost say abuse, of children, by witnessing, for example, punitive budget cuts. The subsequent tax credits leave women nourished by the same feast.

47. See for example, Susan Griffin, *Women and Nature* (New York: Harper, 1978), or *Women on War*, ed. Daniela Gioseffi (New York: Simon and Schuster, 1988).

48. Nancy Chodorow, *The Reproduction of Mothering: Psychoanalysis and the Sociology of Gender* (Berkeley: University of California Press, 1978).

49. In believing, as the early Marx would have it, that one's consciousness is determined by the relationship to the means of production, I have argued for this view in print as well. I am aware that this paper represents a rethinking of my own views.

50. Daniel Boyarin, "Dialectics of Desire: The Evil Instinct is Very Good," in his *Carnal Israel: Reading Sex in Talmudic Culture* (Berkeley: University of California Press, 1993).

51. See *Genesis Rabbah*, Bereshit, IX, 7.

52. *Babylonian Talmud*, Yoma 69b. Cited by Boyarin, "Dialectics of Desire," 61.

53. Martin Buber, *Images of Good and Evil* (London: Routledge & Kegan Paul, 1952).

54. Ilona Karmel, *An Estate of Memory* (New York: The Feminist Press, 1969).

55. Ibid., 270.

56. Hence the question of child murder becomes strangely applicable: how can a motherland murder its children?

57. Hannah Arendt, "Totalitarianism," in *The Portable Hannah Arendt*, ed. Peter Baehr (New York: Penguin Books, 2000), 134.

58. Ibid.

59. Ibid., 135.

60. See Hannah Pitkin, *The Attack of the Blob: Hannah Arendt's Concept of the Social* (Chicago: University of Chicago Press, 2000), 2.

61. Ibid., 405.

62. Hannah Arendt, "The Life of the Mind," as excerpted in Baehr, *The Portable Hannah Arendt,* 407.

63. A friend, not in the field, whom I spoke with whilst I was writing this paper listened to my analysis of evil and then asked, "So, now what do we do about it?" I admitted that beyond theological exhortation, I hadn't figured that out yet, but that by focusing on the problem clearly and by raising this series of questions I hope to begin to alter the nature of the discourse.

64. See Baruch Brody, *Life and Death Decision Making* (New York: Oxford University Press, 1988); Albert Jonsen and Stephen Toulmin, *The Abuse of Casuistry: A History of Moral Reasoning* (Berkeley: University of California Press, 1988); and David Thomasma and Edmund Pelligrino, *For the Patient's Good: The Restoration of Beneficence in Health Care* (New York: Oxford University Press, 1988).

65. It is almost more than I could do to write this paper: to speak of evil is itself difficult. In thinking about this problem, Kathleen Sand's comments are helpful. In reflecting with her (November 1995) about the problem of the feminist who writes of women's evil, we came to agree that it is almost a participation. It was far easier to write of friendship, of witness, and of virtue than of the grimness of evil choices.

66. A note here: recent advances in human neuroscience have raised serious new questions for this research that will need to be explored more fully. How do we understand the relationship between the structural biology of the brain, the uses of aggressive and protection in primates, and the way the programming of the elastic growing brain in childhood affects behavior? What are we to make of new research in brains, genetics, proteins, and behaviors? I did not want to take a position here beyond that of raising questions.

NINE

NANCY K. LEVENE

Judaism's Body Politic

*The human arts are arranged in accordance with nature in three ways.
1) Some of them help nature to do its work—like tilling the ground and
the art of medicine and the like. . . . 2) There are arts that differ from,
and are alien to, nature, for they make things in which nature plays no
role—like most of the productive arts, such as the making of clothing,
house-building, shipmaking, and others. . . . 3) The third way of the
arts is opposed to and against nature—like throwing a stone upward or
causing fire to go downward. Also like this, among men, is the attempt
of some to domineer over others and to subjugate some to others, though
nature has made men free and equal at their birth.*

— ISAAC ABRAVANEL[1]

*Whoever thinks that the halakhah is frozen, and that we may not de-
viate from it right or left, errs greatly. On the contrary, there is no flexibility like that of the halakhah. . . . Only by virtue of this flexibility
were the Jewish people, relying on numerous and useful innovations introduced by the hakhamim {wise ones} of Israel, each in his generation,
able to walk in the path of Torah and its commandments for thousands
of years. If the hakhamim of our {own} generation will have the courage to introduce halakhic innovations true to Torah, with utter faith-
fulness to the body of Torah as written and received, then the halakhah
will continue to be the path of the Jewish people unto the last generation.*

— HAYYIM DAVID HALEVI[2]

*Those who look upon the Bible, in its present form, as a message for man-
kind sent down by God from heaven, will doubtless cry out that I have
committed the sin against the Holy Ghost in maintaining that the Word
of God is faulty, mutilated, adulterated and inconsistent, that we possess
it only in fragmentary form, and that the original of God's covenant
with the Jews has perished. However, I am confident that reflection will
at once put an end to their outcry; for not only reason itself, but the assertions of the prophets and the Apostles clearly proclaim that God's eter-*

Judaism's Body Politic

nal Word and covenant and true religion are divinely inscribed in men's hearts—that is, in men's minds—and that this is the true handwriting of God which he has sealed with his own seal, this seal being the idea of himself, the image of his own divinity, as it were.

— BARUCH SPINOZA[3]

🕎 Introduction: Feminism, Judaism, and Political Philosophy

Of all the sub-fields in Jewish philosophy, political philosophy is one of the most promising areas for feminist research. For one thing, the political sphere has occupied a central place in feminist thinking generally, and feminist philosophers have followed suit in this regard. If the very core of feminism was from the outset a critique of social and political inequality, feminist philosophers have contributed to this critique by moving from the inside out, as it were, challenging conventional assumptions about knowledge, language, and experience and thus creating the possibility for political arrangements that do more than simply equalize the inherited ones. For its part, Jewish political theory has also been preoccupied with questions addressed to living as a minority (or a disempowered group) in a majority culture, as well as to majority–minority relations within its single culture. But it is also true that there are rich overlaps with feminist philosophical questions and strategies. For while Jewish philosophical reflection on the nature of political existence has naturally varied enormously over time, it has shared with many contemporary feminist philosophies a resistance to an abstract or procedural reasoning that would depict the citizen unencumbered before the law by linguistic, religious, cultural, or sexual identities. In other words, it has been in thinking about a body politic that Jewish thinkers have displayed the most willingness to challenge the purified notions of reason and the intellect that are otherwise so dominant in Jewish philosophy, especially in the Middle Ages.[4] Thus Jewish political thought is potentially very fertile ground on which to nourish feminist philosophical insights.

These insights and their connections have not yet adequately been pursued, and in this essay I seek to do so only in outline and in a preliminary manner. But it is also worth beginning by challenging what might be a covert assumption that the *Jew* and the *woman*—as marginalized groups—necessarily share some identifiable experience. It has become axiomatic that one of the edifying signatures of rabbinic Judaism, over against its Greek and Christian interlocutors in antiquity, is its emphasis on forms of particularity, whether legal, historical, and geographical situatedness or simply "carnality," bodily exigencies. Jewish life has been figured as a body politic ("carnal Israel") in more than the casual sense of this phrase—a political and religious entity obsessed with bodies, a bodily entity obsessed with the politics of tradition, genealogy, and blood. That this is not the case in much ancient and medieval Jewish philosophy, which sought to de-emphasize the body's role in intellection, virtue, and the attainment of wisdom, is a mark of the disparate voices in the tradition, and perhaps especially demonstrated by the contrast between rabbinic world-views and medieval philosophical ones. It is also fair to observe the degree to which the image of Jewish carnality—wrested with new-found pride from generations of Christian anti-Jewishness and often standing not only for rabbinic Judaism but also for the tradition *tout court*—is conditioned by a desire to present Judaism as liberatory to contemporary post-Enlightenment sensibilities.[5]

It has become almost as equally axiomatic that feminist philosophy is a philosophy concerned with the exigencies of bodily integrity and the effects of embodiment on cognition, experience, memory, and identity.[6] This focus has taken the forms of a critique of philosophical language and the creation of novel discourses "written on the body,"[7] a rejection of the perceived bellicose nature of conflict resolution that characterizes much reasoning and a turn to an ethics of care and nurturance focused on the other, akin to parenting (to mothering in particular),[8] and an emphasis on philosophically underrepresented human faculties and skills, especially those that have traditionally been discarded by male philosophers as effeminate (often synonymous with the irrational), such as desire, the emotions, imagination, and rhetoric.[9] Here, too, there is an element of reclamation involved in revisiting such discarded discourses, or in emphasizing dimensions of personhood that have been overlooked. And there is a similar project enacted simultaneously to re-imagine historically damaging stereotypes as well as more simply to expand the creative and productive potential of a contested subject.

However much merit these axioms possess, it is surely inadequate simply to assume them from the outset, as a feminist Jewish political philosophy might be tempted to do. My interest, in any case, is not in bodies per se, but in bodies politic, namely in how Israel corporately constructs and views the significance of the political realm, and in so doing how it constructs the relationships between persons. This latter question has several facets. Turning to the quotation from Abravanel in the epigraph above, one sees articulated the claim that "nature has made men free and equal at their birth." Notwithstanding the fact that one can safely assume this statement refers only to men and not to the generic human, it was a quite provocative thing to say in the medieval Jewish philosophical circles where Platonic notions of hierarchy held sway.[10] The question is, what are the legal and political implica-

tions of this insight? Is it illegal to contravene nature in this regard?
Immoral? Politically unwise? Or is it sometimes necessary? What is the cost
of doing so (i.e., what force does the "natural" have here)? As it happens,
Abravanel is the only medieval Jewish thinker with what Abraham
Melamed calls "democratic leanings."[11] That is, he departs from philosophers such as ibn Rushd and Maimonides in being suspicious of monarchy,
holding that royalty is an illegitimate usurpation of divine authority.[12] This
doesn't make him a liberal democrat in the modern sense. But it means that
he was highly critical of the human hierarchies that his Muslim and Jewish
cohorts took for granted.

One might therefore fruitfully, if speculatively ask: what would be the
status of Abravanel's statement concerning equality if one made his words,
regardless of his own intentions, gender inclusive? Would the notion of
male–female equality "at their birth" change how legal and political relationships could be cast, or would it, does it, in fact make little difference?
One thinks, for example, of Genesis 1:27 that has men and women created
at the same time, a narrative that has done nothing to dislodge the sway of
hierarchical images in the tradition, not least, of course, because of the proximity of Genesis 2, in which woman is created from man as his helper. But
it is hardly a stretch to predict this outcome, even without Genesis 2. For,
turning to the second epigraph, the view of the contemporary Sephardi ju-
rist Hayyim David Halevi eloquently expresses an important thread in Jewish self-reflection when he writes that the halakhah is tremendously flexible:
as he puts it, it can enable the generations to "walk in the path of Torah and
its commandments for thousands of years," adapting itself to circumstances
(and opinions) as they change. This is surely a profound strength, and will
immediately strike many modern readers as intrinsically progressive. But
the flexibility of halakhah is also double edged, making possible both a re-
institution of the status quo as well as a critique of it. If Abravanel grounds
his politics at least partly in nature, Halevi grounds nature in politics:
halakhah and the human relationships it mediates can do exactly what we
want and need them to do.

What makes these two quotations so striking when read together (albeit completely out of context) is that both display commitments on the one
hand to something stable, eternal, and immutable (natural equality, the Torah), and on the other hand to something changeable, flexible, and innovative (human "arts," halakhah). Halevi's wording is especially fascinating in
this regard: total fidelity to the Torah as written and received through the
route of flexibility and innovation. Alongside these two statements,
Spinoza's words have the effect of expressing this tension without resolving

it. For Spinoza, God's eternal word and covenant—the law—is "divinely inscribed in men's hearts." What is given in nature (the heart, the mind) is
also what is transformed by covenantal inscription; what is revealed through
the covenant is nothing more or less than what is natural. For Spinoza there
is no natural realm that is not also already inscribed; no inscriptions that exempt us from the natural.

When taken together, these comments, it seems to me, form the challenge at the heart of Judaism's body politic throughout history: to forge a
connection with changing historical circumstances by continually reiterat-
ing what is true; to continually refine what is true by forging ever more precise arts in concert with historical vicissitudes; to remain faithful to what is
given (in nature, in the body) and what is received (the covenant, the law)
by remaining connected to what is made and re-made (a just polity, a community of righteous citizens); and, finally, to juggle the legal and the natural
in such a way that both are liberating. One can understand the issue in more
overtly political terms: Zion, what is stable, eternal, immutable as ideal,
alongside *galut,* diaspora, what is creative, made and re-made, changeable,
flexible, innovative. Between Zion and *galut,* neither one nor the other; both
one and the other: that, perhaps, is where the Jewish body politic has most
richly flourished in all its tensions.

I want to argue, then, that whatever affinities exist between the subjects of feminist philosophy and Jewish political philosophy, affinities that
are visible by regarding the political fate of the Jews from the outside, they
only go so far toward articulating what is truly at stake in the creation of a
feminist Jewish political philosophy. What is at stake, in my view, is the
evaluation of the ways in which—internally—Jewish philosophy and Jewish politics (together with their synthesis) have articulated (or failed to articulate) not only feminist questions narrowly construed (i.e., questions
concerning the status of women and the nature of gender), but questions
more generally of equality, the toleration of differences, the function of
other group identities, and the critique of the status quo in whatever form.
These latter are what I will mean here when I speak of *feminism* or *feminist
theory,* for it seems to me all but useless in the Jewish context to analyze and
evaluate questions related to women and gender without at the same time
looking at theoretical problems of equality. It is not that equality is the
only issue relevant to Jewish feminists. But for all the literature it has generated in feminist political theory, it remains an important, vexed, and still
unplumbed issue in Jewish political theory.

The task consists of subjecting Jewish political theory to a set of questions that concern its most basic parameters: how does it conceive person-

hood, political agency, freedom? To borrow the dilemma from the Israeli Declaration of Independence, a dilemma that is surely at the heart not only of the quagmire that is contemporary Israel but the Jewish political quagmire per se: what is or can be the relationship between democracy and peoplehood; between a Jewish state (polity, community, sociality) and a democratic one? This question concerns not only how Jews treat non-Jews in a context of Jewish sovereignty, but also how and to what extent Judaism per se can organize Jews (male and female, gay and straight, and so on) democratically. Despite the fact that oligarchic strains have clearly predominated in the tradition throughout the ages, are there also, as Melamed puts it, democratic leanings beyond the exceptionalism of Abravanel? What is or can be the relationship between halakhah and sexual equality—how does the tension between exclusiveness and inclusiveness resolve itself? Is the tension productive, or is it merely the signature of a dead end? These are questions Jewish feminists have always asked. What I bring to this project here is a focus on the political dimensions of the Jewish body.

I begin by listing some basic conceptual conundrums in the overlapping fields that comprise feminist Jewish political philosophy, seeking to highlight challenges both descriptive and normative. I then turn to an exploration of one foundational concept in Jewish political philosophy, the covenant, in order to assess its dimension of exclusivity and inclusivity. It is this tension contained in the notion of covenant, as well as the covenant's undecidable identity as both a religious and a political act, that present the most potential for a feminist Jewish political philosophy. It is within the margins of these tensions that feminists can connect simultaneously to the stable and the revolutionary, and can participate in a critique of a tradition that presents its own self-criticism from the outset. Following out the democratic potential of such a critique, I look at Spinoza's political theory to pursue the possibility of holding together the Jewish and the democratic, the feminist and the halakhic. I also briefly explore the paradigm of the medieval *kehillot* as one example of a religio-political environment that contained certain democratic threads. I conclude with some reflections on directions future research might take.

🟤 *Conundrums*

Feminist Jewish political philosophy emerges at the nexus of several problematic fields: feminist philosophy, Jewish philosophy, feminist Jewish philosophy, feminist political philosophy, and Jewish political philosophy. These fields are problematic in ways having to do with definition, method, and/or substance: they may all be seen in different degrees as lacking what William James (in the second chapter of the *Varieties of Religious Experience*) so resonantly referred to as a "circumscription of the topic." I will take up three of these issues below.

a) What Is Feminist Philosophy?

Feminist philosophy is by now a burgeoning and even conventionalized field, which spans the gamut of philosophical sub-fields traditionally exclusive of gender-oriented questions: philosophy of mind, philosophy of language, theories of knowledge, metaphysics, philosophies of science, religion, ethics, and social and political philosophy.[13] Yet this proliferation has failed to stem either methodological or substantive perplexities that arise whenever there is an effort to identify the precise task of feminist philosophy. Is it merely a temporary righting of the wrongs committed in the past under the seemingly generic, yet covertly patriarchal name of philosophy—the exclusions and blindnesses that have been perpetrated by male-centered assumptions and premises? Or is it a subject matter in its own right, with a set of irreducible problems revolving around the consideration of human gendered identity, problems that will provide philosophers with challenges of analysis and comprehension long after such wrongs have been adequately righted? In part due to this ambivalence concerning the aims of the field, certain conceptual tensions arise again and again, such as how to avoid dichotomous thinking—a major feminist philosophical preoccupation. Dichotomies, even those that do not explicitly refer to sexual differences, are seen to be saturated with metaphysical assumptions that are damaging to women.[14] Since thinking with dichotomies nevertheless remains an important tool of philosophical analysis, there can be a sense of unease about what it is one is doing when one thinks philosophically with gender in mind—that is to say, when one seeks to generate a novel philosophical standpoint, as opposed to simply exposing the poverty of someone else's.

b) What Is Jewish Political Philosophy?

There are crucial foundational questions that inevitably arise before a Jewish political philosophy can get underway. In his recent book on the "persistence of the political in Judaism," Alan Mittelman puts the issue succinctly: in what way or to what extent does the political survive in a tradition whose political reality has been so insecure—whose actual sovereignty has historically been so circumscribed and exceptional?[15] Is the persistence of the political a mere residue of the biblical past—the past of the united monarchy and its great political and prophetic figures—devoid of substance, power, and efficacy? Is nationhood, or at least territorial integrity the *sine qua non* of political self-determination and if not, what is? Is political self-determination even a *desideratum* in Judaism, and if so, how does one continue to account for the tradition's bifurcation between Zion and diaspora?

While it would be difficult to argue that Judaism was ever first and foremost concerned with political matters, it is equally difficult to deny that there has existed a rich tradition of political reflection throughout Jewish history. To be sure it is the stock in trade of the modern political theorist to distinguish between civil society and the political, namely between the laws and norms that regulate the realms of commerce and everyday life and the institutions (executive, legislative, judicial) that oversee the protection of life and territory in a commonwealth. But this distinction is exactly what many theorists of Jewish political life have contested.[16] For the Jews, if certainly not unique, do not fit easily into this model. First, as "strangers" in foreign lands, they have almost always possessed a measure of communal integrity that distinguished them as a body from the surrounding political entity—as a part of this entity but not solely reducible to it. Second, regardless of the largesse of any given foreign power, Jewish identity has historically been forged primarily through adherence to Jewish law. Even in times of the greatest pressure to convert, assimilate, or otherwise mute their distinctiveness, this identification makes the Jews quite constitutively unable to disentangle Jewishness from some degree of legal and thus communal autonomy.

Among the questions that arise from the Jewish political case, then, are the following: what role does the (until 1948) single Jewish experience of sovereignty play in Jewish political theory? How might one nuance the distinction between civil and political life in such a way so as to capture not only Jewish diasporic communal autonomy but also the relationship between Jewish peoplehood and the non-Jewish state, whether secular or religious? What role have norms of host states played in Jewish internal affairs, and what role should they play, according to Jewish political theories? Alternatively, how has Jewish political thought had an impact on notions of authority, identity, consent, and community outside the Jewish sphere of interest? Finally, has Jewish life been sufficiently open to the political in ways that have kept pace with modern democratic society?

The one topic that immediately asserts itself as deserving of special notice in thinking about Jewish political theory is that of Zionism and the contemporary state of Israel. Yet it seems to me that the state of Israel—as a secular state—does not fundamentally challenge the ambiguities involved in the questions above. That is, unless one sees contemporary Israel as a partial fulfillment of the messianic notion of a final ingathering of the dispersed around the globe, its status as a special kind of political entity entirely revolves around its struggle for identity, consensus, and legitimacy. This struggle makes it fundamentally not unlike any other struggling new state in which ethnic and/or religious identity is a factor in the construction of citizenship. It may be noted, of course, that the contemporary states struggling with this issue *other* than Israel—states such as those in the Balkans, in central and western Africa, in the former Soviet Union—are by no means automatically seen by North Americans as allies in the same way that Israel is. But this only serves to magnify what is most poignant about Israel, namely its dual allegiance—its commitment, on the one hand, to Euro-American concepts of democracy, and, on the other, to the tribal integrity and homogeneity of the Jewish state. This does indeed put Israel in the category of the special, but not only for the reasons it often articulates, e.g., providing shelter for a subject people or of furthering the common destiny of the Jews. It is also special because it is (so far) a political failure of a very particular kind: a "Jewish and democratic state," as the Declaration of Independence hopefully asserts, in which democracy always threatens to disable its Jewish identity no less than its Jewishness perpetually and systematically disregards its democratic identity. It is special because this fact is about internal combustion. But this combustion just *is* (i.e., it does not change) the persistence of the political problem in the tradition per se.

c) What Is Feminist Jewish Political Philosophy?

Feminist Jewish political philosophy contains the same tension as Jewish political philosophy, namely the tension between the insularity and coherence of a single system (Judaism, halakhah, Jewish identity) and the critical standpoints (democracy, feminism) that disrupt that singularity, even if they come from within. If feminist political philosophers have to worry about aspects such as the relationship between gender identities and constitutional freedoms and protections, feminist Jewish political philosophers have a markedly more intractable domain of analysis. Indeed, one might observe that feminist political philosophy only comes close to dealing with what feminist Jewish political philosophers have to deal with when it leaves the safe haven of Euro-American concepts of the state for, say, the constitution of contemporary Egypt or Iran. It is only in those contexts, in other words, that one can find analogies (whether structural or customary) to Jewish law, that is, where there are analogies to a layered system of metaphysical, institutional, and attitudinal barriers to classical feminist concerns.[17]

This is not a very common perspective on the challenges facing Judaism even from a feminist perspective, because, however oppressive it may seem to feminists, Judaism is overwhelmingly seen as a religion, not a political entity, albeit one that is focused on practice more than belief. What this has meant is that feminist Jewish philosophy has focused almost entirely on the theological (and to a lesser degree metaphysical) obstacles to female voices in the tradition, and very little on the political ones. Within this reading, Jewish law is primarily a spiritual and ritual entity, not a communal–political constitution. Yet this perspective not only potentially leaves obstacles unchallenged. The question is also how Jewish law can become empowering if it is conceived outside the realms of worldly power— if it is seen to concern only what women and men do and think in their private spiritual lives and not in their public civil lives as members of multiple polities, as one is in a democracy. This question highlights one of the paradoxes of thinking about feminist Jewish political philosophy, because arguably the tradition can only become empowering if its own power beyond the private mental and ritual realm is acknowledged, and yet the immediate translation of halakhah into political terms is not something most feminists would *prima facie* desire—halakhah is inegalitarian, whereas most of our political commitments are egalitarian and democratic.

What I would like to suggest, however, is that dividing one's commitments into strict and exclusive spheres of the religious and the political is not only unsatisfactory in the sense that one settles for a bifurcated, and potentially contradictory, self. It is also unnecessary. In fact, Jewish law looks a great deal more amenable to democratic concerns when seen in its political, and not only religious or metaphysical guises.

This is good news for feminism, which is inexorably aligned with the struggle for democracy—that is, democracy is inherently a feminist project and feminism must be, *inter alia,* concerned to facilitate democratic conditions. This is not to imply that the tasks are identical. Each has its own purview, and in particular feminism will focus on the ways in which democracies fail in practice to ensure the freedom and opportunities of women, including exploring other possible barriers such as race/ethnicity, class, and sexual orientation. But I do reject any attempt to exempt issues of sexual equality from the larger political equations within which they are negotiated.[18] The important question of whether democracy is *enough* to achieve feminist goals is another matter, one that has given rise to a very rich discussion in feminist political theory.[19] Here, though, my concern is with allowing democratic ideals to percolate to the surface in a tradition that does not always highlight them.

In this light, I am conceiving democracy as involving a social contract in which each member commits at least minimally to the healthy functioning of the whole. This vision is sometimes labeled *communitarian* for its focus on a society revolving around notions of a common good or goods, in contrast to a perspective that focuses on the rights and protections of individuals. To my mind, this makes it very much an ideal not realized even in modern Western secular democracies, due to inequalities both sexual and economic, among others. But it is one that squares well with Jewish concepts of communal integrity, and it is therefore the best route into the democratic dimensions of Judaism.[20] The upshot is simple: unless and until there is a commitment to full equality within Judaism itself—where, to be sure, neither the form nor the content of equality is presupposed in advance and where the specificity of a Jewish law/polity over against a secular one is affirmed—there can be no Jewish feminist political philosophy in a constructive sense that is of any value.

🌣 Considering the Covenant

Jewish political theory encompasses reflections on both an integrated Jewish polity as well as more diffuse political arrangements. On the one hand, it is squarely focused on biblical narratives of covenant and kingship, and on the question of how these concepts bear on contemporary political questions.[21] Covenant has consistently been proclaimed the pivotal political notion in Judaism—and indeed it is almost as often asserted that this notion is pivotal to all the nations of the West, who are thereby understood to get their constitutions from the primitive case of the Israelites. Kingship has been a preoccupation less because of its continued relevance and more due to the simple fact that the ancient Jewish monarchies of Saul, David, and Solomon represent the only time in Jewish history (until the present) when Jews lived solely under Jewish sovereignty. The much debated question of whether or to what extent this ancient state of sovereignty is actively to be reconstituted has not detracted from the centrality the model has had in thinking about who Jews are as a people and what is their appointed or desired destiny.

On the other hand, perhaps precisely because the greatest proportion of Jewish history has taken place outside of the context of sovereignty, there is a wealth of materials—rabbinic and beyond—that seek to construct and refine political existence in a more piecemeal environment. One could argue, in fact, that, between the extremes of a triumphant monarchy and the travails of living as strangers in hostile lands, there exists a robust, complex, and fruitfully malleable Jewish politics and political theory in the semi-autonomous Jewish communities (*kehillot*) that emerged beginning in the tenth century and continued until the period of the emancipation at the end of the eighteenth century.[22] It is here that one can see Jewish law put to the test (and to the risk) of contingent political exigencies in a way that enables it to seem like the living, creative entity it is often touted as being by some of its modern and postmodern defenders.[23] Indeed, it is perhaps only when, post-emancipation, halakhah becomes divorced from any connection to civil/political life and becomes predominantly the vehicle for religious devotion and communal reproduction that it calcifies into something that cannot easily be challenged or changed.

This is, in fact, an important dimension of my reflections here, namely that a truly liberatory Jewish politics might very well need to make concrete reference to the conceptually entangled connections between religious law and politics in the tradition. More specifically, the challenge would be to connect the biblical covenant that establishes Israel as a holy people with the continual renewal of this covenant and continual redefinition of holiness through many ages and contexts. This loose intermingling of political and religious identities is extremely difficult to conceive, mainly because what becomes *religion* in the modern period (confessionalism, faith, theology, ritual) gets banished from the political sphere. My argument is not to encourage the erosion of the divisions between *church* and *state* or even to call them into question as they currently stand in modern democracies. What I am after instead is a concept of community (within a plurality of communities) that is at once more substantively political than the bare religious associations that pass as the only option for Judaism in the diaspora, yet less permanent than the current state of affairs in Israel. Ironically, what Israel and the diaspora precisely share is a certain rigidity with respect to law, in the first case due to the need to preserve a Jewish majority and in the second to the concentration of religious authority in the hands of a few who have much invested in impeding change. What the *kehillot* present is possibly something altogether more attractive, not something necessarily importable *tout court* into our current world, but a model for conceiving Jewish politics as creatively as philosophers have conceived Jewish ideas, virtues, foundational beliefs, and so on. The difficulty is how to, as it were, "thicken" the tradition without straining the Euro-American pluralism and democracy that precisely frame and enable it today.

Considering the covenant helps to focus attention on the dynamics at work in the tradition's political foundations. It also provides a way of thinking about the *desiderata* of difference and inclusion so fundamental to feminist political philosophy.[24] The broadly ancient Near Eastern custom of covenant-making has been much commented upon, including especially its contractual and thus reciprocal dimensions.[25] But as Daniel Elazar points out, in Mesopotamian and West Semitic covenants, the parties to the agreement were understood to be limited by the association, which was entered into for a specific political goal external to each entity. There was no expectation that the covenant would change the internal structure of the parties involved. In the case of the Israelites, however, the covenant with God was understood to bring about an entirely new community, one based upon a conception of both internal and external shared goals. The example Elazar invokes is that of the relationship between David and Jonathan, who make a covenant (*brit*) with each other because each loves the other as he loves himself—their souls, the verse tells us, become attached to one another and it is this attachment that the covenant both symbolizes and perpetuates (I Sam. 18:1–4).[26]

While love is one way of articulating the nature of the Israelite covenant, the dimension of it that political theorists make the most of, following ancient and medieval commentators, is the conception of consent involved.[27] Consent per se is not unique in the Israelite case, but it takes on a special dimension when the identity of the parties to the covenant is taken into account. It is, after all, God with whom the Israelites enter into agreement, and presumably God could have engineered such an agreement without the consent of human partners. In other words, what makes the Israelite case so unusual is not so much that it is God with whom an agreement is made, but that God acts in such a way as to self-limit in order to enable human partners to attain a sovereign position.

Indeed, in the famous passage from the Babylonian Talmud (Shabbat 88a) explicating the verse "And they took their places at the foot of the mountain" (Exod. 19:17), the rabbis make clear that any notion that the covenant was forced upon the Israelites nullifies it. What is especially interesting is that there is no overt hint in the verse from Exodus that they cite, nor any of the surrounding verses, that the covenant may indeed have been enacted coercively. This coercion is, rather, created by the rabbis themselves as an exegesis of Exod. 19:17: "Rabbi Avdimi b. Hama b. Hasa said, this teaches that the Holy One held the mountain over them like a tub and told them: 'If you accept the Torah—well and fine; otherwise, you will be buried right there.'" Perhaps it is enough that it is God with whom the Israelites

are covenanting to suggest the possibility, or even probability, that the covenant cannot have been completely free. But in any case, the point for the
rabbis, the one they set up the exegesis to make, is that if this is the case,
then the covenant cannot be in force: "Rav Aha b. Jacob said: This furnishes
a powerful disclaimer [*moda'a*] regarding the [acceptance of] Torah. [Rashi:
So if He arraigns them, demanding 'Why have you failed to observe that
which you accepted?' they can respond that the acceptance was coerced]." In
order to respond to this scenario properly, i.e., to show that indeed the covenant is properly in force, a seemingly totally unrelated verse from the Book
of Esther is brought to bear, namely that in the days of Ahasuerus, "the Jews
confirmed and accepted" (Esther 9:27)—they confirmed that which they
had already accepted, or in other words, they freely consented to the covenant, thus rectifying its nullification.[28]

The question of consent is not the only matter that bothered readers of
the Sinai covenant. There was also the issue of permanence: how could the
covenant bind the Israelites beyond those who were literally present at Sinai?
When Moses ascends the mountain to hear what God will say, and comes
down to "[tell] the people all the commands of the Lord and all the rules
. . . all the people answered with one voice, saying: 'All the things that the
Lord has commanded, we will do'" (Exod. 24:3).[29] But what of the generations that came afterward, and what of those Jews (such as lesbians and
gays) who have often been excluded from "the entire people"? According to
the terms of the covenant, God enters into it "not with you alone [i.e.,
those immediately present], but both with those who are standing here
with us this day before the Lord our God and with those who are not with
us here this day" (Deut. 29: 13–14).[30] Yet how exactly do "those who are
not with us here this day" include themselves in this "we will do," or alternatively, if they are automatically included, how does this affect the question of needing consent?

In his short commentary on the Sinai covenant in *The Jewish Political
Tradition,* Bernard Levinson notes that "what is striking in the biblical account of the Sinai covenant is that the promulgation of law is embedded in
a larger narrative, without which it is incomplete: the covenant exists in history."[31] What the historical setting ensures is that the covenant is both free
and extremely fragile. It is neither created once and for all in such a way that
it needn't be renewed nor is it any kind of guarantee against the dissolution
of Israel. All depends on the assent of each generation, members of which
will say, as the original community did, "All that Yahweh has spoken, we
shall do" (Exod. 19:8). Indeed, Levinson suggests, the covenant shows more
strongly that, in the biblical world-view, "existence is a moral postulate."

One can exclude oneself from such a covenant only by failing to ensure that the covenant itself can be heard by all. In this sense, it is not only that God is revealed "publicly to an entire nation, cutting across boundaries of class, gender, and ethnicity." It is also that the assent such a covenant requires "must finally include the assent of the reader, who is invited to enter the narrative of election and who, in the direct address of the Decalogue, is summoned to participate in the covenant."[32] The direct address is to each particular individual, who is spoken to by God using the "intimate singular form rather than the expected plural"; the invitation is to extend that address outwards, to the neighbor, the stranger, the friend.[33]

This claim, that the covenant at Sinai addresses not only each Israelite, not only all of Israel together, but each reader and all readers together, preserves both the covenant's historically specific nature (without which it cannot function as an event of freedom) and also its potential inclusiveness. What Levinson's analysis enables one to contemplate anew is the identity of the Sinai covenant as a constitution, whereby what is constituted is peoplehood through personhood—a democratic collectivity precisely of citizens whose citizenship demands a critical posture toward the formation of communities of exclusion. In this, Levinson is tapping into something quite primordial in Jewish self-consciousness, namely the sense that the covenant between God and the Israelites is incomprehensible insofar as it is purged of its dialectical relationships between individual and community, between Israel and the nations, between sovereignty and diaspora. With these dialectical relationships in play, the covenant is nothing less than the constitution of a body politic—civil, political, spiritual—forever destabilized inside and out by the terms of freedom it demands from its participants.

In this light, conceiving of Judaism in loosely communitarian terms is not a stretch. As Barbara Arneil has summarized it, the communitarian position has three main features, all of which include both descriptive and normative dimensions. In contrast to its main conceptual interlocutor, liberalism, it presumes first that the self should be understood in terms of its cultural, social, religious and other contexts—the self is (and should be seen as) "situated," not "unencumbered," taking its ends from this situatedness and from its web of relationships with others. Second, it holds that democratic societies are (and should be) formed on the basis of public shared goods and a sense of civic virtue, and that these goods can easily be obscured by the pure pursuit of individual interest and the protection of individual rights. Third, it stresses the ability of local communities to temper the anonymity and instrumentalism of larger governments and bureaucracies.[34] As Michael Sandel puts it, "communitarians worry about the concentration of power in both the corporate economy and the bureaucratic state, and the erosion of those intermediate forms of community that have at times sustained a more vital public life."[35]

Although a tradition like Judaism is complex enough to be described in potentially endless ways, the above features seem to me to resonate with foundational notions of Jewish identity: the aspect of being part of a community first (this communal identity is what is enacted at Sinai), of participating in goods wider than individual ones, and of conceiving Jewish community as "an intermediate form" that enriches life below the screen of national or corporate identities. Whether this makes Judaism (at least partly) communitarian, or communitarianism (at least partly) Jewish is not the point. What is clear, however, is that covenantal notions of community enable the tradition at its best to contain, without domesticating, the tension between membership and inclusiveness, without which one is left either with a closed ethnocentrism or a vapid universalism. This does not make covenant a communitarian idea any more than it makes it a liberal one; it simply suggests that the tension between the positions these terms name is something quite indigenous to Judaism.

What makes covenant a fruitful feminist political construct is that it both highlights some classic feminist issues, such as the critique of unimpeded free market-oriented individualism, and relieves some of the concerns feminists have had with communitarianism as a political ideology. In particular, as Arneil notes, feminists have worried about the conservative qualities of community, especially the romanticized communities extolled by religions (with their focus on traditional notions of the family). They have also asked whether the quest for common purposes and goods has obscured the ability of individuals, and of women in particular, vigorously to critique and challenge social, political, and cultural norms. Finally, they have wondered to what extent the emphasis on local community has shifted the burden of certain kinds of work from public bodies to unpaid volunteers, many of whom are women.[36]

These are serious concerns, and they are far from allayed in Judaism as it is currently practiced. Jewish feminists, in fact, rightly point to the tradition's culpability in all three areas. However, it is also the case that foregrounding the covenant in terms of the dialectics above leaves open the possibility of addressing these concerns in a concrete way. It leaves open the possibility of reconceiving gender roles, notions of family, common goods, and the weight of local community over national identity without appealing solely to individual rights, which often seem to come from outside the tradition. Indeed, it is often said, even by feminists, that values like egalitarianism are modern Western importations into Judaism, albeit necessary ones. Reconsidering the covenant enables one to imagine feminist questions as inextricably bound up with the questions of Jewish politics, community, and identity. Without completely dissolving the specificity of gender, there is also a value in insisting that there are no Jewish political questions that are not also feminist questions. This is a substantial gain over simply tinkering with halakhah or attempting to find ancient and medieval precedents for female equality or female role models, as important as these tasks are. What the covenant suggests, or can suggest, is instead something more basic: that the connections between liberty and community, equality and difference, sovereignty and creative dispersion, are those that richly inform Judaism's body politic as it emerges from the very beginning.

🏵 *Spinoza: The Democratic Standard*

These dialectical tensions form the core of Spinoza's political theory, as articulated in the *Theologico-Political Treatise* (TTP), one of the only sustained political treatises in the entire tradition. For our purposes here, the most important dimension of the TTP concerns Spinoza's argument that democracy is the standard in both religion and politics: both are constituted through covenants (pacts) such that all participants are both free and equal. What makes his argument for democracy so relevant to feminist Jewish political theory is that, on the one hand, it is *prima facie* at the cost of orthodoxy, since Spinoza believes that Jewish law as conceived by the rabbis ought not be obligatory in the post-biblical world. On the other hand, were halakhah to have the reach that biblical law had to constitute a polity (or an analogous sub-state entity), it could legitimately obligate on Spinoza's grounds as one kind of human law among many. In other words, insofar as halakhah is politically as well as religiously construed, in touch with community constitution and the issues of power and authority that are thereby negotiated, it could conceivably square with the freedom that Spinoza thinks is enshrined in the two covenants. Unlike some liberal Jewish critiques that have left feminists without a robust tradition to think with, Spinoza does not jettison Jewish law so much as revise it by rethinking its connection to its biblical democratic roots. The advantage for feminist perspectives is this two-fold move: to preserve Jewish law (the "thickness" of the tradition) by reconceiving its connection to political life, and to highlight its fluidity, egalitarianism, and openness.

By religion, or more specifically, the divine law, Spinoza does not mean what either Christians or Jews take to be the revealed, community-specific contents of their traditions. These Spinoza includes among what he calls human laws, those laws, in other words, that are dedicated to the preservation of a particular community and that have to do with divine law only indirectly, providing security and good health, the material conditions within which the divine law can be instantiated (or even the material instance of divine law).[37] The divine law, namely "the universal law that consists in the true way of life," properly belongs to all human beings as individuals, and thus cannot be the sole purview of any particular community.[38] What is interesting about the way Spinoza makes this division is, first, that both divine and human laws are entered into as pacts, that is, they are both acts that express freedom and effort, not natural endowment—they are made, not found. So in other words, human law does not mean "humanly-made" as opposed to divinely ordained. Both the human and the divine laws are "humanly-made," that is, expressive of humanly recognizable values as opposed to being naturally fated or divinely imposed.[39]

Second, religion in fact straddles both divine and human laws. On the one hand, it comprises a set of universal values (justice and charity) that enables human beings to flourish alongside their neighbors. Yet on the other hand, religion re-appears in the context of human laws, which, as I said, are differentiated from divine laws by virtue of having reference to the peace, security, and flourishing of communities, not individuals.[40] Human laws, in other words, can include what are considered both civil or public law and religious or private law. This is not to ignore Spinoza's genuine critique of religion; but it is to cast this critique in more nuanced terms than are often proffered. It is not that Spinoza believes in a universal religion over against particular forms. It is that the particular forms, like all human laws, have as their task the promotion of security and good health for their members, and insofar as they do not, they will neither create the conditions for more refined pursuits nor will they be likely to last very long.[41]

To some degree Spinoza has Judaism in mind here, since its law is a system that can be seen to revolve around the promotion of security and good health. This at least has been true at moments in Jewish history when the Jews had some degree of political autonomy. But it is less and less true when the focus of the law becomes not on how to enable a community to flourish but on how to achieve individual salvation through ritual. When Spinoza therefore disparages "ceremony" as being completely irrelevant to blessedness, he means those dimensions of religion that have become divorced from political life and power—religion as individual and communal ritual rather than as social and political constitution.[42]

Thus, Spinoza's well-known critique of Judaism and especially of the ancient rabbis is complicated by the fact that the Jewish tradition also contains within itself a conception of law that he finds powerfully relevant to the critique of his own Christian society in seventeenth-century Holland, where religion seems to him entirely about strife, controversy, and the distinctions between human beings that foster them. For Spinoza, it is the Hebrew commonwealth before the monarchy that illustrates the connection between religion and the state that he thinks is most valuable. It is not that he thinks the Hebrews exemplify humankind. But their state—founded as it was on a pact with God—perfectly illustrates the tensions that result from the intrinsic pull between the commands of God, the divine law, and the commands of any and every historical state, in which he includes Jewish law, both secular and sacred. The Hebrews are paradigmatic because, despite the fact that it is ultimately Moses who acts in God's place as ruler, it is not Moses with whom the Jews enter into a pact at Sinai, but God. Thus, he writes, the Jews "make an absolute transfer to Moses of their right to consult God and to interpret his decrees" only after they had transferred their right "not to any mortal man, but to God alone" . . . "freely, not by forcible coercion or fear of threats . . . as in a democracy."[43] It was "our God" that they begged Moses to interpret for them when, at Sinai, they were afraid to approach the mountain: "our God," the one with whom they had first covenanted (Deut. 5: 22–23).

What the Hebrews thus illustrate at Sinai is the simultaneity of universal values and their instantiation in particular laws. In a manner of speaking, God is thereby the signature of human equality, written between the lines of the Hebrew constitution. What human beings can never forfeit to a human sovereign or human laws, including religious law, is the covenant they have already made with God. Or at least, in Spinoza's terms, one forfeits this covenant at the cost of security and good health. But the pact with God is thus a critique of tyranny and injustice only insofar as it is left "theoretical," unconditional, absolute, meaning that it is a limit concept to which the human ideals of justice testify, just as ideals of freedom presuppose a theoretical social contract.[44] The moment one attempts to make the pact with God historical—as does a theocracy—its power as a critique is weakened.

What is crucial to see, according to Spinoza, is that the divine law of the Hebrews is inscribed not solely in their particular laws but also in their hearts, for the demolition of their polity was not the demolition of God's pact, the one that commands justice and charity absolutely. The survival of halakhah alone, in other words, is of little consequence to him since he holds it to be essentially political as much as religious. Thus Spinoza turns the survival of the Jews on its head: it is not that the Jews survive because of the law; it is that they survive despite the loss of it in its fullest capacity. Yet on the other hand, and perhaps more importantly, we learn that justice and charity do not exist outside some nation or other. What the Hebrews show us, through the force of their distinctiveness vis-à-vis others, is that a people can indeed survive even though "scattered and stateless"—they can cling to the law unmoored from its polis.[45] What disturbs Spinoza about this is not at all the distinctiveness of a people per se, i.e., the constitution of a *natio* with its own laws and customs. What Spinoza laments is that an unequivocal good—the "organis[ation of] a society under fixed laws, [the] occup[ation of] a fixed territory, and [the] concentrat[ation of] the strength of all its members into one body, as it were, a social body," is entirely substituted with what is only ever a necessary evil—the intensification of piety as a form of social cohesion.[46] The priests and pontiffs get religion wrong not simply because they lust for tyranny and secrecy over clarity, democracy, and accessibility. They get religion wrong because they fail to learn from Moses and the Hebrews—to make explicit what is always implicit— that, whatever power they possess is political in addition to religious. The political is the condition for religion to be true; and it is also, then, the condition for religion to be false—in other words, tyranny is the exactly the same whether in the *ecclesia* or in the *civitas*. One cannot critique tyranny in one realm without doing so in the other.

The Kehillah: *Repoliticizing Religion*

It is difficult to translate Spinoza's position easily into contemporary terms. We who live in Western democracies are used to seeing religion as radically separated from matters of politics (however much in practice this line gets fudged), and indeed it is Spinoza who was in his own way *the* early-modern champion of the kinds of rights and freedoms (of conscience, opinion, and belief) that members of modern democracies take for granted. We attribute these in part to the separation of church and state, but their Enlightenment provenance is more tangled. There is no easy translation because in Spinoza's day religious authority constituted the single most dire threat to the liberties he envisioned precisely because it set itself up as a competing power to the state. To Spinoza, the separation of church and state was the problem, not the solution—a free citizenry should not, he held, have to regard itself as beholden to a divided kingdom, and therefore the solution was to subordinate the religious realm to the political one.

To contemporary readers, however, things look entirely different, due at least in part to the withering of the power of religion in public life. One could say that religious power, even without the checks and balances that cordon it off from the political sphere, does not threaten the authority of the state in the ways it once did, though this judgment can greatly vary depending on one's standpoint and the context in which one is making it. The point is that modern democracies have already successfully subordinated religion even as they separate it off: religion is no longer a threat because it has precisely been privatized, been made a matter of personal belief and conscience. While it might be tempting to give Spinoza the credit for this state of affairs too, his view was more complex than this, for he held that personal belief ought indeed be sacrosanct, but that laws, religious or otherwise, are to some degree public and must therefore wrestle with their connections to the larger polity. At the very least, religious law cannot constitute a pocket of unfreedom and inequality, even if the larger society that permits it to flourish is itself innocent of this charge.

For Spinoza, ultimately there was no way to salvage the Jewish tradition in the diaspora, where it had become something that "discourages manliness," that is, it had become purely about religious ritual (Spinoza was no proto-feminist).[47] But he did not explore the possibility of conceiving Jewish life in ways other than the either/or of diaspora or Zion (a reconstituted commonwealth), despite the fact that there is in Jewish history a very rich tradition of doing so. I refer to the medieval *kehillot,* the semi-autonomous communities that arose in the diaspora in the tenth century with the decline of the centralized rabbinic authorities in Babylonia and the Land of Israel, spreading ultimately to North Africa, Italy, Germany, Spain, France, Turkey, the Balkan countries, Poland, and Lithuania.[48] The *kehillot* present to contemporary readers an opportunity to explore precisely a kind of intermediary "state" of the Jews, one in which the lines between the religious and the political intermingled to produce a cluster of remarkably creative communities.

As Menachem Elon describes it, the *kehillot,* though subject to the whims of its host state, had a surprising amount of power, "cover[ing] the entire range of its members' activity, shaping their social life and spiritual image."[49] The challenge that such communities had to overcome was not only how to constitute a polity on the basis of Torah and halakhah, but also how to conceive of authority in a context in which it had always stemmed from leaders such as kings or prophets. The community in theory does not possess the power to compel obedience to public norms and laws without each member's specific consent. What the *kehillot* thus had to figure out was how to generate communal authority from sources that did not seem automatically to support it—they had to figure out how to govern the public realm, albeit one within a larger realm over which they had no control. What is interesting about this "problem," though, is precisely the consensual character of the *kehillah* and its respect for the individual. This does not by any means imply that the *kehillot* were democratic in our modern sense of this term; it simply suggests that communal consent was something that the elders of the *kehillot* felt they could not simply banish in the constitution of their community— in fact, it formed their most potent obstacle in such a way that the very nature of their authority had to be reconfigured to take account of it.

The method of governing that the rabbis of the *kehillot* initially had available to them was to appeal to custom and to rabbinical decisions and ordinances (*takkanot*). However, situations arose (fiscal, legal, political) for which no existing ordinance applied. The solution was found in the decision of halakhic scholars "to consider the community, from a legal point of view, as equivalent to those bodies included within the scope of Jewish public law, such as the King or Nasi [prophet] and, most importantly, the Court, or even the High Court." What is most revolutionary is the analogy to a court, and indeed the claim that the community functions *as* a court, "with each and every member a judge."[50] There is no precedent for this in talmudic halakhah or *aggadah*. It is simply asserted by post-talmudic scholars without "any legal-halakhic argument to support [it]."[51]

The implication of the analogy to the courts is clear: for the halakhic authorities of the *kehillot,* the point was not simply about the establishment of governing authority (through setting up elected and appointed offices), but about transforming laws to make them more amenable to a given communal situation. Yet these transformations were not arbitrary. For as Elon notes, among the principles established during this period were principles of justice and equity, according to which *halakhic* scholars articulated a framework of Jewish law that could not be contradicted by communal *takkanot,* including things like "equality before the law, protecting the rights of the minority or the weak, [and] improving the social order."[52] What this suggests, in however miniature a form, is that, when forced to become malleable enough to govern itself as a political entity, Jewish law can be seen to tend towards egalitarianism in a loose sense: at least one can observe a consciousness of the power, both religious and political, of what Spinoza regarded as a primordial covenant of all Israelites with God.

🕎 Conclusion: Women and Jews

The question is, how relevant are these examples from the tradition for reflecting on Jewish political life today, and in particular feminist Jewish political life? What I am trying to bring to the fore throughout this essay are ways of looking at Judaism, and halakhah in particular, not only as antithetical to a democratic outlook (which they undoubtedly are in many respects) but also as significantly in line with it—to see in particular the modern Israeli hope for a Jewish and democratic state as not hopelessly contradictory. To do this, I am claiming, one needs to be creative in the imagination of what counts as religion, and skeptical especially of the effort to cordon it off from political life. This is crucial in Judaism not only because religion and politics were once, in antiquity, bound up with each other. What is at stake is the possibility—and it can be no more than a fruitful possibility here since I have surveyed only the tiniest fraction of material—that in aligning the tradition both with the liminal period of the Hebrew commonwealth and with the equally liminal, though longer-lasting period of the medieval *kehillot,* contemporary Jews can find new lenses with which to address the problem of gender equity and the body politic. What this means, though, is that feminist Jewish political philosophy is dependent on re-imagining what Judaism is, not simply on re-arranging the parts that women get to play. The feminist critique cannot take place in the synagogue alone because Judaism does not really happen there for anyone, male or female. This has become a truism especially in Orthodox circles, which are wont to emphasize the religious sanctity of everyday life centered in the home. My view is a version of that emphasis, without the romanticized, gender-differentiated roles that it institutionalizes. My question is, rather, what would it be like to re-politicize religion?

As I have noted, this question cannot be about dissolving the separation between religion and politics in the public sphere, either in America or in Israel (where of course they are not so separate). In that case, what is it that I am envisioning here—a politicized religion that yet remains part of a diverse and indeed secular public sphere? This seeming contradiction shares a great deal with the feminist desire both to insist that the private is public, namely that the home is not a space that can be exempt from the kinds of liberties that one takes for granted in the public sphere, and also properly to retain the privacy that allows one the freedom to make one's life as one chooses, despite public disapproval or sanction. This is possible for women only if they hold onto the notion that politics is not something one enters into and out of, but rather that politics is the context within which all human choices are made. It is no more or less than the basic framework of human interaction, and in the case of a democracy, it is the claim that all persons are equal before the law and have the right to be treated as such. For a woman thus to hold her personal relationships to the standard of her public ones is simply to insist that her life is not bifurcated between how she is valued in public and how she is valued in private. Beyond that structure, she can construct her life in as many different ways as she can envision.

The case of religion is not perfectly analogous, but what is important to see is three-fold. First, it is that women *in* religious communities should not be asked to leave their political commitments behind, regardless of how rich, particular, and idiosyncratic any given tradition is. It is often argued that religious beliefs and systems should not be controlled by the political powers that be, and this is no doubt a desirable state of affairs. But this is not the same thing as saying religion should not be political, that is, subject to, and even a contributing voice in shaping, the norms and values one takes for granted in the larger public realm. In this light, it should be no more legitimate to say that religion ought not to be politicized than that any private choice should be—in other words, religious commitments, like any imaginative life choice, involve our identity as political beings who have chosen particular societies to live in (or find ourselves chosen by them), and these commitments should not be seen as exempt from these societies. I cannot take on here the challenge that politicizing religion strips it of its cultural and symbolic richness, except to insist that this is not at all a necessary by-product of what I am claiming. What is being claimed is that religious engagement within a particular set of customs and laws should not function as a kingdom within a kingdom—it should not force its members to give up something they cherish in one kingdom for membership in another. This either/or has been particularly acute for women who belong to non-egalitarian religious communities. Politicizing religion for such women involves principally the claim that the focus of critical reform should not only be the synagogue or other rituals but also the continuities between the ritual/religious and the political, or between what is lawful or customary in a particular tradition and that which is lawful or customary in wider political life. The latter is no more a threat to the sovereignty of the former than vice versa—ideally, at least, they are two sides of the same coin, the multifaceted coin, that is, of one's modern and postmodern identities.

Second, as members of religious communities, those with feminist goals should be at the frontlines of the effort to make more integrated the religious and the political sides of Judaism in particular, which contains such rich overlaps in these areas. A Jewish feminist political philosophy, in other words, must be one that resists the post-emancipation attenuation of the tradition and looks for sources to enrich those areas of halakhah and *aggadah* that reference our common lives with each other and not only our ritual lives. Feminism has always been a political project, which is to some degree why the nomenclature of *feminist political philosophy* is redundant.

Again, this does not mean that religious commitments cannot be private. It means only that the private need not be seen as utterly divorced from the values one holds elsewhere. Even if one holds that one's religious commitments come before one's political ones, according to the logic, perhaps, that one's relationship with God overrides the secular realm, a feminist perspective will be one that seeks to minimize the conflicts between these two realms.

Third and finally, clearly it is not just any politics that needs to be made more continuous with Judaism as a religious tradition. It is perhaps one of the most damaging blows to the Jewish feminist project to claim that democracy is fundamentally a secular Western ideology that need not override one's more ancient commanded traditions. To insist on living in two incompatible worlds, in other words, when one of those worlds is modern Western democracy, is to deprive Jewish feminist political philosophy of its most crucial insights, namely that Judaism itself has traditions of democracy that animate its political thinking from the very beginning. Many of these threads have not been widely pursued, especially for the implications they have for feminist philosophy. But what is clear is that this is not a matter of importing contemporary external values into a tradition that cannot absorb them. This is about finding indigenous trajectories, whose paths have not yet been creatively pursued. The implication is that the feminist perspective on Jewish political philosophy is one that fastens on Jewish democracy, and imagines what the tradition might look like with this concept at its center rather than at its periphery. This is nothing less than a re-imagination of what Judaism is and can be, not only a critique of its absences or oppressions. All Jews, in other words, would benefit from making it possible to extend the tradition beyond our ritual lives—to make it possible to say Jewish and democratic, not only in the land of Israel but in the diaspora as well.

There is, then, a noteworthy tradition of equality in Judaism, precisely when it makes contact with the political in the widest sense. To be sure, there are also profound inequities in the halakhah, particularly concerning women. But what we learn from the *kehillot* is the elasticity of law. Of course it is anachronistic to imagine that the *kehillot* were democratic in our sense; but there is clearly a strong notion of consensus and equality, nevertheless, that emerges from them. No doubt this did not apply to women; but the conception of halakhic flexibility is nevertheless incredibly useful in precisely this regard now.

The wording of the Israeli Declaration of Independence hovers over these reflections: a state both Jewish and democratic. The almost haunted quality to this hope is one of its most compelling features. It is obviously hard to bring about—but intuitively worth doing. So too the tension between gender egalitarianism and halakhah, or Judaism more widely: as with the Israeli declaration, so here too there is the question of whether the tension is fruitful or simply a dead end. Indeed, a great deal rides on these two tensions, and they are conceptually related: both struggle with the internal and the external, the particular and the general, what changes and what must remain the same. Making halakhah work for women is the same as making it work for men: what is a corrosive and unfree contradiction must become an elastic and generative tension that produces new laws, new customs. The challenge is how to ground Judaism in the political without losing its ritual value, without insisting that ritual is the only way to live Jewishly, and most importantly, extending the political insights of the tradition to frame a community that is neither pure diaspora nor total Zion, fluid but fixed.

This is a task concerning Judaism's body politic, but in the end it is also about bodies, for the anti-democratic strains in the tradition are the same strains that identify wisdom with something disembodied. To be engaged in the struggle for democracy, then, is to be engaged with embodiment in all forms, both individual and social. This is not a necessary entailment; simply a commitment to the recognition that one's individual fate—one's security, good health, and wisdom—are wrapped up in the fate of others and that, as Spinoza puts it, "a [person] who is guided by reason is more free in a state, where [s]he lives according to a common decision, than in solitude, where [s]he obeys only [her or] himself."[53] I look forward to the work ahead.

NOTES

1. "Commentary on the Bible," in *Medieval Political Philosophy,* ed. Ralph Lerner and Muhsin Mahdi (Ithaca, N.Y.: Cornell University Press, 1963), 258.

2. *Aseh Lekha Rav* (Tel Aviv, 1986), vol. 7 section 54, 238. Quoted in *The Jewish Political Tradition,* ed. Michael Walzer, Menachem Lorberbaum, and Noam Zohar (New Haven, Conn.: Yale University Press, 2000), 295. Hereafter JPT.

3. Baruch Spinoza, *Theologico-Political Treatise,* trans. Samuel Shirley, introduction and notes by Seymour Feldman (Indianapolis: Hackett Publishing Co., 1998), 149. Hereafter, TTP.

4. An illuminating recent treatment of the political in the Middle Ages is Menachem Lorberbaum, *Politics and the Limits of Law: Secularizing the Political in Medieval Jewish Thought* (Stanford, Calif.: Stanford University Press, 2001).

5. Daniel Boyarin's research into the emergence of rabbinic culture has stressed these themes. See especially *Carnal Israel* (Berkeley: University of California Press, 1993).

6. A good survey of these issues is Susan Bordo, *Unbearable Weight: Feminism, Western Culture and the Body* (Berkeley: University of California Press, 1993). For influential treatments of embodiment, culture, and discourse, see Judith Butler, *Gender Trouble: Feminism and the Subversion of Identity* (New York: Routledge, 1990) and *Bodies that Matter: On the Discursive Limits of "Sex"* (New York: Routledge, 1993).

7. The locution is Jeannette Winterson's, from her novel of this name (*Written on the Body* [London: Jonathan Cape, 1992]). But it refers more generally to the work of French feminists such as Hélène Cixous, Catherine Clément, and Luce Irigaray, who have focused attention on the need to rewrite philosophy in a language sensitive to women's experience. See Clément and Cixous's *The Newly Born Woman,* trans. C. Porter (Minneapolis: University of Minnesota Press, 1986).

8. On conflict as a paradigm of reasoning, see Janice Moulton, "A Paradigm of Philosophy: The Adversary Method," in *Women, Knowledge, and Reality: Explorations in Feminist Philosophy,* ed. Ann Garry and Marilyn Pearsall (New York: Routledge, 1996), 5–20. On the ethics of care, see, for example, Nel Noddings, *Caring: A Feminine Approach to Ethics and Moral Education* (Berkeley: University of California Press, 1984), and Sarah Ruddick, *Maternal Thinking: Towards a Politics of Peace* (Boston: Beacon Press, 1989). Much of the feminist literature surrounding the discourse of care and nurturing is responding in one way or another to the work of Carol Gilligan, whose book *In a Different Voice: Psychological Theory and Women's Development* (Cambridge, Mass.: Harvard University Press, 1982) charted the ways in which women and men respond differently to the demands of work and relationships.

9. On desire, see Luce Irigaray, *The Sex Which Is Not One,* trans. C. Porter and C. Burke (Ithaca, N.Y.: Cornell University Press, 1985), and Eileen O'Neill, "Representations of Eros: Exploring Female Agency," in *Gender/Body/Knowledge: Feminist Reconstructions of Beings and Knowing,* ed. Alison M. Jaggar and Susan R. Bordo (New Brunswick, N.J.: Rutgers University Press, 1989), 68–91; on the emotions, see Alison M. Jaggar, "Love and Knowledge: Emotion in Feminist Epistemology," in *Gender/Body/Knowledge,* 145–71; on image and the imagination, see Donna Wilshire, "The Uses of Myth, Image, and the Female Body in Re-Visioning Knowledge," in *Gender/Body/Knowledge,* 92–114; on rhetoric, see Susan Shapiro, "A Matter of Discipline: Reading for Gender in Jewish Philosophy," *Judaism since Gender,* ed. Laura Levitt and Miriam Peskowitz (New York: Routledge, 1997), 158–73.

10. For an overview of these attitudes, see Abraham Melamed, "The Attitude toward Democracy in Medieval Jewish Philosophy," in *Commandment and Community: New Essays in Jewish Legal and Political Philosophy,* ed. Daniel H. Frank (Albany: State University of New York Press, 1995), 173–94.

11. Ibid., 188.

12. For an account of Abravanel's republicanism, see Reuven Kimelman, "Abravanel and the Jewish Republican Ethos," in *Commandment and Community,* 195–216.

13. The articles in Blackwell's *A Companion to Feminist Philosophy,* ed. Alison M. Jaggar and Iris Marion Young (Oxford: Blackwell, 1998), give a good overview of the territory.

14. A short treatment of gender dichotomies in the canon of Western philosophy is Genevieve Lloyd, *The Man of Reason: "Male" and "Female" in Western Philosophy* (Minneapolis: University of Minnesota Press, 1984). See also Hilda Hein, "Liberating Philosophy: An End to the Dichotomy of Spirit and Matter," in *Women, Knowledge, and Reality,* 293–311. For a Jewish theological perspective on the negative impact of dichotomies, see Judith Plaskow, *Standing Again at Sinai* (San Francisco: Harper & Row, 1990).

15. Alan Mittelman, *The Scepter Shall Not Depart from Judah: Perspectives on the Persistence of the Political in Judaism* (Lanham, Md.: Lexington Books, 2000).

16. The work of Michael Walzer, Daniel Elazar, Stuart Cohen, and Ella Belfer is exemplary in this regard.

17. I refer here to everything from excluding women from being counted in a *minyan* (prayer quorum), serving on a *beit din* (religious court), observing the so-called time-bound commandments, and being able to initiate divorce proceedings against their husbands, to the laws of *kiddushin* (marriage), in which a woman is "acquired" by a man, and *niddah* (ritual purity surrounding menstruation and the use of the ritual bath) and the customs of *tsniut* (modesty). There are many ways of interpreting the legal differences between men and women. My point here is simply that they are on their face incompatible with a feminist perspective that stresses equality. My thanks to Aryeh Cohen for discussing these issues with me. I also benefited from reading his book *Rereading Talmud: Gender, Law and the Poetics of Sugyot* (Atlanta: Scholars Press, 1998).

18. For a succinct treatment of the complexities involved in the goal of equality, see Alison M. Jaggar, "Sexual Difference and Sexual Equality," in *Theoretical Perspectives on Sexual Difference,* ed. Deborah L. Rhode (New Haven, Conn.: Yale University Press, 1990), 239–54.

19. See especially the work of Alison Jaggar, Iris Marion Young, Virginia Held, and Anne Phillips.

20. For an argument as to why feminist ideals are better served by a more substantive or communitarian democracy, see Anne Phillips, *Democracy and Difference,* especially Chapter 6. I discuss this issue below.

21. The most incisive treatment of this question is Daniel Elazar, "Covenant as the Basis of the Jewish Political Tradition," in *Kinship and Consent: The Jewish Political Tradition and its Contemporary Uses,* ed. Daniel J. Elazar (Washington, D.C.: University Press of America, 1983), 21.

22. See Jacob Katz, *Exclusiveness and Tolerance: Studies in Jewish–Gentile Relations in Medieval and Modern Times* (New York: Behrman House, 1961).

23. See, for example, the work of Robert Cover, Rachel Adler, Emmanuel Levinas, and David Hartman.

24. See Diemut Bubeck, "Feminism in Political Philosophy: Women's Difference," in *The Cambridge Companion to Feminism in Philosophy,* ed. Miranda Fricker and Jennifer Hornsby (Cambridge: Cambridge University Press, 2000).

25. Jon Levenson, *Sinai and Zion* (Minneapolis: Winston Press, 1985), contains a good discussion of the issues.

26. Elazar, "Covenant," 22–23.

27. JPT gives a wide range of these commentaries, from biblical rabbinic texts to Abravanel, Judah Loewe (the Maharal of Prague), and Spinoza. See 10–46.

28. JPT, 28–29.

29. JPT, 13.

30. JPT, 14.

31. JPT, 24.

32. JPT, 26.

33. JPT, 26.

34. Barbara Arneil, *Politics and Feminism* (Oxford: Blackwell, 1999), 144–47.

35. Michael Sandel, "Introduction," in *Liberalism and Its Critics,* ed. Michael Sandel (New York: New York University Press, 1984), 7, quoted in Arneil, *Politics,* 147.

NANCY K. LEVENE

36. Arneil, *Politics,* 147–51.

37. TTP, 38.

38. TTP, 60.

39. For Spinoza's discussion of the two pacts, see Chapter 16. For his account of the "man-made" dimension of both human and divine law, see Chapter 4.

40. TTP, 60.

41. TTP, 184.

42. See TTP, Chapter 5.

43. TTP, 195–96.

44. See TTP, 170–85 for Spinoza's discussion of the origins of society and the democratic state in particular.

45. TTP, 47.

46. TTP, 38.

47. TTP, 47.

48. Menachem Elon, "Power and Authority: Halakhic Stance of the Traditional Community and its Contemporary Implications," in *Kinship and Consent,* 184.

49. Ibid., 184.

50. Ibid., 189.

51. Ibid., 190.

52. Ibid., 193.

53. Spinoza, "Ethics," *Collected Works,* IV: 73, 587.

TEN

SUZANNE LAST STONE

Feminism and the Rabbinic Conception of Justice

This essay presents a detailed analysis of a rabbinic narrative that deals with the tension between justice and mercy, both divine and human, in terms of gender imagery.[1] I dissect the narrative on two levels: first, as a meditation on the emotional attitudes that underlie the legal concepts of justice and mercy in rabbinic thought, and second, as a window onto the role of the feminine in the rabbinic tradition. The essay is a response to the challenge of feminist legal philosophy to take gender categories seriously in thinking through how law historically has been shaped and what shape law may take in the future. It is also a challenge to feminist legal philosophy that has all too often traced the "patriarchal" aspect of modernist law to the rabbinic tradition's supposed emphasis on a "male" God of justice and of impersonal law and rules, who man must emulate.

I. Feminist Legal Philosophy and Jewish Legal Thought

The emergence of feminism as a field of intellectual inquiry in law has given rise both to a new set of legal questions framed around sex and gender and also to a new set of theories about the philosophical underpinnings of law, collectively referred to as feminist jurisprudence.[2] Feminist jurisprudence, which is rooted in ideas derived from both feminism and poststructuralist philosophical discourse, is a significant part of the larger effort in the legal academy to criticize and reconstruct the fundamental categories, methodology, and self-understanding of Western law and legal thought.[3] The feminist investigation of law can be divided into two distinct inquiries. The first focuses on the effect of existing norms and doctrines of the legal system on the actual lives of women. This effort grows out of the initial aspiration of the feminist legal project to establish justice by advancing the legal equality of men and women. Liberal feminists regard modern, liberal law as potentially capable of overcoming patriarchal patterns. The task is to extend the neutrality of law to encompass not only race and ethnicity but also sex. The attempt to desexualize law, however, soon raises the question whether women are, in fact, different from men. If women have unique needs not shared by men, then the law must take account of women's different viewpoints and situations in order to render true justice. The "difference question" has enlarged the discipline of feminist jurisprudence, leading feminist scholars to grapple not only with legal norms and doctrine but also with a larger set of philosophical and anthropological questions. How are women different from men and how do we know these differences? Is sex identical to gender? Is gender given or is it socially constructed, produced by law and culture? If the latter, where do our images of women come from?

The effort to provide an account of the differences between men and women early on converged with the larger scholarly project of providing a critique and reconstruction of law itself. Thus, the second line of inquiry of feminist jurisprudence is to trace the essential features of modernist law, analyze how these features reproduce cultural ideals that are gendered, and show how law might be imagined differently. Feminist legal philosophers argue that the modernist conception of law—a system of universal, abstract, objective rules applied and elaborated by dispassionate judges adhering to standard criteria of legal rationality, which emphasizes formalism, consistency and certainty, and addressing a legal subject conceived as autonomous and self-sufficient—is itself gendered. It is a vision of law produced by men and reflective of traits historically associated with men. Feminist theory has been particularly forceful in analyzing how we traditionally define the other over against the self through the construction of contrasting traits. Indeed, from its inception in the work of Simone de Beauvoir, feminist theory has linked the issue of gender to the larger problem of dualism in Western metaphysics.[4] The duality of Self and Other in terms of male and female is replicated in a series of binary oppositions, in which male and female are contrasted and asymmetrically valued in terms of characteristics such as reason and emotion, abstract justice and mercy, impartiality and passion, the universal and the particular. Because in all these sets of opposed terms the former is the privileged one in modern legal culture, we have an impoverished view of the possibilities for law. "Difference feminists" seek to incorporate into law and judging an "ethic of care," a jurisprudence of "compassion," or even "maternal thinking," to counter the masculine focus on rights and rules. These jurisprudential theories share a "basic thesis of connection," resting on a vision of the feminine self as forming its identity through relationships, and an attention to the intuitive aspects of legal decision-making and to the emotional attitudes that lie behind legal and philosophical concepts.[5] Thus, one of the aims of feminist jurisprudence is to break down the rigid dichotomies between reason and emotion, justice and mercy, or the masculine and feminine, in order to rescue law from its cold abstraction and to inject into law a broader spectrum of human attributes, emotions, and modes of knowledge.[6]

In contrast to the remarkable inroads made by feminism in the field of general legal philosophy, feminism's impact on the study of Jewish law and legal philosophy is marginal. Indeed, feminist jurisprudence is as troubling for Jewish legal theorists as it is potentially enriching. Because Jewish law is at once a precursor of and an alternative to Western legal systems, Jewish law is both the object of feminist critique and a potential ally of the larger goal of feminist jurisprudence to offer an alternative model of law. To date, feminist engagement with Jewish law, emanating from within the Jewish tradition, largely has been limited to noting women's legal inequality under the halakhah and their exclusion from positions of authority in the ongoing process of articulating and elaborating the norms of the Jewish legal system. Far less attention has been paid to the underlying philosophical and religious assumptions, ideals, methodology, and self-understanding of the halakhah. But it is at this more theoretical level that a complex dialogue between Jewish legal philosophy and feminist jurisprudence should emerge.

The incipient encounter between Jewish and feminist jurisprudence thus far has produced two radically disparate and exaggerated claims. Feminist scholars who seek to make visible the theological and gender assumptions that underlie modernist law view Jewish law as the cultural ground from which Western liberal law emerged. Modernist law, they contend, replicates "masculine" authoritarian patterns inherited from the religious realm, particularly from the "patriarchal," monotheistic tradition of Judaism. These writings build on the feminist criticism of the monotheistic idea, which argues that in monotheism, precisely because there is only one God, there is room only for the projection of male experiences onto the divinity. Monotheism, conceived as a cold, masculine, monistic, hierarchical abstraction, is pitted against the idea of pluralism and all that it implies: an openness to the diversity and variety of human emotions and passions, competing perspectives, pluralist law, and pluralist conceptions of truth. Ancient Judaism figures prominently in these analyses as the inaugurator and purest form of the monotheistic idea.[7] Consider, for example, Jean Elshtain's provocative essay titled "Sovereign State, Sovereign God, Sovereign Self," which attempts to construct a politics of monotheism.[8] The monotheistic idea posits a single, indivisible, divine (male) sovereign, who has absolute dominion over domestic space. The political structure of the modern state, with its insistence on one law for everyone enforced top-down, replicates the monotheistic structure, with its focus on one final will "brought to bear on cacophony and chaos."[9] This idea of a unified will, whether that of the "male" God of the monotheistic tradition or that of the state, is also tied, Elshtain argues, to the "masculine" conception of the self as autonomous and sovereign. Similarly, various feminist writings draw a connection between the "masculine," hierarchical structure of monotheism and modernist theories of judging that stress objectivity, impartiality, and the pre-eminent role of reason in adjudication.[10] Taken together, these writings raise the important question whether it is possible for modernist law to break free of a cultural system that is so strongly linked to the image of the dispassionate, impartial, unified, "male" God of justice whom man emulates.

These depictions of the monotheistic idea of the Bible suffer from the fact that the rabbinic tradition is largely unknown in Western culture. Thus, Jewish thinking about political order or divine justice and mercy is identified exclusively with the Bible, unmediated by later Jewish writings and shaped by centuries of Christian reading. Because of the common juxtaposition of the biblical God of vengeance and justice, who punishes every violation of his law, with the New Testament God of forgiveness and love, all too often the cultural origin of the idea of compassion and mercy is ascribed to Christian sources.[11] This tendency continues to influence feminist writings, much of which—even in the American legal academy—are situated in a Christian context. German feminist writings, as described by Susannah Heschel,[12] have gone so far as to locate the mentality of Nazism in the male God of vengeance of the Old Testament that culminated in the rabbinic tradition, with its supposed emphasis on impersonal law, rules, and authoritarianism. And they contrast this patriarchal vision with the "female" values of compassion, love, and interpersonal relationships introduced by Jesus.

Contemporary Jewish legal theorists, by contrast, point out that the Jewish legal system as rabbinically elaborated is not a precursor of Western law, which translated biblical themes through Christianity into liberalism, but rather an alternative model to Western law and thus a conceptual source for both criticizing modernist, liberal law and re-imagining its possibilities.

Recent comparative legal scholarship has pursued the thesis that Jewish law, despite its male-centeredness, incorporates many features and ideas that feminists seek to incorporate into law. The Jewish legal model, these scholars contend, is decentralized and pluralistic rather than statist and monistic, communitarian rather than individualistic, addressed to a legal subject embedded in relationships rather than to the autonomous and self-sufficient subject of liberalism, and organized around interpersonal, particularistic responsibilities rather than abstract, universal rights.[13] One writer has gone so far as to describe Jewish law as "written in a feminist voice"; that is, Jewish law, in emphasizing an ethic of care and compassion and duties motivated by love and friendship, anticipates many of the underlying goals of feminist jurisprudence.[14] Although, as I argue elsewhere, some of these depictions of the Jewish legal model are more wishful than accurate,[15] they, nonetheless, suggest that feminist jurisprudence would benefit from a less polemical, more nuanced confrontation with the rabbinic legal tradition. At the same time, Jewish legal studies would be enriched by incorporating feminist methodologies that take gender categories seriously in understanding law and that focus on the emotional and socio-sexual aspects of law.

In this essay, I explore rabbinic legal culture in light of one important line of inquiry pursued by feminist jurisprudence: how our definitions of justice are informed by ideas about the quality of justice exercised by a model divine being.

II. Gender and the Rabbinic Conception of Justice

In Exodus 34:6–7, two descriptions of God are counterposed. The first portrays God as forgiving and compassionate; the second highlights his retributive punishment, inaugurating a tension between justice and mercy. This tension, dealt with in the Bible through a temporal division (sometimes God acts justly and at other times mercifully), is handled in the Christian tradition through a role division. Strict justice is attributed to God (and later judges) and mercy to the figure of Christ (and later the Church as intercessor for pardon after judgment).[16] Yet, the role division that Christianity introduced reinforces the philosophical dichotomy between reason and emotion in law, the very problem feminist theory seeks to correct. Law becomes the affair of judges who are to emulate a Christian picture of the impartial biblical God of justice while mercy becomes a matter of grace, achieved through the Church. The rabbinic tradition, in contrast, pursues the biblical description of God as both compassionate and vengeful. Mercy and justice are combined in one divine figure possessed of two distinct attributes—strict justice (*din,* which also connotes law, argument, logic, and punishment) and mercy (*rahamim*). Justice and mercy are two polarities, two opposites cooperating, within a unified divine whole. According to rabbinic thought, the various names of God appearing in scripture refer to these two attributes of God,[17] which encompass virtually every aspect of existence. Sometimes these attributes are depicted in midrash as engaged in a struggle within God; at other times, the two attributes appear as almost fully independent beings at war with one another; at still other times, the attribute of strict justice is depicted as at war with God himself. These different literary representations of the two attributes in midrash also may reflect different conceptions of the precise relationship between justice and mercy.[18] The struggle within God connotes an evenly balanced judgment that encompasses both qualities, whereas the struggle of justice against God himself portrays mercy as a nullification of justice.

The rabbinic conception of justice and mercy as interdependent attributes of a single divine figure raises several interesting questions. Is the attribute of mercy an aspect of justice, or is it an act of divine grace outside the sphere of justice? If the latter, what triggers divine mercy? What are the emotional attitudes that make justice and mercy possible? Are the two attributes of God reflective of implicit role divisions, such as God the sovereign and God the creator? And, finally, can these two attributes be distinguished along gender lines? I address these questions through a detailed analysis of one midrash, a story about a heavenly trial to decide the fate of the exiled Jews. But when read in light of various rabbinic texts and traditions condensed within the narrative, the midrash emerges as an exploration of the concepts of justice and mercy, which are treated as manifestations of the emotional attitudes of jealousy and love. Midrash should be read on many levels, including as religious discourse and commentarial art. The great attraction of midrash for feminist legal scholars, however, is that it may be read as a metaphoric discussion of legal and moral concepts, one that transcends the traditional dichotomies of law and literature or reason and emotion. This method of reading midrash also was adopted by medieval rabbinic commentators because it posed a solution to the problem of anthropomorphism. Thus, midrash emerges as the philosophical expression, whether foregrounding or subtle critique, of the more concrete halakhah.

A. THE MIDRASH IN ITS OWN VOICE

The midrash is drawn from rabbinic commentaries on the biblical book of Lamentations.[19] Its setting, as in Lamentations, is the realm of the destruction of the Temple and the exile of Israel for her sins. But while Lamentations is dominated by despair, the rabbinic commentary emphasizes hope.[20] The question occupying the narrator is whether God will restrain his anger, temper strict justice with mercy, and forgive Israel. The literary drama at the center of our midrash is the gradual unfolding of the full personality of God. The story begins with the description of an impartial and indifferent sovereign who exacts retribution for violation of the legal regime of the Torah. The angels and the patriarchs weep, but God is uninvolved. The suffering Jews are the children of the patriarchs; God has no relationship with them. Abraham asks God why he has punished "Abraham's children" so severely and God answers that "your children" deserved this punishment. They violated the entire Torah and each of the twenty-two letters of the alphabet of which the Torah is composed. The narrative immediately dissolves into a trial scene, with God as both judge and prosecutor, calling the Torah and the Hebrew alphabet to testify against Israel. This is a dispassionate God who judges man literally by the book and in accordance with the letter of the law.

Abraham, however, manages to persuade the Torah and the alphabet not to testify against Israel, reminding each witness that Israel was the only nation willing to accept the Torah. Next, the three patriarchs and Moses appear to intercede on behalf of Israel, pointing to various meritorious acts that they performed. Abraham recalls his willingness to sacrifice his only son Isaac in accordance with God's command. "I made myself into a cruel person and did not take pity upon him. Why then do you not remember this deed and take pity on my children?" Abraham asks God. Isaac asks God to remember that he stretched his neck toward the knife when father told him: "God will provide the lamb for the burnt offering—my son" (Gen. 22:8). Jacob recalls his willingness to sacrifice his life in place of his sons whom Esau sought to kill. "And now my children, who caused me so much grief and for whom I suffered the pain of raising children, are handed over to their enemies like sheep to the slaughterhouse. Why then do you not remember this deed and take pity on my children?" Finally, Moses reminds God that he was a "faithful shepherd" to Israel for forty years in the desert and nonetheless God decreed that he could not enter the land of Israel. Throughout this portion of the narrative, God is unresponsive.

Moses then turns to Jeremiah and says: "I will gather them back." But all hope of redemption is dashed by a heavenly voice proclaiming that "This exile is a decree from me!" Moses returns to the patriarchs, providing them with a graphic picture of the fate of Israel in the hands of their captors. He beseeches the captors not to murder cruelly. "Do not slay a son in his father's presence, or a daughter in her mother's." The captors ignore Moses and this section ends with the murder of a child before its mother and the mother's tears and lamentation.[21] At this point, Moses asks God how he can countenance the slaughtering of Jewish children together with their mothers when God himself, in the Torah, forbade Jews to kill an ox or a lamb in the same day as their offspring. God still does not respond.

Finally, the matriarch Rachel pleads on Israel's behalf. She does not present a legal argument, nor does she ask that her deeds count in this time of judgment. Instead, she begins with a story: the story of how she conquered her jealousy. In the biblical account, Jacob worked seven years for Laban, tending sheep, in order to marry Laban's younger daughter Rachel. But on the wedding night, Laban tricked Jacob into marrying his elder daughter Leah. According to the midrash, Jacob distrusted Laban and gave Rachel signs to use on the wedding night so that Jacob would know that his veiled bride was, indeed, Rachel. Rachel, out of pity, conquered her jealousy and shared the signs with Leah. Rachel then turns to God and asks:

> And if I, who am flesh and blood, dust and ashes, was not jealous of my co-wife and did not permit her to be shamed and humiliated then you, Oh living King, why are you jealous of idols that have no reality, and why have You exiled my children and allowed them to be killed by the sword and permitted their enemies to do as they wished with them?

"Immediately," the narrative recites, "God's pity was stirred" and he agreed for the sake of Rachel to restore Israel to their places. This, the narrative concludes, is the sense of Jeremiah 31:14–17: "Thus says the Lord; A voice is heard in Ramah, lamentation and bitter weeping—Rachel weeping for her children. She refuses to be comforted for her children who are gone. Thus says the Lord; Keep your voice from weeping, and your eyes from tears; for your work shall be rewarded. And there is hope for your future, says the Lord: Your children shall come back again from the land of the enemy."

God is finally transformed from a force, an impersonal, affectless, and unrelenting judicial figure, into a person "whose pity is stirred"—a God who can add the emotional traits of "compassion, care, concern, nurturance, identification, and sympath[y]" to the process of judging.[22] This transformation is effected through human persuasion and argument. But why do the pleas of the patriarchs and Moses fail to move God and why does the narrator designate Rachel to be the sole cause of divine transformation?

B. THE MIDRASH'S CONCEPTION OF DIVINE JUSTICE AND MERCY

Several scholars view this midrash as a critique of divine justice, ascribing it to a "bold author" who is willing to portray the destruction and exile not as just punishment for Israel's sins, but, rather, as meaningless suffering caused by God's "arbitrary" decree or petty jealousy of idols.[23] In my view, the narrative is concerned, instead, with elucidating the quality of divine mercy and describing the emotional attitudes that make mercy possible. Looked at from this perspective, the narrative calls the reader to work through the various failed attempts to persuade God to alter his judgment in order to learn why Rachel prevails.

Moses begins by describing the fate of the Jews in poignant terms. They are fettered in irons, and children are slaughtered together with their mothers. But this imagery is not followed by an appeal from Moses for pity for the suffering Jews. Instead, Moses lodges a legal complaint against God, a common midrashic argument that is based on the view that God, too, is bound by the law. God ruled in the Torah that one may not slaughter animals together with their mothers. How then can he permit such slaughtering of Israel? Although there is a subtle critique of God's justice here, the focus of the midrash is on the failure of Moses to present a proper ground for mercy. Instead, Moses has limited himself to rational arguments based on legal analogy and the need for consistency with prior norms.

The second argument presented at the trial is based on the rabbinic doctrine of imputed merits. The patriarchs ask God to take account of their individual meritorious deeds as well as Israel's prior acceptance of the Torah in assessing the degree of punishment appropriate for Israel's current sins. Is this a legal argument rooted in just desert or is this a request for an act of divine grace? The doctrine of the merits of the fathers, like the biblical idea of delayed punishment, is in tension with other rabbinic traditions that God punishes each individual in accordance with his or her sins. In the latter conception of divine justice, every human act elicits a response from God that parallels the gravity of the act. Yohanan Muffs argues that the doctrines of delayed punishment and merits of the fathers mediate between the demands of strict justice, on the one hand, and mercy, on the other.[24] Muffs posits three conceptual models of sin and punishment. In the first, sin has an objective quality that inexorably brings about retributive punishment, which cannot be delayed or mitigated on account of the merits of the fathers. In the third, sin has a subjective quality that can be cured or canceled through repentance. In this model, mercy is bestowed upon a repentant who, viewed in his or her moral entirety, deserves it. In the second model, "[t]he attribute of strict justice makes its demands and the attribute of mercy makes its demands."[25] Justice requires that punishment ensue while mercy urges the cancellation of punishment because the sinner has repented. This tension is resolved by delaying punishment or mitigating it in light of the merit of the fathers. The doctrine of the merits of the fathers, in this view, tips the scales toward and "personifies" mercy.[26] As the mishnah states, the patriarchs have the duty to stand before God as defense counsel because they have the power to transform the divine attribute of justice into the attribute of mercy.[27]

This understanding of the patriarchs' appeal to God, however, shatters the narrative's structure as I have reconstructed it. The reader is left wondering why the patriarchs' appeal for mercy is rejected. Possibly, our narrative assumes that the doctrine of the merits of the fathers is not an aspect of mercy but, rather, an aspect of just deserts when punishment is visited not on a single individual but, rather, as in this midrash, on the collective of Israel.[28] From the collective perspective, all the generations are interwoven. The concept of merits can be seen as a legal demand by the collective on the sovereign to fulfill prior promises based on the notion of corporate justice. Moreover, the doctrine of the merits of the fathers was often contested.[29] The *tannaim* were wary of this concept, popular among the masses, fearing that it might undermine the sense of the obligation to fulfill the commandments in the present.[30] Other stresses on the doctrine emanated from outside the tradition. A common polemic against the Jews centered on why the merits of the fathers did not aid them in their current time of need. And when Christianity placed at the center of its system the concept of vicarious atonement, rabbinic concerns about the doctrine were heightened.[31] At some point after the ascendance of Christianity, rabbinic literature began to assert that the merits of the fathers functioned as a basis for divine mercy only up to a particular point in Israel's history.[32] Indeed, both Lamentations Rabbah, the midrashic collection of which our midrash is a part, and Rabbi Samuel ben Nahman, to whom our midrash is attributed, are generally opposed to this doctrine.[33] Significantly, the very chapter of Jeremiah from which the concluding verses of our midrash are taken is an indictment of vicarious atonement and delayed punishment. Jeremiah cites but rejects the proverb about fathers who eat sour grapes and whose children's teeth are set on edge. Instead, the prophecy of Jeremiah cited in our midrash offers a new conception of justice and mercy for the post-exilic period, proclaiming that "everyone shall be put to death for his own transgression" (Jer. 31:28–29).[34] Our midrash follows the substantive thrust of Jeremiah in rejecting the merits of the fathers as a basis for challenging the divine decree. Instead, the midrash offers an alternative conception of mercy and links this conception to Rachel.

The midrash's literary symbolism and its allusions to Jeremiah provide important clues to the reader that its concern is the nature of divine mercy, which Rachel will elicit. A single metaphor is woven through the narrative, that of the ewe lamb and the shepherd.[35] Israel is portrayed as a lamb led to slaughter and Moses as its shepherd. Moses's argument to God also analogizes Israel's punishment to the laws concerning the slaughtering of lambs. Both Abraham and Isaac recall the aborted sacrifice of Isaac, replaced by the sacrifice of the ram. Most importantly, the Hebrew word *Rachel* is not only the name of the biblical matriarch, but also the word for ewe or lamb, a pun the rabbis elsewhere make explicit.[36] The lamb is a symbol for God's trait of mercy (recall the biblical paschal lamb whose blood averted God's slaughter of the Israelites)—a symbol borrowed by Christianity from Jewish sources. And, indeed, a ewe is also referred to as *rachmin,* from the Hebrew word for mercy. This repeated literary symbolism orients the listener both to the central dilemma of the midrash—the need to locate the source and nature of divine mercy—and to its eventual resolution through the character of Rachel.

The prophetic traditions of Jeremiah, to whom rabbinic tradition assigns authorship of Lamentations, provide the basic framework for our midrash in its entirety. The midrash remains faithful to Jeremiah's substantive message about divine justice and mercy, while transforming Jeremiah's literary images. It is from Jeremiah 11:19 that the image of a "lamb led to slaughter" is taken. Moreover, Jeremiah frames his prophecy around the figure of Rachel, the ancestor of the house of Northern Israel that had been defeated and exiled in an earlier period, who is heard weeping bitterly for her children in Ramah. Ramah is the place of Rachel's tomb but it also means, literally, "on high," giving rise to our midrashic siting of Rachel crying in heaven. Jeremiah tells Rachel to stop crying because God will be moved to pity and will have mercy on "his darling child Ephraim" (Jer. 31:20). Thus, Jeremiah's reassurance of Rachel, a figure for Northern Israel, of God's eventual mercy becomes transformed in our midrash into an etiology of how God "learned" to be merciful from Rachel, a figure for a person involved in the emotional complexities of jealousy and love.

From our narrator's perspective, then, it is fitting that Rachel's argument to God should evoke the attribute of mercy. But what precisely does divine mercy entail in our midrash? Rachel shows God what mercy entails by recalling how she restrained her jealousy out of love for her sister. Mercy is thus conceived as an activity, rather than an attitude—the restraint of jealousy activated by love, within the context of a pre-existing personal relationship. In the view of our midrash, then, mercy is not an aspect of a complex form of judgment that encompasses both attributes; rather, mercy is outside the sphere of justice. It is an act of nullification of the divine decree that is undeserved, and made possible solely because of a prior love relationship in which the actors are embedded. This conception of mercy as an act of love rather than an aspect of justice is represented elsewhere in midrashic thought, most notably by the idea that God's keeping of covenantal promises does not arise from a contractual obligation. Rather, God's keeping of promises is dependent on a divine act of self-restraint and, as such, is an expression of the attribute of mercy latent in God's power.[37]

The "moral intuition"[38] that jealousy and love within the context of a personal relationship are the emotional manifestations of the normative categories of justice and mercy is a "deep structure" of rabbinic thought that both continues and transforms the biblical model. In their study of the sin of idolatry, Moshe Halbertal and Avishai Margalit note that the meaning of idolatry in the Bible is "anchored on all levels in the analysis of marital relations, betrayal, and jealousy."[39] Idolatry is depicted as adulterous betrayal, the worship of strange gods. The God of Israel is a jealous God who demands loyalty and honor from Israel, just as a husband demands these qualities of his wife. The metaphoric representation of idolatry in the Bible as betrayal of the husband is dependent on certain "attitudes toward the family and societal obligations" that justify public forms of retribution and restitution, including death.[40] The biblical conception of jealousy and honor, Halbertal and Margalit argue, became transformed in classical rabbinic culture. "As a result of this conceptual transformation God is seen as possessing dignity rather than honor, and God's honor becomes associated primarily with his ability to restrain himself, rather than with his ability to demand restitution when he has been insulted."[41] Our midrash, Halbertal and Margalit point out, is exemplary of this changed attitude toward jealousy and honor in social relations. God's ability to curb "destructive jealousy" and replace it with "restraint and generosity" still is represented metaphorically through images of marital relations.[42] But now God is represented as a female, a wife, who is able to conquer jealousy of her co-wife, the idol, within the context of a pre-existing, loving relationship.

In a society that emphasizes dignity rather than honor and the preeminence of loving rather than loyalty relationships, the notion of restraint and the substitution of love for jealousy serve as a filter through which a variety of norms, including justice and mercy, is perceived. Justice is no longer perceived as vengeance for betrayal but as a more abstract idea pursuant to which punishment is measured out in accordance with the gravity of the act performed, while mercy is perceived as a nullification of justice based on the priority of loving relationships. This later conception of mercy may also derive from the acute sense of the gravity of Israel's offense that developed with the passage of time. Unlike the first destruction, where return and rebuilding followed almost immediately, the second destruction lingered on with-

Feminism and the Rabbinic Conception of Justice

out solace. Israel was beset by the thought, generated both internally and by its external rivals, that God had finally abandoned the Jews for good reason. By the time of our midrash, reconciliation and return is now thought to depend on a special and immense act of divine mercy, grace, or love—despite the fact that the covenantal promise itself guaranteed the eventual end of exile. This mood is captured in our midrash, which dwells on God's absence and unresponsiveness throughout the lengthy and numerous appeals by the human protagonists to mitigate his decree. The promise of redemption finally comes when least expected, through the surprising appearance of Rachel.

C. THE GENDER OF JUSTICE AND MERCY

The midrash presents the tension between justice and mercy, or retribution and emotional love, in terms of gender imagery. The full realization of the attributes of strict justice and mercy is achieved in the midrash through a clear-cut division of roles between the male and female protagonists. The male protagonists question the justness of the divine decree through logical argument or an appeal to established doctrinal grounds for mitigating punishment. Rachel, by contrast, invokes divine mercy by embodying the emotional manifestations of this normative category. Moreover, the standard biblical depiction of God as male is reversed. In biblical marriage metaphors, God is always the husband. In this midrash, God is portrayed through metaphoric extension as a merciful female, a co-wife, who is, in turn, the model for all human behavior. Is Rachel, then, a figure in rabbinic thought for a feminine attribute of God as dispenser of mercy, or is Rachel a figure for humanity, the "other" to the masculine deity, on whom God's conduct in this narrative is modeled? And, in either case, is the narrative choice of Rachel to give voice to the quality of mercy and its emotional manifestation, the substitution of love for jealousy, a reflection of rabbinic assumptions about feminine characteristics or roles?

These issues are briefly treated by David Stern, who rejects the idea that God's yielding to Rachel's plea in our midrash testifies to the "emergence of a feminine presence within God himself," or a feminine softening of "[h]is masculine hardness." God does not become feminine merely because he is persuaded by a female. Rather, Rachel's femininity "epitomizes humanity, while God's utter masculinity is the sign of divinity."[43] Thus, for Stern, Rachel functions as a generic human model of mercy that transcends gender. A preference for analogies drawn from human relationships, "homey metaphors and anthropomorphic analogies," also explains why, in a later period in Christian thought, one finds increasing usages of maternal imagery to describe Jesus.[44] But, as Caroline Bynum points out, "it also reflects the fact that what medieval authors assumed the female to be coincided with what they increasingly wished to emphasize about God the creator and about the Incarnation."[45] In addition to wishing to stress God as loving and accessible, these medieval writers wished to soften the authority and rule of God "with that for which the maternal stood: emotion and nurture."[46] Thus, one must still ask whether the qualities that the rabbis wished to emphasize about God in this particular midrash, his ability to restrain his jealous anger, coincided with characteristics they assumed to be identifiably feminine—even if they are also feminine aspects of men. For "the female (or woman) and the feminine are not the same. The former is a person of one gender; the latter may be an aspect of a person of either gender."[47]

In attempting to assess the significance of the gender imagery in our narrative, one must proceed cautiously because numerous factors influence the narrative choice of Rachel to give voice to the divine attribute of mercy, and, by extension, to portray God as occupying the female role. The association of Rachel with the quality of mercy is, on one level, a product of wordplay: the equation of *rachel* with ewe lamb and lamb with mercy. On another level, it is the product of local exegesis. First, as noted, our midrash is implicitly commenting on Jeremiah, who assures Rachel that her weeping will be remembered when God shows mercy to her children, and on related traditions stemming from Jeremiah that transform Rachel into a feminine figure of mercy. Second, the suffering of the collective Israel is personified in the biblical Lamentations as a woman in distress and a mother whose child is slaughtered. Symmetry is maintained in the midrashic comment on Lamentations by placing the source of consolation in the voice of a woman. God, too, is possibly made to occupy the female role in response to local exegetical needs. The feminine representation of God here "makes the sin of idolatry less severe" because it is equated with the addition of a co-wife, which is legally permitted, "in contrast to the representation of idolatry as the wife's betrayal of the husband, which is a sin punishable by death."[48] But these examples do not exhaust the condensation of traditions and of ideas about the feminine that occur in our midrash.

1. RACHEL, MERCY, AND THE CO-WIFE

The theme of jealousy, love, and substitution found in our midrash are already present in the biblical stories about Rachel.[49] Laban substitutes Leah for Rachel as Jacob's bride. Rachel is Jacob's beloved and Leah, Jacob's co-wife, is jealous of that love. In turn, Rachel is jealous of Leah because the latter bore Jacob sons and Rachel is barren. Leah views her sons as substitutes for Jacob's love and gives them names to reflect that reality. Rachel, in turn, substitutes a night of Jacob's love for mandrakes that Leah's son gathered. Jacob tells Rachel that she is substituting him for God when she asks him to provide her with children. This constellation of jealousy, love, and substitution is given a different emphasis in various midrashic traditions about Rachel and Leah. They stress the women's capacity to substitute love for initial jealousy, a theme that is absent in the biblical text. Rachel conquers her jealousy of Leah out of love for her sister when she gives Leah the signs that enable her sister to marry Jacob. Leah, in turn, conquers her jealousy of Rachel and prays that her sister will bear a child. In a marvelous example of midrashic wordplay, the midrash parses the words of two biblical verses according to their visual and auditory sense in order both to connect them and fill in gaps in the text. The first verse relates that "after, Leah had a daughter that she named Dinah." The second verse relates that God remembered (*va-yizkor,* a word that also can be read as "to make male") Rachel and listened to her (*eilehah,* which can also be heard as "to Leah") and opened Rachel's womb (*rachmah,* a word also connoting mercy).[50] The midrash explains the gap in the text suggested by the word *after* as follows: After Leah realized that she was pregnant again, she prayed that her child would not be a son, so that Rachel would be able to bring forth as many tribes as had the handmaidens. God substituted Leah's male fetus for a female fetus, Dinah, her judgment. God said to her: You are a merciful person, and so I will be merciful to her. God listened to jealous Leah's loving prayers for Rachel, and switched the fetus, and also remembered jealous Rachel's loving act toward her sister, and gave Rachel a son.[51]

The midrash condenses this dynamic by placing Rachel, the co-wife, at the center of God's substitution of his jealousy with love. Just as Rachel substituted her jealousy of her co-wife with love for her abandoned sister, so does God substitute his jealousy of idols with love for the abandoned Israel. The midrashic reworking of the biblical themes turns jealousy into a positive force. It emphasizes that jealousy is a product of the intimacy of the family relationship that exists between Rachel and Leah, and by extension, between God and Israel. Because this relationship is also suffused with love, jealousy can be overcome. Moreover, in our midrash the emotional dynamic that constitutes the attribute of mercy, the ability to substitute love for jealousy, is shared by both God and humanity. This assumption should be compared to the biblical treatment of this theme, which emphasizes that what distinguishes divinity from humanity is the former's ability to conquer jealousy. In

Hosea, God explains that he can conquer his anger and forgive Israel's betrayal "[f]or I am God, not man." (Hos. 11:9). The differences in the biblical and midrashic treatment of this issue—the former implying that man cannot conquer jealousy and the latter, illustrating how Rachel and Leah, women, are capable of this emotional transformation—suggests that the ability to replace jealousy with love is viewed in the rabbinic schema as a distinctly feminine characteristic.

I would like to speculate why this emotional capacity may have been associated particularly with females within the matrix of rabbinic culture. Rabbinic society, unlike biblical society, was by and large monogamous. Thus the particular emotional capacity of the co-wives highlighted in these various narratives would seem to rest on superseded forms of personal relationships and emotional trials. Yet rabbinic society did perpetuate a particular triangular relationship within the marital domain that must have created emotional trials similar to those experienced by the co-wives. As Daniel Boyarin points out, "[t]he absolute and contradictory demands of marriage and commitment to study of Torah remained one of the great unresolved tensions of rabbinic culture."[52] On the one hand, the law commands that men must marry in order to have children. On the other hand, life-long devotion to Torah study was perceived as not only obligatory but erotic. The Torah, the law—which is invariably imaged as female—was a "jealous mistress," or, in Boyarin's words, "the other woman."[53] This triangle of rabbi, Torah, and wife can be analogized to the social institution of polygyny. If so, the perception that the emotional trait of substituting love for jealousy was a distinctly feminine capacity stemmed not solely from rabbinic reflection on the biblical matriarchs' lives. It also rested on personal observation, as wives restrained their jealousy of the husband's more figurative co-wife out of their own love for the Torah. The talmudic paradigm for this form of marriage is that of Rabbi Akiva and his wife, identified in the tradition as Rachel. And, as Boyarin points out, there are significant parallels between the midrashic story of Rabbi Akiva's marriage and that of the biblical Jacob and Rachel.[54]

2. RACHEL, MERCY, AND MATERNAL LOVE

Although our midrash focuses explicitly on the emotional aspects of mercy in terms of jealousy and love, an undercurrent in the narrative places mercy within a different, although complementary, emotional context: the love that a parent feels for a child, which enables the parent to mitigate the harshness of rules and discipline. The midrash begins with a depiction of

God as sovereign ruler, uninvolved in any familial relationship with Israel. The Jews are "your children," God says to Abraham. But at the midrash's conclusion, through citation to the verses in Jeremiah, God's mercy is also analogized to that of a parent. The narrative choice of Rachel to give rise to the attribute of mercy highlights this aspect of the quality of mercy because there is a pre-existent and stable conception of Rachel in midrash as a maternal figure of mercy.[55] Rachel possesses a distinctive "voice." She is the mother who weeps for mercy for her children, Israel, and at whose tomb observant Jews pray to this day for merciful intercession with the divine.

Does our midrash also condense a pre-existent and stable rabbinic tradition that associates the divine attribute of mercy with the feminine quality of maternal love? Scholars have long sought to find a conception of the two attributes along gender lines in midrashic and talmudic circles, but the evidence is suggestive, at best.[56] Yet, even if the midrashic sources do not attest directly to a gendered conception of justice and mercy, the two attributes of God do seem strongly linked to role divisions that we moderns, at least, have come to associate with traditional gender constructions. The midrashic depiction of mercy and justice seems to correspond to the two basic roles of God, creator or parent, on the one hand, and sovereign ruler or royal figure, on the other. These two divine roles correspond to the two relationships humanity has with God: a parent–child relationship epitomized by love, and a master–servant relationship epitomized by fear and reverence. As our midrash suggests, the quality of strict justice is equated in midrashic thought with the biblical description of God as a "jealous God," in the sense of an exclusive sovereign who does not permit the worship of other gods and who judges such transgressions harshly.[57] The midrashic equation of mercy with the biblical description of God as creator-parent is a commonplace. Commenting on the obvious question raised by Genesis 1:26, "And God said: Let us make man . . . ," the midrash explains that God foresaw that wicked people would arise from Adam. Therefore, God joined with the attribute of mercy in order to create man.[58]

Again, the midrashists were simply extrapolating from scripture. As noted, in depicting the gravity of Israel's sins and the righteous anger of God, the prophets employed the metaphor of God, the jealous, sovereign husband, betrayed by his bride, Israel, the idolatrous-adulterer. This metaphor made forgiveness problematic because biblical law forbids a husband to take back an adulterous wife. Jeremiah notes the problem (3:1) and solves it by substituting a different metaphor of familial relationships. Israel can be forgiven because God is also the parent who shows mercy and Israel is his child (3:19–22).[59] The question left unanswered is whether the rabbis viewed this role division explicitly along gender lines. Apart from our midrash, the evidence is in fact slight. The sovereign ruler God, the attribute of justice, is invariably associated with the masculine. The creator-parental God, the attribute of mercy, however, is only on occasion explicitly associated with the feminine. In a few places, the Bible does refer to God as a woman who conceives, carries, and suckles. The word *rachamim*, mercy, is etymologically related to the word *rechem*, womb, and various cognates of the latter are used to connote the maternal instinct. This linguistic relationship reinforces the connection between the idea of God as creator and the attribute of mercy. But the linguistic connection does not necessarily connote that the aspect of mercy is in itself viewed as feminine nurture. Rather, as we saw before, the opening of the womb by God is viewed as an act of mercy. Mercy, when conceived in terms of the emotional dynamic of a parental relationship, is apparently viewed as a characteristic that is shared by the two sexes. In the rabbinic worldview, paternal and maternal affection is equated. The image of God as a loving father is both common and eminently understandable.

D. The Gender of Human Mercy and Stereotyping in Rabbinic Culture

So far, we have seen that God's quality of mercy, when viewed from the perspective of parental affectivity, is not identified as a particularly feminine trait. On the other hand, the ability to conquer jealousy and replace it with love does seem to be expressed as a feminine characteristic. But the strongest evidence that mercy in the rabbinic schema has a feminine association comes from rabbinic statements scattered throughout the Talmud that identify certain human characteristics as stereotypically female. It is the nature of women to be compassionate, the Talmud asserts, implying in this context that women are by nature more merciful than men.[60] Chastity or modesty also was seen as a special female virtue. Yet elsewhere, the Talmud states that compassion and chastity are the special virtue of the entire nation of Israel.[61] These statements testify to a blurring of gender traits, concomitant with the rabbinic willingness to use gender imagery in a relatively fluid fashion.

One reason for this blurring of gender traits, no doubt, hinges on the central rabbinic concept of *imitatio dei*. As God embodied both justice and mercy already in his biblical portrayal, man who was created in his image also was to act justly and mercifully, even if acting mercifully is associated with the feminine. Once a quality is seen as a religious or ethical virtue, it must be embodied in both sexes. At the same time, the fact that mercy is seen to be one of the essential defining features of the community of Israel testifies to the centrality of this moral ideal in rabbinic thought.

Did the rabbis view the two genders, then, as essentially the same or, at least, complementary, rather than one the opposite of the other? Rabbinic traditions about the androgynous nature of the first human creation also would seem to support the idea that men and women were not marked as a contrasting pair. And, yet, while the genders do not seem to be dichotomous in rabbinic thought, there is an asymmetry in the treatment of the genders in one important respect. Traditional male characteristics such as judgment, reason, logic, rule, and discipline were, to my knowledge, not imputed to females nor described through feminine imagery in the classical rabbinic period. Although God's intimacy and mercy may give God a feminine attribute, God's transcendence and sovereignty are not portrayed through the use of feminine imagery. On the contrary, there are more than a few rabbinic statements alluding to women's frivolity and lack of seriousness, disqualifying them from the discipline of legal study. What we do see here, then, is the sharing of what the rabbis themselves labeled as quintessentially feminine characteristics by men. But some of the traits most valued in rabbinic society, the capacity for legal reasoning and judging, are exclusively male. Thus while there is not a strong sense of males and females as binary opposites in classical rabbinic thought, the rabbis did associate specific personality characteristics or roles with one or the other sex. Were these differences in personality and role viewed as fixed, essential characteristics or as culturally conditioned, necessitated by the need to accomplish larger religious goals, including ensuring procreation, a religious obligation, and creating a system of support for Torah study? Put otherwise, is gender stereotyping and gender imagery in the midrash the product of rabbinic views about the essentially different nature of women and men, or is it motivated by the need to define and mold their behavior in different arenas in order to accomplish larger ends? These are sensitive questions because legal norms may revolve around rabbinic statements that are treated as normative assumptions about human nature, including the essential differences between the sexes.

The question of whether the behavioral assumptions that ground various legal norms or influence gender imagery in midrash are based on "permanent ontological principles," intrinsic features of the human situation, or on culturally and historically determined conditions, is one that divides the present Jewish community, just as it divides contemporary schools of feminist thought. Although I shall take no position on these questions, I would like to speculate about two very different processes of differentiation within rabbinic society, one facing inward, involving the differentiation between men and women, and the other facing outward, involving the differentiation between Jewish men and a different "other"—non-Jews. The nature and function of gender stereotyping and gender imagery in the classical rabbinic period, which has yet to receive full scholarly treatment, must be considered in light of both these processes.

In classical rabbinic culture, self-identity was expressed primarily through defining itself in opposition not to the female but, rather, to the gentile community. It is significant that the statement identifying the essential characteristics of Israel as mercy, chastity, and charitableness, is in the context of a midrash explicating why the Gibeonites, who sought to hang the sons of Saul to avenge Saul's earlier acts of violence against them, were unfit to join the assembly of Israel.[62] The quality of mercy was viewed as the distinctive ideal around which not only Israel's self-identity as a people was forged, but also around which its model of justice was measured. Not only is Israel uniquely merciful, but the rabbis asserted that its model of justice is *uniquely* merciful. As I have described elsewhere, rabbinic legal theory posits two distinct legal orders organized around two different models of justice: the Noahide and the Sinaitic.[63] In rabbinic thought, the Noahide obligation to dispense justice (the obligation of *dinin*), which applies to non-Jews, corresponds with the justice of conventional sovereign polities. Conventional justice is dedicated to the preservation of social order through pragmatic and coercive means. It is exemplified by the attribute of strict justice and is suited to the violent nature of its subjects. The Sinaitic system of justice, which is exceptionally lenient to the accused, flows from the special familial relationship that exists between God and Israel. The Sinaitic model reflects divine justice, which combines strict justice with mercy, a system suited to the merciful character of Israel.

These ideas proliferated within a community under foreign rule, in which gentile violence was always a possibility and sometimes a reality. Such conditions, Max Weber claimed, invariably lead to the exaltation and adoption of feminine virtues. One must at least consider the possibility that the fluid characterization of mercy, in contrast to that of strict justice, as both a female and male virtue, is part of a process of rabbinic assimilation of traditional feminine roles and virtues in its differentiation of itself from the genuine other: non-Jews. In doing so, the rabbinic conception of itself emerges, as Jeanne Schroeder put it in a different context, as a partial "deconstruction of the traditional masculinist definition of the masculine self."[64] Historical studies reveal that the assignment of gender to a characteristic or quality is far more unstable and fluid than much feminist theory presently admits. This is because the masculine, like the feminine, is constantly being redefined. "Feminism historicized," to use Schroeder's term, shows that in medieval Christian circles various traits or qualities associated with the feminine often became redefined as masculine virtues in response to different ideological pressures. The abandoned masculine trait then was attributed to females.[65] In rabbinic circles, this process of definition and differentiation was played out, in terms of dichotomous relationships, vis-à-vis the non-Jew. The feminine trait of mercy was also defined as a masculine virtue while the more traditionally aggressive masculine characteristics, such as vengeance and violence, were attributed to non-Jews.

We can also catch a glimpse of this continuing process of differentiation in the medieval Kabbalah, which is replete with gender images of the divine. The Kabbalah, unlike classical rabbinic thought, does see the genders as dichotomous. The mystical kabbalistic tradition explicitly assigns a gender to the attributes of strict justice and mercy. But mercy is identified as masculine and strict justice as feminine. In the kabbalistic schema, the active, merciful, overflowing male must contain the passive, judgmental, constraining female.[66] The traditionally feminine characteristic of mercy, which became so intrinsic to Jewish identity, is now a masculine virtue while the trait of justice is now assigned to the female. Gender imagery in the kabbalistic sources reflects the more androcentric norms and gender stereotypes of general medieval European culture,[67] in which theosophic Kabbalah flourished. But it is possibly also the logical culmination of an internal process, in which a formerly feminine virtue becomes redefined as masculine and then the abandoned masculine trait is eventually assigned to the female. In the Kabbalah, too, we see the interplay of this process of differentiation in terms of the two "others" in rabbinic culture. The nations of the world are also "characterized as severity and harsh judgment" and symbolized by the image of the non-Jewish woman who, in contrast to the Jewish woman, can never exercise mercy.[68] Thus, even in the Kabbalah, the genuine other is the non-Jew. In classical rabbinic thought, in contrast to the Kabbalah, however, the adoption of the trait of mercy as a defining characteristic of Israel does not lead to the imputation of its opposite to females. On the contrary, females simply embody an intensified form of this trait. Thus, one of the noteworthy aspects of classical rabbinic gender treatment is that it treats the genders as complementary, rather than as studies in contrast. And if gender asymmetry, nonetheless, is maintained, it seems to be less a function of asymmetrical valuing of the genders themselves than that, as in any androcentric society, men will elevate the importance of the role they believe they are obligated to perform.

🕎 III. Conclusion: Feminist Jurisprudence and the Rabbinic Conception of Mercy

Feminist jurisprudence wishes to expose the theological and gender assumptions that underlie modernist, liberal law in order to re-imagine law's possibilities and redefine the forms of justice to which men and women should aspire. A major focus of this effort, as noted, is to detach law from its ancient roots in a conception of divine (male) justice that stresses objectivity, impartiality, retributive forms of justice, and impersonal rules, which humans must emulate. Rabbinic reflections on divine justice complement the feminist legal project by offering an alternative model of divine and, hence, human justice. The God the rabbis seek to emulate is a deeply personified being, who reflects both the "feminine" capacity to displace justice with mercy and the human, parental capacity for compassion. Mercy may be, as the midrash depicts, undeserved and outside the sphere of ordinary, strict justice. Yet the capacity to act mercifully, to substitute love for jealousy or retribution, is an ideal because it inaugurates reconciliation between partners to a pre-existing relationship. The rabbinic model thus shares with feminism a basic vision of connectedness, and of the primacy of human relationships.

How would such a transformed conception of justice and judging alter the law's approach to critical contemporary issues of justice? Should retributive justice be limited by an ideal of mercy? What are the legitimate bounds of punishment and hatred, especially as a response to collective violence? What is the proper role of amnesty or pardon in the face of atrocities? There is a rich body of philosophical literature that discusses mercy's relationship to justice. But this literature does not reflect feminist or related poststructural philosophical concerns. Two recent discussions of current responses to collective violence and war crimes, however, offer a preliminary vision of how such a reformed conception of justice may be incorporated into law. Martha Minow argues that forgiveness in the form of amnesty or pardon, though it cannot be commanded, is an act of restraint that is possible "if legal and cultural institutions offered other avenues for individuals or nations."[69] Such paths include the therapeutic, promoting the process of healing for victims, bystanders, and even offenders through truth commissions and other means, as well as the political, promoting reconciliation across social divisions created by or causing collective violence. In stressing both the therapeutic and reconciliatory goals of truth commissions and amnesty programs, Minow envisions a new role for law and justice beyond the conventional, liberal emphasis on trials, retributive punishment, and just desert. The focus on reconciliation as a goal of pardons places human inter-relationships at the center of law. At the same time, Minow eschews a more radical conception of mercy, recently explored by Jacques Derrida.[70] Derrida traces the idea of amnesty and pardon in modern law and politics to "an equivocation" in the Western heritage of the religious idea of forgiveness and mercy. On the one hand, true forgiveness is pure and paradoxical. It consists in "forgiving the unforgivable," untainted by any form of exchange. On the other hand, forgiveness is conceived as conditional on repentance, recognition of fault, or the desire for reconciliation. Conditional forgiveness assumes an anterior power of the sovereign or victim to judge and punish. This irreconcilable and indissociable tension is carried over into law. Yet pure forgiveness remains a possibility for the future, Derrida argues, even in law and politics.

Engagement with the rabbinic model offers both support and a basis for an initial critique of this new direction in the law's attempt to come to grips with the legitimate bounds of hatred and punishment as a response to collective "sin" or acts of violence. The rabbinic conception of mercy, although not limited by the gravity of the offense, denies that mercy is possible untainted by any form of exchange. Instead, mercy, in the rabbinic model, is conditioned on the existence of a prior relationship and on the possibility of reconciliation. Mercy is embedded in a complex of pre-existing familial relationships, whether husband and wife, sisters, parent and child, or covenantal partners. This conception comports with the familial, particularist, and covenantal structure of Jewish law, where deeper obligations of social solidarity are owed to communal fellows, covenantal partners, than are owed to strangers.[71] This familial relationship between Jews is replicated on the divine–human level through the idea of chosenness, and instantiated in the covenantal relationship between God and Israel. It is precisely this stress on a pre-existing loving relationship and on the importance of its continuation that makes mercy possible. Thus, forgiveness remains a possibility when it serves to reconcile former partners with one another or to heal social divisions among groups with a pre-existing positive relationship. But whether it is possible to replicate such a conception of mercy within a universal legal system, where the circles of solidarity are widened to encompass strangers, remains to be seen.

This conversation is only now beginning. The hope is that, through studies such as this one, the rabbinic tradition will come to be seen as a rich resource for contemporary feminist discourse while feminism's call to rethink the gender of law and, with it, what it means to be human, will inform scholarship in Jewish legal thought.

NOTES

1. A version of this essay first appeared in *Cardozo Studies in Law and Literature*. See Suzanne Last Stone, "Justice, Mercy, and Gender in Rabbinic Thought," *Cardozo Studies in Law and Literature* 8, no. 1 (1996).

2. See generally Katherine T. Bartlett and Rosanne Kennedy, eds., *Feminist Legal Theory: Readings in Law and Gender* (Boulder: Westview Press, 1991); Katherine T. Bartlett, "Feminist Legal Methods," *Harvard Law Review* 103 (1990): 829.

3. See Dennis Patterson, "Postmodernism/Feminism/Law," *Cornell Law Review* 77 (1992): 254.

4. See the discussion of de Beauvoir's *The Second Sex* in Judith Butler, *Gender Trouble: Feminism and the Subversion of Identity* (London: Routledge, 1990), 12.

5. See Judith Resnik, "On the Bias: Feminist Reconsiderations of the Aspirations for Our Judges," *Southern California Law Review* 61 (1991): 1877.

6. See Martha Minow and Elizabeth Spelman, "Passion for Justice," *Cardozo Law Review* 10 (1988): 37, 39; Benjamin Zipursky, "DeShaney and the Jurisprudence of Compassion," *New York University Law Review* 65 (1990): 1101, 1129–37.

7. See, e.g., Mary Daly, *Beyond God the Father* (Boston: Beacon, 1973); Rosemary Ruether, *Sexism and God-Talk: Toward a Feminist Theology* (Boston: Beacon, 1983).

8. Jean Elshtain, "Sovereign State, Sovereign God, Sovereign Self," *Notre Dame Law Review* 66 (1991): 1555.

9. Ibid., 1571.

10. For an excellent summary of these theories, see Resnik, "On the Bias."

11. See, e.g., Lawrence Blum, "Compassion," in *Explaining Emotions,* ed. Amélie Oksenberg Rorty (Berkeley: University of California Press, 1980), 509.

12. See Susannah Heschel, "Configurations of Patriarchy, Judaism and Nazism in German Feminist Thought," in *Gender and Judaism: The Transformation of Tradition,* ed. Tamar M. Rudavsky (New York: New York University Press, 1995), 135–54.

13. See Suzanne Last Stone, "In Pursuit of the Countertext: The Turn to the Jewish Legal Model in Contemporary American Legal Theory," *Harvard Law Review* 106 (1993): 813.

14. Steven F. Friedell, "The 'Different Voice' in Jewish Law: Some Parallels to a Feminist Jurisprudence," *Indiana Law Journal* 67 (1992): 915.

15. See Stone, "In Pursuit of the Countertext."

16. See John T. Noonan, Jr., "Heritage of Tension," *Arizona State Law Journal* 22 (1989): 39.

17. On the association of divine names with the divine attributes, see N. Dahl and A. Segal, "Philo and the Rabbis on the Names of God," *Journal for the Study of Judaism* 9 (1978): 1.

18. See Ephraim E. Urbach, *The Sages: Their Concepts and Beliefs,* vol. 1, trans. Israel Abrahams (Jerusalem: Magnes, 1975), 420–48.

19. See *Lamentations Rabbah,* ed. S. Buber (Vilna, 1899), 25–28. The entire narrative, with its uplifting coda, is included only in Sephardic manuscripts of the midrash. For other scholarly treatments of this midrash, see Alan Mintz, *Hurban: Responses to Catastrophe in Hebrew Literature* (New York: Columbia University Press, 1984), 57–62; David Stern, "Imitatio Hominis: Anthropomorphism and the Character(s) of God in Rabbinic Literature," *Prooftexts* 12 (1992): 151, 160–68; David Kraemer, *Responses to Suffering in Classical Rabbinic Literature* (New York: Oxford University Press, 1995), 143–46; Moshe Halbertal and Avishal Margalit, *Idolatry* (Cambridge, Mass.: Harvard University Press, 1992), 33–35.

20. See Shaye J. D. Cohen, "The Destruction: From Scripture to Midrash," *Prooftexts* 2 (1982): 18, describing the theology of *Lamentations Rabbah.*

21. The shorter version of the midrash ends here. See Buber's edition of *Lamentations Rabbah,* 28, n. 23.

22. Resnik, "On the Bias," 87.

23. See Kraemer, *Responses to Suffering,* 146; Stern, "Imitatio Hominis," 166–68.

24. See Yohanan Muffs, "Who Will Stand in the Breach?: A Study of Prophetic Intercession," in his *Love and Joy: Law, Language, and Religion in Ancient Israel* (Cambridge, Mass.: Harvard University Press, 1992), 16–24.

25. Ibid., 17.

26. Gordon M. Freeman, *The Heavenly Kingdom: Aspects of Political Thought in the Talmud and Midrash* (New York: University Press of America, 1986), 28. See also Arthur Marmorstein, *The Doctrine of Merits in Old Rabbinical Literature* (New York: KTAV, 1968), 14–29.

27. Mishnah Sotah 5:5. Cf. Talmud Bavli, *Yevamot* 64a; Talmud Bavli, *Sukkah* 14a; *Genesis Rabbah* 44:5; *Song of Songs Rabbah* 1:14.

28. Rabbinic thought veers between a corporate conception of divine justice and an individualist conception. See Kraemer, *Responses to Suffering,* 160.

29. For a succinct summary of the tensions, see Solomon Schechter, *Aspects of Rabbinic Theology* (New York: Schocken Books, 1961), 170–98.

30. See Urbach, *The Sages,* 497.

31. On the relationship between Christianity and the rabbinic doctrine of merits, see Shalom Spiegel, *The Last Trial: On the Legends and Lore of the Command to Abraham to Offer Isaac as a Sacrifice* (Woodstock, Vt.: Jewish Lights Publishing, 1993), 77–120.

32. For a fuller account, see Marmorstein, *The Doctrine of Merits.*

33. Ibid.

34. See Michael Fishbane, *Biblical Interpretation in Ancient Israel* (Oxford: Clarendon Press, 1985), 337.

35. Daniel Boyarin shows how this metaphor operates in another midrash centering on the name Rachel. See Daniel Boyarin, *Carnal Israel: Reading Sex in Talmudic Culture* (Berkeley: University of California Press, 1993), 151–55.

36. Talmud Bavli, *Ketubot* 63. See Boyarin, *Carnal Israel,* 154.

37. See the discussion in Urbach, *The Sages.*

38. Halbertal and Margalit, *Idolatry,* 10.

39. Ibid., 30.

40. Ibid.

41. Ibid., 33.

42. Ibid., 34.

43. Stern, "Imitatio Hominis," 163.

44. Caroline Walker Bynum, *Jesus as Mother: Studies in the Spirituality of the High Middle Ages* (Berkeley: University of California Press, 1982), 134.

45. Ibid.

46. Ibid., 154.

47. Ibid., 167.

48. Halbertal and Margalit, *Idolatry,* 34.

49. See Genesis 29–30.

50. Genesis 30:21–22.

51. Talmud Bavli, *Berakhot* 60a; Midrash *Tanhuma* (Buber, ed.), 79. This midrash is

beautifully explicated in Geoffrey H. Hartman, "Jewish Tradition as/and the Other," *Jewish Studies Quarterly* 1 (1993/94): 89.

52. Boyarin, *Carnal Israel,* 134.

53. Ibid.

54. Ibid., 151–54.

55. See *Genesis Rabbah* 71:3 (Theodor Albeck, ed.), 824 (attributed in one variant to the designated author of our midrash); *Genesis Rabbah* 82:10 (Theodor Albeck, ed.), 988.

56. On the implicit relationship of the two names of God and the attributes of justice and mercy, defined as masculine and feminine, in Midrash Tadshe, see Moshe Idel, *Kabbalah: New Perspectives* (New Haven, Conn.: Yale University Press, 1988), 128–36.

57. On the tetragrammaton, which Philo and later kabbalistic sources assign to the attribute of strict justice, as meaning jealous, see S. Goitein, *Iyyunim ba-Mikra* (Tel Aviv: Yavneh Press, 1957), 318–31, quoted in Halbertal and Margalit, *Idolatry,* 256 n. 17.

58. *Genesis Rabbah* 8:3.

59. See the discussion in Halbertal and Margalit, *Idolatry,* 18–20.

60. See, e.g., Talmud Bavli, *Megillah* 14b.

61. Talmud Bavli, *Yevamot* 79a ("this nation is known by three characteristic features; they are merciful, chaste, charitable").

62. Talmud Bavli, *Yevamot* 79a.

63. See Suzanne Last Stone, "Sinaitic and Noahide Law: Legal Pluralism in Jewish Law," *Cardozo Law Review* 12 (1991): 1157.

64. Jeanne L. Schroeder, "Feminism Historicized: Medieval Misogynist Stereotypes in Contemporary Feminist Jurisprudence," *Iowa Law Review* 75 (1990): 1135, 1170.

65. Ibid., 1136.

66. See Elliot R. Wolfson, "Woman—The Feminine as Other in Theosophic Kabbalah: Some Philosophical Observations on the Divine Androgyne," in *The Other in Jewish Thought and History: Constructions of Jewish Culture and Identity,* ed. Laurence Silberstein and Robert L. Cohn (New York: New York University Press, 1994).

67. Ibid.

68. Wolfson, "Woman—The Feminine as Other."

69. Martha Minow, *Between Vengeance and Forgiveness* (Boston: Beacon Press, 1998).

70. Jacques Derrida, *On Cosmopolitanism and Forgiveness* (New York: Routledge, 2002).

71. See Suzanne Last Stone, "The Jewish Conception of Civil Society," in *Alternative Conceptions of Civil Society,* ed. Simone Chambers and Will Kymlicka (Princeton, N.J.: Princeton University Press, 2002).

Reconstructing Divine Power: Post-Holocaust Jewish Theology, Feminism, and Process Philosophy

Introduction

No other event has crystallized the problem of evil and problematized power more than the Holocaust. In a midrash on Leviticus 21:1–3, 10–12, in which the priestly caste is forbidden from making contact with corpses for fear of a loss of their trust in God, Shlomo Carlebach wrote, "Ever since the Holocaust we are all like priests who have become contaminated by death."[1] Indeed, the faith of many modern Jews has been corrupted by contact with the corpses of the Holocaust. Though modern science and philosophy had spun their disenchantments on Jews as much as on anyone else, the Holocaust was an unequivocally Jewish tragedy that multiplied by immeasurable degree the crisis of meaning that gripped Europeans and Americans in the twentieth century. Where had the all-powerful, all-good God of the covenant been at Auschwitz?

What had been hoped for, even expected, had not happened. The classic Jewish hope is for a world that is in accord with God's will—a world made meaningful by standards of justice, the fulfillment of promises, and an increase in holiness and peace. Jewish covenantal expectations have revolved around the understanding that each partner in the divine–human relationship has specific responsibilities and duties and although the human partners may, indeed will, fall short of their obligations, it is understood that God will hold true to the partnership despite humanity's failures. It goes without saying, then, that the relationship between divine justice, love, and power has been, for Jewish thinkers, the theological and philosophical challenge of the hour. In the struggle to make sense of either justice or love in the face of the Holocaust, divine power plays a pivotal role.

Post-Holocaust Jewish theologians have probed the meaning of divine and human power, seeking to understand how power could have become so deeply perverted in the mid-twentieth century. What is striking is that power continues to be understood by and large, in traditional terms: most thinkers assume divine omnipotence (even if they opt for divine self-limitation) and assume power's primary form to be coercive.

Important critiques and reconstructions of power have come from two quarters: feminist thought and process philosophy. Having assessed modernity as a particularly egregious advocate and sponsor of the use of dominating power, they have provided sophisticated analyses that have helped to unveil the complex dynamics of power. Feminist thinkers have been masterful in exposing the absences on which power thrives as well as in detailing the privileges and exclusivity of power that is bonded to patriarchy. Process thinkers have focused on modernity's marriage to mechanism and materialism and the subsequent uses and abuses of power. Both feminist and process thinkers have developed a thorough critique of dominating power, but this critique has had little impact on the construction of post-Holocaust theodicies by Jewish thinkers.

This essay brings feminist thought and process philosophy into conversation with Jewish theology on the topic of divine power and covenantal relations in a post-Holocaust era. It begins with an examination of "divine hiddenness" and "divine self-limitation" as responses to the Holocaust with specific attention given to the writings of Eliezer Berkovitz and Irving Greenberg. For both thinkers, God is assumed to be omnipotent and to wield coercive power but to voluntarily become less powerful in order to accommodate human freedom.

The second part of the essay is a critique of the idea of "divine hiddenness" based on feminist re-evaluations of power and powerlessness. Feminist scholars have given considerable attention to documenting alternatives to dominating power—alternatives drawn from the life experiences of those who have survived generations of oppressive conditions. In so doing, they have illustrated, on the one hand, that "hiddenness" is not "powerlessness" when power is expanded to include such powers as come with affection and relational interdependence. On the other hand, it is also clear that although the status of being invisible is not without its power, it is nonetheless indicative of an oppressive imbalance of power. When the negative consequences of the "hiddenness" of women are acknowledged, "hiddenness" as a theological strategy becomes suspect.

The third section offers an analysis of power based on the principles of process philosophy. In ascribing the powers of self-determination and causal efficacy to all experiencing beings, process philosophy insists on the metaphysical necessity of power at the same time that it favors persuasive power as the form of power most in line with freedom and relationality. A process understanding of power offers ways to name the power of "hiddenness" positively—as *persuasive* power—and, in fact, to assert that such power is not a compromise, but a fundamental characteristic of divine action.

Taken together, feminist critiques of dominating power and explications of the "hidden" power of the oppressed, and process philosophy's reconstruction of divine power based on a relational metaphysics, have important implications for the development of post-Holocaust theodicies and theologies.

I. Divine Hiddenness in Post-Holocaust Jewish Theology

The notion of divine hiddenness can be traced to the ancient Jewish mystical tradition. For Jewish mystics (particularly those influenced by Merkabah mysticism), hiddenness qualifies the character of God's noumenal being. *Eyn-Sof,* "that which is infinite," is impersonal because unknown, and unknown because unrevealed. That is, God is a *deus absconditus* insofar as God is inconceivable; God in Godself is unknowable and hence hidden.[2] The mystical concept of *Eyn-Sof* indicates that God's hiddenness is an ontological fact. It is not until hiddenness is interpreted as a divine judgment or response to the created world that it becomes associated with divine providence, justice, and theodicy. Hiddenness is a theological strategy only in relation to the revealed God who acts in the world as a personal, covenanting being. For example, in the midst of great suffering, prophets and psalmists alike raised the question, "Wherefore hidest Thou Thy face, and forgettest our affliction and oppression?" (Ps. 44:24) The Prophet Isaiah declared, "Verily Thou art a God that hidest Thyself" (Isa. 45:15), and Job, the model of innocent suffering, echoed that entreaty, asking God, "Why do you hide your face and treat me like an enemy?" (Job 13:24). These inquiries express, at one and the same time, an expectation regarding God's action in the world and confusion in the face of an expectation unfulfilled.

Where the expectation is for divine intervention to end evil or suffering, divine hiddenness has given rise to two main interpretive paths. It has been understood as a form of divine punishment for human sin; God withholds God's presence in response to human failures of faith, judgment, and action. In this interpretation, divine non-action can be understood as evidence of God's goodness, justice, and merciful restraint. In contrast is the much more difficult scenario in which suffering afflicts those who meet the standards of innocence. God's absence appears as mysterious indifference to both undeserved pain and injustice. For, as the classic statement of the problem of evil dictates, an all-good, all-powerful God would not remain passive in an encounter with undeserved suffering. And yet history is a chronicle of such suffering, and Jewish history is an especially exemplary narrative. It is here that *hester panim,* the hidden face of God, becomes an exquisite challenge to covenantal faith.

Why would an all-good, all-powerful God choose to be silent in the face of suffering, particularly in the face of the suffering of those who have a relationship of partnership with God? Though this question has biblical and talmudic precedents, it is the theological focal point of much post-Holocaust thinking. Its poignancy is captured by Arthur Hertzberg who once recalled: "[screaming] at Buber himself in his home in Jerusalem, what right had God to go away, or to permit Himself to be eclipsed, while my grandfather and all of my mother's brothers and sisters and their children were being murdered?"[3]

In the post-Holocaust period of his writing, Buber has continued to hold fast to his dialogical theology, proposing that although God's presence was in eclipse, God was yet the Thou who could be met in encounter.[4] The dialogical relationship with God, he argued, had been obscured by the impersonal, manipulative instrumentalism of modernity, but the failure was more humanity's than God's. Buber's answer to God's absence at Auschwitz was unacceptable to Hertzberg because it did not satisfy Hertzberg's expectations about God's power and hence God's responsibility for the events of the world. From Hertzberg's perspective, what needed to be explained was why God's power could not overcome cultural patterns of instrumental abuse, regardless of how strongly embedded those patterns had become. This is the theological coil to which our attention is drawn. How is the absence of divine intervention in response to evil to be explained?

Although "absence theologies" differ in various ways, they serve as strategies that release God from the culpability of inaction. They do so by counterpoising divine occultation with the diminishment of divine power. In his book, *Evil and Suffering in Jewish Philosophy,* Oliver Leaman writes,

It might be argued that there is not much difference between a God who hides his face and a God who is not there at all. Yet a God who hides his face gives his creatures the opportunity to take responsibility for the actions of themselves and the natural world, in so far as the latter is under their control. . . . What the Holocaust demonstrated was the need to move towards a more sophisticated notion of the relationship between God and the world, a relationship which places far more reliance upon the ability of the world to go awry *without the direct intervention of the deity.*[5]

Leaman captures the theistic options assumed by absence theologians: either God exists as wielding omnipotent, physical power, or God exists as a passive presence who does not intervene *directly* into human affairs. Though he raises the possibility that suffering provides evidence for "a different kind of deity, one which relates to the world in more subtle and indirect ways," he immediately quotes Emmanuel Levinas who speaks of suffering as the revelation of "a God who, renouncing all helpful manifestation, appeals to the full maturity of the integrally responsible man."[6] In this view, God must restrain God's power, else human freedom and the covenantal relationship are undercut. The polarity between God as omnipotent and God as helpless (or unhelpful) structures the discussion. God's hiddenness or the absence of divine intervention is, in fact, God's presence. More precisely, what is hidden is not God, but God's omnipotence. In the hands of absence theologians, what had been perceived as a bald breach of covenantal expectations becomes instead evidence *for* covenantal relationality.

While the relationship between God's power and God's presence is inverted by absence theologians, what is most significant to note is that the meaning of power goes largely unchallenged. The continuing assumption is of power as coercive, brute force. The use of such power does, indeed, undermine the integrity of beings with lesser power. If divine power is presumed to be overwhelming in quantity and in quality, then in addition to the question of God's indifference to suffering (as evidenced by God's inaction), is the question of the existence and preservation of human freedom. Absence theologians propose a limitation on the quantity of divine power (albeit as a divine *self*-limitation), but they nonetheless maintain the traditional assumptions about the *kind* of power that God wields. Such power is often portrayed as the supernatural interruption of natural events, experienced primarily through the sensory modalities of sight and sound. The principal examples are the Exodus and Sinai events. In Egypt, God turns Moses's staff into a snake, brings down the plagues, and parts the waters of the sea; at Sinai, God thunders and the mountain quakes. God overpowers the natural forces and hence demonstrates divine action as a supernatural impact on the visible world. When absence theologians speak of the "hiding" or self-limiting of divine power, they anticipate that an unlimited God, out of hiding, would act in ways that would not only violate human freedom but would also breach the natural order of the physical world.

Though Eliezer Berkovitz and Irving (Yitz) Greenberg accept Buber's absence theology, albeit in different ways, their theodicies also serve as examples of the above argument that absence theologians limit God's quantitative power, but continue to assume that the primary form of divine power is coercive.

ELIEZER BERKOVITZ'S THEOLOGY OF DIVINE HIDDENNESS

Berkovitz acknowledges that "Auschwitz does not stand by itself." Though it may be the "most horrifying manifestation of divine silence," it is but one of numerous episodes in Jewish history bereft of a divine revelatory presence.[7] On the relation between God's justice and the suffering of innocent beings, then, post-Holocaust theology is akin to Jewish theology throughout the ages; undeserved suffering has always raised the question of God's presence in history.[8]

For Berkovitz, God's presence in history cannot be understood apart from God's decision to create a particular kind of world, one in which freedom is given precedence even over goodness. It is here that God's culpability for evil resides, although Berkovitz provides several reasons for mitigating any condemnation (including both the possibility of great human good and the existence of a "dimension beyond history" in which redemption occurs). God chooses to create a world in which there are creatures who "strive for value" and who have the power to choose to be ethical. Such power requires freedom and responsibility that together constitute "the very essence of man." Two conditions follow from the fact that human beings are human by virtue of their freedom. First, freedom brings with it the risk that humans may choose evil over good. Second, God cannot contravene human freedom in order to prevent evil without destroying humanity itself. As a consequence of creating free agents, God is placed in the position of tolerating evil for the sake of humanity. Thus Berkovitz says, "The question therefore is not: Why is there undeserved suffering? But, why is there man? He who asks the question about injustice in history really asks: Why a world? Why creation?"[9]

In a world that is home to human beings, God resists the use of "physical omnipotence" in order to honor the conditions that define humanity. Berkovitz continues to refer to God's omnipotence, but it is omnipotence shackled and restrained. "Given man, God himself could eliminate moral evil and the suffering caused by it only by eliminating man, by recalling the world of man into nothingness."[10] God *could* eliminate moral evil, but self-limits divine power in order to preserve humanity. That self-limitation is described by Berkovitz as hiddenness or absence and refers to a God who refrains from exercising omnipotent, physical power.

> If man is to be, God himself must respect his freedom of decision. If man is to act on his own responsibility, *without being continually overawed by divine supremacy,* God must absent himself from history.[11]

Divine hiddenness, then, is a way to hold on to both divine omnipotence and human freedom. God is absent from history only in the sense that God's omnipotent power is hidden in order to sustain human freedom. When Berkovitz says that God "hides His presence," he means that God acts in history "as if he were powerless":

> it is impossible for God to be present in history by using his physical omnipotence. . . . Man can only exist because God renounces the use of his power on him. This, of course, means that God cannot be present in history through manifest material power. Such presence would destroy history. . . . The rabbis in the Talmud saw the mightiness of the almighty in that he controls his inclination to judge and to punish and behaves in history as if he were powerless. To curb the use of power where infinite power is at hand, to endure the mocking of one's enemies when one could easily eliminate them, that is true strength. Such is the mightiness of God. God is mighty, for he shackles his omnipotence and becomes "powerless" so that history may be possible. . . . God is mighty in the renunciation of his might in order to bear with man.[12]

God is a hidden or absent God insofar as God does not act with unlimited power in human history. In Berkovitz's theology, God is present only when God is omnipotent; God is absent when God is, "as it were," powerless.

Hence divine absence is a structural requirement that protects human existence in relation to divine omnipotence. But Berkovitz adds an emotional dimension to this structure when he shifts from language of "absence" to language of "abandonment," acknowledging the psychological impact of an inactive God. On the one hand, he constructs a theology in which God must not intervene in human history; on the other hand, he declares the Holocaust to have been "injustice absolute, injustice *countenanced by God.*"[13] Though he holds to a theological logic that explains why an omnipotent, all-good God would not participate in arresting evil, Berkovitz also wishes to recognize the reality of tragedy and the real suffering of individuals. He thus settles for what he calls "the inescapable paradox of divine providence."

> While God tolerates the sinner, he must abandon the victim; while he shows forbearance with the wicked, he must turn a deaf ear to the anguished cries of the violated. This is the ultimate tragedy of existence: God's very mercy and forbearance, his very love for man, necessitates the abandonment of some men to a fate that they may well experience as divine indifference to justice and human suffering. It is the tragic paradox of faith that God's direct concern for the wrongdoer should be directly responsible for so much pain and sorrow on earth.[14]

God abandons the world out of respect for human freedom, no matter how misused. But this abandonment is predicated on the assumption that an omnipotent God can only act in a physical, over-powering way that will destroy not just evil, but all beings with lesser allocations of power. God-in-the-world is either omnipotently violent or "as it were," powerless.

Berkovitz thus adopts the imagery of "hiddenness" to speak of a God who is omnipotent in essence, but impotent in the realm of history. The equation of power with omnipotence and physical demonstration is so deeply ingrained in Berkovitz's thought that even when he speaks of God as "present without being indubitably manifest" and proposes ways in which God is non-coercively active—as, for example, "guiding," "forbearing," "suffering with," and "protecting"—he does not identify these activities as having anything to do with power. Power that influences but does not determine is not acknowledged as power. In Berkovitz's theological system, God is either omnipotent, bearing coercive power, or powerless.

Although God's absence from human history is primarily the consequence of divine impotence, it is reinforced by Berkovitz's conception of God as perfect and hence complete. He writes, for example, that "God is perfection. Yet because of his very perfection, he is lacking—as it were—one type of value; the one which is the result of striving for value."[15] In understanding God as perfect in this static sense of perfection, Berkovitz makes it impossible for God to be responsive to the struggles of humanity, particularly in its efforts to achieve justice, love and peace (the very values that God embodies). Truly, such a God *is* absent from meaningful engagement with history. Berkovitz acknowledges that "God's presence in history must remain—mostly—unconvincing."[16] He is more right than he may have intended, for when perfection thus understood is combined with omnipotent, dominating power, God is not only hidden, but entirely removed from the historical arena and covenantal engagement.

IRVING GREENBERG AND GOD AS SELF-LIMITING

Irving (Yitz) Greenberg's reconstruction of theology after the Holocaust is based on an analysis of power, both divine and human. Like Berkovitz, he speaks of God as having chosen to limit divine power in order to preserve human freedom. Without divine self-limitation, there could be neither covenant nor divine–human partnership, for the kind of power that God possesses overwhelms human freedom and destroys human responsibility. In line with Berkovitz's conception, what is "hidden" from the historical arena is the power of divine omnipotence. God is present in history, but not as an omnipotent, supernatural being.

For Greenberg, however, it is not simply the fact that divine omnipotence destroys humanity that moves him to speak of divine hiddenness. He proposes a covenantal process in which, "step-by-step," human partners become more and more responsible for the events of history and more and more able to reflect the image of God. God's efforts are aimed at the perfection of the world; as covenantal partners, humans are to engage in this same effort. But they cannot be coerced to do so without undercutting the covenantal relationship that calls for freely chosen participation in the created world. According to Greenberg, "the Divine self-limits to enable humans to attain perfection with dignity."[17] Dignity entails free choice and, moreover, a maturity that comes with the risk of increased power. In the biblical stage, the period of covenantal infancy, God was physically manifest in history, most visibly in the events of Exodus, delivering the Jewish people from oppression "almost against its will." By the time of the destruction of the Second Temple in 70 C.E., the covenantal relationship had entered its second stage, characterized by real partnership, and requiring fuller human participation. "The lesson of the Destruction was not that God had abandoned Israel, but that God was deliberately hiding in order to evoke a greater response, a greater participation in the covenantal way."[18] In order to increase human participation and responsibility, a "manifest God" showing "overwhelming power" must become less obviously visible. Greenberg writes, "The deepest paradox of the Rabbis' teaching was that the more God is hidden, the more God is present."[19] While during the biblical period God was most manifest in the Temple, in rabbinic times God could be found in synagogues throughout the world and thus, though God's power was more hidden, God's presence was more accessible. This shift is captured by the rabbinic valuation of Purim as the "great redemptive event of the Hidden God," paralleling the Exodus story and yet never mentioning God's name. Here divine redemption occurs through human agency, by political action and even "bedroom intrigue." Greenberg adds, "This is not clean, not neat, not like the good old days when God did it all." Rather it is indicative of how God acts in the world as human partnership matures. "In this stage, God is more hidden, Judaism is more worldly."[20]

With Auschwitz, Judaism enters the third and current stage of covenantal relations. God is most hidden, depending on humans to be the bearers of covenantal power and to use it to move the world toward perfection. When humans act in ways that redeem the world, God is thereby present as a redemptive God. For Greenberg, the re-establishment of the State of Israel is the clearest instance of the hidden Presence of God working through the responsible action of God's human partners. "This moment of revelation is fully human; this moment of redemption is humanly fully responsible in the presence of God."[21] Thus, in answer to the question, "What was God's message when God did not stop the Holocaust?" Greenberg writes,

> Let us venture to say that God was calling humans to take full responsibility for the achievement of the covenant. Judaism is entering a third stage; the Judaism of both biblical Israel (in which God initiated events) and of the rabbis (in which humans met God halfway) has now led to the understanding that the ultimate logic of covenant is for humans to take full responsibility.[22]

The logic of the covenant is to increase human responsibility and hence human power. This entails a shift from God as the central agent of power to humans as the primary actors in the world.

Greenberg's pedagogical model of covenant is offered in the face of "the overwhelming testimony of the six million [which] is so strong that it all but irretrievably closes out religious language." His dialectical approach to faith after the Holocaust leads him to argue that, on the one hand, we are in a period of covenantal renewal and, on the other hand, we live in "an age when one is ashamed or embarrassed to talk about God in the presence of the burning children."[23] In this time when the most we can manage is a "moment faith," fluctuating between belief in God's ongoing redemption and despair over the great evil of the Holocaust, Greenberg proposes that the religious enterprise is fundamentally an effort to "create, save, and heal the image of God wherever it still exists—lest further evidence of meaninglessness finally tilt the scale irreversibly."[24] While the model of covenantal pedagogy may be a too simple strategy for accounting for evil, it is based on a vivid awareness of the despair that permeates Jewish thought after the Holocaust. Greenberg's pedagogical model for covenantal renewal represents the side of his theological dialectic that nurtures faith in the living presence of a redemptive God. The model belongs to his efforts to salvage the covenant by emphasizing "the testimony of life" as evidence of and responsiveness to God's continuing redemptive work.

Like Berkovitz, however, Greenberg never directly renounces either the concept of divine omnipotence or the assumption that power is primarily coercive. In his tack toward hiddenness, he maintains both of these elements. Who is hidden? A God who is omnipotent, who has the power to intervene supernaturally in history, and whose power, when visibly manifested, overwhelms the free choice of human covenantal partners. When Greenberg poses the question, "What was God's message when God did not stop the Holocaust?" and gives as his answer, "God is calling humans to take full responsibility for the achievement of the covenant. It is their obligation to take arms against evil and to stop it," he opens up the opportunity to declare that omnipotence is no longer a meaningful divine attribute. But rather than doing this, he maintains the existence of divine omnipotence, yet declares it to be hidden. God participates in the secular world solely through the activities of human agents; the divine presence is indistinguishable from natural and secular forms.[25] Though God remains all-powerful in essence, in actuality God's power is severely curtailed.

Likewise, though Greenberg moves toward an image of God who does not act in coercive ways, he continues to think of God's power as fundamentally evident through physical force. He interprets the founding of the modern State of Israel as "renewed testimony to Exodus," witnessing to God's redemptive presence.[26] It is the example par excellence of the covenantal renewal in which "full human responsibility" manifests God's redemptive presence. Reflected in this example is the assumption that divine power, even when channeled through human agency, remains the power to visibly reshape the physical landscape. But there is irony here as well. As God's human partners have stepped up to the challenge of increased responsibility, an imbalance arises between human action and divine responsibility. Modern Israel is a "moment of redemption [that] is humanly fully responsible in the presence of God."[27] Because this model of the contemporary covenantal relationship precludes God's ability to act independently of human agency and because power is interpreted solely as physical force, Greenberg does not offer a way to understand divine "presence" as power-bearing. God's activity is superintended by human agency; hence, the covenantal dialectic is subverted.

❁ II. Feminist Critique of Dominating Power

In asking for clarification of the difference between a God who restrains the use of power and a God who is actually limited in power, Steven Katz makes the sardonic observation that, "If the non-presence, non-power, non-involvement of God proves his Presence, then by a similar demonstration we could 'prove' all sorts of entities and attributes into existence."[28] Indeed, the strategy of hiddenness, insofar as it continues to assume divine omnipotence and limit the expression of power to physical force, is unable to fulfill its intentions.

Though absence theologians like Berkovitz and Greenberg hold on to traditional notions of divine power, they verge on proposing an alternative understanding of power, both human and divine. When they speak of the presence of the "hidden God" as guiding, nurturing, and caring, they are identifying alternative notions of power. Were these alternative forms of divine activity recognized as forms of power, it would be possible to develop a theodicy that does in fact fulfill the intention of upholding covenantal relationality.

Feminist thought has revolved around a critique, dissection, and reconstruction of power. An ongoing fugue, played and replayed through the voices of many women, power is the major theme composing feminist inquiry. Power is acknowledged to be both the instrument of oppression and the means of liberation. Feminists have evaluated the power of power as it appears in political and social institutions, cultural traditions, and by way of tacit knowledge, including the "anonymous," "unbound," disciplinary power that permeates cultures.[29] In the most general terms, feminist examinations of power can be divided into two broad categories: (1) various critiques of dominating power, and (2) illuminations of multiple forms of alternative power.

It is dominating power, power "over," that is the trademark of patriarchy and the hallmark of women's experience in patriarchal cultures. Undergirding dominating power is a dualistic and hierarchical vision of reality: the world is divided along gender lines into two kinds of beings—men who are superior and women who are inferior—and operates hierarchically, with those who are superior having power over those who are inferior. In a patriarchal framework, it is assumed that power is a limited commodity so that power relations are understood as competitive, with a gain on one side yielding a loss on the other. Moreover, power is used to exact privilege from those who might not otherwise oblige; it is, to put it simply, coercive.

When feminists have turned to an examination of religion and power, they have focused attention on such issues as God-language, authority structures, and textual and ritual traditions. Feminist theologian Nancy Howell has pointed out that "Feminists do not seem particularly preoccupied with the topic of divine omnipotence."[30] And yet, the traditional doctrine of divine omnipotence is absolutely central to the reconstruction of a non-patriarchal theology. For divine omnipotence has been construed as congruent with patriarchal power and hence both mirrors and anchors the power relations that are found in social and political settings. Even in a largely secular culture, images of God, whether accepted as literal or literary, give support to deep-seated messianic hopes, nationalistic desires, and interpersonal relations. Thus, when God is conceived of as warrior, king, and supreme ruler, men have hoped to attain such status and both women and men have accepted the roles of soldiers and servants of God. When God is described as masculine, men have been given normative status and women perceived as "other." And when God is imaged as an all-power being whose power takes the form of overwhelming coercion (e.g., through "signs and wonders"), then those who desire to act in consonance with the divine image learn to hope for unlimited power and to mimic divine dominance.

To feminist thinkers we owe significant insights into the power of language to shape our expectations and experiences. As Carolyn Merchant has written about the cultural shift that occurred in early modern attitudes toward nature, "Descriptive statements about the world can presuppose the normative; they are ethic-laden. . . . The norms may be tacit assumptions hidden within the descriptions in such a way as to act as invisible restraints or moral ought-nots."[31] Language and images of God's power as dominance belie an ethic of brute power and a world in which relationality is contingent and autonomy is valued over interdependence. The tacit assumption behind a conception of God as an omnipotent being who wields aggressive, imperious, even tyrannical force, is a theology of domination. Judith Plaskow, the Jewish feminist theologian who has so cogently addressed gender relations, cites with approval the insight of Rosemary Radford Ruether that "Such images of God's dominance give rise to the terrible irony that the symbols Jews have used to talk about God as ultimate good have helped generate and justify the evils from which we hope God will save us."[32] Even when God is cast as a loving parent, Plaskow notes, it is as an authoritarian father who demands obedience, punishes independence, and shows little restraint in using power to achieve this.

Once the alignment between divine omnipotence and patriarchal power is acknowledged, the significance of feminist critiques of power for post-Holocaust Jewish theology becomes clear. For it is patriarchal power that continues (unnamed) to inform the thought of most post-Holocaust theologians. Omnipotent power is taken to be dominating power, and thus both violent and competitive. In the theologies of Berkovitz and Greenberg, we are given images of a God who fears that without self-restraint, not only evil but the very structure of human existence will be destroyed.

An oppositional dynamic is in place in which God must self-limit in order to allow for human freedom. Thus we are presented with a flawed emancipatory project, based on the idea of power as a zero-sum game, in which one party's gain in power entails the other party's diminishment.

In a patriarchal model, power connotes physical presence and effect and powerlessness connotes invisibility. When absence theologians couple divine hiddenness with powerlessness, God joins the ranks of many women who have suffered the same fate under the conditions of patriarchy. While humanity gains power, God takes up the classic female role of suffering both with those involved in power struggles and because of them. Berkovitz describes the hidden God as long-suffering and patient; Greenberg speaks of the self-limited God as "suffering, sharing, participating, calling." These are attributes that have been assigned to women and are associated with helplessness. Although it will be argued momentarily that such attributes are in fact bearers of non-dominating power, here it is important to note that in connecting hiddenness and helplessness, Greenberg and Berkovitz repeat the pernicious conditions for silencing that women have experienced.

ALTERNATIVE FORMS OF POWER

In contextualizing power so that it is understood as something that functions differently in different circumstances, feminist analyses have led to the realization that dominating power is neither the singular nor the superior species of power. Attention is given to more complex forms of power, identified as relational or empowering power. In contrast to "power over," alternative forms of power speak of influence, interdependent relationality, and mutual empowerment.

The contrast with oppositional power is striking. "Formal male power" has been described as "a form of compulsion" and as "direct pressure on a social actor to perform a specific action." Such power becomes a "'thing in itself,' measurable like amps on an electricity meter."[33] Operating as an external force "on" another being or object, formal power takes place between independent, separate beings and results in an effect that is visible and measurable. Informal, female power, by contrast, functions as influence, which has been described as "in-fluence," in which the effect of another "is not working *upon me* so much as *into* me; influence is that which flows in."[34] Its effect is internal and thus may not be immediately or even ever discernible in the same way as dominating power. It is often the quiet, gentle power of sympathy, patience, care and support. Moreover, because it is cooperating power, it does not overwhelm, but rather increases capacity and competence.[35] And empowering power is abundant, contributing to the power of another without diminishing the power of those who enter a relationship. Relational power takes many forms. It can, for example, guide, encourage, cooperate, and respond. Its hallmark is sensitivity to the other and thus, in this sense, it is contingent power. In its most intimate form, it is the power of love, expressed by parents, friends, children, lovers—and by God. Such power *is* real power, but it is so different from the paradigm of dominating power that it is often not recognized to be an alternative power, let alone the most elemental, pervasive power at work in the world.

Because Berkovitz and Greenberg limit their interpretation of power to dominating power, they remove God from the world in order to make room for human freedom and responsibility. Though they wish to strengthen the covenantal relationship, they actually undercut it. God is bereft of power and humanity is bereft of a response-able relationship with God. The mutual participation and responsibility required by covenant is dissolved. Were Berkovitz and Greenberg, however, to attribute the power of influence and relationality to the "powerless presence" of the hidden God, they would actually gain expressed corroboration of their own insights. Invisibility does not necessarily mean powerlessness; nor does "powerlessness" require invisibility. Power has its hidden, quiet forms; and those deemed invisible because excluded from formal power structures, have always had informal power.[36] The naming of "invisible" power as real power also maintains a continuum of responsibility throughout all relationality, thus breaking the dualism between power and responsibility and powerlessness and irresponsibility. For when divine hiddenness is equated with powerlessness, God is excused from responsibility because God is helpless to act. Non-dominating power assumes the ability to act, albeit in non-coercive ways, and thus entails responsibility as well.

Feminist proposals for understanding relational power offer important correctives to the theological strategy of divine hiddenness. Based on an examination of women's experiences as more or less hidden from the formal, public domain, and yet not dispossessed of power, not helpless, and not irresponsible, alternative forms of understanding divine activity in the world become available. God may indeed be in the world, actively guiding it and responding to it without overwhelming human freedom or undercutting human responsibility.

🏵 III. Process Philosophy on Divine Power

Based on the thought of Alfred North Whitehead (1861–1947) and Charles Hartshorne (1897–2000), process philosophers have developed a detailed analysis of power as relational and a model of divine agency that affirms neither dominating nor omnipotent power. God's power is redefined in two ways: (1) God is understood as the most powerful existent being, but because other creatures have some power, power is not confined to the God-head, and (2) God's power is the power of persuasion, not the power of brute force; were God to act with violence toward any creature, God would violate a vital aspect of what is implied in the image of God as a perfect being.

Process philosophy, unfortunately, has received only limited attention in contemporary Jewish thought, even though some leading Jewish think-ers in the twentieth century were indebted to it. Max Kadushin in his 1938 book, *Organic Thinking: A Study in Rabbinic Thought,* spoke of Whitehead's philosophy as "the most comprehensive philosophy of organism" and pro-posed that many of Whitehead's "metaphysical concepts can be taken as generalizations of the characteristics of rabbinic theology."[37] The scholar of Gnosticism and philosopher of science, Hans Jonas, expressed strong appre-ciation for and affinities with process thought, calling it a philosophy "whose intellectual force and philosophical importance are unequaled in our time."[38] Jonas embraced the process emphases on becoming over being, on freedom and value as characteristic of all of life, and on limits to divine power. In the 1950s, Milton Steinberg spoke of his indebtedness to Charles Hartshorne's "neo-classical" reconception of divinity in which God is neither immutable nor omnipotent. Rabbi Levi Olan, too, adopted Harts-horne's reinterpretation of divine perfection in which "'be ye perfect' does not mean 'be ye immutable!'"[39] Most recently, Rabbi William E. Kaufman has contributed a book on *The Evolving God in Jewish Process Theology* and David Griffin and I have published a collection of essays entitled *Jewish The-ology and Process Thought.*[40]

The starting point for process philosophy is an analysis of power as a fundamental characteristic of *all being.* The primary units of reality ("actual occasions" or "events") are understood to be *subjects* for themselves and as such, to include some degree of self-determination. Because to be is to have some power (perhaps only infinitesimal) of self-determination, there is free-dom or creativity throughout the system.

Whitehead substitutes *the process of becoming* for the idea of substance. Subjectivity, then, is not a state but a process (hence the term, *process philos-ophy*). The process of becoming is a process of *feeling* the world; Whitehead's term is *prehension. Feeling* or *prehending* the world means entering into rela-tionship with it. A subject does not exist before feeling, but emerges from feeling the world. Feelings are the direct connections between units of real-ity; they are the "food" on which subjectivity feeds and as sustenance, are incorporated into the becoming subject. The basic process of reality is the process of becoming a subject by becoming "internally related" to the world. Feminist process philosopher Catherine Keller notes, *"Relation, in other words, is more than a feminine or feminist preoccupation; it is the best metaphor for the nature of the universe."*[41]

But how the becoming subject feels the given world and how the given world is incorporated into the becoming subject is not strictly determined. Relations, process thinkers explain, involve "in-fluence"; in the process of becoming, every actual occasion experiences the power of the past and the power of possibilities—not as determinative, but as influential—and shapes itself in response to these influences. The given world—which, for process theologians includes God—is "felt" by the becoming actuality and thus becomes constitutive of the arising subject. But again, though subjectivity arises in relation to the given world and though this relation is internal to the subject, there is always some degree of novelty and freedom at work in the emergence of subjectivity.

It is thus the case that as occasions of subjectivity arise, they are affected (influenced but not determined) by the power already at work in the universe. In perishing, they contribute to the welter of the past and become part of the influences inherited by the next becoming occasions.[42] As Whitehead writes, "It belongs to the nature of every 'being' that it is a potential for every 'becoming.'" Thus relational power is at the root of the dynamic of becoming: all beings have the capacity both to influence others and to be influenced by others.[43] In other words, every creature possesses two forms of creative power: the power of self-determination and the power of efficient causation. That this is so has important ramifications for the status of divine power.

A PROCESS THEODICY

In this metaphysical landscape of freedom and influence, the picture of divine power is significantly modified from that given in traditional theologies. God's power exists in a world of power and is, like all power, fundamentally relational. As with biblical, rabbinic, and kabbalistic theologies, process theology assumes the reality of human freedom and responsibility. It does so, however, without relying on the compromise of logic that characterizes classical Western religious thought, where divine omnipotence is upheld simultaneously with human freedom. The principle behind omnipotence is sustained: God is that being who influences *all* beings. God is omnipresent and omni-influential.

The process discussion of divine power takes place with full cognizance of the problem of evil. As Whitehead himself noted, "All simplifications of religious dogma are shipwrecked upon the rock of the problem of evil."[44] The process encounter with theodicy begins with the admission that genuine evil exists—that there are events without which the world would be better. And it affirms the two-fold power that is definitive of every creature. These set the parameters of the process reconception of divine power. In answer to the question, "How is the occurrence of any genuine evil compatible with a perfectly good creator *who could have unilaterally prevented all genuine evil while still making possible all the good?*" process theism answers that because there is freedom and power throughout the created world, God does not act unilaterally.[45] Evil occurs because some degree of self-determination, that is, some degree of power, exists in beings who are inter-related with God, but not fully determined by God's will. It is the metaphysical consequence of the existence of free beings who are limited in (among other things) understanding, vision, energy, and sensitivity.

Moreover, as David Griffin has made clear, there is an evolutionary pattern that may be described as the "law of the variables of power and value" such that an increased capacity for feeling is related to an increased capacity to experience both good and evil and to contribute both positively and negatively to the experience of others. Such capacity is accompanied by a correlative increase in the power of self-determination, including the power to act contrary to God's direction.

> This doctrine means not only that God cannot occasionally interrupt the world's causal nexus. It also means that the divine purpose to bring about a world rich in value cannot—*metaphysically* cannot—be carried out without the risk of great evils. In this way, process philosophy is able to reconcile the facts of our world, as horrible as they often are, with belief in the wisdom and perfect goodness of this world's creator.[46]

This assessment of God's power resolves the classical problem of evil by revising the proposition that God is all-powerful and thus could single-handedly (so to speak) prevent evil events. Omnipotence is abandoned as an illogical concept in a system in which relationality is necessary rather than contingent. Omnipotence, process philosophers maintain, is both logically meaningless and theologically objectionable. A "monopoly theory of power," as Charles Hartshorne points out, is meaningless because power is by definition a relational term; divine power, existing in relationship with creaturely power, cannot be omnipotent.[47] God's power is "absolutely maximal, the greatest possible, but even the greatest power is still one power among others."[48] Hans Jonas, who formulated his theodicy in conversation with process philosophy, also objects, on the same philosophical grounds, to the notion of omnipotence.

> From the very concept of power, it follows that omnipotence is a self-contra-dictory, self-destructive, indeed, senseless concept. . . . Absolute, total power means power not limited by anything, not even by the mere existence of something other than the possessor of that power. . . . Absolute power then in its solitude, has no object on which to act. But as objectless power it is a powerless power, canceling itself out: "all" equals "zero" here. In order for it to act, there must be something else, and as soon as there is, the one is not all-powerful anymore, even though in any comparison its power may be superior by any degree you please to imagine. The existence of another object limits the power of the most powerful agent at the same time that it allows it to be an agent. In brief, power as such is a relational concept and requires relation. . . . In short, it cannot be that all power is on the side of one agent only. Power must be divided so that there be any power at all.[49]

To this metaphysical paradox, Jonas adds his theological objections, arguing that "We can have divine omnipotence together with divine goodness only at the price of complete divine inscrutability." Jonas holds that the only Jewishly appropriate solution is to deny omnipotence, rather than divine goodness or intelligibility. A god who is hidden from human understanding, is a "profoundly un-Jewish conception," undercutting revelation and covenant.[50] Hence, with other process philosophers, Jonas rejects omnipotence.[51]

In rejecting omnipotence, process theologians do not thereby propose a powerless, passive, or hidden God. The second characteristic of a process theodicy involves the kind of power that God possesses and the way in which God intervenes in the world. Process philosophy speaks of God's nature as dipolar, distinguishing between God's "primordial" nature, which is eternal and necessary, and God's "consequent" nature, which is contingent and responsive. In both cases, God is ever-present and ever-active in the world without violating creaturely freedom or the defining patterns of the natural world. God's power is understood as creative–redemptive power, operating as persuasive agency within each occasion and responding to the decisions of every occasion.

In the process of *concrescence* (Whitehead's term for *becoming*), every arising subject is influenced both by the past and by the possibilities inherent in the universe. Those possibilities are given in an ordered form to each occasion by God. In this way, God functions as "the organ of novelty" and the "lure for feeling," apart from which there could be neither novelty nor order in the world. This is what is termed the activity of God's "primordial nature" and it is one way in which God directly participates in the constitution of every subject. At every moment, God is present and efficacious, offering possibilities in line with God's goals of goodness and beauty. Because every creative act is by definition not fully determined by external agencies (else it would lack freedom and creativity), God's power cannot be coercive. God must work in tandem with other causal influences and with the element of self-determination that defines each occasion. Yet God is felt as an immanent power, responding to creaturely freedom with an influx of possibilities and thus actively working to shape the world.

In addition, process philosophers speak of God's consequent nature which is effected by the decisions made—at every moment—by those actualities in the process of concrescence. All that is decided, all that comes to be, finds everlasting effect in the immediacy of God's own life.[52] At every moment, the possibilities that God can offer the world are reintegrated in response to the actual decisions taking place within the world. Through God's integrative activity, all lives are remembered and continue to influence both God and the world. In this aspect of God's nature, God changes in response to the world.[53]

How, then, does God act in a world that is constituted by beings with some degree of self-determination, in which heightened sensitivity and complexity carry the possibility of both increased good and evil and in which God, therefore, is metaphysically constrained? "God's role," Whitehead writes, "is not the combat of productive force with productive force, of destructive force with destructive force. It lies in the patient operation of the overpowering rationality of his conceptual harmonization."[54] In a world in which all creatures have the two-fold powers of self-determination and efficient causation, God does not have either omnipotent or coercive power. But neither is God helpless. God has persuasive power over *all* things and, in fact, this kind of power *is* unlimited.[55] *Persuasion is power,* but it is power exercised in response to the integrity of other beings. Its manifestation is felt, but is not necessarily physically visible. For it is a kind of power that relies on the openness of individuals and acts internally. To speak of power in this way presumes a world that is not conceived of as mechanical, materialistic, or deterministic, that is, a world in which power can only be external and coercive. Rather, it is to think of the world as home to real subjectivity and freedom; in this kind of world, power is not control over but the capacity to influence the decisions of another. If human beings are in some way free and hence have some amount of power, then God works in a complicated world of relationships of power. And since process thinkers hold that it is not only human beings who have freedom and power, but that power and freedom are characteristics of the entire system of life, God is active in a world that is deeply complex. At every moment, God intervenes for good in the world, but at every moment God encounters the power that defines free and responsible creatures. Evil happens not because God allows it to happen, but because of the choices that are made by other free creatures who freely choose to ignore or oppose God's will.

Thus divine activity that is not coercive or omnipotent need not be equated with divine inactivity or powerlessness. Indeed, Buber's description of messianic activity—described as "hiddenness" but nonetheless clearly redemptive and creative—is expressive of the divine activity as it is framed in process metaphysics.

> Hiddenness is the unannounced work that brings the Kingdom of God into the concrete forms which define the everyday, "hiding" the sacred within the profane world and thereby redeeming the world without unraveling it. Hiddenness is the means for continuity, for the continuity of creation— there is no break between redeemed and unredeemed time—where there is no saving knowledge, every act of the individual has bearing on the cre- ative-redemptive process. The paradoxical nature of "hiddenness" is this: it is in concealment that the redemptive process reveals itself.[56]

Creative–redemptive power does not unravel, demolish, obliterate, or con- sume. It operates as persuasive agency, luring the world toward goodness and beauty and repairing the world as it fails to reach those goals.

❦ *Conclusion: A Jewish Feminist Process Theology after the Holocaust*

At the heart of Judaism is a divine–human partnership through which value and meaning become intimately known. The covenant is both a rela- tionship of asymmetrical power in which God is in all ways understood as superior, and yet in which there exists a partnership. It is a relationship en- tered into by free subjects who regard each other as co-committed to an in- terpersonal relationship of trust, responsibility, and shared expectations. Within these parameters, what kind of power makes sense? Where there is both an extreme power differential and yet the requirement of mutuality, what kind of power is involved?

Clearly, coercive power violates covenantal mutuality. Though there is biblical affirmation of such power, there are important biblical, rabbinic, and kabbalistic renderings of divine power that point a different direction, toward the quiet, hidden work of non-violent responsiveness. When the rabbis of the post-Second Temple period reshaped Judaism, they did so in response to the failure of their military strength. They created a Judaism that could survive without political power and they remade their image of God within this new context. The God who is in exile with the Jewish People is a God who rejoices in a different kind of mastery: the mastery of texts, of *mitzvot,* and of prayer. They did not give up earlier conceptions of God's power as dominance, but that kind of power was deferred to a messianic future; in the present, imitation of God included, instead, the sustaining activities of study, prayer, and the doing of good deeds.

Post-Holocaust Jews face a situation akin to that of the rabbis who survived the destruction of 70 C.E. Both process philosophy and feminist thought can contribute to that part of the rabbinic tradition which recognized the need for a reconstruction of divine power and human power, of the way God acts in the world and the way humans ought to act. What the rabbis came to understand—though they held this insight in tension with the tradition of dominating power—and what feminists and process thinkers have since affirmed—is that it is persuasive agency that empowers most fully. And the most powerful form of this kind of agency is love—love that encourages both the self-determination and the continuity of all beings. When God's power is conceived of as persuasive power, the language of love is given philosophical support. Bringing a process philosophical understanding of power and a feminist critique of patriarchal forms of power to bear on Jewish thought can lead to a more adequate way of imaging God's steadfast love in a post-Holocaust world.

Theological models of divine silence and invisibility continue to promote the very patterns of power that they mean to condemn. Eliezer Berkovitz and Irving Greenberg both oppose divine coercive omnipotence because it devalues human life. Yet divine silence in the form of passivity or hiddenness also devalues human life—as well as divine life—for God is denied significant participation in it. To exist and not be recognized, to have one's power denied or trivialized, to be called to suffer but to lack the ability to prevent suffering: these are characteristics that have unjustly marked women's lives. Women have risen up against these conditions now recognized as the outcome of degrading human relationships. Heeding women's experience, what is to be gained by a model of divine powerlessness that promotes the very corruptions women have rejected?

Theological models of powerlessness are built on a patriarchal understanding of power. Feminist critiques have exposed such an understanding of power to be inadequate. All too often, such power leads to abuse. In response, feminist thinkers have proposed a re-conception of power as relational, non-competitive, and ideally, non-coercive. The feminist critique of power is supported by a process metaphysics in which power characterizes all of life. Feminist alternatives to patriarchal power and process claims about the structure of reality have much to contribute to Jewish theologians who are searching for alternative ways to understand God's power and activity in the world. They offer ways to conceive of God as powerful without being coercive and as active in the world without overwhelming human freedom. In so doing, these alternatives offer an image of God that may in fact be deserving of *imitatio dei.*

NOTES

1. Cited in Rodger Kamenetz, *The Jew in the Lotus: A Poet's Rediscovery of Jewish Identity in Buddhist India* (Northvale, N.J.: Jason Aronson, 1995), 157.

2. Gershom G. Scholem, *Major Trends in Jewish Mysticism* (New York: Schocken Books, 1941), 12–13.

3. "A Lifelong Quarrel with God," *The New York Times Book Review,* May 6, 1990, cited in David Wolpe, "*Hester Panim* in Modern Jewish Thought," *Modern Judaism* 17, no. 1 (1997): n. 38.

4. Martin Buber, *The Eclipse of God* (New York: Harper & Row, 1952), 38.

5. Oliver Leaman, *Evil and Suffering in Jewish Philosophy* (Cambridge: Cambridge University Press, 1995), p. 232, my emphasis.

6. Ibid., p. 232. Levinas citation is *Difficile liberté,* p. 102.

7. Eliezer Berkovits, *Faith after the Holocaust* (New York: KTAV Publishing House, 1973), 135.

8. Ibid., 94.

9. Ibid., 105.

10. Ibid., 105–106.

11. Ibid., 107, my emphasis.

12. Ibid., 108–109.

13. Ibid., 94, my emphasis.

14. Ibid., 106.

15. Ibid., 105.

16. Ibid., 107.

17. Irving Greenberg, "The Relationship of Judaism and Christianity: Toward a New Organic Model," in *Twenty Years of Jewish–Catholic Relations,* ed. Eugene J. Fisher, A. James Rudin, and Marc H. Tanenbaum (New York: Paulist Press, 1986), 195.

18. Ibid., 203.

19. Ibid., 204.

20. Ibid., 205, 206.

21. Ibid., 210.

22. Irving Greenberg, "The Shoah and the Legacy of Anti-Semitism," in *Christianity in Jewish Terms,* ed. Tikva Frymer-Kensky, David Novak, Peter Ochs, David Fox Sandmel, and Michael A. Signer (Boulder: Westview Press, 2000), 35–36.

23. Irving Greenberg, "Cloud of Smoke, Pillar of Fire: Judaism, Christianity, and Modernity after the Holocaust," reprinted in *Contemporary Jewish Theology: A Reader,* ed. Elliot N. Dorff and Louis E. Newman (Oxford: Oxford University Press, 1999), 406.

24. Ibid., 406–407.

25. See Greenberg, "The Relationship of Judaism and Christianity," 209. "One must find God in the street, in the hospital, in the bar."

26. Greenberg, "Cloud of Smoke," 410.

27. Greenberg, "The Relationship of Judaism and Christianity," 210.

28. Cited in Wolpe, "*Hester Panim* in Modern Jewish Thought," 26.

29. Sandra Bartky, "Foucault, Femininity and the Modernization of Patriarchal Power," reprinted in *Feminist Philosophies,* ed. Janet A. Kourany, James P. Sterba, and Rosemarie Tong (Englewood Cliffs, N.J.: Prentice Hall, 1992), 112.

30. Nancy Howell, *A Feminist Cosmology: Ecology, Solidarity, and Metaphysics* (New York: Humanity Books, 2000), 107.

31. Carolyn Merchant, *The Death of Nature: Women, Ecology, and the Scientific Revolution* (San Francisco: Harper & Row, 1980), 4.

32. Judith Plaskow, *Standing Again at Sinai: Judaism from a Feminist Perspective* (San Francisco: Harper and Row, 1990), 132.

33. Jean Bethke Elshtain, "The Power and Powerlessness of Women," in *Beyond Equality and Difference: Citizenship, Feminist Politics and Female Subjectivity,* ed. Gisela Bock and Susan James (London: Routledge 1992), 112.

34. Catherine Keller, *From a Broken Web: Separation, Sexism, and Self* (Boston: Beacon Press, 1986), 27.

35. This point is nicely made by Rachel Adler in *Engendering Judaism: An Inclusive Theology and Ethics* (Philadelphia: Jewish Publication Society, 1998), 94. It is, however, important to note that not all non-coercive power is affirming or empowering power. For example, Miriam Peskowitz details the use of the feminine gaze and women's gossip/storytelling to control women in obedience to patriarchal standards. She writes, "In the absence of more formal modes for enforcing rabbinic visions of culture, law, and society, the informalities of public gazes and chatter are not to be underrated," in *Spinning Fantasies: Rabbis, Gender, and History* (Berkeley: University of California Press, 1997), 149.

36. See, for example, Leila Ahmed's now almost classic essay "Western Ethnocentrism and Perceptions of the Harem," *Feminist Studies* 8, no. 3 (Fall 1982): 521–34, in which she describes some aspects of the power and control available to women in separatist structures. For example, she writes, "Although in its explicit formulations, Saudi society gives individual men control over individual women, nevertheless, the *shape* of that society allows men considerably less control over how women think, how they see and discuss themselves, and how they see and discuss men." (p. 528).

37. Max Kadushin, *Organic Thinking: A Study in Rabbinic Thought* (1938; reprint, New York: Bloch Publishing Co., 1976), 247–50.

38. Hans Jonas, *The Phenomenon of Life: Toward a Philosophical Biology* (Chicago: University of Chicago Press, 1966), 96.

39. Charles Hartshorne, "Philosophical and Religious Uses of 'God,'" in *Process Theology: Basic Writings,* ed. Ewert H. Cousins (New York: Newman Press, 1971), 111–16. See Steinberg, quoted in Simon Noveck, *Milton Steinberg: Portrait of a Rabbi* (New York: KTAV Publishing House, 1978), 87, 262. On Levi Olan's affinities with process thought, see his essay, "The Prophetic Faith in a Secular Age," reprinted in *Jewish Theology and Process*

Thought, ed. Sandra B. Lubarsky and David Ray Griffin (New York: State University of New York Press, 1996), 25–34.

40. William E. Kaufman, *The Evolving God in Jewish Process Theology* (Lewiston, N.Y.: Edwin Mellon Press, 1997); Lubarsky and Griffin, *Jewish Theology and Process Thought.*

41. Catherine Keller, "Postpatriarchal Postmodernity," in *Spirituality and Society: Postmodern Visions,* ed. David Ray Griffin (Albany: State University of New York Press, 1988), 75.

42. "The 'effects' of an actual entity are its interventions in concrescent processes other than its own. Any entity, thus intervening in processes transcending itself, is said to be functioning as an 'object.' It is the one general metaphysical character of all entities of all sorts, that they function as objects. It is this metaphysical character which constitutes the solidarity of the universe." Alfred North Whitehead, *Process and Reality: An Essay in Cosmology,* corrected edition, ed. David Ray Griffin and Donald W. Sherburne (1929; reprint, New York: Free Press, 1978, 220).

43. This is Bernard Loomer's definition of relational power, cited in Nancy Howell's *A Feminist Cosmology,* 116.

44. Alfred North Whitehead, *Religion in the Making* (1926, reprint, Cleveland: World, 1960), 74.

45. David Ray Griffin frames the question as cited in his book *Reenchantment without Supernaturalism: A Process Philosophy of Religion* (Ithaca, N.Y.: Cornell University Press, 2001), 224–25.

46. Ibid., 230.

47. Charles Hartshorne, *A Natural Theology for Our Time* (La Salle, Ill.: Open Court, 1967), 119.

48. Charles Hartshorne, *Divine Relativity: A Social Conception of God,* 2nd ed. (New Haven, Conn.: Yale University Press, 1964), 138.

49. Hans Jonas, "The Concept of God after Auschwitz," reprinted in Lubarsky and Griffin, *Jewish Philosophy and Process Thought,* 151–52.

50. Ibid., 152.

51. Among the few contemporary Jewish thinkers who have rejected divine omnipotence, most have done so under the influence of process philosophy. Such thinkers include Harold Schulweiss, William Kaufmann, Hans Jonas, Arthur A. Cohen, Levi Olan, and Milton Steinberg.

52. Whitehead, *Process and Reality,* 346. "He [God] saves the world as its passes into the immediacy of his own life."

53. The distinction between God's primordial and consequent natures is spoken of by both Whitehead and Charles Hartshorne as "di-polar" and affords a way of thinking of God as having both unchanging and responsive aspects.

54. Whitehead, *Process and Reality,* 346.

55. This very idea was insisted on by Rabbi Levi Olan in his essay "The Prophetic Faith in a Secular Age," reprinted in *Jewish Theology and Process Thought* 30: 25–34, in which he wrote that "Power need not be coercive; it can be persuasive and unlimited."

56. Martin Buber, *The Origin and Meaning of Hasidism,* ed. and trans. Maurice Friedman (New York: Harper Torchbooks, 1966), 109.

TWELVE

RANDI RASHKOVER

Theological Desire: Feminism, Philosophy, and Exegetical Jewish Thought

Now that we are well into the twenty-first century, it is an appropriate time for Jewish thinkers to reflect upon the character and objectives of postmodern Jewish thought. I believe that the most central issue in postmodern Jewish thought is how simultaneously to lend a philosophically savvy reading to classical Jewish sources *and* to appreciate this critical activity as a religious task. In what follows, I present a model for how Jewish thought can meet these two objectives. More specifically I argue that postmodern Jewish thought must couple the philosophical rigor in Jewish feminism with the theological commitment introduced into postmodernism through the return to the texts movement.

Over the past two decades, Judaism has participated in the linguistic turn by advancing a non-apologetic, text-centered approach to Jewish thought. However, despite its best intentions, exegetically oriented Jewish thought is insufficiently critical of Jewish textual authority and ignores the complex configurations of human inter-subjectivity that appear in the texts and their interpretations. Briefly stated, the return to texts has too quickly divorced itself from the critical rigor of philosophical analysis. Moreover, I believe that it is exegetical Jewish thought's lack of critical rigor that explains why few self-proclaimed Jewish feminist thinkers have identified themselves with this movement.

It was of course Hegel who recognized human life as the perpetual engagement of selves with other selves in dramatic encounters of recognition and mis-recognition. In her now famous work *Mourning Becomes Law: Philosophy and Representation,* the late Gillian Rose reintroduces Hegel's appreciation of the inter-subjective character of human life and identifies Hegel's phenomenology of the self with the life of law. Contemporary thought must, Rose insists, readmit philosophical awareness of the inter-subjective character of human knowledge into all of its analyses and most specifically into its hermeneutical methodology. I believe that Rose's philosophically oriented hermeneutics offers a crucial corrective to the contemporary Jewish exegetical tradition.

However, if we define philosophical labor as the conscious reflection upon the drama of human inter-subjective engagement, we can appreciate much Jewish feminist thought as philosophical. More specifically, I want to argue that both Rachel Adler and Miriam Peskowitz present hermeneutical methodologies that bear much in common with Rose's hermeneutics and therefore provide the kind of philosophically rigorous analysis of the inter-subjectivity of human knowledge lacking in exegetical Jewish thought.

Finally, Jewish postmodernism seeks not only philosophical rigor but religious meaning as well. If feminism helps Jewish theology recognize the need for a philosophically informed hermeneutics, then Jewish feminism must recognize human inter-subjectivity as the site of theological desire and therefore as covenantally significant. To substantiate this claim, I will draw from David Novak's analysis of natural law as the testament to human anxiety and as the desire for God. Novak's analysis will illuminate the theological ramifications in Rose's philosophy of human inter-subjectivity and by extension, Peskowitz's and Adler's critical hermeneutics. In the end, I seek to offer a model for contemporary Jewish thought that appreciates and facilitates philosophically critical analysis as theological desire.

I. Contemporary Jewish Thought and the Exegetical Turn

Following in the wake of Rosenzweig's and Buber's German-Jewish renaissance, much of late twentieth and early twenty-first century Jewish thought has sought to retrieve the meaning and value of classical Jewish texts for liberal Jews. At the risk of over-generalizing, one can identify a few common characteristics of the postmodern return to the sources. First, it is assumed that classical Jewish sources are sacred. More specifically, the sanctity of the sources is expressed through their plurality of meaning, that is, their interpretability. Second, this school commonly believes that the

Jewish sources present a unique metaphysical orientation that differs from the classical Greek and modern European models. Third, text thinkers assume that the metaphysical difference between classical Jewish sources and the Greek and European models concerns the role of the Word and its interpretability in the sources and that exegetical activity functions as the primary mode of philosophical discernment.

The return to the texts movement has helped many Jews become acquainted with classical Jewish sources. Nonetheless, this movement has become myopically focused on the texts and maintains an insufficiently critical faith in their authority. Consequently, the exegetical school of Jewish thought has lost sight of extra-textual dynamics that influence the writing and interpretation of these texts. In what follows, I will back up this claim by examining the hermeneutical approach of the most influential of the exegetically oriented thinkers, Emmanuel Levinas, and then review the exegetical approach in American Jewish thought through a review of the works of Susan Handelman and Peter Ochs.

EXEGESIS AND ETHICS AS FIRST PHILOSOPHY

At the heart of Emmanuel Levinas's work is his concern to demonstrate the marriage between Jewish thought and exegesis. Levinas maintains that traditional Jewish learning stages vital opportunities for the ethical engagement with an other.

The encounter with the other presupposes the self who approaches the world and appropriates it as its own. But how can the self know anything outside itself if it appropriates the world into its own representations? Truth emerges for Levinas only in an encounter with the living, expressing, face of an other who simultaneously requires my attention but resists my signification. "The life of expression consists in undoing the form in which the existent, exposed as a theme, is thereby dissimulated."[1] Exceeding my representation, the face compels me to recognize its exteriority. "This presence dominates him who welcomes it."[2]

According to Levinas, the self is preserved in Desire, a Desire generated by the other, for the other. This desire, "originates from its 'object' . . . is absolutely non-egoist; its name is justice."[3] The self is preserved and affirmed only so far as it attends to the other. "[I]n discourse I expose myself to the questioning of the Other, and this urgency of the response—engenders me for responsibility; as responsible I am brought to my final reality."[4] Desiring goodness, "the I appears still higher, since it can sacrifice to its Desire its very happiness."[5] Fulfilled by this release of its happiness for the sake of goodness for the Other, the self knows peace. "Peace must be my peace, in a relation that starts from an I and goes to the other, in desire and goodness, where the I both maintains itself and exists without egoism."[6] But peace is eschatological. History's narratives erase the details of individuals, subsuming them in the currents of epochal change. The moral encounter preserves individuality and judges totality. It is beyond history, politics, and war. "The eschatological vision breaks with the totality of wars and empires in which one does not speak."[7]

Levinas's concern with Torah study derives from this ethical phenomenology. According to Levinas, the sacred texts are vehicles of divine revelation because they invite hearers to acts of listening. Jews are commanded to *hear* the Word of God and interpret it. The Word of God becomes the multiple Word heard by its listeners. "The totality of the true is constituted from the contribution of multiple people: the uniqueness of each act of listening carrying the secret of the text."[8] But, how does one guard against arbitrary subjectivism?

Levinas argues that in Judaism, individuals interpret the Word of God together with others, around the study table. Interpretation of the Word must happen, Levinas says, "in the context of the Whole,"[9] in the context of the tradition of commentaries and rabbinic discussions. The polysemic character of the Word of God feeds the other person's interpretation and in study I encounter this interpretation and am humbled and commanded to recognize it.

> Man is . . . simultaneously him to whom the word is said, but also him through whom there is Revelation. Man is the place through which transcendence passes. . . . In the event of revelation, the prophets are succeeded by the *chakham*. . . . He is taught and he teaches.[10]

The individual's obedience to the text and to the Word of God is the individual's obedience to the Word as spoken and interpreted through the other person and consequently, the obedience to this neighbor. On account of its plurivocity, Torah stages an opportunity for ethics and for peace.

Levinas's exegetical approach privileges the classical Jewish sources. For Levinas, the texts offer the formal opportunity for non-violent ethical fulfillment; the texts are also sacred. While Levinas opens the door to a critique of contemporary society ("my" interpretation is challenged by the face of the other with whom I study), the authority of the Torah remains unchallenged. Furthermore, even if text study affords a chance for a critique of contemporary society, Levinas's portrait of the ethical engagement that results from text study waxes utopian, its critical potential absorbed and thereby dissolved into a kind of messianic peace that leaves any awareness of the complexities of contemporary social and political realities behind.

POST-LEVINASIAN CONTEMPORARY EXEGETICAL JEWISH THOUGHT

One of the first contemporary American Jewish works positioned outside of the modern Jewish project, Susan Handelman's *The Slayers of Moses: The Emergence of Rabbinic Interpretation in Modern Literary Theory* attempts to earmark the difference between the Greek and Western philosophical tradition and show how Judaism's metaphysical position emerges from its exegetical life.

Drawing directly from the groundbreaking work of Jacques Derrida and Paul Ricoeur, Handelman avers that the Western European philosophical tradition devalues the metaphysical value of word and text. Following Derrida, Handelman challenges Aristotle's view of substance and the univocal view of knowledge and language that results. Instead, Handelman claims that knowledge is metaphorical because it emerges when we discover that a particular entity or concept is like and dislike something else. By perpetually forging these relations, we disorder and expand upon our former understanding of what things are. "Metaphorical movement is a 'disordering' . . . which simultaneously destroys and creates new order."[11] Therefore, truth is dynamic and meaning is plurivocal. Language is no longer viewed as a poor attempt to copy reality. Language produces reality.

Handelman debunks Western metaphysics because she sees an overlap between the contemporary challenge to it and the Jewish (biblical and rabbinic) world-view. Recalling Eric Auerbach's famous comparison between Homer and the Bible, Handelman argues that the Bible portrays the world as created and contingent—the product of divine word. As God's word, the Bible presents an authoritative narrative that claims the reader's participation. The Bible does not refer to an outside reality but generates reality: "The biblical narrative claims an authority which subsumes our own reality and everything that happens in our own world."[12] Furthermore, as God's Word, the biblical text is mysterious, demanding interpretation. Given the Bible's authority as God's word, interpretation of the text becomes the means of comprehending one's own world. "[B]y interpretive extension, all new facts become fitted into its account."[13] To discern ultimate reality, a Jew does not look to nature and then to the Bible. She looks into the Bible's "own network of relations, of verbal and temporal ambiguities."[14] Echoing Auerbach, Handelman concludes the Bible maintains an authority unparalleled by Greek literature: "There is no ultimate outside point of view."[15]

By locating reality in the Word of God rather than in forms or substances, the Hebrew Bible, according to Handelman, can present multiple views of reality. The biblical text does not try to pictorially represent the way the world really is. Rather, it speaks and asks its readers to listen to what it says. Unlike seeing, listening is multi-toned and always retains the moment of difference between the speaker and the hearer.

While Handelman celebrates the all-absorbing character of the Torah text, Peter Ochs recognizes the potentially uncritical character of this position. In an article titled "Scriptural Logic: Diagrams for a Postcritical Metaphysics,"[16] Ochs claims that exegesis is not only the process of entering into the Torah but also the process through which the Torah encounters the world. The Torah text, Ochs says, has a transformative dimension that enables it to speak to the needs and challenges of generations of readers. Torah is a composite of symbols that acquire meaning by the rule-regulated relation they maintain to other words established by interpreting communities. Since changing interpretive communities can interpret symbols according to new rules, symbols become "agents of pragmatic inquiry"[17] that encourage diverse communities to contest their meaning. Consequently, Ochs's hermeneutics grants more latitude for the outside world to present challenges to the text than does Handelman's.

Like Levinas, Handelman's and Ochs's exegetically oriented approach to Jewish thought preserves the unchallenged authority of the Jewish textual tradition. Despite her effort to draw attention to the Jewish sources as expressions of metaphysical difference, Handelman's celebration of the polysemic character of the sources endows them with an unparalleled authority that nullifies the possibility for external voices to challenge the worlds generated by the text.

Ochs claims that the symbolic nature of the classical sources provides a built-in mechanism that ensures their own critique. Nonetheless, implicit in Ochs's hermeneutic is the assumption that exegetical meaning derives from the question–answer dynamic between texts and readers. Readers approach texts with questions and challenge the sources. Nonetheless, meaning emerges when, shaped by the contours of the questions asked, the text offers a claim; that is, the text provides an answer. In *Reasoning After Revelation,* Ochs says,

> we are prepared to receive the words as behaviorally and epistemologically authoritative. . . . Rather than placing rationality over and against textual-

ity . . . we may redescribe rationality as both servant and consort of the text.[18]

According to this hermeneutics, the text expands with each new challenge, becoming an ever richer authority on all life matters. Consequently, more than a guard against the text's oppressiveness, the text's indeterminacy bolsters its own authority, prohibiting the possibility of radical critique.

🏵 II. Readmitting Philosophy into the Contemporary Jewish Conversation

When interpretation of texts is understood as the perpetual discernment of a surplus of meaning, no room remains for a critical analysis of how that meaning is scripted and how it is interpreted. Of course, it was Hegel who challenged Kant's presuppositions regarding the cognitive subject and first appreciated the complex dynamics of human inter-subjective relations and their impact on the construction of knowledge. The groundbreaking insight of the *Phenomenology of Spirit* is that an individual's apprehension of the world is the product of the dialectical character of its experiences in the world and with others. Consciousness, Hegel tells us, approaches its world with its assumptions regarding truth only to meet with experiences that negate these assumptions. Consequently, the self's unification with Absolute Spirit is its recognition of the role of others in its own construction of knowledge. Knowledge happens when "self-consciousness has its own self-certainty in the other free self-consciousness, and possesses its truth precisely in that 'other.'"[19]

Hegel also recognizes that individuals will attempt to disregard the reality of inter-subjective relations and posit the truth of their own particular perspectives. As Hegel's famous description of the master–slave relationship attests, these efforts to deny the reality of the other are the source of inequitable power relations between individuals. Of course, Hegel tells us, the master needs the slave as much or more than the slave needs the master. While we can try to ignore the influence of others on our knowledge, we cannot erase such influence. Nonetheless, Hegel avers that individuals must pass through this stage in order to learn the nature of inter-subjectivity: "They must engage in this struggle, for they must raise their certainty of being for themselves to truth . . . [namely,] that its essential being is present to it in the form of an other."[20]

Hegel's recognition of the dynamics that underlie the production of knowledge is missing from exegetical Jewish thought. Perhaps the most provocative and compelling thinker to appreciate this was Gillian Rose. Rose's neo-Hegelian epistemology and hermeneutics offers an invaluable corrective to contemporary exegetical thought. While Rose's death-bed conversion to Christianity might lead Jewish thinkers to reject her thought, I believe, unlike Rose, that contemporary Judaism need not fall prey to anti-philosophical trends.[21] In fact, I will show how contemporary feminist Jewish thought engages in the kind of philosophical analysis Rose advocated.

RECOGNITION, LAW, AND DESIRE

Gillian Rose's work is an ardent attempt to resuscitate philosophy against the current of what Rose takes to be postmodernism's "renunciation of reason."[22] Needed, Rose argues, is a "reassessment of reason, gradually rediscovering its own moveable boundaries . . . a way to conceive learning, growth and knowledge as fallible and precarious, but risk-able."[23] Offering what she labels an aporetic reading of Hegel's *Phenomenology of Spirit,* Rose argues that knowledge is a social reality, the by-product of a self's recognition that its self-awareness is always mediated through its awareness of an other. Selves are always "enraged and invested"[24] in one another. However, according to Rose's reading of the Hegelian phenomenology, the journey of consciousness does not culminate in an absolute realization in and with the other. Rather, the *Phenomenology* charts the *misadventures* of the self who "comes up against again and again, its own positing of the world, discovering outcomes the inverse of what it intended."[25] Sometimes the self recognizes the positive role of the other in the cultivation of the self's own knowledge. Under other circumstances, it refuses to acknowledge the other's import. In either case, knowledge is mediated through the third moment that is neither the immediate product of self or world but the moment between the two when I reflect back on what I have learned in the encounter with the other.

Knowledge is the product of inter-subjective relations. But the form of my inter-subjective relations is law. For Rose, self-cultivation begins with the self's desire to project its view of the world onto the world. However, a self's projection *always* meets with the response of others. It *must* always be mediated. This is the law of human life. "Existence is already . . . commanded."[26] My power is always limited. Still, to live is to live in law for there are no other conditions under which I can assert power; if there is no assertion of power, there is no self.

Consequently, through law I learn that life is a perpetual process of desire, risk, engagement, and investment with others. According to Rose, the givenness of law does not secure the outcome of a self's engagements. Law establishes the possibility of justice if selves achieve mutual recognition. However, law can also lead to injustice if selves refuse to acknowledge the import of others in their own self-relations and attempt to stabilize inter-subjective relations through the imposition of structures of domination. Such structures are abuses of power; they fail to recognize the finite nature of human power. Justice presupposes an appreciation for the precariousness of knowledge.

> [M]y relation to myself is mediated by what I recognize or refuse to recog-nize in your relation to yourself; while your self-relation depends on what you recognize of my relation to myself . . . and to fix our relation in domi-nation or dependence is unstable and reversible, to fix it as 'the world' is to attempt to avoid these reverses . . . and deny the broken middle.[27]

READING TEXTS PHILOSOPHICALLY

According to Rose, hermeneutics must be philosophical. To interpret events or texts is to chart the process of law and the actualities of power as they appear to the interpreter. Additionally, Rose maintains, hermeneutical critique is also critique of hermeneutics—that is, all the while that an inter-preter assesses the dynamics of a work, she must also allow herself to become aware of the uncertainty of her own assertions.

Rose applies this methodology to her interpretation of rabbinic texts. Contrary to popular efforts to pose text study as the converse of and anti-dote to mainstream political life,[28] Rose maintains that like all texts, rab-binic texts are expressions of law and the politics of power. More specifically, she argues, the sages developed a unique form of exegesis in order to project their own perspective of reality on and in relation to mem-bers of the traditional Jewish authority (priests and prophets) as well as to non-Jewish sovereigns. "Learning in this sense mediates the social and the political: it works precisely by making mistakes, by taking the risk of ac-tion and then by reflecting on its unintended consequences, and then tak-ing the risk, yet again . . . and so on."[29]

Furthermore, Rose maintains, an appreciation of rabbinic texts as the misadventures of the sages helps contemporary readers appreciate the drama of our own misadventures in law and politics. In interpreting the rabbis, we learn that rabbinic exegesis is a political response to the loss of Jewish political power after the destruction of the Temple. But what hap-pens to the need for rabbinic exegesis in modernity when political power rests with individuals and Judaism is privatized? Rabbinic Judaism appears to lose its political basis. It may assume authority, and yet its authority is only as powerful as the individuals who acknowledge it. "Under these modern circumstances, Midrash can tell the truth about its loss of truth."[30] Interpreting rabbinic texts today should awaken us to the complexities of our own political and social environment—that is, it should encourage our own philosophical reflection. Like the rabbis, Jews today must risk seeking the universal and hope to arrive at a just engagement with the world.

Unfortunately, Rose maintains, postmodern Jewish thought has renounced the labor of reason, positing instead a sundering of law and ethics, history and messianism. Of course Rose believes that postmodernism's mission to locate a non-violent arena of pure ethics results only in its opposite, namely, the persistent presence of the forces of power devoid of the mediation of philosophical reflection. Power is mediated by the work of reason. To dismiss reason is to ensure the unregulated reign of forces of power. Philosophy must be readmitted into the discourse of contemporary thought.

III. Feminism's New Philosophical Work

Despite the pervasiveness of exegetical Jewish thought, few Jewish feminists identify themselves with this school of thought. From a feminist point of view, the fundamental problem with this approach to Jewish thought is its uncritical celebration of the classical Jewish sources as authoritative and secure homes for all Jews. After thirty years of Jewish feminist work, it is easy to understand why casting classical Jewish sources as authoritative is deeply problematic for Jewish feminists. Women have far fewer legal rights and responsibilities in the classical Jewish sources.[31] Furthermore, the classical Jewish sources often describe women negatively.[32] From a feminist perspective, exegetical Jewish thought is insufficiently critical.

Leery of modern philosophy's effort to guise its own political and social interests in the name of metaphysical and epistemological certainty, Jewish feminists largely have disassociated themselves from identifying with the modern/Jewish philosophical canon. Nonetheless, if we understand philosophy in the terms Rose established, that is, as the analysis of the agonistic character of human life bound by the law of its inter-subjective relations, it becomes clear that strands of contemporary Jewish feminism are readmitting philosophical analysis into Jewish thought.

The relatively new philosophical impulse found in feminist thinkers differs from the earlier feminist concern with theology, best represented by Judith Plaskow's work. Plaskow's analysis focuses on the construction of concepts relating to experiences of the divine. The feminist thought I am examining considers the construction of human knowledge apart from sacred experiences. As will become clear, I believe that there is an inextricable relationship between philosophical and theological work. Nonetheless, one must separate the strands of the two analyses prior to assessing their interdependency. In what follows I will illuminate this philosophical impulse in Miriam Peskowitz's *Spinning Fantasies: Rabbis, Gender and History* and Rachel Adler's *Engendering Judaism: An Inclusive Theology and Ethics,* by comparing their work to Gillian Rose's analysis of the construction of knowledge in order to illuminate the kind of philosophical corrective that I believe exegetically oriented thought needs.

RABBINIC FANTASIES

Miriam Peskowitz's *Spinning Fantasies: Rabbis, Gender and History* is a historical analysis of rabbinic texts. Nonetheless, implicit within Peskowitz's historical work is a philosophical analysis of human knowledge as the site of desire and anxiety that bears deep resemblance to Rose's hermeneutical approach. One of the objectives of Peskowitz's *Spinning Fantasies* is to display the soft and uncertain underbelly of rabbinic perspectives on gender, what Rose would call the *agon* of authorship. Readers of rabbinic texts often assume that the rabbis were confident in their knowledge regarding the differences between men and women. Peskowitz argues that the rabbis wanted their views to appear ordinary and self-evident. Careful readings of rabbinic texts suggest, however, that the rabbinic writers had to go to some lengths to construct their halakhic positions on gender. In fact, Peskowitz argues, far from self-evident, rabbinic knowledge and halakhah regarding gender was a product of the rabbis' anxious negotiation with women in their society, a negotiation that often resulted in patriarchal dominance.

Peskowitz's analysis of Mishnah Ketubot 8.1 offers a good example of her hermeneutics. Mishnah Ketubot 8.1 concerns the issue of women's control over property in circumstances of betrothal and marriage. According to Peskowitz, this Mishnah seeks to expand a husband's rights over his wife's property in ways not indicated by the Bible. Reviewing Peskowitz's reading, I will focus only on her analysis of the second part of the text that asks whether or not a woman who acquires property during her betrothal has the right to sell it or give it away as a married woman. According to the text, both Hillel and Shammai argue against her right to do so. However, the Mishnah also presents a position attributed to Rabbi Gamliel that argues that her husband does not have control over her acquired property. Rabbi

Gamliel's disagreement is based in his claim that a husband's control over his wife's old property (that is, the property she acquired during betrothal) presupposes the legality of his control over her new property. But the latter claim, Gamliel argues, is not legally self-evident and needs its own justification. Consequently, Gamliel cannot consent to the former claim. As Peskowitz tells us, the Mishnah refutes Gamliel's position and sides instead with Hillel and Shammai.[33] Seen in this light, Gamliel's position provides an important minority opinion.

However, in Peskowitz's interpretation, Gamliel's position is valuable because it allows readers to realize how rabbinic positions on women's issues were not self-evident. Had they been self-evident the Mishnaic rabbis would not have bothered to argue against Gamliel's position. Rabbinic "knowledge" of women and gender is constructed and the Mishnah's refutation of Gamliel's position reveals the seams in the fabric of their position on women and property. When we juxtapose Peskowitz's exegesis with Rose's view of law and society, it becomes clear that rabbinic texts are built on agonistic relations. Peskowitz reads the rabbinic texts as expressions of the rabbis' confrontation with others in their society—in this case with women—and their anxious desire to project their own view of the other onto their environment. Peskowitz says,

> [a]s the passage yields its legal story about how to extend the privileges of husbands, it reveals a rabbinic anxiety about the foundations for their law . . . an anxiety about gender and male authority. If they needed to argue for it, masculine authority was not an entirely automatic and naturalized part of life . . . the Mishnah implicitly acknowledges the plasticity of masculine privilege.[34]

Gamliel is important to Peskowitz's reading for a second reason. It is tempting, Peskowitz acknowledges, to read Gamliel as a hero for women—a sign that the rabbinic texts contain resources for feminists. One could read this text and argue that in its day and from the perspective of the community's own interpretive rules, *Ketubot* 8.1 might have been read as an affirmation for a husband's control over his wife's property. Today, however, the text does not make sense to us in this way, in view of our feminist concerns. Pragmatically speaking, we can and must (the text's semantic indeterminacy mandates it) apply our own rules of understanding to find its meaning. In other words, we must read the text from the perspective of Gamliel's views on the protection of women and not from the position of Hillel and Shammai. As plurivocal, and thereby sacred, the text contains the seeds for its own healing.

Although Peskowitz acknowledges the temptation of a pro-feminist reading, she rejects it for its failure to appreciate the social and political complexities at play in the rabbinic text. This strain of Jewish thought, Peskowitz avers, suffers from nostalgia—the naïve faith in the ability to secure home. Furthermore, Peskowitz argues, efforts to find a home in this text by latching onto Gamliel's position keep readers from facing the politics in Gamliel's position itself. From Peskowitz's perspective, Gamliel's dissent from Hillel and Shammai is not an expression of a higher, pro-feminist, emancipatory morality. Gamliel is anxious about foundations. He is caught in the same struggle as Hillel and Shammai—the desire to project his view of authority in the face of the challenges raised by others.

Peskowitz's reading offers the philosophical awareness I believe these texts require. Implicit in Peskowitz's hermeneutics is the conviction that the rabbis are not blank slates onto which the divine word is written, but human beings, invested and engaged with others. Like all of us, they are the comedic heroes of their own misadventures—misadventures that sometimes result in justice and sometimes result in evil. If we fail to appreciate this, Peskowitz says, "we [will] replicate [their] patterns and terms,"[35] and unknowingly endorse unjust power structures.

It is natural, Rose maintains, that selves seek to project their view of the world. But life is the endless cycle of the search for home, the meeting with another outside one's home and the return from mediation. Recollection, nostalgia, and utopianism—the grand narratives that most of us script in order to secure a home—only betray the cycle of risk. For Rose, it is philosophy's task to take note of law and the endless repetition of its perpetual cycle from desire to loss to reflection, back to desire. If we cannot recognize the complexities in our texts, we will not be able to take responsibility for the negotiations with others in our present. Peskowitz's hermeneutics strives toward the same goal. We ought not, she argues, read

> rabbinic texts for answers and for temporary allies . . . this way we gain no practice in looking closely at evidence, in taking apart its assumptions and logics, in finding historic contexts and in figuring out the mechanisms of how masculinism worked. . . . Demanding these kinds of answers situates us as people who will countenance no ambivalence and little complexity.[36]

It is high time that exegetically oriented Jewish thought conquers its nostalgia and makes room for this kind of philosophically inspired hermeneutics.

LAUGHING AT/WITH THE RABBIS

One of the greatest contributions to contemporary Jewish thought, Rachel Adler's *Engendering Judaism*, also advances the kind of philosophical challenge to postmodern exegetical theologies that I am advocating. Like Peskowitz and Rose, Adler avoids reading the rabbis as heroes or oppressors. Ideological readings betray complexity; they lack rigor. Also like Peskowitz (and Rose), Adler reads the classical sources as testaments to the misadventures—what Adler refers to as the comedy of rabbinic reason.

At times, Adler reads from the perspective of an object relations theory that bears striking resemblance to Rose's aporetic reading of the Hegelian consciousness. Drawing from the work of Jessica Benjamin and others, Adler argues that individuals are strung between the conflicting desires for power and recognition. At once, we seek to project our view of the world and another's acknowledgement of it. We are destined to an inter-subjectively conditioned, finite freedom. A healthy life mediates between one's desire for self-expression and the desire for recognition from another. In Rose's terms, a healthy life is a philosophically reflective life. However, like Rose, Adler recognizes that individuals often seek greater security than the healthy life affords. Structures of domination and submission result. When present in texts, such structures demonstrate the need for an analytically rigorous hermeneutics that can unveil the anxiety underneath the apparent inviolability of these structures. In *Engendering Judaism,* Adler applies this hermeneutical approach to a variety of rabbinic stories.

Adler's reading of Berakhot 51b provides a good example of her hermeneutic of comedy. Berakhot 51b tells the tale of a dinner at the house of R. Nahman and his wife Yalta. Also present at the meal is a male guest named Ulla. The meal is finished and the moment comes for the guest Ulla to pass the cup of blessing to those collectively participating in the grace after meals. R. Nahman asks Ulla to pass the cup to R. Nahman's wife. Ulla, citing biblical texts that establish the male as the source of fertility, argues that if women's fertility is dependent on men, so her blessedness derives from men as well. He therefore refuses to pass the cup to Yalta. In response, Yalta goes down to the wine cellar and smashes four hundred jars of wine. Afterwards, R. Nahman repeats his request that Ulla pass her the cup. Ulla passes the cup but tells Yalta that he is passing her the ancient equivalent of a plastic cup. He mocks her. She, in turn, mocks him, saying "from travelers come tall tales and from ragpickers lice."[37]

Adler tells us that this story occurs in the context of a talmudic discussion concerning the laws of who participates in the grace after meals. Adler doesn't flesh out the meaning of the passage in this context. However, to appreciate Adler's hermeneutical approach it is worth playing out some aspects of this more traditional reading. Interpreted in the context of the halakhic discussion concerning participation in grace after meals, the story helps form the apparently stable edifice of rabbinic positions regarding women and their participation in ritual activity. For our purposes (or Adler's), it makes no difference whether the story buttresses Nahman's or Ulla's position. What matters are this reading's assumptions. First, it assumes that it is normal for there to be a special conversation regarding women's participation. This suggests that women are not, somehow, the norm. Second, the story presupposes that men rightfully make the decisions about women's participation. Third, the story assumes that men's decision-making takes place in a conversation that excludes women. (Yalta does not participate in the conversation—she goes away from the table to smash the wine jars.) Read in this context, the rabbis appear to have a stable basis of knowledge of the topics of men, women, and law.

Adler's hermeneutics challenges this apparent certainty, highlighting instead the insecurity of rabbinic knowledge and the comedy of the rabbis' efforts to assert their desired positions. Like Rose's, Adler's hermeneutics casts a philosophical doubt on rabbinic consciousness. Unlike the traditional interpretation of the tale, Adler's interpretation focuses on Yalta. From the halakhic standpoint, Yalta is incidental. The main action happens between R. Nahman and Ulla as they play out the details of halakhah. However, when we focus attention on Yalta, everything changes. Two men debate the right a woman has to receive a ritually important glass of wine. They talk, they cite texts, they talk some more. All the while the woman removes herself from the drone of their exchange, goes to the wine cellar and smashes four hundred wine jars. So much for the blessing over the cup—how are you going to make a blessing when there's no wine? What looked like a rational engagement between two thinking men concerning a legal problem now looks like a comedy of fools.

The boldness of Yalta's act challenges each of the assumptions above described. First, by smashing the wine jars, Yalta challenges the peripheral, non-normative status assigned her. She creates a situation where her position (not being able to participate in the ritual) becomes the situation for everyone since there's no more wine. Second, since her act determines the outcome of the situation, it challenges the assumption that men control legal decisions. Finally, her deed defies the paradigm of Torah conversation as the vehicle for legal determination. And Adler says, "as destabilizer of law, she exposes its hidden meanings and debunks its mystifications."[38] By debunking the rabbinic assumptions at work in a traditional reading, a reading that focuses on Yalta exposes the precariousness of the rabbinic legal edifice. Sounding like Rose, Adler says,

Our feminist hermeneutic re/members the storytellers and their homosocial world, their frantic scramble to preserve a patriarchal power they saw as infinitely fragile,. . . . All that . . . is naked here. . . . And we laugh.[39]

As we have seen, Handelman, Ochs, and Levinas maintain that the Hebrew Scriptures offer an inexhaustible pool from which readers may gather the scripts of their collective memories and their future utopias—the ongoing tales of creation, revelation, and redemption. Adler's hermeneutics negates the assumption that the classical Jewish sources may generate perpetual meaning. She encourages contemporary readers to find incongruities in the text—to appreciate "the subversive potential in laws' foundational narratives."[40] However, like Rose, Adler rejects melancholia. Neither denies the need to mourn the injustices in these texts. But neither believes our mourning places us in a privileged position. Injustice never stands alone but always implies the possibility of its opposite and vice versa. In contrast to Derrida's "I mourn, therefore I am,"[41] Rose calls for a "completed mourning"[42] that returns to the site of injustice and standing there takes up law's challenge to right former wrongs. Likewise, Adler maintains that neither can we cozy up in these texts nor escape from them. We must live with them, appreciating them for the misadventures they portray:

> Being human, none of us can see very far. . . . I choose to walk through stories searching . . . the hidden springs of laughter that well up once we are willing to relinquish the suffocating security of the dominator or the smoldering grudge of the victim.[43]

Moreover, as Rose does, Adler insists that we return to the site of these injustices if only to be inspired to create our own just norms.

Rose, Peskowitz, and Adler agree that texts presuppose the values of those who script and interpret them. Hermeneutics should document this play rather than strive to move beyond it. We cannot escape a life in law. We can tell funny stories about old law and "by means of feminist jurisgenesis, . . . regenerate a nomos, a world of legal meaning in which the stories, dreams and revelation of Jewish women and men are fully and complexly integrated."[44]

🕎 IV. From Philosophy to Theology

One crucial point distinguishes Adler's philosophically minded hermeneutics from that of Rose and Peskowitz. In her epilogue to *Engendering Judaism,* Adler reads from the first chapter of the talmudic tractate

Berakhot that tells the story of how Rabbi Yose, on the way to Jerusalem, stops by "one of the ruins of Jerusalem"[45] to pray. Immediately thereafter, Yose encounters the prophet Elijah who informs him that he has erred—he should not have gone into the ruin, he should have prayed on the road, and he should have said the short prayer. Elijah then asks Yose if he heard a voice in the ruin, and Yose responds that he "heard a divine echo, a 'bat kol' and she was moaning like a dove"[46] over the sins of her children and their exile. Elijah responds by telling Yose that God moans like this three times a day, but when God's children enter a synagogue and pray the kaddish there, God follows his moaning by expressing relief over their praise to him and says, "happy is the king who is praised in his house like this. What's to become of a father who has exiled his children and alas for the children exiled from their father's table?"[47]

Adler ends her book with this story because it is a testament to the rabbinic negotiation with its own misadventures. The story does not read this way at first. Elijah reprimands Yose for entering the ruin. He tells him he ought to have prayed the short prayer on the road. But the story does not end there. Elijah inquires into and listens to Yose's experience in the ruins. Yes, Elijah acknowledges, God bemoans our past injustices. We have sinned. This is why, Elijah says, Jews must now pray in synagogues. There, too, we hear God's wailing, but in synagogue we can offer the kaddish—we can confront the injustice that led to our ruination and now incorporate our awareness of it into a new practice. Jews can revisit their former ruins, and by inhabiting them, can take up the challenge of justice that their ruination implies. Here, Adler says, the rabbis "encode the capacity for remaking justice and for tender reciprocity with the divine Other. . . . God's human partners regrew their shattered nomos and cultivated a new world they and God could inhabit together."[48] Most noteworthy about Adler's interpretation is her identification of the rabbis' effort for "remaking justice" and "their tender reciprocity with the divine Other." Somehow, although Adler does not spell it out, there is a relationship between "remaking justice" and our relationship to God. The mourning that becomes law has theological implications.

Earlier in Engendering Judaism, Adler reprimands liberal Jews for not attending to the theological implications of their halakhic positions. While I agree with Adler's theological critique of much of liberal Judaism, Adler's own theological position is conspicuously absent from Engendering Judaism. The closest that Adler comes to enunciating a theological position occurs when she refers to the salvific character of a comedic feminist hermeneutic. Unlike Peskowitz or Rose, Adler does not shy away from using a language of redemption. In her "Introduction," she says,

I am concerned not only with critiquing androcentric structures . . . but also with mending and healing Judaism by encountering renewing and reclaiming the holiness in texts. The theological questions I ask of a text are designed to interrogate its moral universe, to hold the text accountable, and to redeem the text by learning Torah from it.[49]

Clearly Adler sees theological import in her hermeneutical approach. It offers a path that somehow, Adler's interpretation of the beginning of Berakhot 1 suggests, brings us into a closer relation to God. Adler's suspicions are right. Unfortunately, *Engendering Judaism* does little to spell them out.

Engendering Judaism's theological silence illuminates what I believe is the most central issue in postmodern Jewish thought, an issue that a Jewish feminist philosophy must also confront, namely, how simultaneously to lend a philosophically savvy reading to classical Jewish sources *and* to appreciate this critical activity as a religious task. If, despite their best efforts, Handelman, Ochs, and Levinas fail to carve out a sufficient space for the role of philosophy in Jewish hermeneutics, the philosophically rigorous feminist hermeneutics I have explored must inquire into the theological/religious implications of its position. In what remains of the essay I will articulate the theological implications of the agonistic philosophy I am supporting and have identified in Rose's, Adler's, and Peskowitz's thought.[50]

THE LAW: HUMAN OR DIVINE?

Despite her virulent attack on what Rose refers to as theologies of "holy cities,"[51] Rose often waxes theological in her writing. In *Mourning Becomes Law,* Rose portrays law as a source of solace and strength rather than as a mundane evil to be overcome. Even those afflicted by unjust applications of law, Rose avers, must return to the law. Mourning must become the law. "To acknowledge and to re-experience . . . justice and . . . injustice is to accept the law, it is not to transgress it—mourning becomes the law."[52] But why return to the law? Rose says that the mourner returns

> to carry out that intense work of the soul, that gradual rearrangement of its boundaries, which must occur when a loved one is lost . . . and hence fully to be regained beyond sorrow. . . . The mourner returns to negotiate and challenge the changing inner and outer boundaries of the soul and of the city; she returns to their perennial anxiety.[53]

How can a return to perennial anxiety allow one to move "beyond sorrow?" Rose explains that mourning draws on transcendent but representable justice, which makes the suffering of immediate experience visible and speakable. When completed, mourning returns the soul to the city, renewed and reinvigorated for participation, ready to take on the difficulties and injustices of the existing city.[54]

As risk, engagement, and return, law is the site of transcendence.

Rose's *The Broken Middle* is replete with proclamations regarding the liaison between law and grace. "Without law, no sin: without sin, no grace."[55] By cryptically referencing Paul, Rose means to say that God is present and expressed in law, law that gives rise to virtue just as easily as it gives rise to sin. "Law is abundant and abounding: it is not the contrary of grace. . . ."[56] The implication here is that God's revelation transpires where the self participates in the perennial anxiety of its life in law. Revelation happens in the self's comedic journey toward and away from its home. One could conclude, therefore, that when postmodern Jewish thought ignores the dimensions of human anxiety it becomes atheistic. This is certainly ironic, given much of postmodernism's commitment to the centrality of revelation.

THE THEOLOGICAL DIMENSION OF LAW

Rose does not unpack the logic behind her theology of law and grace. Her occasional references to a Hegelian-styled divine comedy do not account for her comments regarding transcendence. The God implied in her analysis is more than Hegel's immanent dialectical Spirit. Rose needs the help of theology to articulate how law, as the site of human risk and anxiety, is also the site of divine transcendence. David Novak's conception of the relation between philosophy and theology provides an invaluable tool for this work.

Like Rose, Novak challenges the modern/contemporary identification between Judaism and ethics as found in thinkers such as Cohen, Buber, and Levinas. For Novak, the identification of Judaism with Jewish ethics reduces the covenantal relationship established at Sinai between God and the Jews to an inter-human relationship as is evidenced by Cohen's correlation, Buber's I-Thou encounter, and Levinas's encounter with the other. The ethics–Judaism equation collapses revelation into creation. "Theologically, the error here is that revelation is essentially reduced to the supreme awareness of an order already present in creation."[57]

Furthermore, *implicit* in Novak's work is an additional critique, that is, when thinkers like Cohen, Buber, and Levinas equate revelation with human ethics, they misconstrue the nature of human ethics. More specifically, they deny its character as an expression of human desire and finitude. In my earlier discussion of Levinas's ethical phenomenology, we saw that while for Levinas my encounter with an other requires a critique of my self, the self who responds to the commanding other finds a peace in that relationship and loses interest in her own desires by assuming the desire of an other. For Novak, this is a flawed understanding of human–human relationships. To see why, we must understand Novak's position on the nature of human ethical engagement.

NOVAK'S PHENOMENOLOGY OF NATURAL LAW

Though commonly misunderstood, Novak's interest in natural law is less concerned with affirming a body of set norms and more concerned with establishing the finite character of human life. For Novak, as for Rose, law is that which is already there. Both Novak and Rose respect the notion of human freedom. However, both thinkers appreciate that human freedom is always mediated through others. It is always conditioned by law. Novak says,

> Humans are already contained within a world fundamentally not of our own making. Nature is the order of that world in which we find ourselves. . . . What is within the world is what humans can choose, but they cannot choose the world itself . . . justice is a natural necessity.[58]

Novak's discussion of Cain and Abel provides a useful illustration. The biblical text indicates that God holds Cain accountable for the murder of his brother. Nonetheless, the text does not indicate that Cain has been taught that murder is immoral. On what grounds is he guilty? According to Novak, Cain ought to have known that it is immoral to harm Abel because the law is implicit in the fact that he and his brother "share a common humanity."[59] Novak locates law in the same place as Rose. By claiming that law is present in Cain and Abel's common humanity, Novak simply means that human selves never exist alone, but always exist in relation to others. But, if we exist in relation to others, then one's relation to one's self is always informed by one's relation to others. In the order of things, human selves mutually define and therefore de-limit each other. By murdering Abel, Cain expressed his disregard for the humanity of his brother and exhibited his belief in the superiority of his life over his brother's. He denied his human finitude; he denied the reality of law and was guilty.

Novak and Rose agree on another essential feature of law—namely that lawfulness creates anxiety and a sense of homelessness in human beings. Although one might think that human beings would feel secure by dwelling in an already ordered world, Novak and Rose maintain the opposite. In *The Election of Israel: The Idea of the Chosen People,* Novak argues that

Abraham experiences a deep sense of existential anxiety or homelessness not despite his confidence in the orderliness of the world, but because of it. If law means that my freedom is necessarily delimited by the existence of other people, then law is a testament to my finitude. Law awakens me to my mortality and I become anxious about my existential condition. Am I alone in the world, destined to die alone? "What we soon learn from this order is our own mortal vulnerability."[60] The experience of law is the experience of homelessness. "Abraham the bedouin is looking for his home."[61]

Finally, Novak and Rose both identify awareness of law with philosophical activity or reason. When I participate in law, I participate in the process of self-critique and critique of the world. My perspective and the perspectives of others are mediated through a third—that is the universal. Cain's murder of Abel is immoral and irrational. Awareness of natural law amounts to a skepticism regarding any assertion of absolute human power. It is philosophical doubt. As Novak says, "Hence natural law functions as a philosophical corrective within a culture . . . as the bridge between cultures, preventing any of them from cornering the market on humankind and humanity.[62]

Implicit in Novak's view of natural law is the conviction that not only do Cohen, Buber, and Levinas reduce revelation to creation, but they also divinize human ethics. By so doing, all three thinkers deny the nature of human finitude, the reality of human homelessness, and the nature of reason. Consequently, their assertion of Judaism as ethics results in a disembodied, apolitical and anti-philosophical account of Judaism's reality. Together with Rose, Novak asserts the need to reclaim the place of philosophy and law into the discourse of Jewish thought.

THEOLOGY AND HOME

The fundamental difference between Rose and Novak, a difference that has important consequences for Jewish feminist thought, concerns Novak's analysis of natural law/philosophy as the "precondition"[63] of covenant life. Novak draws out the theological connections implicit in Rose's discussions of law and grace.

Let us return to Novak's discussion of Abraham in *The Election of Israel*. Novak's Abraham is familiar with the laws of the created world but is plagued by loneliness and anxiety about home. What does this have to do with God? Can't Abraham comfort himself by thinking that this world is just a physical representation of a higher, eternal world? This, Novak says, will not help Abraham feel at home *here*. Can't Abraham find strength in himself and attempt to control the world where he feels insecure? He could, but such mastery comes at the price of fighting with the world rather than finding one's home in it. No, says Novak, Abraham does not want to escape from his world or master it. He wants to feel at home in it and in his relations with others. This desire is, according to Novak, theological.

As a person, I feel *compelled* or *claimed* by the other person to respect their co-humanity. I do not *desire* the good. I am compelled by it. Instead, I *desire* to feel at home in the world where I am so claimed. But, since nothing in the world can provide this comfort, my desire to feel at home becomes my desire to feel at home with something that transcends me. Said in other terms, philosophical activity—the activity of doubting one's place in the world that transpires in my relations with others (in law) is the same as theological desire. Theological desire is the existential yearning for a God who creates the world as a home for us *and* who establishes a relationship with us through which we feel secure.

Consequently, for Novak, the philosophical activity of self-delimitation through natural law produces the desire to share intimacy with God—to be known and know God. By knowledge Novak means *yada* or the kind of knowledge Adam has of Eve that Novak says can be sexual but does not have to be. Theological desire is erotic, Novak says, insofar as "true eros is ecstatically self-giving, so much so that the true lover allows himself or herself to be radically affected by his or her beloved."[64]

Novak distinguishes this theological desire from Plato's philosophical eros. For Novak, Plato's philosophical eros is the desire to know the Good—that which is the "summit of the order of eternal, intelligible forms."[65] But the desire to know or participate in a divine order (as the gods do) is not the same as the desire to share intimacy with a God who relates to us and cares for us. Only this unique intimacy affords the sense of home that persons desire.

By claiming that natural law or reason is theological desire, Novak is not presenting a proof of the existence of God, whether through an argument from design or any other argument. Nor is he arguing that we always long for God. We can posit a higher order and escape from the world, or we can try to master the world. We can attempt to deny the character of our lives. However, if we embrace the reality of our homelessness, we position ourselves for covenantal life. We open ourselves to God, and we wait for the creator God to reveal himself and call us to a relationship. We become persons of faith.

With this argument, Novak draws out the theological implications in Rose's work. Moreover, he presents a view of covenantal theology that is invulnerable to a Roseian critique. Because of their failure to recognize the reality of human finitude, Cohen, Buber, and Levinas present covenantal portraits in which human desire and anxiety are overcome. Conversely, Novak not only appreciates human anxiety as theological desire. He recognizes the place of human desire in the covenantal relationship itself. In Deuteronomy we are commanded to "love the Lord your God with all your heart, with all your life, and with all your might."[66] But, Novak asks, "can there be any love without desire?. . . . 'For you O Lord is my whole desire'. . . . Is not God to be served by a 'desiring soul'?"[67] We love God when we desire God as the one who makes my world a home. Covenantal relationship does not nullify human desire as it does for Cohen, Buber, and Levinas. The *world* becomes an authentic place of dwelling not when I transcend my desire but when I direct my desire toward God.

FEMINISM AND THE NEED FOR JEWISH THEOLOGY

Like Handelman, Ochs, and Levinas, Novak identifies himself with the postmodern move back to the sources in Jewish thought. Nonetheless, Novak's move back to the sources derives from his belief that Jewish learning is both philosophically rigorous *and* redemptively meaningful. Like Rose, Peskowitz, and Adler, Novak reads classical Jewish sources as expressions of human risk and anxiety. At first glance, it may seem that Novak, Rose, Adler, and Peskowitz would have precious little to say to one another. Unlike Rose, Adler, or Peskowitz, Novak is a traditional Jew who believes in the divine origin of Torah. This does not mean, however, that the Torah is beyond human critique, for, as he says, "[t]he Torah speaks according to human language. . . . Although God is the Torah's first speaker, humans are its intended recipients, whose task it is to receive this gift in an authentically human way."[68] Consequently, the Torah is God's message conveyed and understood through human reason. Additionally, Novak appreciates extrabiblical rabbinic legislation as an authentic expression of rabbinic risk and finitude and thereby finds it theologically acceptable while Rose, Peskowitz, and Adler would argue that much rabbinic legislation seeks to escape the risk of law becoming, in Novak's terms, idolatrous. Nonetheless, from a philosophical point of view, the two sets of hermeneutical approaches have a good deal in common.

Moreover, Novak's hermeneutics sheds light on the theological implications of Rose, Peskowitz, and Adler's hermeneutics. For Novak, the classical Jewish sources are testimonies to the covenantal life with God *because* they express the anxiety of human life as the desire for God. They are expressions of philosophical activity as theological desire and demand to be read as such. Novak says, "worship is essentially a human reaching to God."[69] As expressions of worship, classical Jewish sources testify to human finitude and the desire for God and call us to do the same.

Novak's articulation of philosophical activity as theological desire explains how Adler views her philosophically rigorous readings as theologically meaningful. More importantly for this essay, Novak's analysis sheds light on the religious significance of a philosophically rigorous feminist hermeneutic. Rose, Peskowitz, and Adler are correct to demand a place for philosophical analysis in contemporary Jewish hermeneutics. Novak's work can help them appreciate this hermeneutics as covenantally meaningful.

🕎 Conclusion

As unlikely as the comparisons between Novak, Rose, Adler, and Peskowitz appear, I believe the conversation among these thinkers helps contend with the problem at the heart of postmodern Judaism—namely, how to relate critical analysis with theological discourse. If as Peter Ochs says, postmodernism seeks a "hermeneutic that preserves the text—or tradition . . . while delimiting its potential oppressiveness,"[70] it must take seriously the philosophical critique found in Rose's thought and in feminist critical discourse.

Nonetheless, philosophical analysis cannot remain distanced from theology. Jewish feminist thinkers today are often critical of their foremothers for their utopianism. Judith Plaskow's work has suffered from this critique. If Plaskow has failed to attend to the ongoing dynamics of power that plague our current society, her work can still remind the younger generation of critically minded feminists about the theological significance of their own work. Of course, contemporary Jewish thought needs thinkers like David Novak to articulate the necessary relationship between philosophy and theology implicit in all Jewish thought. The model I am presenting calls for philosophically rigorous hermeneutical analysis and appreciates this as covenantally *significant* activity. Such a model offers the route to a life of both divine praise and emancipatory analysis.

NOTES

1. Emmanuel Levinas, *Totality and Infinity: An Essay on Exteriority,* trans. Alphonso Lingis (Pittsburgh: Duquesne University Press, 1996), 66.

2. Ibid.

3. Ibid., 62.

4. Ibid., 178.

5. Ibid., 63.

6. Ibid., 306.

7. Ibid., 23.

8. Emmanuel Levinas, "Revelation in Jewish Tradition," in *Contemporary Jewish Theology: A Reader,* ed. Elliot N. Dorff and Louis E. Newman (New York: Oxford University Press, 1999), 167.

9. Ibid., 169.

10. Ibid., 174.

11. Susan Handelman, *The Slayers of Moses: The Emergence of Rabbinic Interpretation in Modern Literary Theory* (Albany: State University of New York Press, 1982), 23.

12. Ibid., 30.

13. Ibid.

14. Ibid., 31.

15. Ibid., 49.

16. Peter Ochs, "Scriptural Logic: Diagrams for a Postcritical Metaphysics," in *Re-Thinking Metaphysics,* ed. L. Gregory Jones and Stephen E. Fowl (Cambridge, Mass.: Blackwell, 1995).

17. Peter Ochs, "Postcritical Scriptural Interpretation," in *Interpreting Judaism in a Postmodern Age,* ed. Stephen Kepnes (New York: New York University Press), 63.

18. *Reasoning After Revelation: Dialogues in Postmodern Judaism,* ed. Stephen Kepnes, Peter Ochs, and Robert Gibbs (Boulder: Westview Press, 1998), 20.

19. G. W. F. Hegel, *Phenomenology of Spirit,* trans. A. V. Miller (New York: Oxford University Press, 1977), 212.

20. Ibid., 114.

21. Martin Kavka also argues this point by providing a philosophical reading of Levinas in his "Saying Kaddish for Gillian Rose," in *Secular Theology: American Radical Theological Thought,* ed. Clayton Crockett (New York: Routledge, 2001), 104–29.

22. Gillian Rose, *Mourning Becomes the Law: Philosophy and Representation* (Cambridge: Cambridge University Press, 1997), 11.

23. Ibid., 11–13.

24. Ibid., 75.

25. Ibid., 74.

26. Gillian Rose, *The Broken Middle: Out of Our Ancient Society* (Oxford: Blackwell, 1992), 86.

27. Rose, *Mourning Becomes Law,* 75.

28. For Rose, Rosenzweig and Levinas are the fathers of this position.

29. Rose, *Mourning Becomes the Law,* 38.

30. Ibid., 97.

31. Tradition holds that women are not commanded to engage in time-bound, positive commandments, including some of the most spiritually central commandments in the tradition. Women are not commanded to wear tefillin (Berakhot 20a–20b), to say the *Sh'ma* (*Shulhan Arukh, Orah Hayyim* 106:2), or to study Torah, arguably the most spiritually significant mitzvah, despite the fact that it is not a time-bound, positive mitzvah (*Kiddushin* 29b). Legally, women are second-class citizens in Judaism. They are "acquired" (*kinyan*) in marriage (*Kiddushin* 2a–b). They cannot issue a divorce (at best they can appeal to a Jewish court to compel a husband to divorce her [*Ketubot* 77a]). Additionally, women are restricted in their capacities as witnesses and as members of the public sector.

32. For examples and further discussion, see Aviva Cantor, "The Lilith Question," in *On Being a Jewish Feminist,* ed. Susannah Heschel (New York: Schocken Books, 1983).

33. Peskowitz explains that Mishnah *Ketubot* 8.1 is followed by Mishnah *Ketubot* 8.2, which argues, against Gamliel, that if a husband knows about property his wife acquired before their marriage, he may control it. Miriam Peskowitz, *Spinning Fantasies: Rabbis, Gender, and History* (Berkeley: University of California Press, 1997), 47.

34. Ibid., 38–39.

35. Ibid., 168.

36. Ibid., 45.

37. Rachel Adler, *Engendering Judaism: An Inclusive Theology and Ethics* (Philadelphia: Jewish Publication Society, 1998), 53.

38. Ibid., 56.

39. Ibid., 17.

40. Ibid., 51.

41. Rose, *Mourning Becomes the Law,* 11.

42. Ibid., 12.

43. Adler, *Engendering Judaism,* 19.

44. Ibid., 35.

45. Ibid., 209.

46. Ibid.

47. Ibid.

48. Ibid., 212.

49. Ibid., xxv.

50. The issue is central to the work of many contemporary Jewish thinkers including Robert Gibbs, Yudit Greenberg, Daniel Boyarin, and David Weiss Halivni.

51. Rose, *The Broken Middle,* 283.

52. Rose, *Mourning Becomes the Law,* 36.

53. Ibid., 35–36.

54. Ibid., 36.

55. Rose, *The Broken Middle,* 86.

56. Ibid., 87.

57. Novak, *Natural Law in Judaism,* 85.

58. Ibid., 46–47.

59. Ibid., 37.

60. David Novak, *The Election of Israel: The Idea of the Chosen People* (Cambridge: Cambridge University Press, 1995), 128.

61. Ibid., 132.

62. Novak, *Natural Law,* 178.

63. Novak carefully distinguishes between natural law as the "precondition, " "what enables a thing to be" (*Natural Law,* 186), of the covenant and natural law as the "ground" or cause of the covenant. Natural law is not the cause of the covenant because covenant does not derive from natural law.

64. David Novak, "Karl Barth on Divine Command: A Jewish Response," unpublished.

65. David Novak, "Law Religious or Secular?" *Virginia Law Review* 86, no. 3 (2000): 579.

66. Deuteronomy 6:5.

67. Novak, *The Election of Israel,* 120.

68. Novak, *Natural Law,* 29.

69. Novak, *The Election of Israel,* 175.

70. Kepnes, Ochs, and Gibbs, *Reasoning after Revelation,* 37.

Contributors

LEORA BATNITZKY is an Associate Professor at the Department of Philosophy in Princeton University. She earned her Ph.D. from Princeton University in 1996 and has been teaching modern Judaism, modern religious thought, religious ethics, and philosophy of religion at Princeton University since 1997. She is the author of *Idolatry and Representation: The Philosophy of Franz Rosenzweig Reconsidered* (2000), the editor of *Martin Buber: Schriften zur Philosophie on Religion* (in press), and the co-editor of *Icon Image and Text in Modern Jewish Culture* (in press).

JEAN AXELRAD CAHAN is a Senior Lecturer in the Departments of Philosophy and Political Science and formerly the Director of the Norman and Bernice Harris Center for Judaic Studies at the University of Nebraska-Lincoln. She holds a Ph.D. in philosophy from Johns Hopkins University with a dissertation titled "An Interpretation of Marx's Metaphor of Base and Superstructure from the Perspective of Methodological Individualism." She has published articles on Marx, Spinoza, and Rosenzweig and is completing a book entitled *Judaism and Naturalism* that uses Spinoza's thought as a starting point to discuss problems in contemporary philosophy and theology.

IDIT DOBBS-WEINSTEIN is an Associate Professor of Philosophy at Vanderbilt University. She earned her Ph.D. in Philosophy and Medieval Studies in University of Toronto in 1987 and since then has been teaching at Vanderbilt University, specializing in the history of Western philosophy, political philosophy, and Spinoza. She is the author of *Maimonides and St. Thomas on the Limits of Reason* (1995) as well as many articles on medieval Aristotelianism and Spinoza. She is currently completing a book titled *An Occluded Philosophical Tradition: A Study of the Transmission and Occlusion of the Arabic and Jewish Aristotelian Tradition*.

CLAIRE ELISE KATZ is an Assistant Professor in the Department of Philosophy at Penn State University, where she teaches feminist theory, philosophy of religion, and Jewish philosophy. She earned her Ph.D. in Philosophy from the University of Memphis in 1999 and since then has published essays in ethics, phenomenology, and philosophy of education. She is the translator of Henri Maldiney's *"Chair et Verbe dans le Philosophie de M. Merleau-Ponty,"* for *Chiasms: The Problem of the Flesh in Merleau Ponty* (2000). Her book, *Levinas, Judaism, and the Feminine: The Silent Footsteps of Rebecca,* was published by Indiana University Press in 2003.

NANCY K. LEVENE is an Assistant Professor of Religion at Williams College. She earned her Ph.D. from Harvard University in 2000 with a dissertation on Spinoza. She is the author of the forthcoming book, *Spinoza's Enlightenment: Religion, Democracy and the Critique of Reason,* and co-editor (with Peter Ochs and David Novak) of *Textual Reasonings: Jewish Philosophy and Text Study at the End of the Twentieth Century.* She has published essays on Spinoza and on Jewish ethics and politics.

SANDRA B. LUBARSKY is an Associate Professor of Religious Studies and the Director of the Masters Program in Liberal Studies at Northern Arizona University in Flagstaff, Arizona. She earned her Ph.D. in religion from Claremont Graduate University in 1986 and is the author of *Tolerance and Transformation: Jewish Approaches to Religious Pluralism* (1990) and the co-editor (with David Ray Griffin) of *Jewish Theology and Process Thought* (1996). Her publications focus on Judaism and process philosophy.

SARAH PESSIN is an Assistant Professor in the Department of Philosophy at California State University, Fresno. She earned her Ph.D. from Ohio State University in 2000 and her dissertation on Solomon ibn Gabirol is forthcoming as a study of *eros* and *apophasis* titled *Embroidering the Hidden.* She has published essays on medieval Neoplatonism (in the Jewish, Christian, and Muslim traditions) in the *Blackwell Companion to Philosophy in the Middle Ages, The Journal of the History of Philosophy, The Stanford Encyclopedia of Philosophy,* and *The Cambridge Companion of Medieval Jewish Thought.*

RANDI RASHKOVER is an Assistant Professor of Religious Studies at York College in York, Pennsylvania. She earned her Ph.D. from the University of Virginia in 2000 with a dissertation in comparative philosophical theology. She has published several articles on postmodernism, philosophical theology, and Jewish–Christian relations and is preparing her dissertation "Franz Rosenzweig, Karl Barth and the Theology of Testimony" for publication.

HEIDI MIRIAM RAVVEN is a Professor at the Department of Religion at Hamilton College. She earned her Ph.D. in Philosophy and History of Ideas at Brandeis University in 1984, and her publications focus on Spinoza,

Maimonides, and Hegel. She is the co-editor (with Lenn E. Goodman) of *Jewish Themes in Spinoza's Philosophy* (2002) and the author of *Spinoza's Rupture with Tradition: His Hints of a Jewish Modernity* (forthcoming).

T. M. RUDAVSKY is Professor of Philosophy and Director of the Melton Center for Jewish Studies at The Ohio State University. She earned her Ph.D. in philosophy from Brandeis University in 1976 and has been teaching and writing on ancient Philosophy, medieval Philosophy, and Jewish philosophy. She is the author of *Time Matters: Time, Creation and Cosmology in Medieval Jewish Philosophy* (2000) and the editor of *Divine Omniscience and Omnipotence in Medieval Philosophy: Islamic, Jewish and Christian Perspectives* (1985), and *Gender and Judaism: The Transformation of Tradition* (1995).

SUZANNE LAST STONE is a Professor of Law at the Benjamin N. Cardozo School of Law of Yeshiva University. She holds a J.D. from Columbia University Law School (1978). After a legal career, she joined the faculty of Yeshiva University in 1983 where she served as Associate Dean from 1987–1990. She has published numerous essays in law journals such as *Harvard Law Review, Israel Law Review,* and *Cardozo Law Review* on Jewish jurisprudence, Judaism and postmodernism, and Judaism and American law.

HAVA TIROSH-SAMUELSON is Professor of History at Arizona State University. She earned her Ph.D. from the Hebrew University of Jerusalem in 1978 in Jewish philosophy and Kabbalah, and her research focuses on Jewish intellectual history in the Middle Ages and the early modern period. She is the author of *Between Worlds: The Life and Thought of Rabbi David ben Judah Messer Leon* (1991) and *Happiness in Premodern Judaism: Virtue, Knowledge, and Well-Being* (2003), as well as the editor of *Judaism and Ecology: Created World and Revealed Word* (2002).

LAURIE ZOLOTH is Professor of Medical Ethics, Humanities, and Religion and Director of Bioethics in the Center for Genetic Medicine at the Feinberg School of Medicine at Northwestern University. She earned her Ph.D. from the Graduate Theological Union in Berkeley in 1976 and has published extensively in the areas of ethics, family, feminist theory, religion and science, Jewish Studies, and social policy. She is the author of *Health Care and the Ethics of Encounter* (1999) and the co-editor of *Notes from a Narrow Ridge: Religion and Bioethics* (with Dena Davis); *Riding on Faith: Religion, Popular Culture and the World of Disney* (with Simon Harak), *Margin of Error: The Ethics of Mistakes in Medicine* (with Susan Rubin), and *The Human Embryonic Stem Cell Debate: Science, Ethics, and Public Policy* (with Karen Lebacqz and Suzanne Holland).

Index